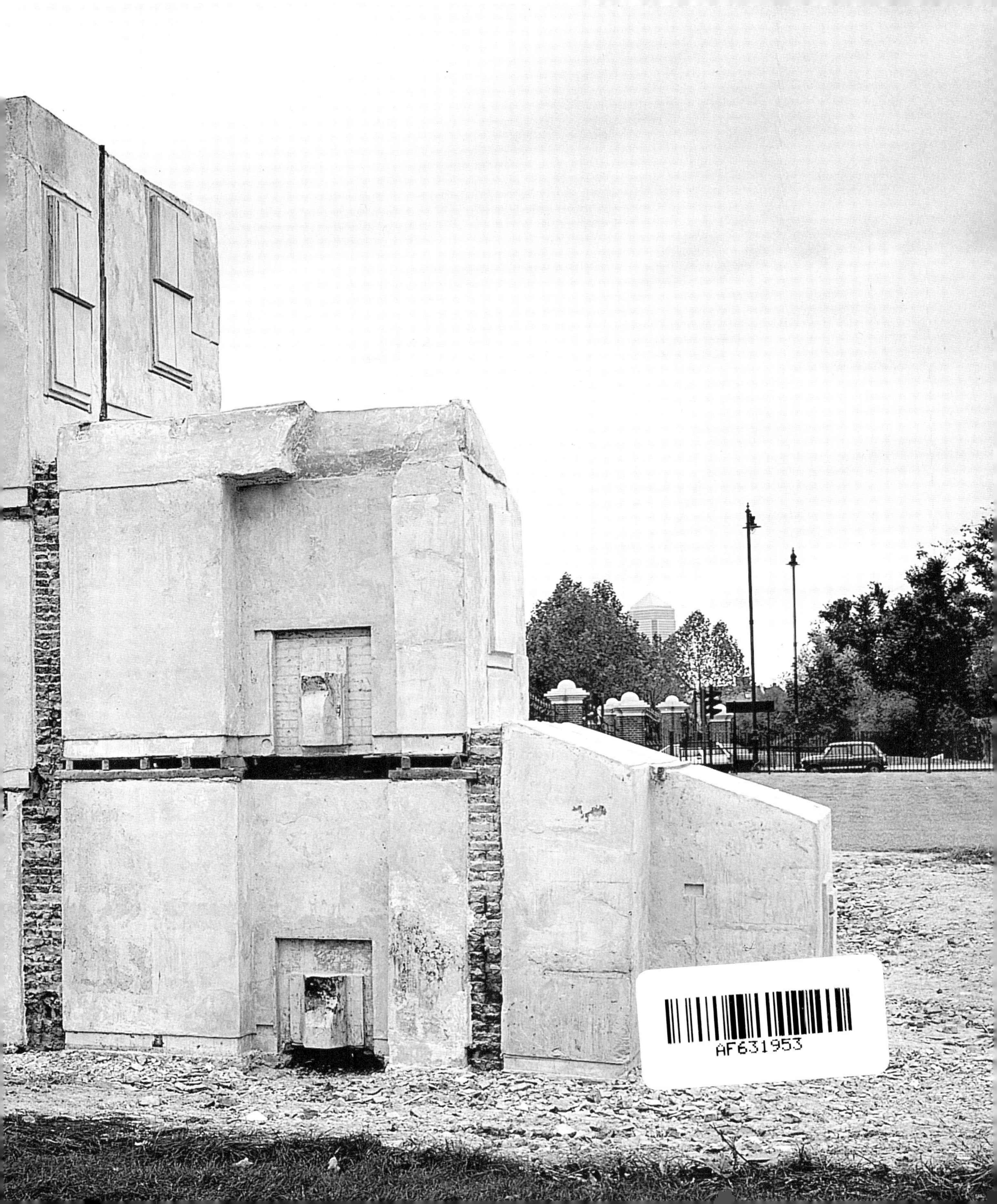

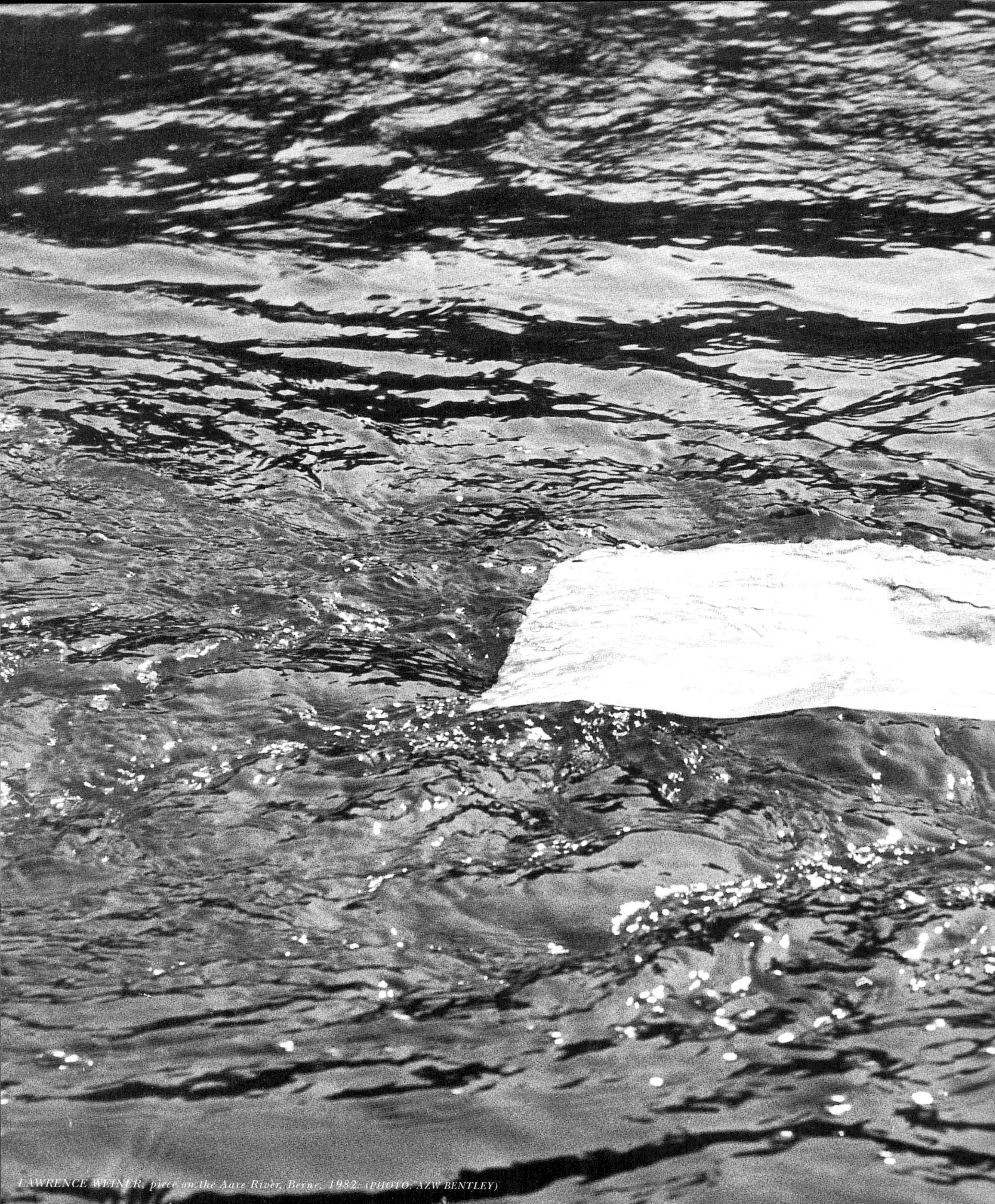

LAWRENCE WEINER, piece on the Aare River, Berne, 1982. (PHOTO: AZW BENTLEY)

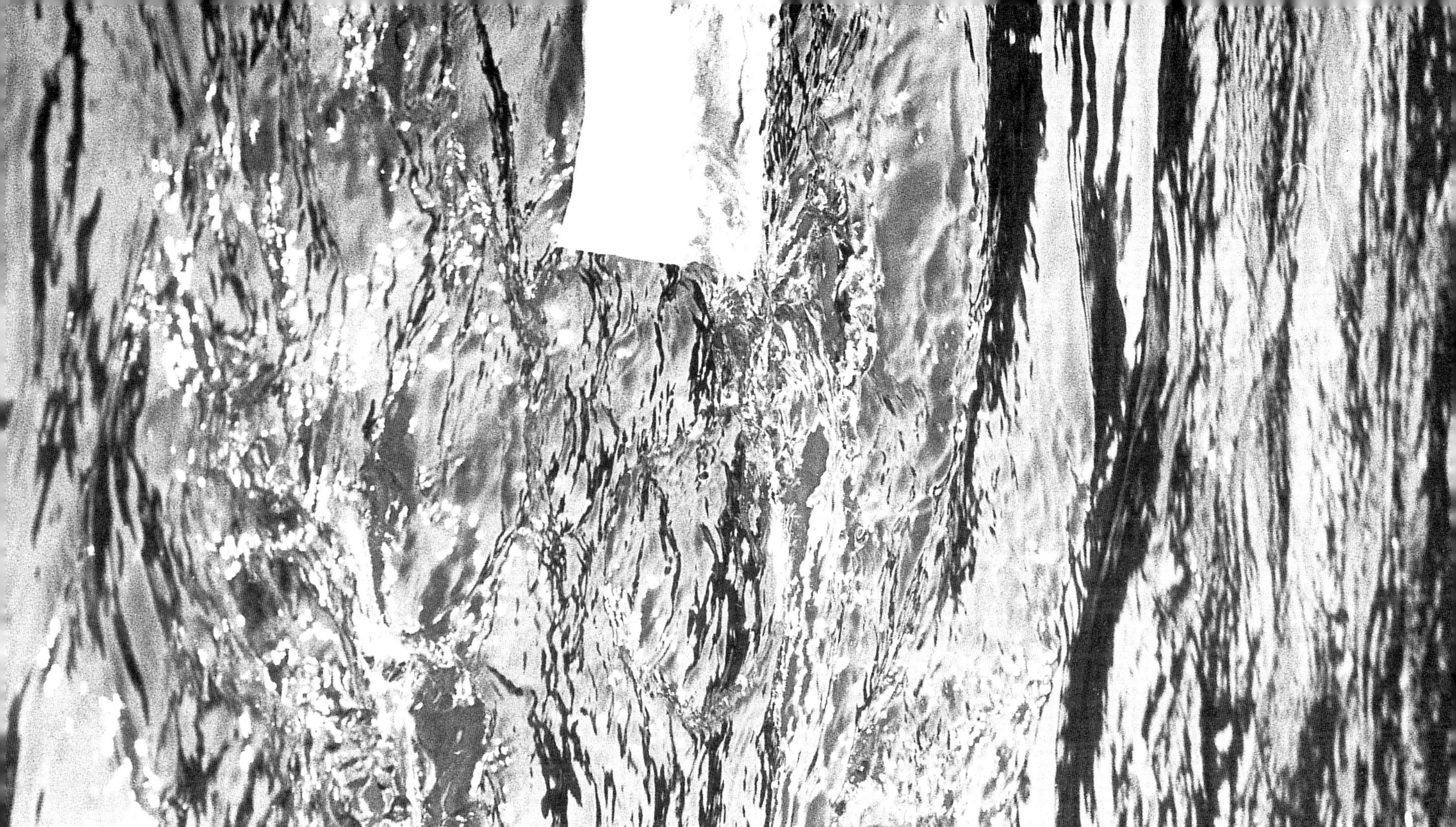

RUHENDES WASSER AUF DEM STROM PLAZIERT   STILL WATER PLACED UPON THE STREAM

DIE PARKETT-REIHE MIT GEGENWARTSKÜNSTLERN
THE PARKETT SERIES WITH CONTEMPORARY ARTISTS

Jede Nummer der Zeitschrift entsteht mit Künstlern oder Künstlerinnen, die eigens für die Leser von PARKETT einen Originalbeitrag gestalten. Diese Werke sind in der gesamten Auflage abgebildet und zusätzlich in einer limitierten und signierten Vorzugsausgabe erhältlich.

Each issue of the magazine is created in collaboration with artists, who contribute an original work specially made for the readers of PARKETT. The works are reproduced in the regular edition and available in a signed and limited Special Edition.

PARKETT – Zürich – New York – Frankfurt

Buchreihe mit Gegenwartskünstlern in deutscher und englischer Sprache, erscheint vierteljährlich. Der Parkett-Verlag gibt auch Bücher heraus.
Book series with contemporary artists in English and German, published quarterly. As an international publication, Parkett chooses to retain its authors' stylistic variations. Parkett also publishes books.

Bice Curiger
Chefredaktorin / Editor-in-Chief
Jacqueline Burckhardt
Redaktorin / Senior Editor
Louise Neri
Redaktorin USA / Senior Editor USA
Susanne Schmidt
Textredaktion und Produktion / Editing and Production
Trix Wetter
Graphik / Design
Hanna Koller
Graphik Assistenz / Design Associate
Claudia Meneghini
Korrektur / Proof Reading
Catherine Schelbert
Englisches Lektorat / Editorial Assistant for English
Katrin Wittneven
Volontariat / Traineeship

Dieter von Graffenried
Verleger / Executive Publisher
Beatrice Fässler
Vorzugsausgaben / Special Editions
Eleonore von Graffenried
Inserate / Advertising
Sibylle Schellenbauer
Abonnemente / Subscriptions
Vera Tremp
Büromitarbeiterin / Office Staff
Frances Richard
Redaktionsassistenz und Abonnemente USA / Editorial Assistant, Administration and Subscriptions US
Adrian Koerfer
Deutsche Verlagsvertretung / German Representative

Herausgeber / Publishers
Jacqueline Burckhardt · Bice Curiger · Dieter von Graffenried
Walter Keller · Peter Blum
Satz, Litho, Druck · Zürichsee Druckereien AG (Stäfa) · Copy, Printing, Color Separations

JAHRESABONNEMENT (VIER NUMMERN)/ANNUAL SUBSCRIPTION (FOUR ISSUES)
SFR. 98.– (SCHWEIZ), DM 108,– (BRD), SFR. 115.– (ÜBRIGES EUROPA), US$ 75.– (USA AND CANADA ONLY)

PARKETT-VERLAG AG, QUELLENSTRASSE 27, CH-8005 ZÜRICH, TEL. 41-1-271 81 40, FAX 41-1-272 43 01
PARKETT, 636 BROADWAY, NEW YORK, N.Y. 10012, PHONE (212) 673-2660, FAX (212) 673-2887
PARKETT-VERLAG AG, ROSSERTSTRASSE 16, D-60323 FRANKFURT A. M., TEL. (069) 17 27 79, FAX (069) 17 27 70

PRINTED IN SWITZERLAND ISBN 3-907509-92-7, ISSN 0256-0917

INHALT / CONTENTS

Umschlagphotos/Cover Photos: Mancia/Bodmer; Karsten Schubert Ltd.

EDITORIAL Diese Ausgabe von PARKETT kann einen zeitweilig an das Motto von «Kunst und Leben», die zu verschmelzen seien, erinnern. Doch nicht in der Art, wie die Forderung in den früheren Jahrzehnten gehört wurde. Hier wird die Vereinigung von Kunst und Leben ohne den aufdringlichen Einsatz der Person des Künstlers vorgetragen. Auch geschieht kein Flug aus dem Fenster à la Yves Klein, der den Künstler als freien Vogel ins Bild rückte.

Kunst und Leben erscheinen bei Weiner und Whiteread als objekthafte, fassbare Fusion, als Schmelzkörper. «I'll be a tattoo on Rachel Whiteread's structures,» sagte Lawrence Weiner, als wir die Gegenüberstellung der beiden Künstler vorschlugen.
Beide haben im öffentlichen Raum gearbeitet, sich einer Reibung mit «der grossen Öffentlichkeit gestellt». Diese Öffentlichkeit mit ihren Meinungen ist in diesem Heft auch zu Gast. In Wien steht mitten in der Stadt ein Flakturm aus dem Zweiten Weltkrieg, der durch Lawrence Weiner seit einigen Jahren eine von weit herum sichtbare Inschrift erhalten hat: ZERSCHMETTERT IN STÜCKE (IM FRIEDEN DER NACHT). Während zu Weiners Arbeit sich einzelne Personen äussern, deren sehr persönlich gefärbte Begegnungen ein emotionales Spektrum aufweisen, das auch die Indifferenz nicht ausschliesst, widerspiegeln die heftigen Reaktionen zu Rachel Whitereads spektakulärer Skulptur HOUSE die starke Bezugnahme auf das Kollektiv, auf eine vergegenwärtigte Gemeinschaft.

Im gleichen Heft beschreibt Vince Leo, wie sich Robert Frank in seinem photographischen Werk im Laufe der Jahrzehnte vom Öffentlichen zum Privaten hin entwickelt habe: «1959 muss es ausgesehen haben, als wäre das ganze Land (Amerika) im Begriff, den öffentlichen Raum aufzugeben.» Gleichzeitig stellt Leo fest: «Privatheit und Imagekontrolle, einstmals Privilegien der Reichen, wurden zur prägenden Kraft in allen visuellen Beziehungen.»

In diesem beschriebenen Spannungsfeld überschreiten im Insert Nan Goldins lebensdurchtränkte Bilder menschlicher Verletzlichkeit jene unbeschriebenen Grenzen, die sich als Thema dieser PARKETT-Ausgabe herauskristallisiert haben.

EDITORIAL This issue of PARKETT evokes the merger of art and life, not as it was propagated in the late sixties, but as an entity freed from the conspicuous involvement of the artist's person. Nor is the artist free as a bird, à la Yves Klein's leap into the void.

In the work of Weiner and Whiteread, "art and life" appear as an objective, tangible fusion, melted into a single body. Both artists have worked in public spaces, and faced the friction of public exposure. "I'll be a tattoo on Rachel Whiteread's structures," Lawrence Weiner said when we suggested juxtaposing the two of them. Public opinion has been given a voice in this issue. An anti-aircraft tower from World War II that stands in the midst of Vienna bears an inscription by Weiner that is visible from afar: SMASHED TO PIECES (IN THE STILL OF THE NIGHT). The personal responses of individuals to Weiner's piece reveal an emotional spectrum that does not exclude indifference, while the intense reactions to Rachel Whiteread's spectacular sculpture HOUSE demonstrate its powerful impact on the community.

By contrast, writer Vince Leo traces the shift of Robert Frank's photographic oeuvre from public to private sphere: "In 1959 it must have looked as if the whole country was in the process of abandoning public space." He goes on to observe that "privacy and image control, once the privilege of the rich, became a guiding force in all visual relations."

Nan Goldin's ardent, vital images of human vulnerability in the Insert cross those unwritten boundaries that have become the subject of the present issue of PARKETT.

Bice Curiger

VINCE LEO

ROBERT FRANK: FROM COMPROMISE TO COLLABORATION

▪ *Compromise* ▪

The first Robert Frank photographs published in America were pictures of women's shoes that appeared in a July 1947 *Harper's Bazaar* article titled "As Skirts Go Lower—Shoes Grow Higher." Even though the variable focus and overall darkness of the pictures offer hints of the gritty, off-center realism that was to become Frank's stylistic trademark, the photographs reveal much more about an artist who understood the rewards of biding his time. These photographs are not by Robert Frank the archetypal photographic outsider, they're by Robert Frank the up-and-coming insider, the man who traded his photographic freedom for a paycheck and a foot in the door.

That trade-off and its effects were the crucible of Frank's discontent and the true subject of his "personal" and commercial photographs for the next ten years. Slowly but surely, Robert Frank would hone a style and a vision out of his life in the belly of the beast. He would also find commercial support for that style and vision. By 1955 he would do a photo story for *Fortune* on the Washington-New York train

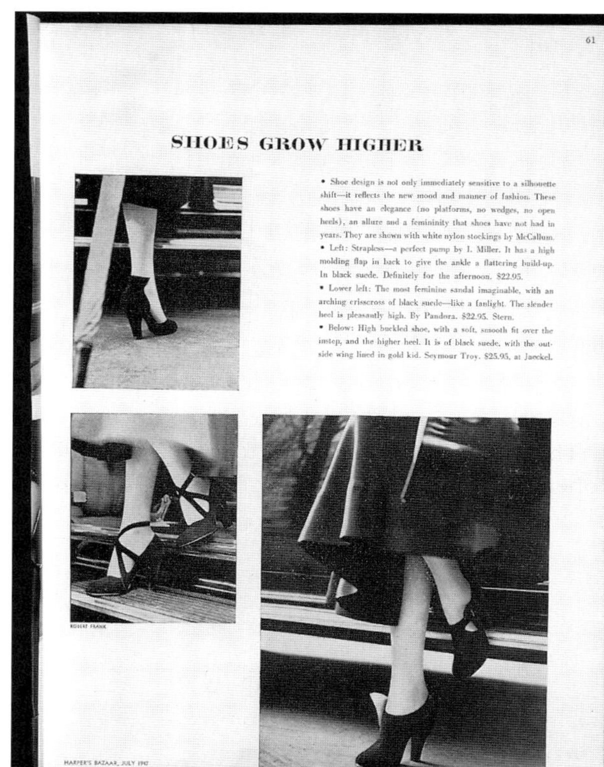
61

SHOES GROW HIGHER

• Shoe design is not only immediately sensitive to a silhouette shift—it reflects the new mood and manner of fashion. These shoes have an elegance (no platforms, no wedges, no open heels), an allure and a femininity that shoes have not had in years. They are shown with white nylon stockings by McCallum.
• Left: Strapless—a perfect pump by I. Miller. It has a high molding flap in back to give the ankle a flattering build-up. In black suede. Definitely for the afternoon. $22.95.
• Lower left: The most feminine sandal imaginable, with an arching crisscross of black suede—like a fanlight. The slender heel is pleasantly high. By Pandora. $22.95. Stern.
• Below: High buckled shoe, with a soft, smooth fit over the instep, and the higher heel. It is of black suede, with the outside wing lined in gold kid. Seymour Troy. $25.95, at Jaeckel.

ROBERT FRANK

HARPER'S BAZAAR, JULY 1947

ROBERT FRANK, "As Skirts Go Lower—Shoes Grow Higher", *Harper's Bazaar*, July 1947.

VINCE LEO is an artist and writer living in Minneapolis.

called The Congressional, one photograph of which would serve second duty in THE AMERICANS. Even in 1958, when his photographs had completely eclipsed the editorial work of the day, he would start on a long-term advertising project entitled NEW YORK IS that would encompass his transition to film by publishing filmstrips instead of individual photographs. It was a long way from photographing shoes, but he was still working on someone else's project, still compromising what he saw for what others wanted him to see.

Even though he traveled and worked on independent projects, Frank worked on assignment for sixteen years. Officially speaking, these sixteen years barely exist. Unlike the magazine work of Walker Evans or Diane Arbus, his commercial photographs have never been the subject of a monograph or exhibition.[1)] The result is a morally uncomplicated Robert Frank who never existed. In possession of a pure vision routinely traced to some early snapshots, this Robert Frank is exactly the kind of pasteboard hero the photographer of THE AMERICANS would call into question. Frank's heroism might be more complicated and more hard-won, but that's impossible to know because we've never been given a glimpse of what it was he had to overcome to achieve what he did. Without the visual evidence of those thirteen years of compromise we can never understand how the romanticism of his snapshots developed into the social critique of THE AMERICANS or COCKSUCKER BLUES; we can't estimate the great price in lost illusions that he paid for his vision of the world. Without those photographs from *Life* and *Look* and *Vogue,* we remain blind to the nature of his personal accomplishment—the way he transformed a willingness to compromise into an ability to forge a complex integrity out of whatever the world had to offer. Compromise, transcribed in fractions of a second and measured by years of survival, is one of the keys to Robert Frank's particular greatness, evidence of his ability to persevere in the face of overwhelming odds and proof that a moral and aesthetic self could survive and grow in the most unexpected places.

▪ *Unpredictability* ▪

There's a story about Robert Frank that may or may not be true. Ralph Gibson was working on a film with him and complaining that everything in photography had been done, there wasn't anything new to do with a camera. Frank replied by taking Gibson's Leica, setting the self-timer, and throwing it as high as he could into the air. After Gibson had caught it, Frank asked, "Ever done that before?"

That story illustrates what is truly unsettling about Robert Frank's photographs from the 1950s. It wasn't only the national or racial or economic politics of his pictures that brought him to national attention, it was also his representational politics. At a time when photographic aesthetics dictated controlling every element of the picture plane from exposure to framing to development, Frank immersed himself in the possibilities of losing control on purpose. He pointed his camera and shot from the hip or the floor into jumbled crowds and backlit rooms. No matter how much the success of this strategy depended on practice, skill, and pure athletic ability, it was all in the service of creating a space for the forces of the world to have a more active part in the making of his photographs. The more he relinquished control, the more the world stepped in to take a hand in its own transcription—creating relationships, destroying tonal visibility, giving up hidden details. Even at his most critical, Robert Frank photographed his own trust in the unpredictable nature of the world and made its power for truth-telling and renewal visible. This is how he was able to make pictures about what he might not be able to see or even know but which was present anyway.

Giving up control meant more than overturning the conventions of photographic aesthetics. Control is the essence of planning and planning was the essence of American utopianism in the 1950s. Plan-

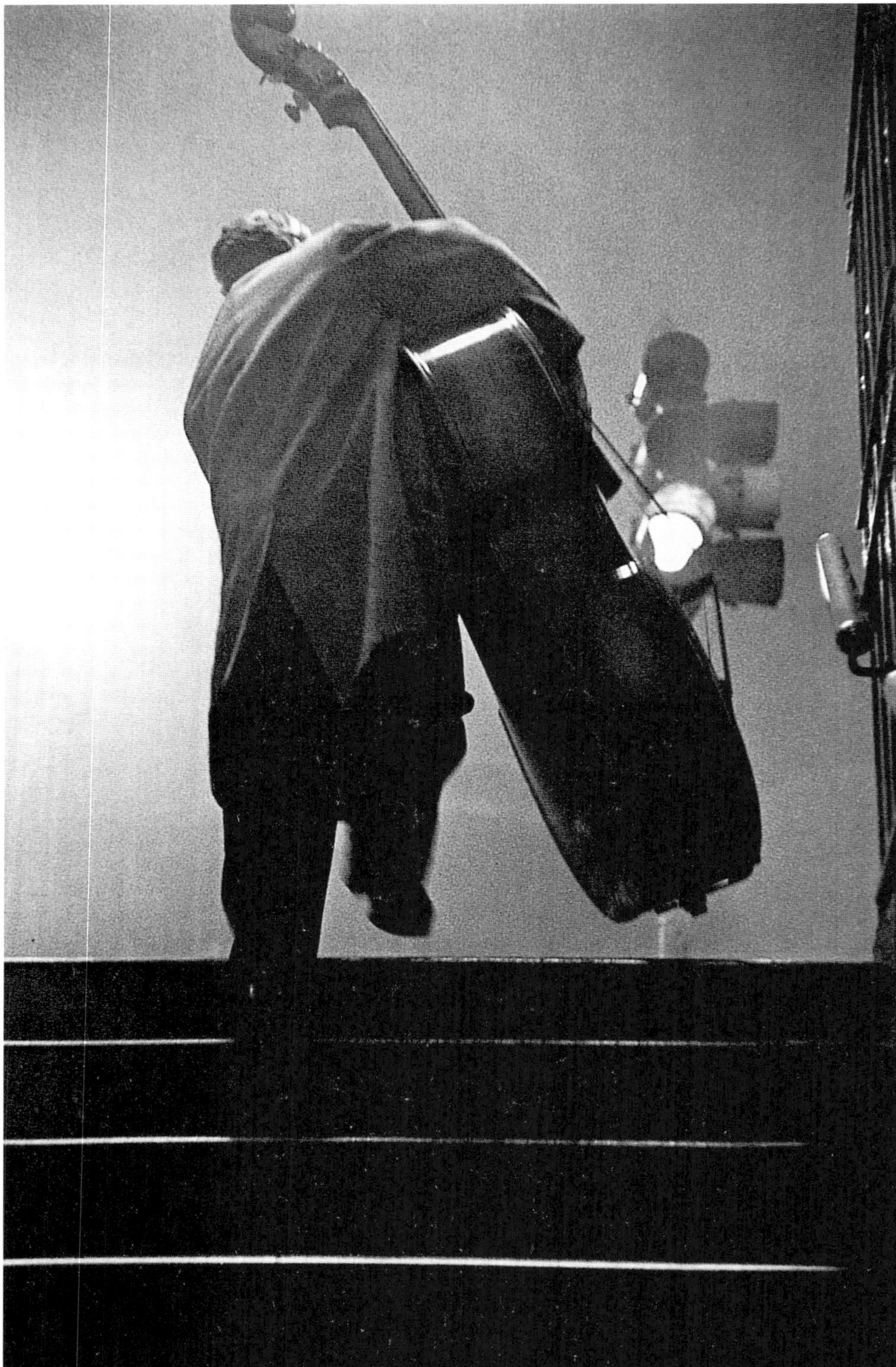

ROBERT FRANK, NEW YORK SUBWAY, 1953.

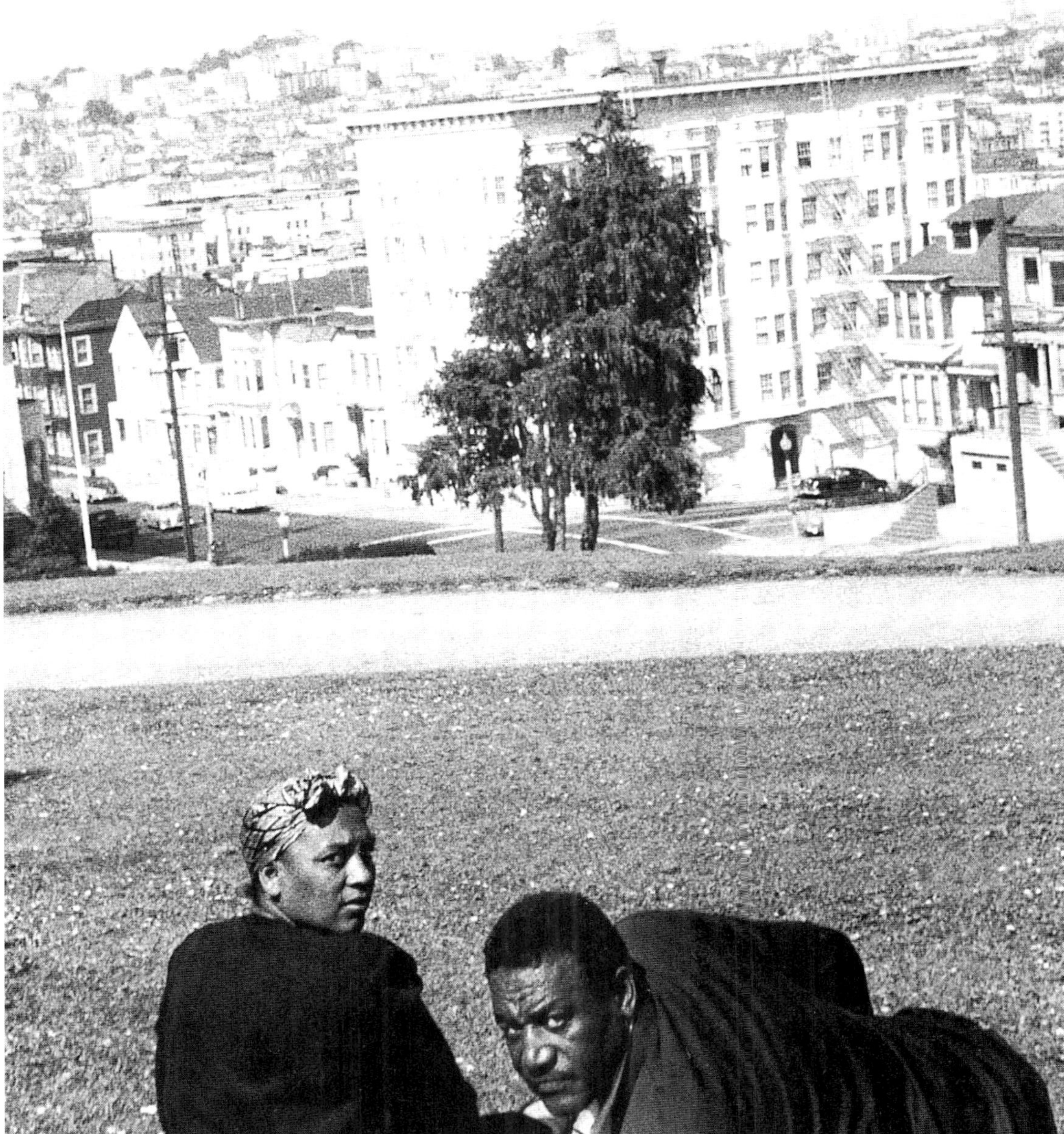

ROBERT FRANK, SAN FRANCISCO, 1955.

ning held up the statistical possibility of keeping the world at bay by denying the power of the unpredictable. Planning would create jobs, save cities, painlessly redistribute wealth, and in the process lay the foundation for the American Century. The cast of characters in Robert Frank's photographs is drawn from this very plan—many of them could have appeared in any one of a number of stories in *Life* or *Look*. But when he breaks with the conventions of photographic control, his subjects break with the visual conventions of the American plan. It's not so much that they don't look happy, contented, or successful—the biggest problem to those who believed in the logic of planning was that Frank's subjects didn't look the way they were supposed to look. They became unpredictable. Willingly, unwillingly, even unknowingly, they entered the unstable field created by Frank's experiments with control and rewrote the way the world worked in America.

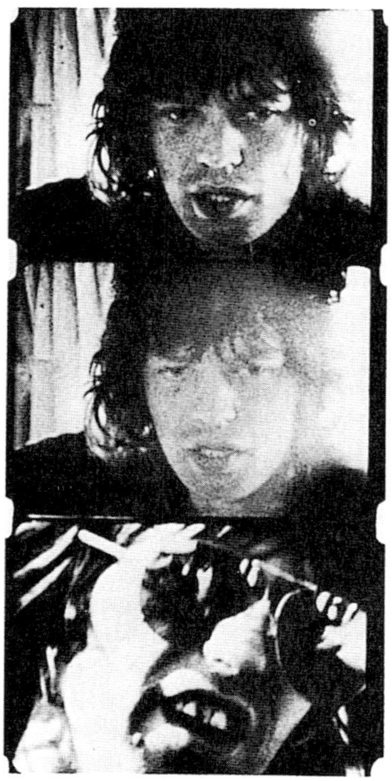

Negotiations I

Most of the photographs in THE AMERICANS look as if they had been made on overcast days. There are few distinct shadows or highlights. Contrary to Frank's famous dictum, "Black and white is the vision of hope and despair,"[2] many of his pictures are a dark and dreary gray. Like a powerful dirge, his bleak tonal range (especially in the versions of THE AMERICANS published after 1969) is the most elemental form of his visual critique of American optimism. By making use of overcast days, Frank replaced the possibilities and eventful drama encoded in directional light with an ambient gray visibility. He turned luminosity—American realism's last and most elemental symbol of salvation—into something that was part helpless accomplice to lackluster lives and part angry witness for a pitiless prosecution. If we feel despair at Robert Frank's pictures, it is the despair we feel over the changelessness of cloudy days.

This is Robert Frank at his most sublime, able to negotiate the very sun and sky into his photographic statements. But sun and sky don't observe the boundaries of the visual field. Consider El Niño, the mysterious Pacific trade wind. When El Niño descends on North America it brings an inordinate number of overcast days and with them an increasing amount of social depression. Maybe El Niño was on the loose in 1955–1956, prowling North America on Frank's shoulder, coloring his photographic palette and his attitude. It's humbling to consider that those winds, locked inside Frank's photographs, are still blowing across America thirty-nine years later, still affecting the emotional tenor of the country, still shaping the direction of representation.[3]

Negotiations II

A friend once said that the reason THE AMERICANS was so important and so good was because Robert Frank had the rare luck to photograph at a time when people actually looked like what they were. It's

ROBERT FRANK, aus dem Film COCKSUCKER BLUES, 1972 / from the film COCKSUCKER BLUES.

ROBERT FRANK, CHARLESTON, South Carolina, 1955.

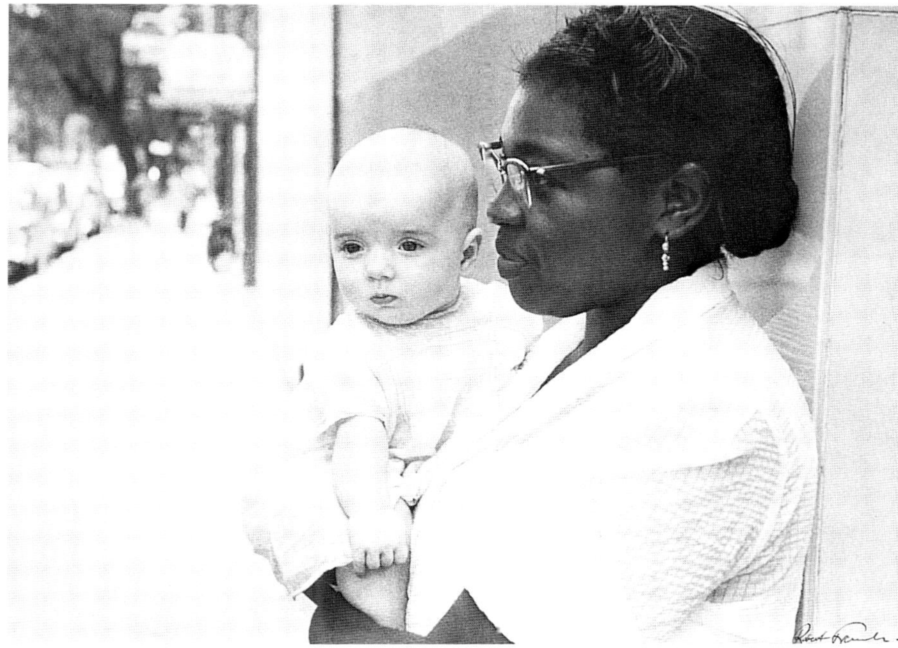

an interesting idea, but the evidence of Frank's photographs suggests that he entered into a much more active negotiation with the world.

SAN FRANCISCO is a photograph of one of these negotiations. Most people would accept that it's a picture about or of the black couple in the center of the frame, but it's also a picture by them. They brought their entire lives to bear on this single moment of exposure. Their dreams and disappointments have physically inscribed the silver grains of Frank's film. SAN FRANCISCO wouldn't exist without these two anonymous collaborators.

And yet Robert Frank is also active in this photographic moment. He isn't just releasing the shutter, he's set the entire emotional context of the picture in motion by surprising these two people, by approaching them from the rear. He doesn't photograph their immediate disorientation, he waits that brief second until they have some idea of what's happening to them. The woman's expression turns to fear and the man's to anger. Fear and anger are the bitter harvest of racism, the emotions produced by hundreds of years of beatings, rapes, and lynchings. The memory of racism is what these two people bring to this photograph; it is Frank who activates that memory and brings it into the present.

The catch is that the only way for Frank to contact the products of racism was to become the figure of the racist. Robert Frank is the threatening white man, become part of the racist world, present in his own photograph as the feared and hated. SAN FRANCISCO is not a photograph about racism, it's a racist incident. In some way Frank brutalized these two people, but together they created one of the truest and most painful representations of American race relations.

One of the subtexts of THE AMERICANS is its exposé of the everyday nature of American racism. But it would take the wisdom of Solomon to decide whether Frank was right or wrong in SAN FRANCISCO, or who the true author of this photograph might be, or whether the pain suffered by all parties was worth it. These questions are the burden of any active photographic negotiation with the world. The fact that Frank assumed this burden only speaks to the good faith of his negotiations and the depth of his hope in an optimistic outcome.

ROBERT FRANK, CAR ACCIDENT, U.S. 66, between Winslow and Flagstaff, Arizona, 1955.

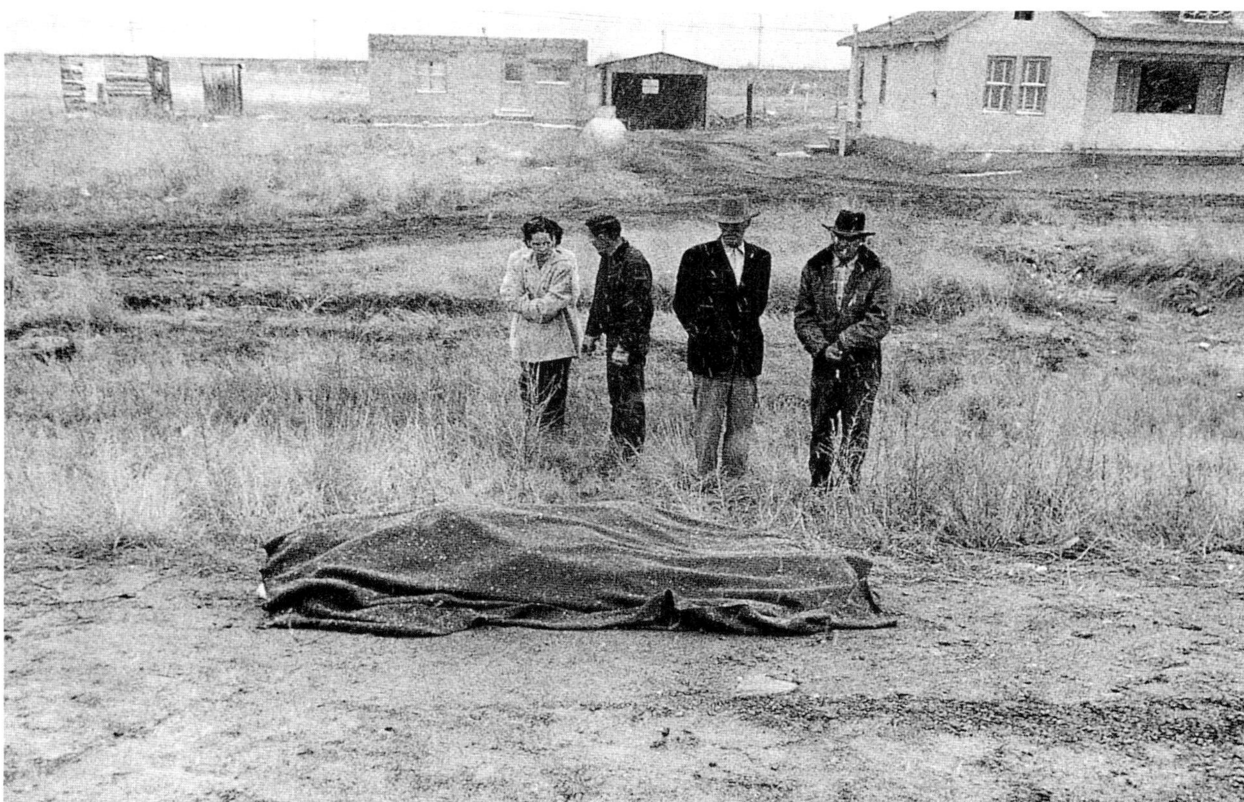

ROBERT FRANK, VIEW FROM HOTEL WINDOW / BLICK AUS DEM HOTELFENSTER, Butte, Montana, 1956.

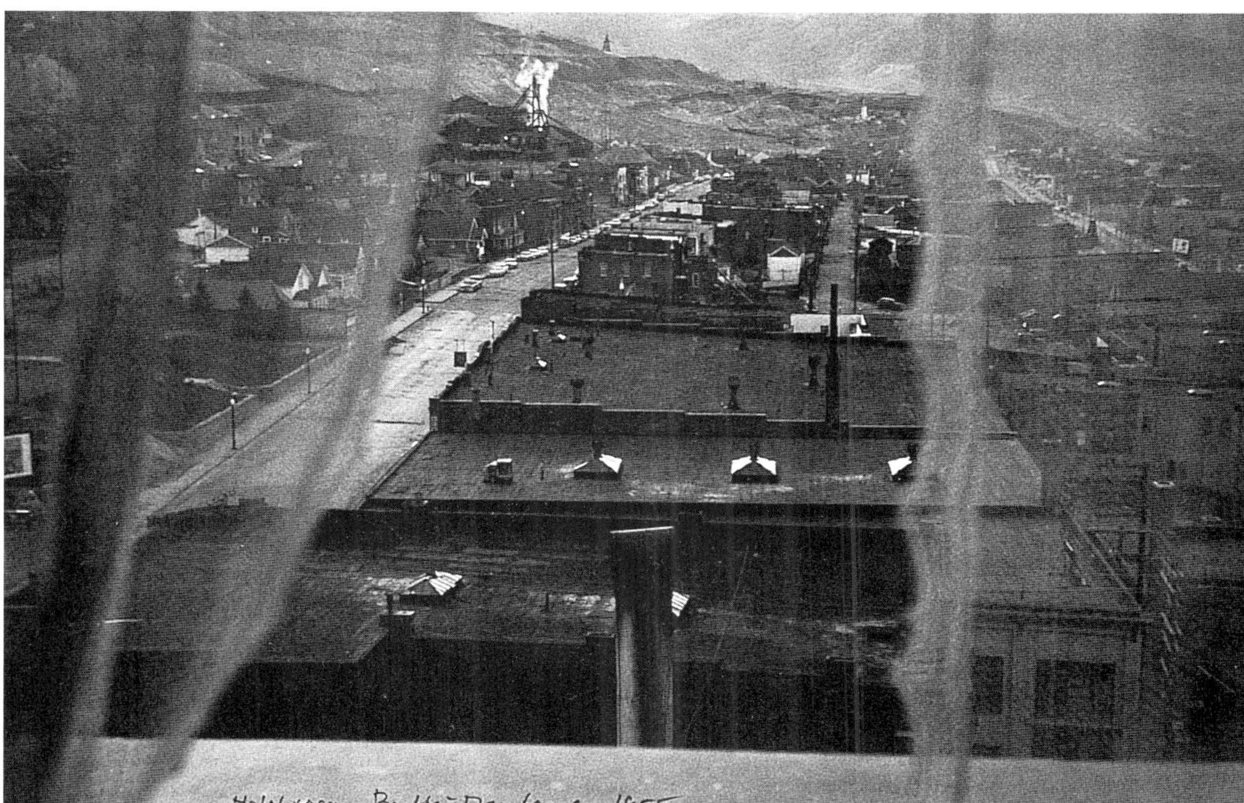

Collaboration

Visually speaking, Robert Frank's movement from still photography to film is barely discernible. Even though the BUS series and ZERO MOSTEL READS A BOOK are constructed from still photographs, they can also be seen as truncated films, jumbled, not-quite-right flipbooks. On the other hand, PULL MY DAISY looks a lot like Frank's still-camera work. His films may have signaled a profound transition in his work but it wasn't profound as a change in media—it was profound as a change in his relationship to his subject. Gone are the anonymous collaborators and chance encounters of his street work. When Frank began to make movies, he filmed for his friends. Friends would become cast and crew, screenwriter and object of fascination. He would eventually return to still photography, but he would remain wary of the anonymous social relations of his earlier work.

The change in subject had started much earlier. A photograph of Frank's wife and son, MARY NURSING PABLO, had won second prize in *Life* magazine's 1951 Young Photographer's Contest and MARY IN BED had been part of THE FAMILY OF MAN in 1955. Most tellingly, the last photograph of THE AMERICANS is a picture of Mary and Pablo made near Del Rio, Texas. They look like a figure for Robert Frank himself, tired of the road, ready to head home. When he returns to still photography he very seldom leaves home, photographing his new partner June Leaf, his surroundings in Nova Scotia, a short trip to the hospital. Even his few forays into public space to photograph the Democratic convention or to film the Rolling Stones are by invitation. The truth is that Frank never really abandoned still photography; he abandoned "the street"—the public space of still photography—and the kind of photographic violence that characterized it.

In 1959 it must have looked as if the whole country was in the process of abandoning public space. Frank's urban and rural street of 1955–1956 was becoming the walled-in private property of malls and suburban developments. The social contract that he questioned and pushed to the limit would soon disintegrate into any and all forms of public violence. Privacy and image control, once a privilege of the rich, became a guiding force in all visual relations.

When Frank moved from the public to the personal he turned the consequences of this shift away from public space inside out. He filmed the street in his own home, followed unpredictability into the most predictable of settings, confronted those most dear to him. It was a whole new America, an America based on community, shared interests, and ongoing commitments. Fragmentary photographic engagements gave way to long-term representational relationships based on the compromised give-and-take of active participation. This was the new world Robert Frank bequeathed to a whole generation of photographers for whom the old America could no longer exist. You can glimpse this new version of THE AMERICANS in the family photographs of Emmit Gowin, the extended family photographs of Nan Goldin, and the community-based photojournalism of Wendy Watriss. In Robert Frank's new America, personal space had become public space and public space had become representational space—larger, more participatory, realized only through compromise and compromised only by the terms of collaboration.

This article is published on the occasion of Robert Frank's 70th birthday. The major exhibition currently on view at the National Gallery in Washington until the end of this year will tour Japan, Switzerland and Holland before returning to the United States.

1) One of these works, an advertisement in the NEW YORK IS- series, appears in Sarah Greenough's discussion of Robert Frank's sequencing of photographs in "Fragments that Make a Whole: Meaning in Photographic Sequences," in *Robert Frank: Moving Out* (Washington: The National Gallery, 1994), p. 118.
2) Ibid, p. 54.
3) Portions of NEGOTIATION I were published in *Camera Austria* No. 40, Fall, 1992, p. 11, and *Fünf amerikanische Fotografen und Edward Hopper*, ed. George W. Költzsch and Heinz Liesbrock, exhibition catalogue (Essen: Museum Folkwang Essen, 1992), p. 162.

VINCE LEO

ROBERT FRANK: VOM KOMPROMISS ZUR MITWIRKUNG

▪ *Kompromiss* ▪

Die ersten Photos, die Robert Frank in Amerika veröffentlichte, waren Aufnahmen von Frauenschuhen in der *Harper's Bazaar*-Ausgabe vom Juli 1947; sie erschienen im Rahmen eines Artikels mit dem Titel «As Skirts Go Lower—Shoes Grow Higher» (Die Röcke werden kürzer – die Schuhe werden höher). Die wechselnde Schärfe und die allgemeine Dunkelheit der Bilder verweisen zwar bereits auf den ebenso eigenwilligen wie abseitigen Realismus, der zu Franks stilistischem Markenzeichen werden sollte. Viel mehr aber verraten diese Photos über einen Künstler, der es versteht, den richtigen Zeitpunkt abzuwarten. Diese Photographien sind nicht von Robert Frank, dem archetypischen photographischen Aussenseiter, sie sind von Robert Frank, dem vielversprechenden Insider, jenem Mann, der seine photographische Freiheit für einen Scheck und einen Fuss in der Tür verkauft hat.

Dieser Handel und seine Folgen waren der Schmelztiegel für Franks Unbehagen und das eigentliche Thema seiner «persönlichen» wie auch seiner kommerziellen Photos in den nächsten zehn Jahren.

VINCE LEO ist Künstler und Autor und lebt in Minneapolis.

Langsam, aber sicher entwickelte Robert Frank aus diesem Leben in der Höhle des Löwen einen Stil, eine Vision. Für beides fand er auch kommerzielle Unterstützung. 1955 schoss er für das Magazin *Fortune* eine Photogeschichte im Zug Washington–New York (man nennt diesen Zug «The Congressional»); eine Aufnahme aus dieser Serie erschien später auch noch einmal in THE AMERICANS. Noch 1958, als seine Photographie bereits weit über die normale redaktionelle Arbeit hinausging, begann er ein langfristiges Werbeprojekt mit dem Titel NEW YORK IS. Anstelle von einzelnen Photos veröffentlichte er Filmstreifen; der Übergang zum Film kündigte sich an. Frank hatte sich bereits weit von jenen Zeiten entfernt, in denen er Schuhe photographierte, aber immer noch arbeitete er für jemand anderen und stellte, was er sah, hinter das zurück, was er sehen sollte.

Wenngleich er reiste und unabhängige Projekte realisierte, führte er doch immerhin sechzehn Jahre lang Auftragsarbeiten aus. In der offiziellen Darstellung fallen diese sechzehn Jahre aber kaum ins Gewicht. Im Gegensatz zu den Zeitschriften-Arbeiten von Walker Evans oder Diane Arbus sind seine kommerziellen Photographien nie Gegenstand einer Monographie oder Ausstellung gewesen.[1] Auf diese Weise ist das Bild eines moralisch völlig unkomplizierten Robert Frank entstanden, der aber so nie existiert hat. Im Besitz einer reinen Vision, die schablonenhaft bis zu ein paar frühen Schnappschüssen zurückverfolgt wird, ist dieser Robert Frank genau jene Art von plakativem Helden, den der Photograph von THE AMERICANS in Frage stellen wollte. Franks Heroismus ist komplizierter und schwer erkämpft, aber davon können wir nichts wissen, weil wir niemals einen Eindruck davon bekommen haben, was er überwinden musste, um die bekannten Ergebnisse zu erzielen. Ohne den visuellen Niederschlag dieser dreizehn kompromissreichen Jahre werden wir nie verstehen, wie sich aus dem Romantizismus seiner Schnappschüsse die Gesellschaftskritik von THE AMERICANS oder COCKSUCKER BLUES entwickelte. Und wir werden nie begreifen, welch hohen Preis an verlorener Illusion er für seine Sicht der Welt zu zahlen hatte. Ohne diese Photos aus *Life* und *Look* und *Vogue* bleibt uns seine persönliche Leistung verschlossen, jene Art, wie er seine Kompromissbereitschaft in die Fähigkeit umwandelte, aus allem, was die Welt zu bieten hatte, ein komplexes Ganzes zu formen. Der Kompromiss, im Bruchteil einer Sekunde eingegangen und in langen Jahren immer wieder überprüft, ist einer der Schlüssel zu Robert Franks besonderem Vermögen, ist Zeichen für seine Fähigkeit, unter erdrückenden

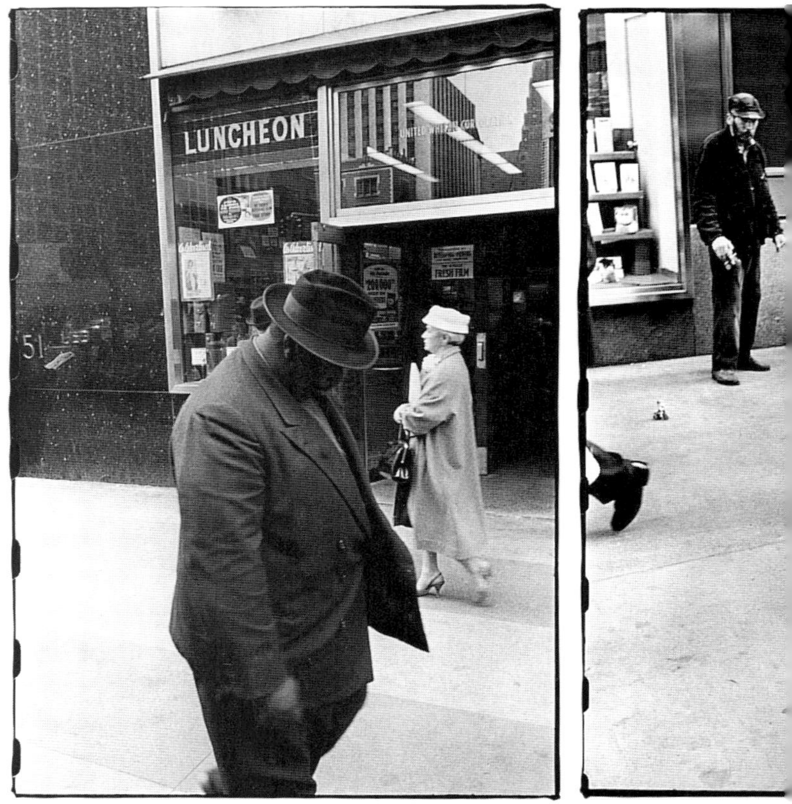

Bedingungen durchzuhalten, Beweis dafür, dass ein moralisch-ästhetisches Ich selbst an den ungewöhnlichsten Orten überleben und sich entwickeln kann.

▪ *Unvorhersehbarkeit* ▪

Es gibt eine Geschichte über Robert Frank, die vielleicht wahr ist, vielleicht aber auch nicht. Ralph Gibson arbeitete mit ihm an einem Film und beklagte sich darüber, dass es in der Photographie alles schon einmal gegeben habe und mit der Kamera nichts Neues mehr zu machen sei. Frank nahm daraufhin Gibsons Leica, setzte den automatischen Auslöser in Gang und warf sie, so hoch er konnte, in die Luft. Nachdem Gibson sie aufgefangen hatte, fragte Frank: «Hast du das schon mal gemacht?»

Diese Geschichte zeigt das eigentlich Beunruhigende an Robert Franks Photographien aus den 50er Jahren. Es waren nicht bloss die nationalen, rassistischen oder ökonomischen Aspekte seiner Aufnahmen, die ihm nationale Aufmerksamkeit eintrugen, sondern auch seine Darstellungsmethoden. Zu einer Zeit, als die Ästhetik der Photographie die Kontrolle jedes einzelnen Elements der Bildfläche von der Aufnahme über die Rahmung bis hin zur Entwicklung vorschrieb, vertiefte Frank sich in die verschie-

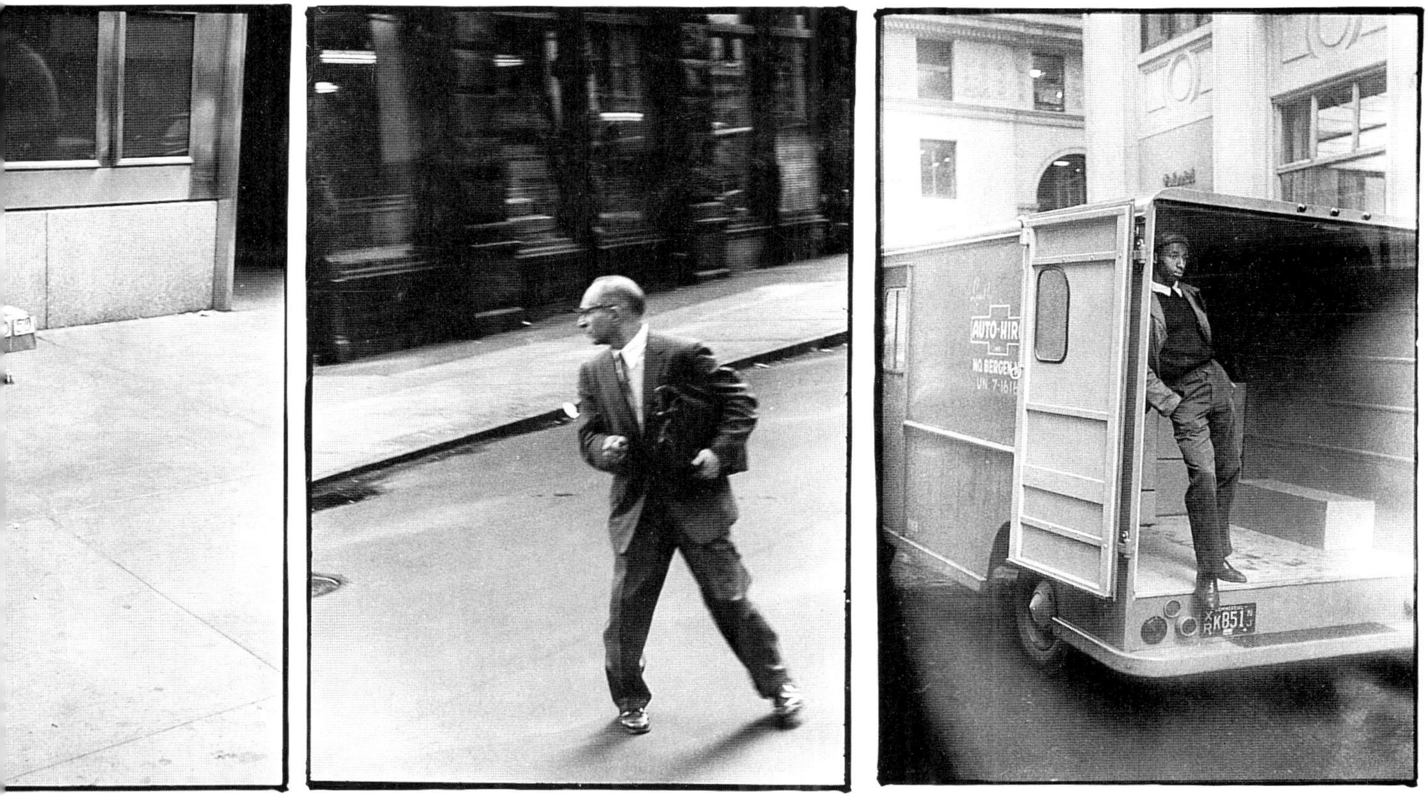

ROBERT FRANK, BUS PHOTOGRAPHS, New York City, 1958.

denen Möglichkeiten, wie man die Kontrolle bewusst aufgeben konnte. Er brachte seine Kamera in Anschlag und schoss aus der Hüfte oder vom Boden in Menschenmengen und Zimmer im Gegenlicht. Gleichviel ob der Erfolg dieser Strategie auf Erfahrung, Handwerk und reinem athletischen Können beruhte oder nicht, immer ging es darum, einen Raum für die Kräfte der Welt zu schaffen, auf dass diese in der Entstehung seiner Photographien eine aktive Rolle spielen konnten. Je mehr er die Kontrolle aufgab, desto deutlicher führte die Welt in seiner eigenen Formulierung Regie – stellte Bezüge her, zerstörte die tonale Differenziertheit, gab verborgene Details preis. Selbst in seinen kritischsten Momenten photographierte Frank sein Vertrauen in die Unabsehbarkeit der Welt und demonstrierte seine Kraft zur Wahrhaftigkeit und Erneuerung. Auf diese Weise gelangen ihm Bilder über das, was er selbst vielleicht gar nicht sah oder wissen konnte, was aber dennoch gegenwärtig war. Die Kontrolle aufzugeben hiess mehr, als nur die Konventionen photographischer Ästhetik über den Haufen zu werfen. Kontrolle ist das Herzstück der Planung, und Planung wiederum war das Herzstück des amerikanischen Utopismus der 50er Jahre. Planung barg die statistische Möglichkeit, die Welt in Schach zu halten, indem man die Macht des Unvorhersehbaren leugnete. Planung sorgte für Arbeitsplätze, für die Rettung der Städte und die reibungslose Umverteilung des Wohlstands, und sie schuf dabei die Grundlage für das amerikanische Jahrhundert. Die Figuren in Robert Franks Photographien entstammen ebendiesem Plan; viele von ihnen könnten jeder beliebigen Geschichte aus *Life* oder *Look* entnommen sein. Doch wo Frank mit den Konventionen der photographischen Kontrolle bricht, brechen seine Personen mit den visuellen Konventionen des amerikanischen Plans. Nicht dass sie unglücklich, unzufrieden oder erfolglos aussähen; das grösste Problem für diejenigen, die an die Logik der Planung glaubten, war die Tatsache, dass Franks Personen nicht so aussahen, wie sie aussehen sollten. Sie wurden unvorhersehbar. Willentlich oder unwillentlich, ja selbst ohne überhaupt davon zu wissen, gerieten sie in jenes instabile Feld, das Frank durch seine Experimente mit der Kontrolle schuf, und zeichneten ein neues Bild der Welt, wie sie sich in Amerika darstellte.

▪ *Austausch I* ▪

Die meisten Photos in THE AMERICANS sehen aus, als wären sie an wolkenverhangenen Tagen aufgenommen. Es gibt kaum klare Schatten oder Lichter. Im Gegensatz zu Franks Maxime «Schwarz und Weiss ist die Vision von Hoffnung und Verzweiflung»[2)] sind viele dieser Bilder in düster-trübes Grau getaucht. Gleich einem machtvollen Klagegesang bildet seine trostlose Grauskala (vor allem bei den nach 1969 veröffentlichten Versionen von THE AMERICANS) die elementare Form seiner visuellen Kritik am amerikanischen Optimismus. Aus strahlendem Glanz – jenem letzten und wichtigsten Heilssymbol des amerikanischen Realismus – wird bei ihm zum einen eine Art hilfloser Komplizenschaft mit dem glanzlosen Leben und zum anderen ein zorniges Zeugnis für gnadenlose Zielstrebigkeit. Die Verzweiflung, die uns bei Robert Franks Bildern beschleicht, ist jene, die wir angesichts der Reglosigkeit trüber Tage verspüren. Hier bringt Robert Frank sein Können auf den Punkt: die Sonne und den Himmel selbst ins Photo zu zitieren. Doch Sonne und Himmel halten sich nicht an die Grenzen des Sichtfelds. Nehmen wir beispielsweise El Niño, den mysteriösen pazifischen Passatwind. Wenn El Niño über Nordamerika weht, bedeutet das zahlreiche wolkenverhangene Tage und damit wachsende Depression in der Gesellschaft. Vielleicht hat El Niño sich 1955/56 ausgetobt, seinen Beutezug durch Nordamerika auf Franks Rücken ausgetragen und dabei auf dessen photographische Palette wie auf dessen Haltung abgefärbt. Es ist desillusionierend zu sehen, dass diese Winde, die Frank in seinen Photos eingefangen hat, 39 Jahre später immer noch über Amerika wehen, die emotionale Stimmung des Landes beeinflussen und die darstellerische Gesinnung prägen.[3)]

▪ *Austausch II* ▪

Ein Freund meinte einmal, THE AMERICANS sei deshalb so gut und wichtig, weil Robert Frank das seltene Glück gehabt habe, zu einer Zeit zu photographieren, als die Leute genauso aussahen, wie sie waren. Das ist ein interessanter Gedanke, doch Franks Photos zeigen selbst, dass er in einen viel aktiveren Austausch mit der Welt getreten ist.

SAN FRANCISCO ist ein Photo mit einem solchen Austausch. Die meisten Leute würden wohl sagen, dies sei ein Bild, das das schwarze Paar am unteren Bildrand zeigt, doch die beiden haben an dem Bild auch selbst mitgewirkt. In diesem kurzen Augenblick der Aufnahme haben sie ihr ganzes Leben zum Tragen gebracht. Ihre Träume und Enttäuschungen sind dem Silberkorn in Franks Film physisch einbeschrieben. Ohne die beiden anonymen Mitwirkenden würde SAN FRANCISCO nicht existieren.

Und doch ist auch Robert Frank in diesem photographischen Moment aktiv. Er drückt nicht einfach nur auf den Auslöser, er hat den gesamten emotionalen Kontext dieses bewegten Bildes geschaffen, indem er sich den beiden Personen von hinten näherte und sie überraschte. Er photographiert nicht den ersten Augenblick der Verunsicherung, sondern wartet jene kurze Zeitspanne ab, bis sie sich eine Vorstellung davon gemacht haben, was mit ihnen passiert. Der Gesichtsausdruck der Frau geht in Angst über, der des Mannes in Zorn. Angst und Zorn sind die bitteren Früchte des Rassismus und der Gefühle, die in Jahrhunderten von Mord, Vergewaltigung und Lynchjustiz entstanden sind. Die beiden Menschen bringen die Erinnerung an den Rassismus ins Bild; und Frank erweckt diese Erinnerung zum Leben, hebt sie in die Gegenwart.

Der springende Punkt dabei ist, dass Frank den Kontakt zu den Produkten des Rassismus nur dadurch herstellen konnte, dass er selbst die Rolle des Rassisten übernahm. Robert Frank ist der bedrohliche Weisse, Teil der rassistischen Welt und gegenwärtig in seinem eigenen Photo als der Gefürchtete, Verhasste. SAN FRANCISCO ist kein Photo über Rassismus, es ist ein rassistischer Übergriff. In gewisser Weise hat Frank diese beiden Menschen brutal behandelt, aber zusammen haben die drei eine der wahrhaftigsten und zugleich schmerzhaftesten Darstellungen amerikanischer Rassenverhältnisse hervorgebracht.

Zu den Anklängen, die in THE AMERICANS immer wieder eine Rolle spielen, gehört die Alltäglichkeit des amerikanischen Rassismus. Aber wer wollte entscheiden, ob Frank bei SAN FRANCISCO richtig gehandelt hat oder wer der eigentliche Autor dieses Photos ist oder ob es das Leid gelohnt hat, das allen Beteiligten hier zugefügt wurde. Diese Fragen sind der Preis jeder aktiven photographischen Auseinandersetzung mit der Welt. Dass Frank diesen Preis gezahlt hat, spricht für die Absicht seines Unterfangens und für seine tiefe Hoffnung auf ein gutes Ende.

▪ *Mitwirkung* ▪

In visueller Hinsicht lässt sich der Übergang von der Photographie zum Film bei Frank kaum ausmachen. Die BUS-Serie und ZERO MOSTEL READS A BOOK sind zwar aus Einzelphotos zusammengesetzt, aber man könnte sie ebensogut für Filmausschnitte halten, für durcheinandergeratene, etwas verunglückte Daumenkinos. Dagegen hat PULL MY DAISY wieder Ähnlichkeit mit Franks photographischen Aufnahmen. Sicherlich markieren die Filme einen tiefgreifenden Wandel in seinem Werk, aber nicht hinsichtlich des Mediums, sondern hinsichtlich der Beziehung zu seinem Gegenstand. Die anonymen Kollaborateure und Zufallsbegegnungen seiner Strassenarbeit gibt es jetzt nicht mehr. Als Frank mit dem Filmemachen begann, drehte er zunächst für seine Freunde. Aus ihnen rekrutierte er die gesamte Besetzung, sie wurden zum Drehbuchautor oder zum Objekt der Faszination. Gelegentlich kehrte er zwar noch zur Photographie zurück, doch hütete er sich vor den anonymen gesellschaftlichen Beziehungen seiner früheren Arbeit.

Der Themenwechsel hatte schon viel früher stattgefunden. MARY NURSING PABLO, ein Photo von Franks Frau und Sohn, hatte 1951 beim Young Photographer's Contest des *Life*-Magazins den zweiten Preis gewonnen, und MARY IN BED wurde 1955 im Rahmen der Ausstellung THE FAMILY OF MAN gezeigt. Interessanterweise ist das letzte Photo aus THE AMERICANS ein Bild von Mary und Pablo, das in der Nähe von Del Rio, Texas, aufgenommen wurde. Die beiden wirken wie ein Abbild von Robert Frank selbst: der Strasse überdrüssig, gen Heimat gewendet. Als er zur Photographie zurückkehrt, verlässt er nur selten sein Zuhause, sondern photographiert seine neue Partnerin June Leaf, seine Umgebung in Nova Scotia, einen kurzen Krankenhausbesuch. Selbst seine kurzen Ausflüge in den öffentlichen Raum, wenn er den Parteitag der Demokraten photographiert oder die Rolling Stones filmt, finden ausschliesslich auf Einladung statt. Tatsächlich hat Frank sich nie wirklich von der Photographie abgewandt, wohl aber von «der Strasse», dem öffentlichen Raum der Photographie, und jener photographischen Gewalttätigkeit, die ihr zu eigen ist.

1959 muss es ausgesehen haben, als wäre das ganze Land im Begriff, den öffentlichen Raum ganz aufzugeben. Aus Franks Stadt- und Landstrasse von 1955/56 wurde der umfriedete Privatbesitz der Passagen und suburbanen Entwicklungen. Der Gesellschaftsvertrag, den er hinterfragte und an seine

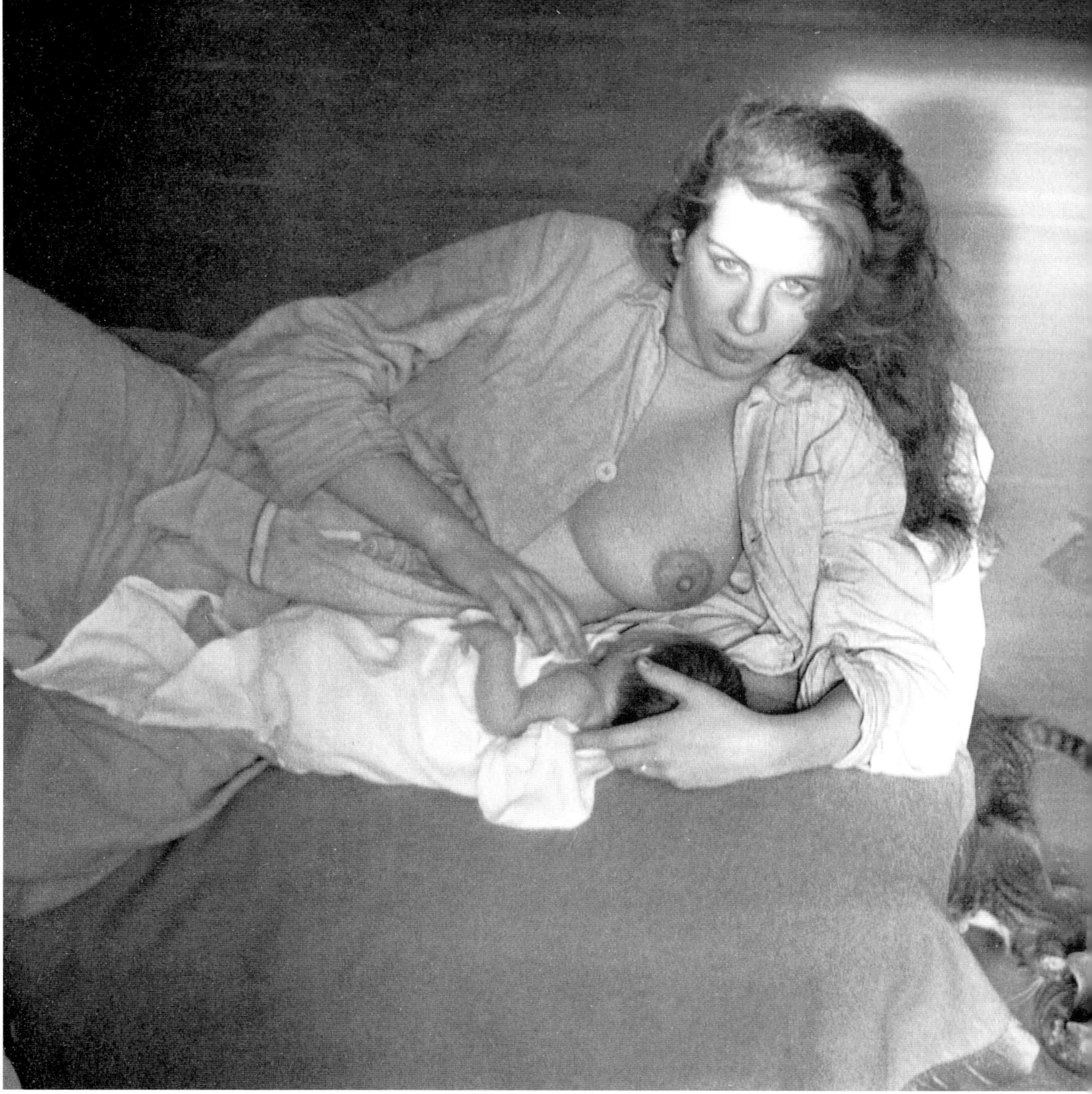

ROBERT FRANK, MARY AND PABLO, New York City, 1951.

Grenzen trieb, sollte sich schon bald in alle möglichen Formen öffentlicher Gewalt auflösen. Privatheit und Image-Kontrolle, einstmals Privilegien der Reichen, wurden zur prägenden Kraft in allen visuellen Beziehungen.

Als Frank vom Öffentlichen zum Persönlichen wechselte, stülpte er die Folgen dieser Abwendung vom öffentlichen Raum von aussen nach innen um. Er filmte die Strasse in seinem eigenen Heim, spürte das Unberechenbare im scheinbar Selbstverständlichen auf und setzte sich mit seinen engsten Mitmenschen auseinander. Es war ein ganz neues Amerika, ein Amerika, das auf Gemeinschaft, gemeinsamen Interessen und festen Bindungen beruhte. Das augenblickhafte Engagement des Photographen wich anhaltenden darstellerischen Beziehungen auf der Grundlage von Geben und Nehmen in aktiver Anteilnahme. Dies war die neue Welt, die Robert Frank einer ganzen Generation von Photographen hinterliess, denen das alte Amerika nicht mehr galt. Dieser neuen Version von THE AMERICANS begegnen wir in den Familienphotos von Emmit Gowin, den erweiterten Familienphotos von Nan Goldin und dem auf der Gemeinschaft aufbauenden Photojournalismus von Wendy Watriss. In Robert Franks neuem Amerika war der persönliche Raum zum öffentlichen geworden, und der öffentliche zum Darstellungs-Raum – weiter, mit grösserer Anteilnahme, hervorgegangen aus dem Kompromiss, und dieser wiederum erzielt im Zusammenwirken.

(Übersetzung: Nansen)

Dieser Artikel erscheint anlässlich von Robert Franks 70. Geburtstag. Gegenwärtig findet bis Ende Jahr in der National Gallery in Washington eine grosse Ausstellung statt, die weitergeht nach Japan, der Schweiz, den Niederlanden und zurück in die USA.

1) Eine dieser Arbeiten, eine Anzeige aus der NEW YORK IS-Serie, ist zu sehen in Sarah Greenoughs Auseinandersetzung mit Robert Franks Photo-Reihen in «Fragments that Make a Whole: Meaning in Photographic Sequences», in *Robert Frank: Moving Out* (Washington, The National Gallery), 1994, S. 118.

2) Ebd., S. 54.

3) Teile aus NEGOTIATIONS I wurden veröffentlicht in *Camera Austria Nr. 40*, Herbst 1992, S. 11, sowie in *Fünf amerikanische Fotografen und Edward Hopper* (Hrsg. George W. Költzsch und Heinz Liesbrock), Ausstellungskatalog, Essen, Museum Folkwang, 1992, S. 162.

Lawrence Weiner

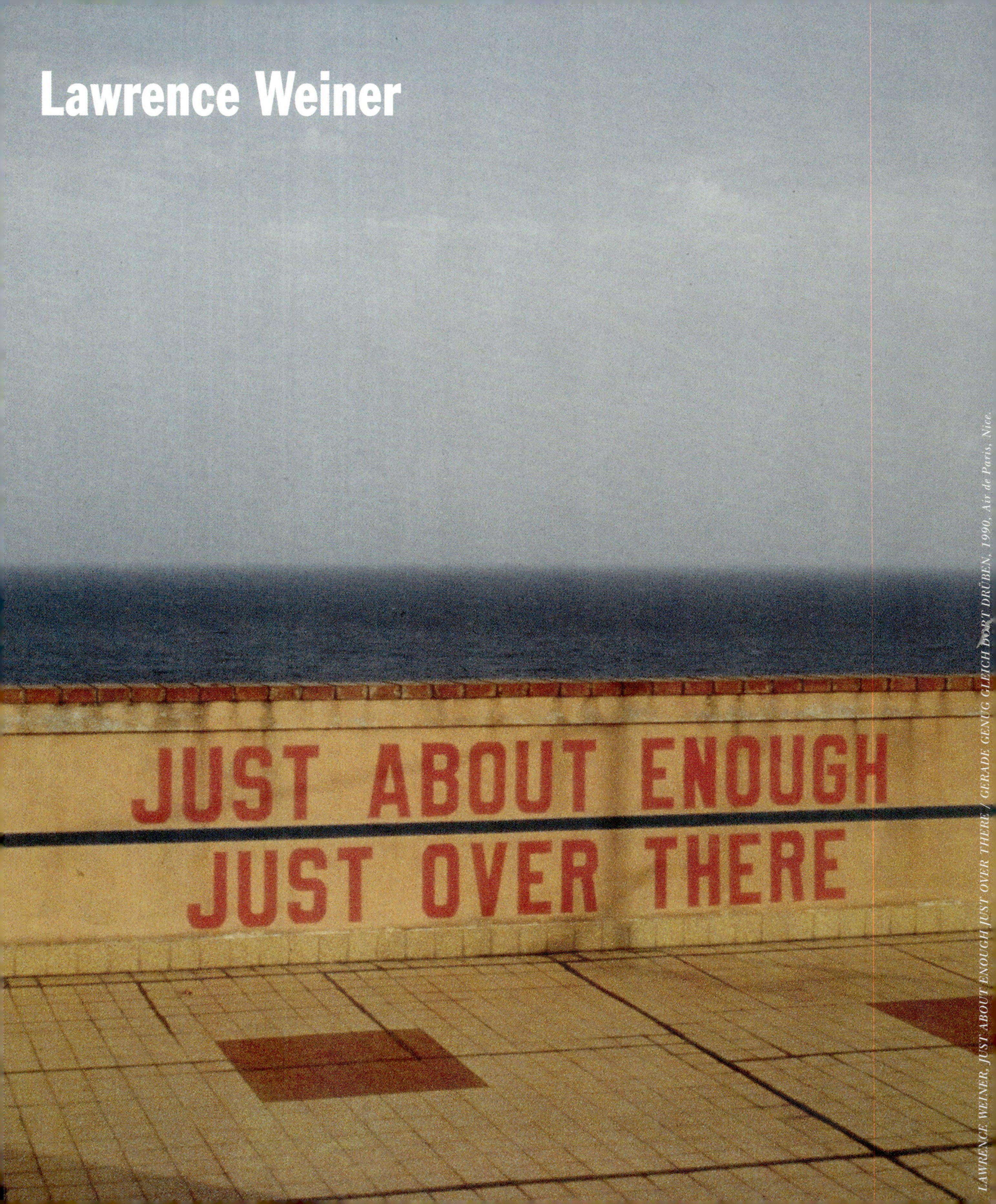

LAWRENCE WEINER, JUST ABOUT ENOUGH JUST OVER THERE / GERADE GENUG GLEICH DORT DRÜBEN, 1990, Air de Paris, Nice.

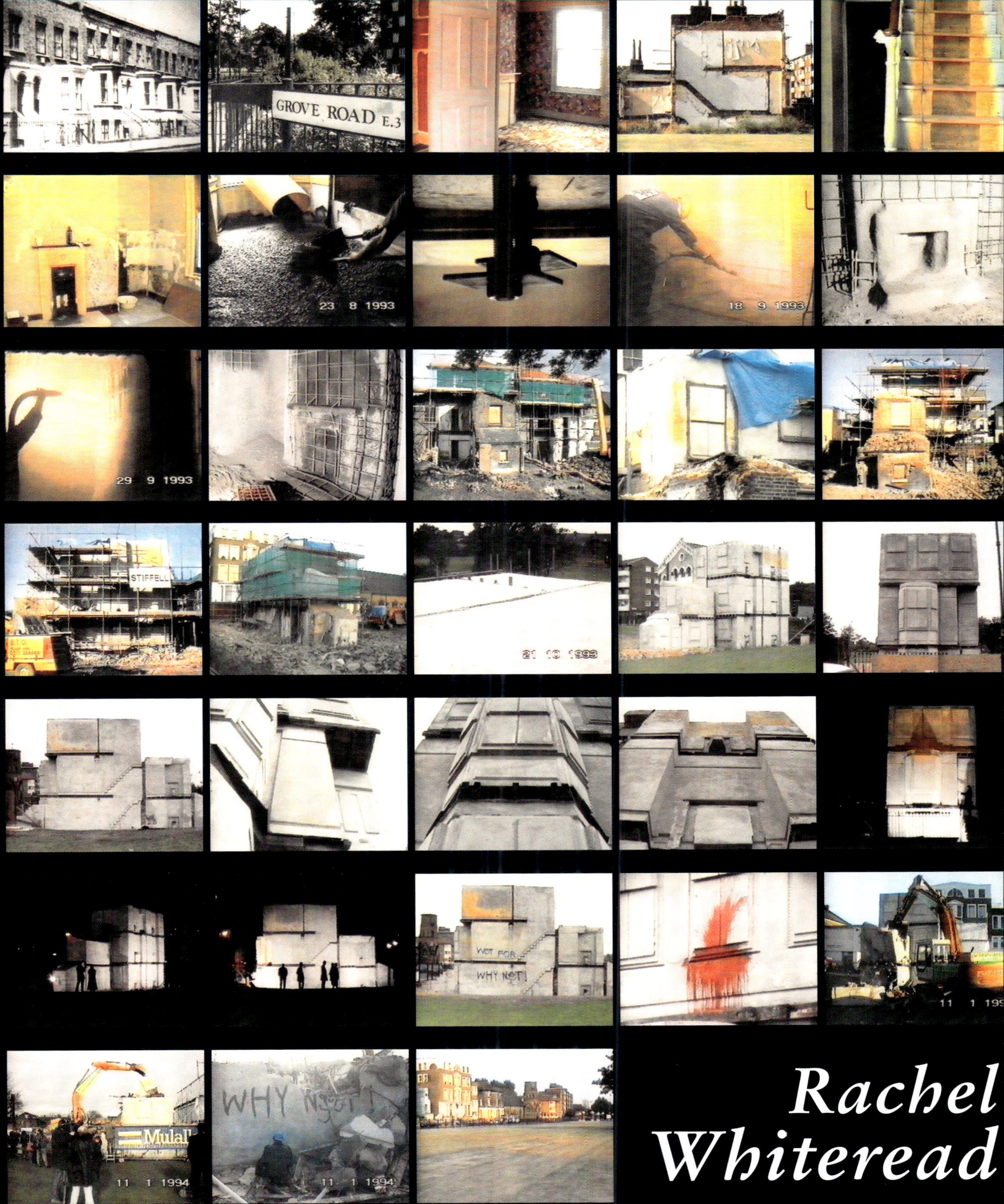

RACHEL WHITEREAD, *HOUSE, prints from the documentary video, August 1993–January 1994, a Hackneyed Production for Artangel.*

Rachel Whiteread

BROOKS ADAMS

Weiner's Werkstätte

I will never forget seeing Lawrence Weiner's 1988 retrospective at the Stedelijk in Amsterdam. Although long familiar with Weiner's works—or so I thought—I was bowled over by their formal diversity and generosity of spirit. The exhibition was an unfurling—room after room—of words, phrases, punctuation riddles, and syntactical fragments, realized in virtually every possible color and typeface. The show as a whole seemed at once prismatic and impressionistic, both euphoric in feeling and soberly egalitarian in its message. At the time, I happened furthermore to be working on an essay about Dutch and Belgian Impressionism and, much to my surprise, here was all that diurnal atmosphere somehow reincarnated in Weiner's concrete wordscapes.[1] Indeed, they all looked like landscapes to me: abstract horizons and vistas of works, as linear and semaphoric as Mondrian's first ecstatic reductions, and, with their rainbow-bright colors, as chromatically alive.

How extremely different this was from perceived versions of Weiner's work that I had more or less taken for granted as a student in the 1970s, and what a sharp contrast to all those received images of mandarin dourness and inscrutability. This artist—whose work has over the years touched on everything from graphic design to concrete poetry, and from film-making to pop-song lyric writing—has for too many years been ghettoized by outdated clichés and characterizations about Conceptualism and the so-called "dematerialization of the art object." "Rediscovered" in the late 1990s, Weiner's art reveals a sensibility that is rooted in a low-down vernacular and yet is almost giddily elevated, one that is as gritty as it is dandified.

It seems to me now that Weiner's work is the very opposite of insular. Ecumenical in its more cerebrated intentions, it also suggests, an array of formal as well as temperamental resonances, overt or subliminal, with visual phenomena including postwar painterly abstraction and film noir, Pop Art and Warholian cinema, along with Earthworks and more recent neo-Romantic displacements.

Weiner's work has itself evolved since 1968, when the artist's Conceptualist manifestoes first appeared. His epochal utterance from 1968, that "the piece need not be built"—a statement invoked and debated ad nauseam by critic-defenders of the dematerialist stance—was qualified by the artist to begin with, and has in any case been superseded by the sheer number and variety of pieces that have in fact not only been built, but also documented in a veritable cavalcade of catalogues raisonnés: one each for the books, the posters, the films and videos, and the word-works. Likewise, the prevailing sense of willful self-negation in Weiner's work of the late sixties,

BROOKS ADAMS is a Contributing Editor to *Art in America.*

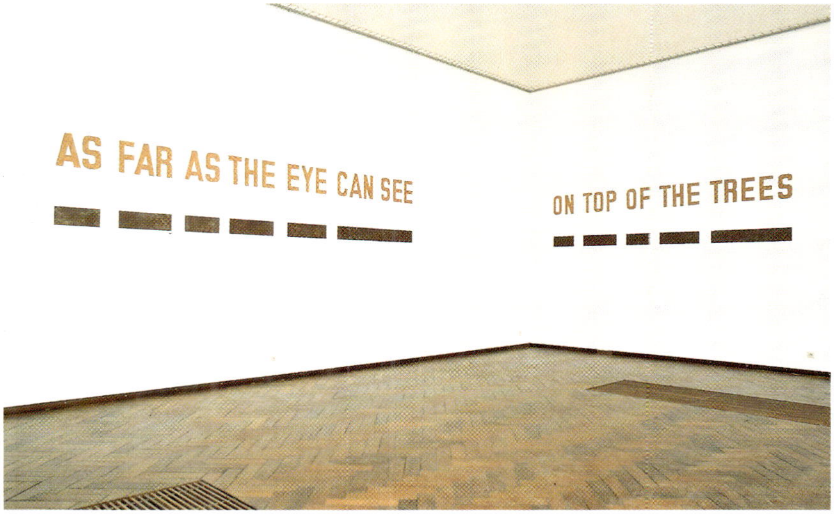

LAWRENCE WEINER,
at the Stedelijk Museum, Amsterdam, 1988.

along with the case for negation in general constructed for and around it as recently as 1986 by the critic Benjamin H. D. Buchloh, have also been superseded by Weiner's own will to realize and proliferate, never more apparent than in recent years.[2)]

The artist's 1993 transformation, for example, of a nineteenth-century weighbridge in the English mill-town of Halifax is an exercise in covert monumentality.[3)] The recast weighbridge, located at the entrance to what was once the largest carpet factory in the world, is now a sculpture, a sort of quasi-Minimalist floor piece emblazoned with the words

SOME LIMESTONE SOME SANDSTONE
ENCLOSED FOR SOME REASON

Thus does Weiner's work proclaim its connection to the spirit of the place, to the matter of the surrounding landscape and, elliptically via "some reason," to the ambiguous welter of private interests, public motives, and historical progressions that over the course of a century led to the initial building of the factory, its eventual obsolescence, and its present, recycled state as a business complex—called Dean Clough—now consecrated by a commissioned work of art. In keeping with nineteenth century convention, the piece is stamped with the date, foundry name, and commissioner (The Henry Moore Sculpture Trust). Weiner's mission here is certainly positive and reclamatory: Essentially he has taken an industrial-age corpse and brought it back to life.

The project continues: After traversing the weighbridge piece—which sits on original, disused railroad tracks—one enters the Dean Clough exhibition halls where the same message may be read, painted directly on the wall. (It is worth noting that due to their environment these wall paintings are often assumed to be tapestries.) Finally, in wall drawings near these latently private/public tapestries are the phrases

STEEL PENNIES DON'T COME
FROM OR GO TO HEAVEN

and

FOR A COPPER OR TWO

Here, conflated and impacted, we find an expanded affirmation of a popular adage merged with the contradiction to a sentimental song title, and a resurrected bit of Victorian bartering slang fused with a double, or even triple entendre that simultaneously alludes to the police and, slyly, to prostitution. This whole project, amplified to the condition of virtual *Gesamtkunstwerk,* is nevertheless classic Weiner: using the givens of a situation, recasting those givens and informing them with a newly relevant public/private iconography, and combining a sense of high moral or historical seriousness with a certain scabrous *je ne sais quoi.*

Today perhaps more than ever, Weiner's public persona evokes the tradition of the socialist aesthete. The artist's appearance, for one, is unique: He reminds me of a traditional Native American he-she, or *berdache.*[4] As scruffy as a sailor gone to seed at sea, yet as highly cultivated as a Talmudic scholar, he further summons up visions of eminent Victorians in portraits by Julia Margaret Cameron. A visit to his house confirmed these eclectic impressions. Almost spartan in its overall decor but ineffably promiscuous in its suggestive powers, it, too, seems at once wholly original and echt-bohemian. There is a 1940s war-time poster in the entrance depicting an heroic male worker, with the caption, "Free Labor Will Win!"; in the large-ish room on the lower ground which serves as Weiner's studio, I noticed a pert triangular pillow inscribed with the words "Camp Fire Girls"—a present given, it turns out, at the time of Weiner's performances (in skirt and high heels) with the all-girl, Vienna-based group *Die Damen.*

Also in the studio were prototypes for several multiples: a new ex-libris for the Kröller-Muller Museum, a letter-opener for a German ad company, a manufacturer's prototype for an edition in progress (in the form of a license plate). At the artist's insistence, the ex-libris which reads SPIRITUS MATERIA will be fixed inside museum book-covers right next to the original ex-libris—designed by Henry Van de Velde—which will be left intact. The knife/letter opener bears the word "lost" on the sheath, and "at sea" on the blade—and presto, we have a quizzical maritime note that is both plangent and almost paradoxically non-violent. The license plate, depending on how you look at it, identifies the hypothetical driver as a goddess or a weakling: Read it one way, you get "Issis" and intimations of Isis, the Egyptian deity and fertility cult heroine; flip it around and you get "sissi," which is a stone's throw away from "faggot." And once again, there is that whimsical insouciance—however you look at it, issis/sissi is a nonsense word—along with a lurking street toughness and an equally characteristic, if somehow loftier preoccupation with deistic essences and the revealed Word.

Weiner is also a significant and underestimated cinéaste. Better known in Europe than in the States, his films and videos of the 1970s and early 1980s provide a funky and unexpectedly Warholian subtext for his cleaner, more exalted wall pieces, installations, and bookworks. Like Warhol, the more hipsterish and hippie-like Weiner can boast a cast of regulars—infrastars perhaps—that includes his wife Alice and daughter Kirsten, as well as friends such as artist Mel Kendrick who, looking very young and androgynous in the *ménage à trois* context of *A First Quarter* (1973), might be said to occupy the Joe Dallesandro slot. With their laconic rhythms and dyspeptic conversations, *A First Quarter* and a number of other Weiner films and videos of this period are also harbingers of the contemporary "slacker" aesthetic.

Indeed collectively, Weiner's camera-works conjure up a brew of raunchy sex and Left Bank patter that could keep any latter-day underground film and video dweeb on his toes. The anatomy of the mind/body split, for example, is the most explicitly illustrated by *A Bit of Matter and A Little Bit More* (1976)—a black and white videotape originally tinted poison-green—in which the droning of some sort of existentialist encounter session is echoed by an ambient semi-soft group-grope largely focused on a lesbian coupling, and counterpointed repeatedly by relentlessly hard-core, close-up genital takes of a heterosexual couple fucking variously on a table.

In *Plowman's Lunch* (1982, color) we find shades of Jack Smith's immortal *Flaming Creatures,* not to mention Jean Vigo's *L'Atalante* and Jean Genet/ Rainer Werner Fassbinder's *Querelle de Brest.* Like much of the artist's own life in Holland, the movie takes place on houseboats in Amsterdam, and features an hysterical cross-dressing character who is raped on board in one scene and, recast as a street tough who assaults a temptress, is himself the aggressor in another. A number of aspects of the artist's life appear to be reflected or refracted here: for instance, his own migratory patterns as an artist, as well as the conceptual process of making art. "The story," Weiner has said, "is about emigration, and emigration is like making art. It's fantastic to find yourself in another place with another logic, having to understand in order to go on."[5]

Many of Weiner's recent works have also assumed a quasi-cinematic presence, even as they maximize the givens of place.

**SHAFTS OF BROKEN MARBLE
SET ON THE GROUND HERE
AND ACROSS THE WATER**

which was installed in Athens in 1987 at Jean Bernier suggests an epic paean to the displacement of ancient art, most notably the Elgin Marbles in London, as well as a virtual form of temple architecture in words. Or take the ruder, funnier, but arguably no less wistful

**WE ARE SHIPS AT SEA
NOT DUCKS ON A POND**

from 1986, a theme the artist would further explore in a book, a floating sculpture in the harbor of Hamburg, and most recently, in lyrics for an album of songs entitled *Ships at Sea, Sailors & Shoes*, recorded *a capella* by Ned Sublette and the Persuasions.

Weiner's individual meaning within art history, along with the larger historical relevance of Conceptual Art in general, is more than ripe for reevaluation and revision. As soon as one relaxes one's own perceived strictures of categorization, many more resonances than have normally been allowed become apparent. The fusion of didacticism and visionary design typically associated with Conceptual Art of course suggests roots that go at least as far back as the eighteenth century and architects and artists such as Ledoux, Boullée and J. L. David.[6] And that same fusion, further nuanced by a private/public attitude much like Weiner's—that of the socialist aesthete—finds a very direct precedent in the life and work of William Morris, the ardent Victorian socialist who wrote and lectured on reformist issues and designed wallpaper.

Implicit in my epiphany at the Stedelijk was the possibility that Weiner's art may at last begin to be seen and read within an even broader art-historical context. Many of Weiner's locational works can be understood as boiled-down history paintings, for instance, or *paysages moralisés*. More immediate formal precedents—including some that may have been anathema to Weiner and other members of his generation—should be reexamined in relation to his work. Weiner's ability to evoke generalized notions of enclosure and location by the simple means of boxed words even suggests a distant kinship with the paintings of Cy Twombly. In Twombly's work, for instance, written allusions to a figure, date or site are often circled, squared or obliterated with a theatrical mock-finality that in a sense mirrors the mock-perishability of Weiner's temporary installations. Then too, in the chromatic intensity and feeling of vista in Weiner's more recent work, the theme of the immanent or latent landscape may again be discerned. Finally, in the presence of his ribboning, unfurling lines of primary-colored words, neither Mondrian nor even the late de Kooning seem all that far away. All in all, Weiner's art is capable of sustaining infinite translation and metamorphosis, a condition which posits an ever-widening audience for his exalted yet populist form of Logos-building.

1) See my "Mussels and Windmills: Impressionism in Belgium and Holland" in *World Impressionism: The International Movement, 1860–1920*, New York, 1990, pp. 248–273.
2) In *Posters, November 1965–April 1986, Lawrence Weiner*, ed. Benjamin H. D. Buchloh (Halifax and Toronto: The Nova Scotia College of Art & Design and Art Metropole, The Nova Scotia Series, Vol. XVII, 1986).
3) For this reading I am indebted to Iwona Blazwick's essay, "Labyrinth," in *Steel Pennies Don't Come From or Go to Heaven* (Halifax: The Henry Moore Sculpture Trust, 1993).
4) See Will Roscoe, *The Zuni Man-Woman* (Albuquerque: The University of New Mexico Press, 1991).
5) In *Show (&) Tell: The Films and Videos of Lawrence Weiner, A Catalogue Raisonné*, Ghent, 1992, p. 31.
6) For an extended comparison of Weiner, Diderot, and Greuze, see Colin Gardner, "The Space Between Words: Lawrence Weiner," *Artforum* Nov. 1990, p. 157.

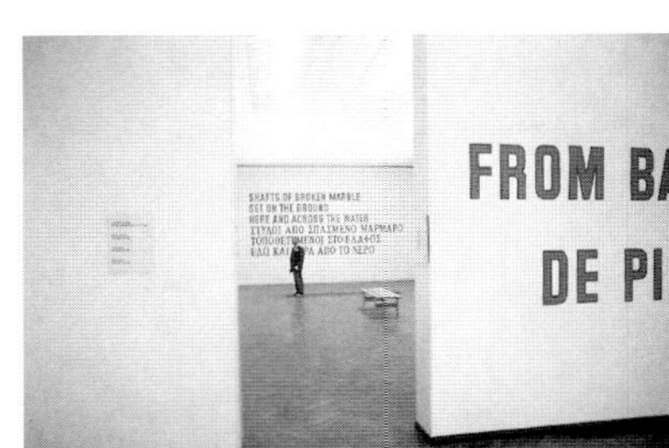

LAWRENCE WEINER, at the Stedelijk Museum, Amsterdam, 1988.

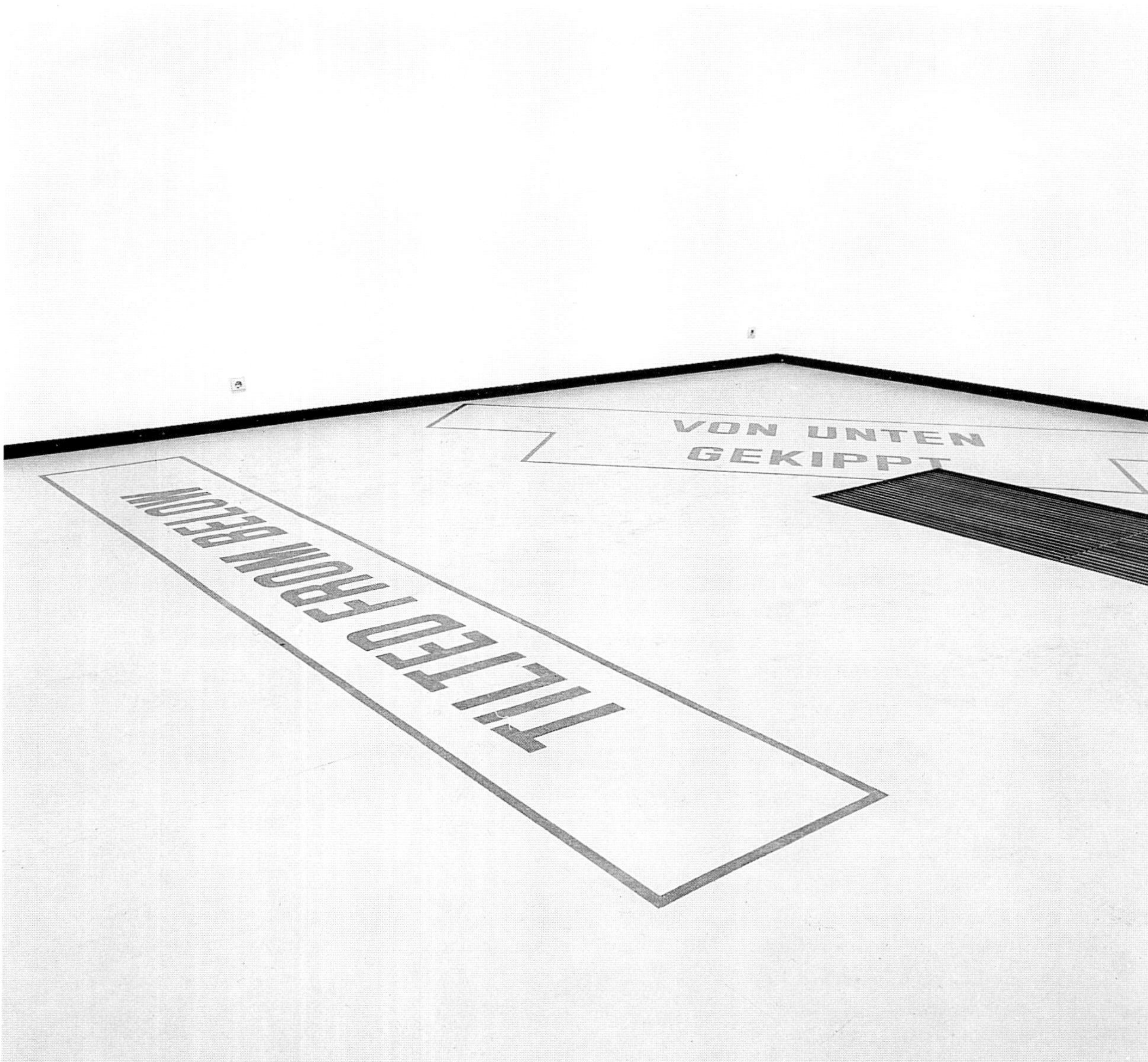

LAWRENCE WEINER, at the Stedelijk Museum, Amsterdam, 1988.

BROOKS ADAMS

Weiners Werkstätte

Ich werde nie meinen Besuch der Retrospektive von Lawrence Weiner 1988 im Stedelijk Museum in Amsterdam vergessen. Obgleich seit langem mit dem Werk vertraut – so glaubte ich zumindest –, war ich von dessen formaler Vielfalt und geistiger Fülle überwältigt. Die Ausstellung war eine Auffächerung – Raum für Raum – von Wörtern, Sätzen, Rätseln der Interpunktion und syntaktischen Fragmenten, realisiert in nahezu jeder denkbaren Farbe und Schriftart. Die Schau als Ganzes wirkte gleichzeitig prismatisch und impressionistisch, vom Gefühlseindruck her euphorisch und zugleich trocken egalitär in ihrer Botschaft. Zu der Zeit arbeitete ich ausserdem zufällig an einem Aufsatz über den Impressionismus in Holland und Belgien, und zu meiner grossen Überraschung war hier in Weiners konkreten Wortlandschaften die ganze tiefländische Tagesatmosphäre irgendwie zu neuem Leben erweckt.[1] Tatsächlich wirkten die Arbeiten auf mich alle wie Landschaften: wie abstrakte Horizonte und Panoramen aus Wörtern, ebenso linear und signalhaft wie die ersten ekstatischen Reduktionen Mondrians und mit ihren strahlenden Regenbogenfarben auch von ähnlicher chromatischer Lebendigkeit.

Welch ein extremer Unterschied zu den Versionen von Weiners Werk, die ich als Student in den 70er Jahren unmittelbar zu Gesicht bekommen und mehr oder weniger als selbstverständlich hingenommen hatte, und welch ein scharfer Kontrast zu all den vermittelten Bildern von mandarinhafter Strenge und Unergründlichkeit. Dieser Künstler, der mit seinem Werk im Verlauf der Jahre alles mögliche von graphischer Gestaltung bis zu konkreter Poesie und vom Filmemachen bis zum Texten von Popsongs aufgegriffen hat, ist seit allzu vielen Jahren durch überholte, klischeehafte Charakterisierungen der Konzeptkunst und der sogenannten Entmaterialisierung des Kunstobjektes ghettoisiert worden. Im Zuge ihrer Wiederentdeckung in den 90ern offenbart die Kunst Weiners eine Sensibilität, die in vulgärster Mundart wurzelt und dennoch von fast schwindelnder Erhabenheit ist, eine, die gleichermassen ungeschliffen wie geschniegelt daherkommt.

Inzwischen habe ich den Eindruck, dass die Kunst Weiners alles andere als insular ist. Ökumenisch in ihren eher durchdachten Intentionen beschwört sie von der Form wie vom Temperament her eine Vielzahl eindeutiger oder unterschwelliger Anklänge an visuelle Phänomene, darunter die gestisch-abstrakte Malerei der Nachkriegszeit und den Film noir, die Pop Art und das Kino Warholscher Prägung sowie Werke der Land Art und jüngere neoromantische Übertragungsäusserungen.

Das Werk hat sich entwickelt seit 1968, als erstmals die konzeptualistischen Manifeste des Künstlers erschienen. Seine epochemachende Aussage von 1968, wonach «die Arbeit nicht realisiert werden muss» – ein Statement, das bis zum Überdruss von Kritikern zur Rechtfertigung des Entmaterialisierungsstandpunktes angeführt und diskutiert worden

---

BROOKS ADAMS schreibt unter anderem für *Art in America*.

ist –, hatte der Künstler schon damals modifiziert, und sie ist so oder so hinfällig geworden durch die schiere Zahl und Vielfalt der Arbeiten, die nicht nur tatsächlich realisiert, sondern auch in einer wahren Kavalkade von Werkverzeichnissen – jeweils eines für die Bücher, die Plakate, die Filme und Videos und die sogenannten *specific and general works* – dokumentiert worden sind. In gleicher Weise ist auch der vorherrschende Eindruck der bewussten Selbstverleugnung in Weiners Werk der späten 60er Jahre – neben den theoretischen Argumenten für die Negation im allgemeinen, die der Kritiker Benjamin H. D. Buchloh noch 1986 dafür anführte – verdrängt worden durch Weiners eigenes Streben nach Realisierung und Produktivität, das in den letzten Jahren so offenkundig ist wie nie zuvor.[2)]

So ist die Verwandlung, die der Künstler 1993 an einer Brücken-Waage aus dem 19. Jahrhundert in der englischen Textil- und Maschinenbaustadt Halifax vornahm, eine Übung in verdeckter Monumentalität.[3)] Die neu gegossene Brücken-Waage, aufgestellt am Eingang der einstmals grössten Teppichfabrik der Welt, ist jetzt eine Skulptur, gleichsam eine Art minimalistischer Bodenarbeit, beschrieben mit den Worten

ETWAS KALKSTEIN ETWAS SANDSTEIN
AUS IRGENDEINEM GRUND ENTHALTEN

Auf diese Weise bekundet Weiners Arbeit ihre Beziehung zum Genius loci, zur Materie der umgebenden Landschaft und, in elliptischer Form durch die Worte «aus irgendeinem Grund», zu dem obskuren Wirrwarr privater Interessen, öffentlicher Motive und historischer Entwicklungen, die im Verlauf eines Jahrhunderts zunächst zum Bau der Fabrik, dann zu ihrer Abwirtschaftung und schliesslich heute zu ihrer Wiederverwertung als – nunmehr durch ein Kunstwerk geadeltes – Büro- und Geschäftszentrum mit dem Namen Dean Clough geführt haben. Wie im 19. Jahrhundert üblich sind der Arbeit Entstehungsdatum sowie die Namen der Giesserei und des Auftraggebers (The Henry Moore Sculpture Trust) eingeprägt. Weiners Mission ist hier zweifellos positiv und bewahrend: Im Grunde hat er einen Leichnam des Industriezeitalters zu neuem Leben erweckt. Das Projekt geht noch weiter: Nachdem man die Brücken-Waage – die auf ausrangierten Originalgleisen aufliegt – überquert hat, betritt man die Dean-Clough-Ausstellungsräume, wo, direkt auf die Wand gemalt, die gleiche Botschaft zu lesen ist. (Interessanterweise wird aufgrund des Standortes der Wandbilder häufig angenommen, es handle sich um Tapisserien.) Schliesslich finden sich in Form von Wandzeichnungen nahe dieser latent privaten/öffentlichen Tapisserien die beiden Statements

PFENNIGE AUS STAHL FALLEN NICHT
VOM HIMMEL, NOCH KOMMEN SIE DORTHIN

und

FÜR EIN PAAR KUPFERMÜNZEN

Hier begegnet uns, amalgamiert und verdichtet, eine erweiterte Bestätigung einer Volksweisheit, verbunden mit der verneinten Form eines Schnulzentitels und eine wiederbelebte Probe viktorianischen Händlerjargons, gekoppelt mit einer Zwei- wenn nicht gar Dreideutigkeit, die gleichzeitig auf die Polizei und hintersinnig auf Prostitution anspielt. Dieses ganze, praktisch in den Rang eines Gesamtkunstwerks erhobene Projekt ist gleichwohl Weiner in Reinform: indem es die Gegebenheiten einer Situation nimmt, sie umgestaltet und mit einer aufs neue relevanten öffentlichen/privaten Ikonographie erfüllt und indem es einen Sinn für hohen moralischen oder historischen Ernst mit einem gewissen schlüpfrigen *Je-ne-sais-quoi* verbindet.

Weiners öffentliches Image erinnert heute vielleicht mehr denn je an die Tradition des sozialistischen Ästheten. Das konkrete Erscheinungsbild des Künstlers etwa ist einzigartig: Es erinnert mich an die traditionelle Figur des *Berdache,* der Mann-Frau bei amerikanischen Indianern.[4)] Ungepflegt wie ein Matrose, der seine besten Tage auf See schon hinter sich hat, und doch hochgebildet wie ein Talmudgelehrter, ruft er zugleich das Bild bedeutender Viktorianer auf Porträts von Julia Margaret Cameron in Erinnerung. Ein Besuch in seinem Haus bestätigte diese eklektischen Eindrücke. Insgesamt fast spartanisch in der Ausstattung, doch unbeschreiblich mannigfaltig in seiner Suggestivkraft, wirkt auch dieses

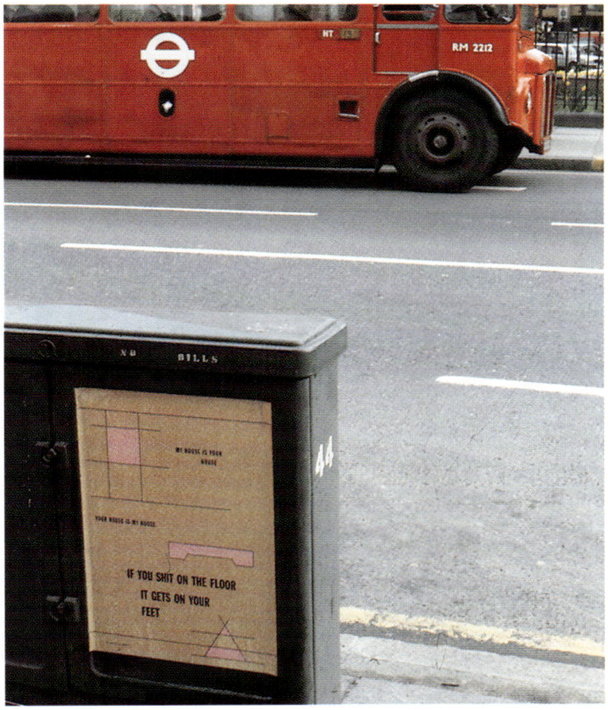

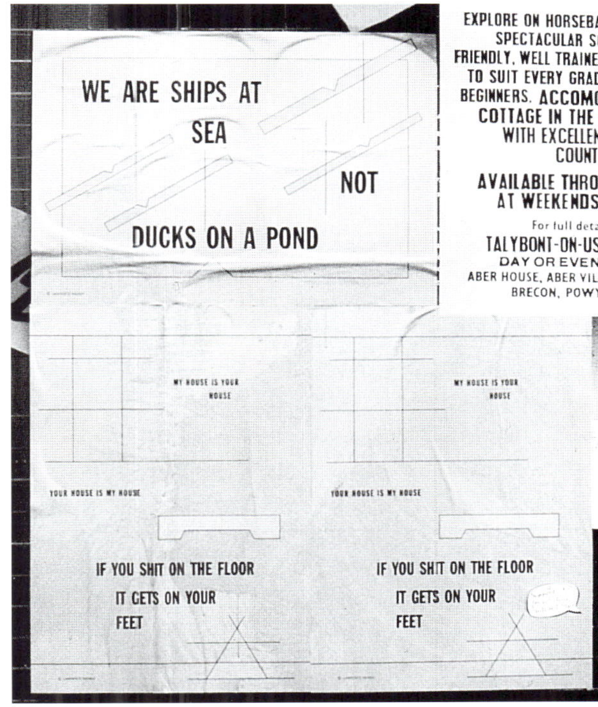

LAWRENCE WEINER, WE ARE SHIPS AT SEA NOT DUCKS ON A POND / WIR SIND SCHIFFE AUF DEM MEER KEINE ENTEN AUF DEM TEICH, Poster, Oxford Street, London. (ARTANGEL TRUST, ICA LONDON)

gleichzeitig ganz und gar originell und echt bohemienhaft. Im Flur hängt ein Plakat aus der Zeit des Zweiten Weltkriegs, das einen im heroischen Stil gehaltenen Arbeiter darstellt und darunter die Worte «Free Labor Will Win!» (Die freie Arbeiterklasse wird siegen!); im grösseren Raum im unteren Erdgeschoss, der Weiner als Atelier dient, fiel mir ein schmuckes dreieckiges Kissen mit der Aufschrift «Camp Fire Girls» auf – ein Geschenk, wie sich herausstellte, aus der Zeit, in der Weiner (im Rock und auf hochhackigen Schuhen) zusammen mit der Wiener Mädchengruppe *Die Damen* aufgetreten war.

Ausserdem lagen im Atelier Modelle für verschiedene Multiples: ein neues Exlibris für das Kröller-Müller-Museum, ein Brieföffner für eine deutsche Werbefirma, ein Herstellerprototyp für eine in Arbeit befindliche Edition (in Form eines Autonummernschildes). Auf ausdrücklichen Wunsch des Künstlers wird das Exlibris, das SPIRITUS MATERIA lautet, auf der Umschlaginnenseite von Büchern im Besitz des Museums unmittelbar neben dem ursprünglichen – von Henry van de Velde gestalteten – Exlibris angebracht werden, das unangetastet bleiben wird. Der messerähnliche Brieföffner trägt auf der Scheide das Wort «lost» (verschollen) und auf der Klinge «at sea» (auf hoher See), und im Nu haben wir eine seltsam maritime Note, die zugleich vom Rauschen der Wellen erfüllt und fast paradox gewaltlos ist. Das Nummernschild charakterisiert den hypothetischen Fahrer je nach Blickwinkel als eine Göttin oder einen Schwächling: Liest man es von einer Seite, ergibt sich die Buchstabenfolge «Issis» mit ihrem Anklang an Isis, die ägyptische Gottheit und Protagonistin des Fruchtbarkeitskults; kehrt man es um, hat man «sissi», was in die Richtung von Schwuchtel geht. Und wieder ist da diese schrullige Unbekümmertheit – von welcher Seite man es auch betrachtet, «issis/sissi» ist ein Nonsenswort –, verbunden mit einer latenten, von der Strasse geprägten Härte und einer nicht minder charakteristischen, wenngleich irgendwie hehreren Besessenheit von deistischen Wesenheiten und dem offenbarten Wort.

Weiner ist auch ein bedeutender und unterschätzter Cineast. Seine Filme und Videos der 70er und frühen 80er Jahre, bekannter in Europa als in den Vereinigten Staaten, bieten einen saloppen, überraschend an Warhol anklingenden Subtext seiner makelloseren, erhabeneren Wandarbeiten, Installationen und Buchprojekte. Wie Warhol kann sich der mehr hipster- und hippieartige Weiner eines Ensembles von Stammschauspielern rühmen – darunter seine Frau Alice und seine Tochter Kirsten sowie Freunde wie der Künstler Mel Kendrick, der, mit seinem sehr jugendlichen und androgynen Aussehen im Ménage-à-trois-Kontext von *A First Quarter* (1973), wenn man so will, den Part Joe Dallesandros einnimmt. Mit ihren lakonischen Rhythmen und misslaunigen Gesprächen sind *A First Quarter* und eine Reihe anderer Filme und Videos Weiners aus dieser Zeit zugleich Vorläufer der heutigen *Slacker*-Ästhetik.

Tatsächlich beschwören Weiners Kameraarbeiten insgesamt ein Gebräu aus billigem Sex und Bohemegeschwätz, das jeden heutigen Undergroundfilm- und Videofreak in Erregung versetzen könnte. Die Anatomie der Spaltung von Geist und Körper wird aufs anschaulichste verbildlicht in *A Bit of Matter and A Little Bit More* von 1976 – einem Schwarzweissvideo, das ursprünglich giftgrün eingefärbt war –, in dem das monotone Geleier einer Art existentialistischer Begegnungsgruppe aufgegriffen wird von einem in der Mitte zwischen hartem und Softporno angesiedelten kollektiven Gegrapsche, das sich im wesentlichen auf eine lesbische Paarung konzentriert und wiederholt kontrapunktiert wird durch schonungslose Nahaufnahmen der Genitalien eines auf einem Tisch kopulierenden heterosexuellen Paares.

In dem 1982 in Farbe gedrehten Film *Plowman's Lunch* finden wir Anklänge an Jack Smiths unvergessliche *Flaming Creatures,* ganz zu schweigen von Jean Vigos *L'Atalante* und Jean Genet/Rainer Werner Fassbinders *Querelle de Brest.* Wie überwiegend das Leben des Künstlers selbst in Holland, spielt der Film auf Wohnbooten in Amsterdam, und als Protagonist tritt eine hysterische Transvestiten-Figur auf, die in einer Szene an Bord eines Bootes vergewaltigt wird

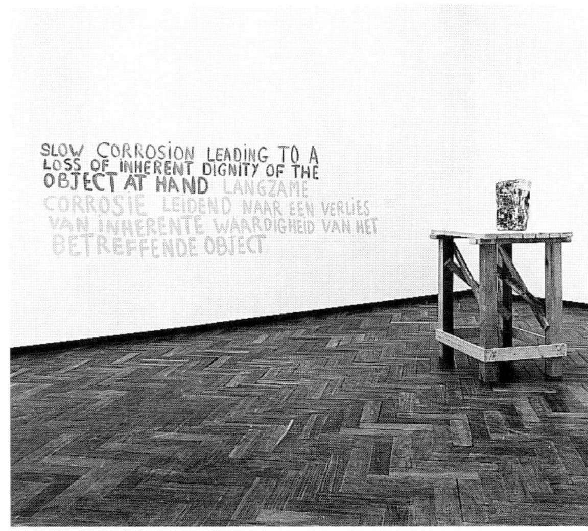

LAWRENCE WEINER, SLOW CORROSION... 1985 und Skulptur WAS AUF DEN TISCH GESETZT WIRD SITZT AUF DEM TISCH 1960 / and sculpture WHAT'S SET UPON THE TABLE SITS ON THE TABLE, Stedelijk Museum, Amsterdam, 1988.

und in einer anderen, in der sie in einer neuen Rolle als Rowdy über eine Verführerin herfällt, wiederum selbst den Aggressor spielt. Verschiedene Aspekte des Lebens des Künstlers spiegeln sich hier offenbar mehr oder weniger gebrochen wider: so etwa das Muster seines eigenen Wanderlebens als Künstler wie auch der konzeptuelle Prozess der künstlerischen Arbeit. «Die Geschichte», so Weiner, «handelt von der Emigration, und Emigration ist vergleichbar mit Kunstmachen. Es ist phantastisch, sich an einem anderen Ort mit einer anderen Logik zu finden und diese verstehen zu müssen, um weiterzukommen.»[5)]

Auch viele neuere Arbeiten Weiners haben eine gleichsam filmische Wirkung angenommen, selbst wenn sie die Gegebenheiten eines Ortes überhöhen.

**SÄULENSCHÄFTE
AUS ZERBROCHENEM MARMOR
ERRICHTET HIER AUF DEM BODEN
UND AUF DER ANDEREN SEITE
DES WASSERS**

eine 1987 bei Jean Bernier in Athen installierte Arbeit, hat etwas von einem epischen Päan auf die Verschleppung antiker Kunst, namentlich der sogenannten Elgin Marbles im British Museum in London, und zugleich von einem verbalen Grundschema von Tempelbauten. Oder nehmen wir die krudere, witzigere, aber, wenn man so will, nicht minder wehmütige Arbeit

WIR SIND SCHIFFE AUF DEM MEER KEINE ENTEN AUF DEM TEICH

von 1986, ein Thema, dem der Künstler noch weiter nachgehen sollte in einem Buch, bei einer schwimmenden Skulptur im Hafen von Hamburg und zuletzt in Texten für eine auf Schallplatte aufgenommene Liedersammlung mit dem Titel *Ships at Sea, Sailors & Shoes*, a cappella gesungen von Ned Sublette and the Persuasions.

Die spezifische Bedeutung Weiners innerhalb der Kunstgeschichte ist, neben der übergreifenden historischen Relevanz der Konzeptkunst im allgemeinen, überreif für eine Neubewertung und Überprüfung. Sobald man das eigene verengende Schubladendenken erkennt und lockert, werden wesentlich mehr Assonanzen sichtbar, als dem Werk normalerweise zugestanden wurden. Die Mischung aus Didaktik und visionärem Entwurf, die charakteristischerweise mit der Konzeptkunst assoziiert wird, lässt auf Wurzeln schliessen, die mindestens bis ins 18. Jahrhundert auf Architekten und Künstler wie Ledoux, Boullée und Jacques-Louis David zurückgehen.[6] Und eben diese Verbindung, zusätzlich nuanciert durch eine bei Weiner ausgeprägte private/öffentliche Haltung – die des sozialistischen Ästheten –, findet ein ganz unmittelbares Vorbild in Leben und Werk von William Morris, dem viktorianischen Sozialisten, der sich in Aufsätzen und Vorträgen zu reformistischen Fragen äusserte und Wandtapeten entwarf.

In meiner Epiphanie im Stedelijk angedeutet war die Möglichkeit, dass Weiners Kunst allmählich endlich in einem gar noch breiteren kunsthistorischen Rahmen gesehen und gedeutet werden könnte. Viele situationsbezogene Arbeiten Weiners lassen sich zum Beispiel als destillierte Historienbilder oder *Paysages moralisés* begreifen. Im Zusammenhang mit diesem Werk ist eine Überprüfung unmittelbarerer formaler Vorbilder geboten, darunter auch solcher, die für Weiner und andere Angehörige seiner Generation möglicherweise tabu waren. Die Art und Weise, wie Weiner einfach dadurch, dass er Wörter in Kästchen plaziert, einen verallgemeinerten Begriff von Einschliessung und Lokalisierung zu evozieren vermag, deutet sogar auf eine entfernte Verwandtschaft mit den Bildern Cy Twomblys hin. So werden in Twomblys Werk geschriebene Andeutungen etwa einer Zahl, eines Datums oder eines Ortes häufig eingekreist, in ein Quadrat plaziert oder getilgt mit einer theatralischen Pseudo-Endgültigkeit, die in gewisser Weise der scheinbaren Vergänglichkeit der zeitlich befristeten Installationen Weiners entspricht. Und in der farblichen Intensität und dem panoramaartigen Eindruck der jüngeren Arbeiten Weiners wiederum ist aufs neue das Thema der immanenten oder latenten Landschaft angedeutet. Schliesslich ist in der Gegenwart seiner sich wie ein Band dahinziehenden und entrollenden Zeilen mit primärfarbenen Wörtern weder Mondrian noch gar der späte de Kooning sehr weit entfernt.

Alles in allem vermag Weiners Kunst endloser Interpretation und Verwandlung standzuhalten, die Bedingung dafür, dass sich ein immer breiteres Publikum für seine gehobene und doch populistische Form von Logos-Arbeit herausbildet.

(Übersetzung: Magda Moses, Bram Opstelten)

1) Siehe meinen Beitrag «Mussels and Windmills: Impressionism in Belgium and Holland», in *World Impressionism: The Internationat Movement 1860–1920*, New York 1990, S. 248–273.

2) Siehe *Lawrence Weiner: Posters, November 1965–April 1986*, hrsg. v. Benjamin H. D. Buchloh, The Press of the Nova Scotia College of Art & Design and Art Metropole, The Nova Scotia Series, Bd. XVI, Halifax und Toronto 1986.

3) Ich schliesse mich hier der Einschätzung Iwona Blazwicks in ihrem Aufsatz «Labyrinth» an, in *Steel pennies don't come from or go to heaven*, The Henry Moore Sculpture Trust, Halifax 1993.

4) Siehe Will Roscoe, *The Zuni Man-Woman*, University of New Mexico Press, Albuquerque 1991.

5) Weiner in *Show (&) Tell: The Films and Videos of Lawrence Weiner, A Catalogue Raisonné*, Gent 1992, S. 31.

6) Ein eingehender Vergleich zwischen Weiner, Diderot und Greuze findet sich bei Colin Gardner, «The Space between Words: Lawrence Weiner», in *Artforum* (November 1990), S. 157.

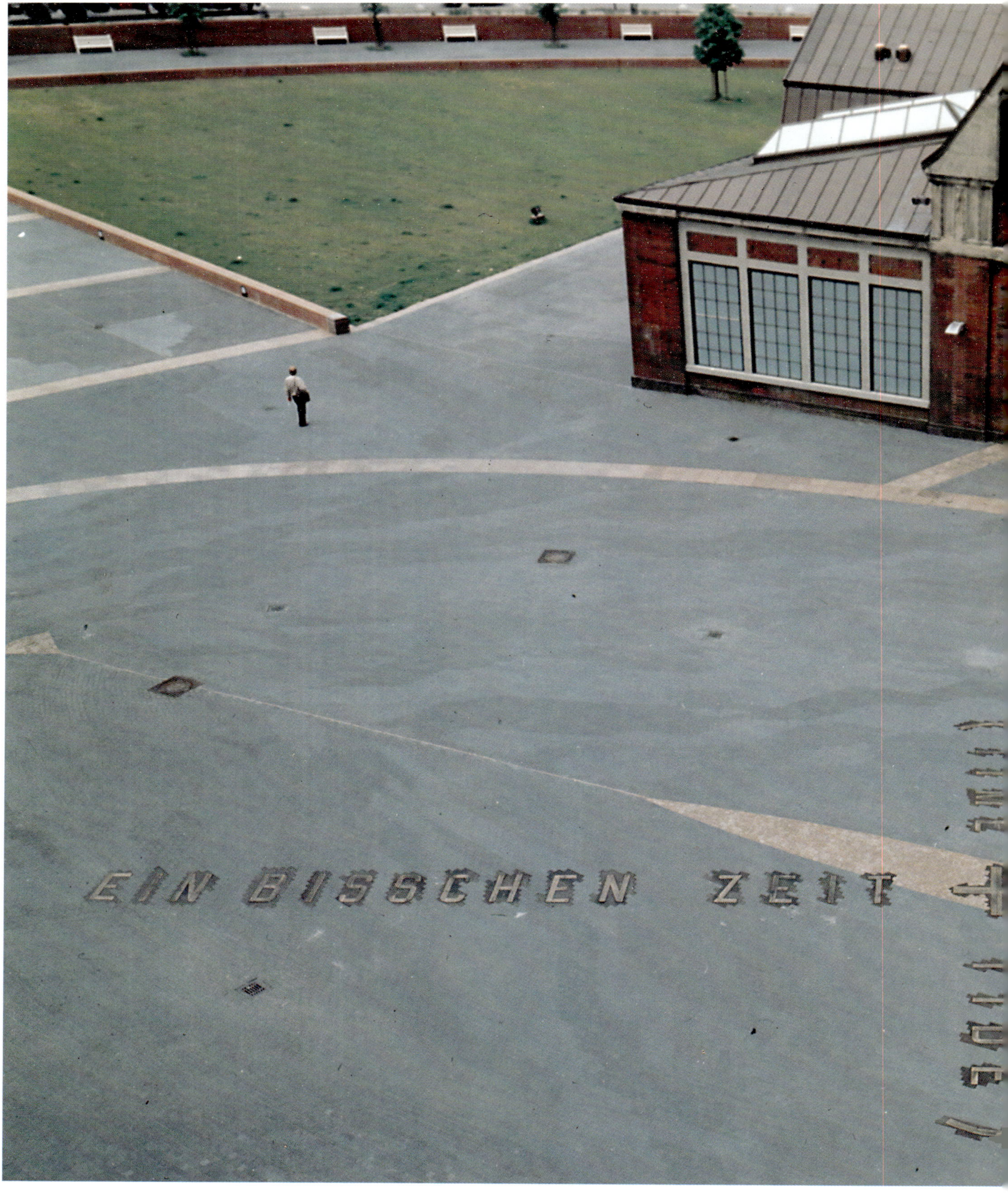

LAWRENCE WEINER, *EIN BISSCHEN ZEIT + GANZ VIEL EBBE (TIME + TIDE) / A LITTLE TIME + A LOT OF LOW TIDE (ZEIT + GEZEITEN), vor den Deichtorhallen, Hamburg, 1990.*

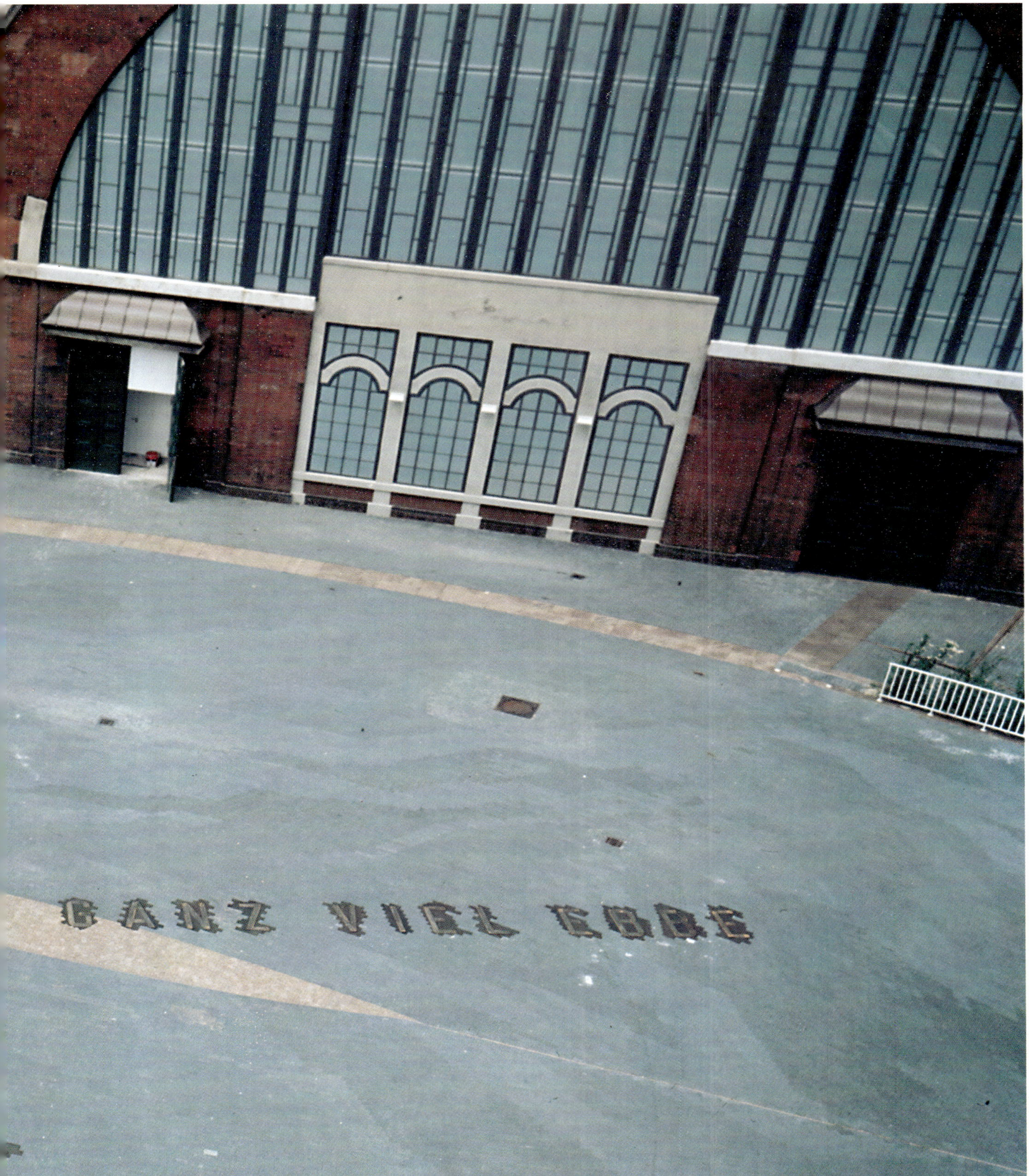
GANZ VIEL ERDE

FRANCES RICHARD

Providing Metaphor Needs: Lawrence Weiner's *Specific & General Works*

Putting up a piece of sculpture I can provide other peoples' metaphor needs, not make a metaphor myself.

– LW in conversation with Iwona Blazwick

Language, because it is the most non-objective thing we have ever developed in this world, never stops.

– LW, *Art Without Space*

The catalogue raisonné of Lawrence Weiner's art, *Specific & General Works,* reads simultaneously like a philosophical treatise, a writer's journal, and the notes of an optimistic but slightly mad carpenter-architect.[1] As a forum for Weiner, who has repeatedly stated that "all you have to remember is the words," the book offers his paintings and sculptures in their most literal state, in sans serif block capitals, in multiple languages, and in several tones of gray ink, on white paper in a matte moss-green paper cover.

As an object, the book, with its uniformly trimmed edges, subdued colors, and utilitarian typography, resembles a Minimalist box. But, upon opening it, the reader realizes that more than a little Pandora has infiltrated the contents. If the nature of visual experience and image-production is called into question by reading Weiner's text-based art on the wall of a gallery or on a plaque in an outdoor installation, then the experience of reading these works in the context of a book—a book without pictures—can only further complicate and layer such questions of visuality. In the specific context of an installation, contextual clues help to narrow the scope of associative fancy. But, in the intimate, diachronic, and portable experience of a book, the latent narratives embedded in each of Weiner's statements are freed from their temporal moorings. With no physical matrix beyond the pages of the book itself, each phrase resonates and expands, spinning out nuances of meaning to fit the individual reader's expectation(s).

This deep investment in the imagination of the receiving audience upsets Minimalism's stern directive that we as viewers see only the materials placed before our eyes. Reading the words

A WALL CRATERED
BY A SINGLE SHOTGUN BLAST

FRANCES RICHARD is a writer who lives in New York. She also works at Parkett.

for example, it is left entirely up to the reader to imagine what kind of wall s/he will see, and then if it is, say, a white interior wall, to imagine the raw hole punched in the plasterboard, the delicate spider-web pattern of surrounding breakage. But how different the image would be if the wall were made of fieldstone, the crater in question little more than a chip lost in the rusticated surface. In each case, it is up to the reader to wonder what has happened: a domestic argument? A hunter's miscalculation? There are as many possible stories as there are perceivers, each one equally invited and thwarted by Weiner's language.

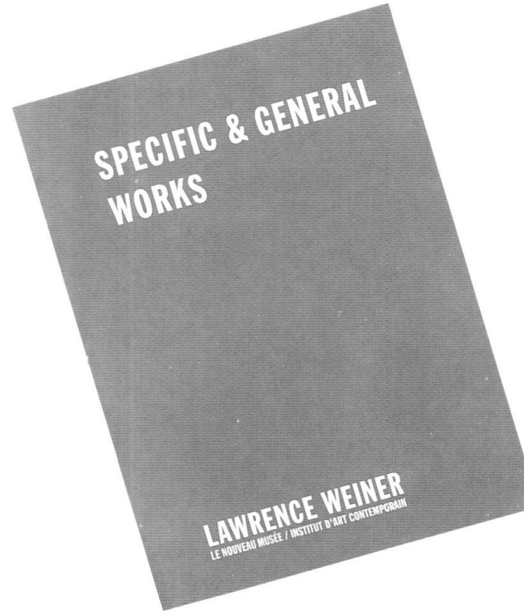

Once the adventuring reader realizes that *Specific & General Works* is more than a list of works whose "real" substance exists elsewhere, the whole text falls open like an enchanted tome and s/he is tempted into an ecstasy of uncertain narration. Individual statements, widely separated in the sequence of pages, mingle their meanings so that (for example)

A RUBBER BALL THROWN ON THE SEA
links with
A TURBULENCE INDUCED
WITHIN A BODY OF WATER
and then links again with
JUST ANOTHER MOVEMENT
OF THE TIDE (IMPAIRED)
Perhaps it is this ball that rocks
TO AND FRO. FRO AND TO. AND TO AND FRO.
AND FRO AND TO.
THE TRACE OF ACTION PAST
(i.e. A WET PLACE)

might now suggest the place where the ball rested on a rock, after the impaired tide cast it back to shore. But this wet trace/active place could, in another story, become so erotic that "to and fro..." would take on another rhythm, another meaning altogether...

The bluntness of the texts, their sometimes stubborn, sometimes coy refusal to cooperate with our urge toward narrativization does not stop us from doing it, but it makes us conscious that we are doing it. As one micro-story after another suggests itself and cannot be completed, Weiner makes us realize a) that the urge toward narrativization can be pathetic in its limitations, b) that this urge to order and catalogue experience perseveres regardless of whether or not it can demonstrate positive results, and c) that no matter what version of the story we choose to tell, other versions are always pushing themselves forward simultaneously. In this way, Weiner's texts remind us of the inherent hopefulness of narrative: Stories are never complete, but the act of telling them allows us to imagine completeness. Since nothing is definitely happening, nothing can be said to have definitely happened, and thus nothing is impossible.

Art critics discussing Weiner's work are careful to avoid "literary" commentary, but it is difficult to ignore the fact that, bound together in one volume, each statement must partially revert from its visual-conceptual duties to become part of a shamelessly "written" whole. Like an epic poem, the book that is Weiner's *Statements* concerns itself with traditional heroic (male?) subjects: building, endeavor, accomplishment, will. But the *Statements* are also stubbornly lyric: describing fantasy spaces or paradises, visions, wishful thinking, desire. As a verbal materialist, Weiner refuses complete sentences, insisting on

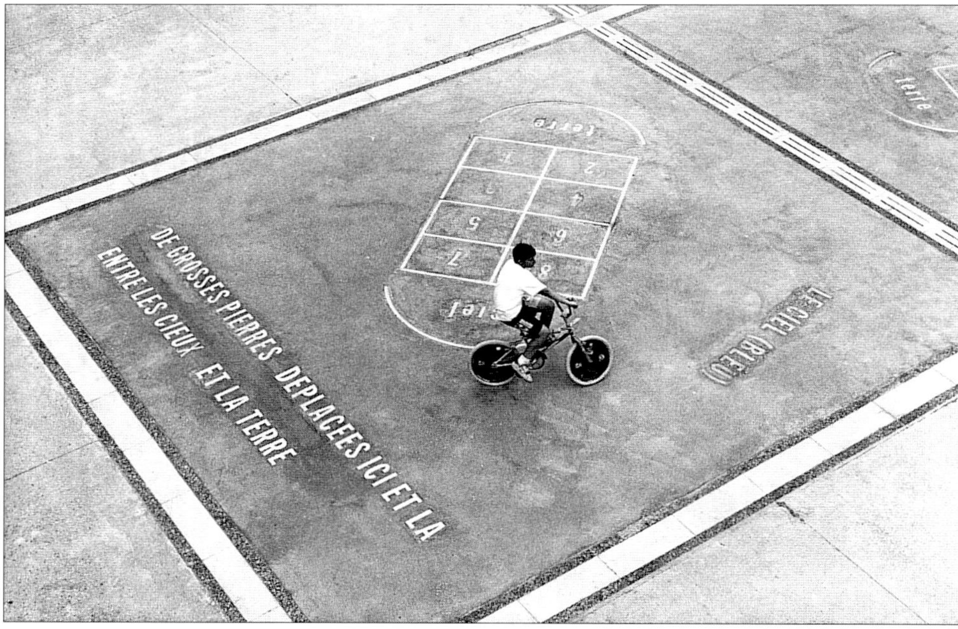

LAWRENCE WEINER, DE GROSSES PIERRES DEPLACEES ICI ET LA ENTRE LES CIEUX ET LA TERRE / BIG STONES MOVED HERE & THERE BETWEEN THE HEAVENS AND THE EARTH, 1990,
Place Mendès-France, Villeurbanne, France.

a diction in which all claims toward a narrating "I" have been expunged. This avoidance of overt subjectivity makes his works simultaneously reticent and enormous: his is a world in which there are many acts, but no actors. The texts are always dynamic because of the intrinsically performative "request" or "demand" made by the materials the texts embody. But no body comes forth to perform. *Statements* is like a story about the disappearance of the hand; about a world constructed by (hardware-loving) fairies or industrious, invisible insects; like the notebook-jottings of God.

In this sense, the conceptualism of language framed as a visual phenomenon flows both backward and forward along the official chronology of aesthetic movements. Erasing the presence of the acting body while simultaneously insisting on actions only a human being could perform (thus calling into question agency, subjectivity, and corporeal integrity) sounds eminently postmodern, but there is something subtly magical, almost premodern, about Weiner's insistence on the potency of naming, of the word as Prime Mover. Weiner has said, "I don't find Duchamp an interesting artist,"[2] and indeed, his works offer a version of the artist's engagement with his/her environment that is almost the opposite of Duchamp's. Weiner's statements are not readymades; they do not re-contextualize chunks of normal experience by articulating them in aesthetic terms. Rather, Weiner's works are *waiting-to-be-mades.* Like a recipe-book, a grammar, or a how-to manual, *Specific & General Works* offers not a résumé of existing objects, but the possibility of their realization.

1) Lawrence Weiner, *Specific & General Works,* Le Nouveau Musée/Institut d'art contemporain, Villeurbanne, 1993.
2) Interview with David Batchelor, in *Artscribe,* March/April, 1989, p. 52.

FRANCES RICHARD

Das Bedürfnis nach Metaphern befriedigen: Die *Specific & General Works* von Lawrence Weiner

Durch die Installation einer Skulptur kann ich das Bedürfnis anderer Leute nach Metaphern befriedigen, ohne selbst eine Metapher zu schaffen. – LW im Gespräch mit Iwona Blazwick

Die Sprache hört, weil sie das Ungegenständlichste ist, was wir jemals in dieser Welt hervorgebracht haben, niemals auf.
– LW, *Art Without Space*

Specific & General Works, das Œuvreverzeichnis der Kunst Lawrence Weiners, liest sich gleichzeitig wie eine philosophische Abhandlung, wie das Tagebuch eines Schriftstellers und wie die Aufzeichnungen eines zukunftsgläubigen, jedoch leicht überspannten Bauplaners.[1] Als Forum für Weiner, der wiederholt zu verstehen gegeben hat, dass «es genügt, sich die Worte einzuprägen», präsentiert das Buch seine Gemälde und Skulpturen in ihrem reinsten Zustand: in serifenlosen Blockbuchstaben, in mehreren Sprachen und in verschiedenen Abstufungen grauer Druckfarbe auf weissem Papier in einem in mattem Moosgrün gehaltenen Pappeinband.

Als Objekt wirkt das Buch mit seinen gleichmässig abgeschnittenen Rändern, seinen gedämpften Farben und seiner zweckmässigen Typographie wie ein minimalistischer Kasten. Doch beim Aufschlagen stellt der Leser fest, dass sich mehr als nur eine kleine Pandora in den Inhalt eingeschlichen hat. Wenn durch das Lesen der textgebundenen Weinerschen Kunst auf der Wand einer Galerie oder auf einer Tafel im Rahmen einer Installation im Freien das Wesen der Bildwahrnehmung und bildschöpferischen Arbeit in Frage gestellt wird, so kann die Konfrontation mit diesen Werken im Kontext eines Buches – eines Buches ohne Bilder – solche Fragen der Bildlichkeit nur noch komplexer und vertrackter machen. Im spezifischen Kontext einer Installation tragen kontextuelle Hinweise dazu bei, den Spielraum der assoziativen Phantasie einzuengen. Beim intimen, diachronischen, handlichen Bucherlebnis jedoch werden die latenten Geschichten, die jeweils in Weiners Statements eingebettet sind, aus ihrer zeitlichen Verankerung gelöst. Jeglicher physischen Matrix ausser den Seiten des Buches entledigt, hallt

FRANCES RICHARD ist Schriftstellerin und lebt in New York. Daneben ist sie für Parkett tätig.

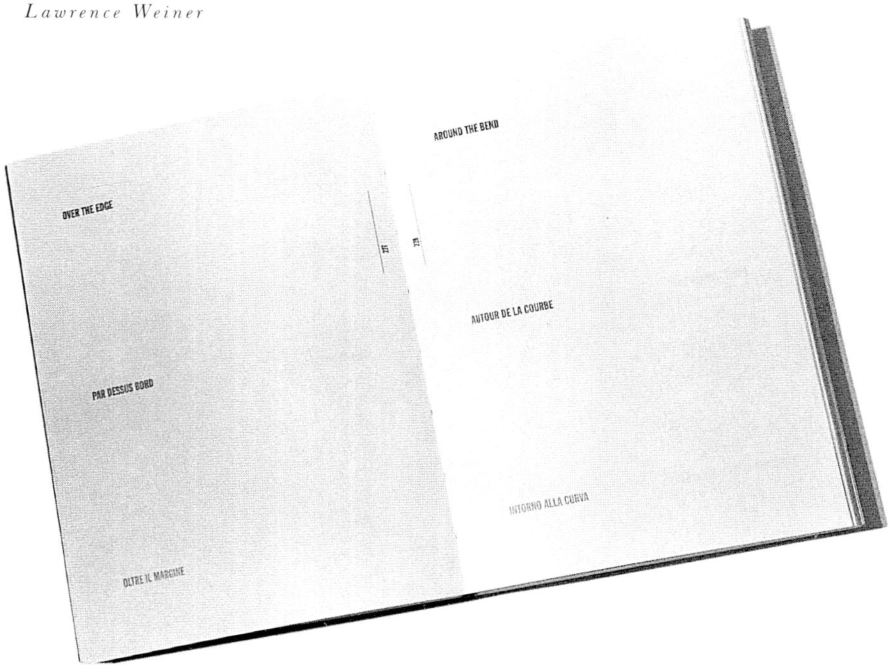

und schwingt jede Wortfolge und schillert in verschiedenen Bedeutungsnuancen je nach den Erwartungen des einzelnen Lesers.

Diese tiefgehende Investition in die Vorstellungskraft des rezipierenden Publikums wirft das strikte Gebot des Minimalismus über Bord, wonach wir als Betrachter nichts anderes als die uns vor Augen geführten Materialien sehen. Beim Lesen etwa der Worte

EINE DURCH EINEN EINZIGEN
SCHUSS AUS EINER SCHROTFLINTE
DURCHLÖCHERTE WAND

bleibt es ganz und gar dem Leser überlassen, welche Art von Wand er sich ausmalt. Im Falle, sagen wir mal, einer weissen Innenwand, stellt man sich vielleicht das unförmig in den Putz gesprengte Loch, das feine Spinnwebenmuster der umliegenden Risse vor. Doch wie anders wäre das Bild, wenn es sich um eine Mauer aus Feldsteinen handelte, in der das besagte Loch nicht mehr wäre als ein kleiner in der unregelmässigen Oberfläche sich verlierender Splitter. So oder so liegt es beim Leser, sich zu fragen, was geschehen sein mag: ein häuslicher Zwist etwa? Ein Versehen eines Jägers? Es gibt ebenso viele Versionen, wie es Betrachter gibt, jede einzelne gleichermassen angeregt wie vereitelt durch die Sprache Weiners.

Sobald der Leser, der sich auf dieses Abenteuer einlässt, erkennt, dass *Specific & General Works* mehr ist als nur ein Verzeichnis von Werken, deren eigentliches, materielles Substrat anderswo existiert, öffnet sich der ganze Text wie ein Zauberbuch, das ihn in einen Taumel offener Geschichten hineinzieht. Einzelne Aussagen, die von der Seitenfolge her weit auseinanderliegen, verschränken sich inhaltlich, so dass sich beispielsweise

EIN AUF DAS MEER
GEWORFENER GUMMIBALL

verknüpft mit

EIN IN EINEM GEWÄSSER
AUSGELÖSTER STRUDEL

und darauf wiederum mit

NUR EINE WEITERE BEWEGUNG
DER GEZEITEN (ABGESCHWÄCHT)

Vielleicht ist dies der Ball, der schaukelt

AUF UND AB. AB UND AUF.
UND AUF UND AB. UND AB UND AUF.

DIE SPUR
EINER ZURÜCKLIEGENDEN HANDLUNG
(d. h. EINE NASSE STELLE)

könnte sich jetzt auf die Stelle beziehen, wo der Ball auf einem Felsen lag, nachdem die abgeschwächte Flut ihn wieder ans Ufer gespült hatte. Doch diese/r feuchte Spur/Handlungsort könnte, im Rahmen einer anderen Geschichte, mit derartiger Erotik aufgeladen werden, dass das Aufundab einen völlig anderen Rhythmus, eine gänzlich andere Bedeutung annehmen würde...

Die Ungeschliffenheit der Texte, ihre einmal störrische, dann wieder spröde Weigerung, unserem narrativen Trieb nachzugeben, hindert uns nicht am Geschichtenerzählen, macht uns aber dessen bewusst. Während sich eine Mikro-Geschichte nach der anderen aufdrängt und nicht abschliessen lässt, bringt Weiner uns zu Bewusstsein, a) dass der Drang zum Geschichtenerzählen in seiner Begrenztheit etwas Jämmerliches haben kann, b) dass dieser Drang, Erfahrung zu ordnen und zu katalogisieren, ungeachtet dessen, ob er positive Ergebnisse aufzuweisen vermag oder nicht, hartnäckig Bestand hat und c) dass, ganz gleich, welche Version der Geschichte wir zu erzählen uns entscheiden, sich gleichzeitig immer andere Versionen in den Vordergrund drängen. Auf diese Weise erinnern uns Weiners Texte an die Erwartungshaltung, die sich von Natur aus mit dem Erzählen verknüpft: Geschichten sind niemals abgeschlossen, sondern der Akt ihres Erzählens erlaubt es, sich eine solche Abgeschlossenheit vorzustellen. Da nichts definitiv geschieht, gibt es nichts, von dem sich behaupten liesse, es sei definitiv geschehen, und folglich ist nichts unmöglich.

Kunstkritiker sind in der Auseinandersetzung mit Weiners Werk sorgsam darauf bedacht, jede «literarische» Kritik zu vermeiden, gleichwohl lässt sich schwerlich die Tatsache ignorieren, dass, gebündelt in einem Buch, jedes einzelne Statement zwangsläufig seinen visuell-konzeptuellen Aufgaben partiell den Rücken kehrt und Teil eines ungeniert «geschriebenen» Ganzen wird. Wie ein episches Gedicht befasst sich das Buch, das Weiners *Statements* bilden, mit traditionellen heroischen (männlichen) Themen: mit Bauen, Streben, Vollbringen, Wollen. Doch die *Statements* sind zugleich eigensinnig lyrisch: in der Beschreibung von Phantasieräumen oder imaginären Paradiesen, von Visionen, Illusionen, Sehnsüchten. Als Wortmaterialist lehnt Weiner es ab, Sätze zu vollenden, und beharrt statt dessen auf einer Diktion, aus der jeder Anspruch in Richtung eines erzählenden Ichs getilgt wurde. Diese Vermeidung unverhüllter Subjektivität verleiht seinem Werk etwas gleichzeitig Stummes und Monumentales: seine Welt ist eine, in der es viele Handlungen, aber keine Handelnden gibt. Die Texte sind stets dynamisch aufgrund der Handlung, die das in ihnen Konkretisierte im Grunde nahelegt oder erfordert. Doch keiner tritt hervor zur Durchführung. Die *Statements* sind wie eine Erzählung über das Verschwinden der Hand, über eine Welt, die von (hardwareverliebten) Feen oder fleissigen, unsichtbaren Insekten errichtet wurde, sie sind wie die Notizbuchaufzeichnungen Gottes.

In diesem Sinn bewegt sich der Konzeptualismus der Sprache, der diese als ein visuelles Phänomen betrachtet, entlang der offiziellen Zeitachse künstlerischer Richtungen gleichzeitig vor- wie rückwärts. Die Strategie, auf die Gegenwart eines Handelnden zu verzichten, gleichzeitig aber auf Handlungen zu insistieren, die nur ein menschliches Wesen durchführen könnte (und so Wirksamkeit, Subjektivität und die Ganzheit des Körpers in Frage zu stellen), klingt ausgesprochen postmodern, doch es liegt etwas untergründig Magisches, etwas beinahe Vormodernes in Weiners Festhalten an der Kraft des Benennens, am Wort als primus movens. «Duchamp», hat Weiner einmal ausgesagt, «ist für mich kein interessanter Künstler»,[2] und in der Tat bietet sein Werk eine Spielart der Auseinandersetzung des Künstlers mit seiner Umgebung, die der Duchampschen Haltung fast diametral entgegengesetzt ist. Weiners Statements sind keine Readymades, sie stellen nicht Segmente der alltäglichen Erfahrung in einen neuen Zusammenhang, indem sie diese in einen ästhetischen Bezugsrahmen einfügen. Vielmehr sind Weiners Arbeiten Hervorbringungen, die ihrer Realisierung harren. Ähnlich wie ein Rezeptbuch, eine Grammatik oder eine Gebrauchsanweisung bieten die *Specific & General Works* keine Auflistung vorhandener Objekte, sondern die Möglichkeit ihrer Verwirklichung.

(Übersetzung: Magda Moses, Bram Opstelten)

1) Lawrence Weiner, *Specific & General Works*. Le Nouveau Musée/Institut d'art contemporain, Villeurbanne 1993.
2) Interview mit David Batchelor, in *Artscribe* (März/April 1989), S. 52.

LAWRENCE WEINER, COVERED BY CLOUDS, 1989, Furkart '89, Switzerland. (PHOTO: CLAUDE JORAY)

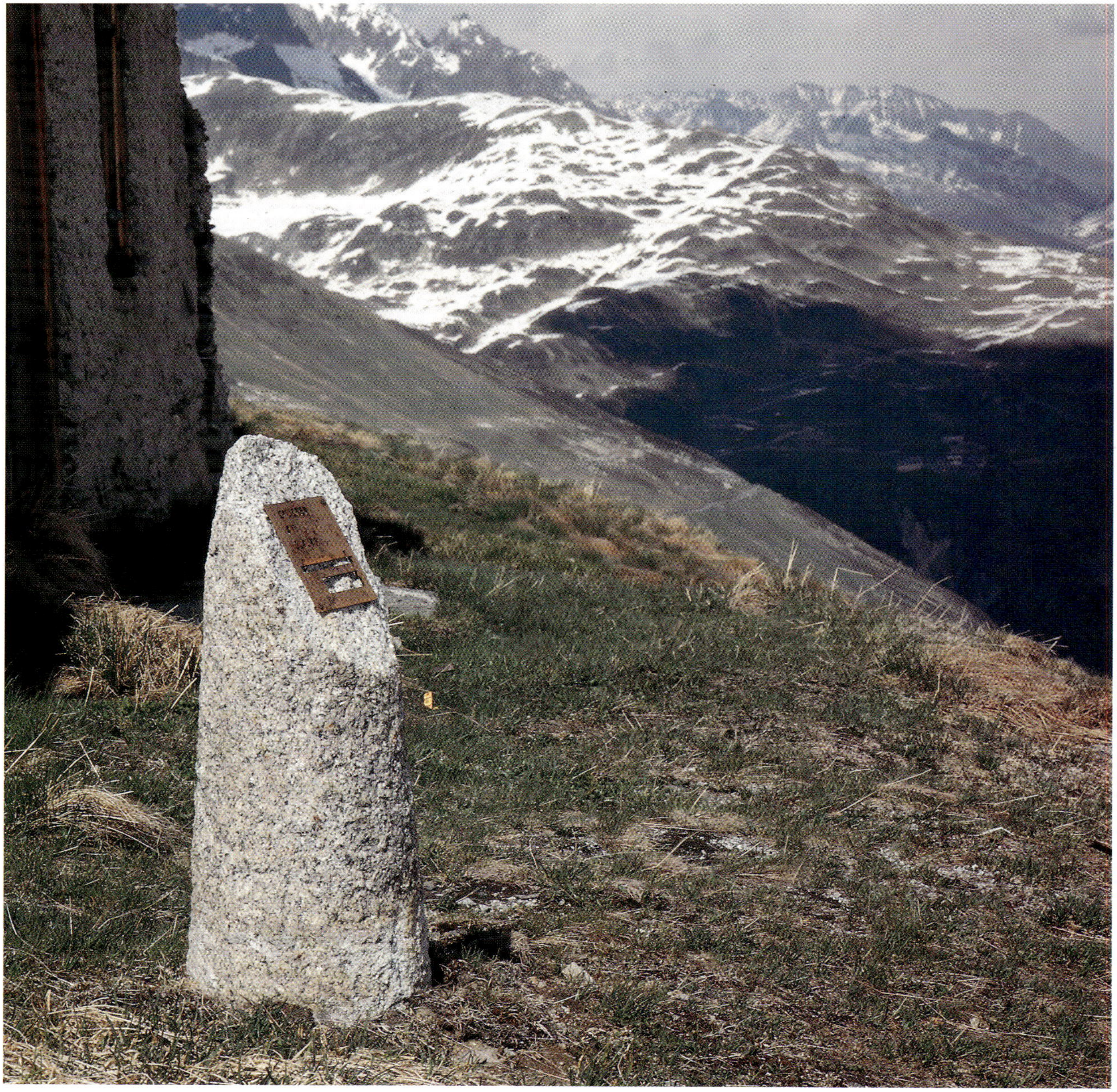

DIETER SCHWARZ

Public Freehold

Vermehrt wurde in den letzten Jahren von sogenannter Kunst im öffentlichen Raum gesprochen, und manche Künstler, darunter Lawrence Weiner, haben Werke sogar für einen solchen spezifischen Zweck konzipiert. Wie kann das sein? Dass Kunstwerke dem öffentlichen Raum besonders zugedacht sein sollen, hat etwas Tautologisches oder Widersinniges an sich, je nachdem wie man dies versteht. Jedenfalls sind Kunstwerke ausserhalb eines öffentlichen Bereichs, das heisst ausserhalb einer Struktur, die neben Autor und Objekt auch den Betrachter einschliesst, undenkbar. Indem ein Werk als solches festgelegt wird, gliedert es sich in die Menge der Äusserungen ein und offenbart damit seine sprachliche Qualität. Selbst dort, wo Privatheit angestrebt wird, steht diese stets in Beziehung zu sozialen und kulturellen Bedingungen, die das Kunstwerk ermöglichen und legitimieren. Der Galerie- oder Museumsraum ist aufgrund seiner Definition ebenso öffentlich zugänglich wie ein anderer Raum, bloss etwas geschützter, das heisst einem besonderen Konsens unterworfen; und dass der private Wohnraum des Sammlers gänzlich von öffentlichen Konnotationen und Anforderungen durchsetzt ist, kann wohl nicht bestritten werden. Also kann eine bestimmte Kultur eigentlich nicht in öffentlichen und nicht-öffentlichen Bereich aufgeteilt werden. Auf der anderen Seite ist im Begriff einer spezifischen Kunst im öffentlichen Raum eine Funktionalisierung und Zweckbestimmung enthalten, die sich nur schwer mit der Afunktionalität und der Zwecklosigkeit des modernistischen Kunstwerks verträgt. Das heisst nicht, dass die Kunst sinnlos ist, es heisst vielmehr, dass sie ausschliesslich von künstlerischen Dingen und von nichts anderem handelt. Befasst sie sich mit einer Aufgabe, dann übernimmt sie eine Hilfestellung und ist beispielsweise Design oder Dokument.

Dieser Sachverhalt spitzt sich zu, wenn wir als Voraussetzung ein Werk Lawrence Weiners wählen, das aus Sprache und den Materialien, auf die sich die Aussage bezieht, besteht. Ein solches Werk hat von Anfang an keinen festen Platz in einem bestimmten Raum, denn es beruht unmittelbar auf der Tatsache, dass die sprachliche Aussage keine endgültige äussere Form besitzt. Sicherlich ist innerhalb einer Sprache eine bestimmte Formulierung für das Werk gegeben, und sie ist auch im englischsprachigen Werkverzeichnis niedergelegt, doch so, wie Weiner seine Arbeit definiert, hat sie nicht einen festen Ort innerhalb einer Sprache, sondern sie kann beliebig von einer Sprache in eine andere transferiert werden. Innerhalb einer jeden Sprache ist aber jeder Ort ein öffentlicher, denn es ist unmöglich, einen bestimmten Teil der Sprache als privaten auszusondern. Die sprachlichen Arbeiten Lawrence Weiners befinden sich also von Anfang an in einem allgemeinen Raum, demjenigen der sprachlichen Gemeinschaft, auf die sich eine Kultur gründet. Dieser Bezug auf einen allgemeinen Raum galt jedoch bereits für Weiners frühe, noch von ihm selber materiell ausgeführten Skulpturen, und Weiner hatte auch 1968 bemerkt: «Die Arbeit hätte überall existiert, wo man sie hingestellt hätte; sie stand in Beziehung zu einem Aussenraum, im Gegensatz zu

DIETER SCHWARZ ist Leiter des Kunstmuseums Winterthur und Herausgeber des *Katalog Raisonné, Bücher Lawrence Weiner,* Köln 1989.

einem spezifischen Aussenraum.»[1] Was die Arbeit in diesem allgemeinen Raum jedoch bedeutet, ist eine Frage, die der Künstler nicht allein beantworten kann.

Die Frage nach Funktionsgebundenheit oder Autonomie des Werks stellt sich deshalb für Weiner auf neue Weise. Man könnte dafür seine Überzeugung von der Übersetzbarkeit der Werke anführen. Diese pragmatische Auffassung gibt vor, das Medium Sprache funktionell einsetzen zu können: die äussere Form des Werks ist gleichgültig, wenn der Inhalt, nämlich die beschriebenen Materialien, derselbe bleibt. Das heisst, dass die materielle Referenz den austauschbaren Sprachsequenzen als Konstante gegenübergestellt wird. Ist diese funktionelle Konzeption nun auf die Plazierung von Weiners Werken übertragbar? Wird das Werk in den Dienst einer Architektur, eines Auftraggebers, einer Sache gestellt, wenn es einmal installiert ist? Nehmen wir an, die Sprache sei nur das Instrument, das den direkten Bezug auf Materialien herstellt, und sie sei darüber hinaus beliebig austauschbar. Dann bewegt sich die Aussage ungehindert von einer Sprache in jede andere. Dann gleitet sie fort, selbst wenn der Satz auf Wände gemalt oder in Tafeln graviert ist. Dann kann ein Satz heute hier stehen und morgen dort:

BROKEN OFF

einmal auf einer Postkarte, einmal auf einer zerbrochenen Ofenkachel, einmal mit Schablone gemalt, einmal aus Mosaiksteinen gesetzt... Und selbst wenn die Schrift stehenbleibt (*scripta manent...*), ist sie stets demjenigen überlassen, der sie liest, gehört sie nie einer Architektur, einem Auftraggeber, einer Sache, das heisst ihrem Träger oder Produzenten. Die materielle Referenz, und Weiner setzt darauf, ist schliesslich nicht ein Gegenstand, sondern sie ist das Material, so wie es in verschiedenen Kontexten durch langjährigen Gebrauch eine Bedeutungsdichte erworben hat. Die ursprüngliche Referenz ist in einem Werk Weiners in eine unabsehbare Menge sprachlicher Aussagen verwandelt.

Im selben Masse wie die Funktionalität dahinfällt, soweit das Werk Sprache ist, ist auch die Autonomie des Werks in Zweifel gezogen. Weiner kam seit seinen frühen Arbeiten immer wieder darauf zurück, dass für ihn in erster Linie das Herstellen eines Kunstwerks von Interesse sei und dass nichts anderes davon ablenken könne, weder der prozessuale Aspekt noch die äusserliche Erscheinung der Präsentation: «Materialistisch bedeutet eine primäre Beziehung zum Material, aber ich beschäftige mich vorrangig mit Kunst. Man könnte sagen, dass das Thema das Material ist, aber seine Daseinsberechtigung geht weit über das Material hinaus zu etwas anderem, und dieses etwas ist Kunst.»[2] Mit der Formulierung von Werken in sprachlicher Form fand Weiner eine Lösung für dieses Problem. Das Werk bleibt materiell gefasst, ohne dass das Material davon ablenken würde, dass das Werk auf etwas anderes als nur auf sich selber verweist. Da es sprachlich ist, kann es gar nicht anders, als ständig auf etwas anderes zu verweisen. Ob das andere, worum es Weiner

LAWRENCE WEINER, BROKEN OFF / ABGEBROCHEN (ODER) AUFGEBROCHEN, 1989, Salzhaus Sindelfingen.

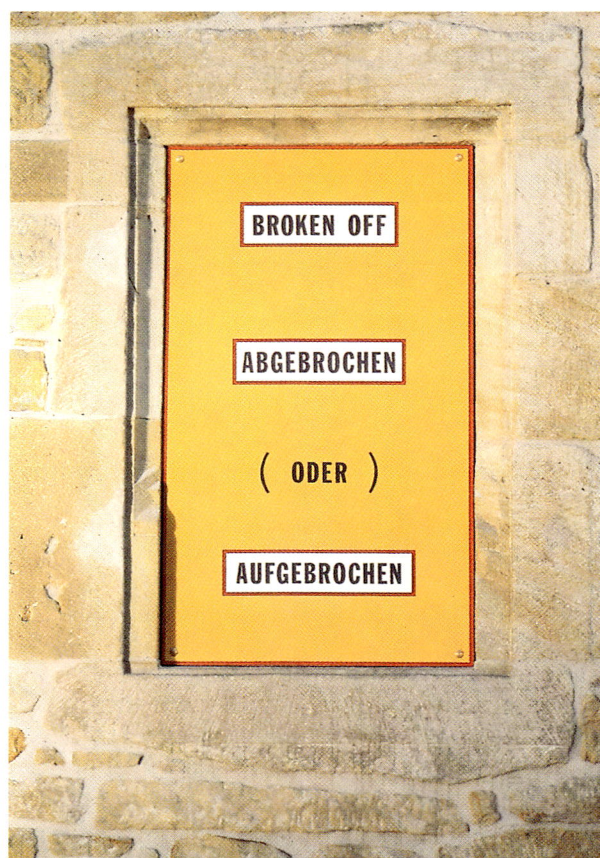

geht, nämlich die Kunst, nun identisch sei mit diesem anderen, worauf die Sprache jeweils verweist, muss offenbleiben. Jedenfalls weist die Sprache weiter, weg von einer direkten Darstellung, weg auch von einem eindeutigen Bezug, wie beispielsweise die Idee der Kunst. Der idealistische Anspruch von Weiners Aussage – der Verweis auf das Abstraktum Kunst – hebt sich also darin auf, dass er seine Werke einem Medium anvertraut, das Gewissheit noch nicht besitzt, sondern sie erst herzustellen hat. Wenn es also im sprachlichen Werk um die «Kunst» gehen soll, dann ist es die Aufgabe desselben Mediums, den Begriff der Kunst überhaupt zu konstruieren. Die Kunst gibt es nicht vor der Sprache, es gibt sie nicht vor dem Werk, das Weiner formuliert. Bedingende Aussage und bedingte Aussage sind voneinander nicht grundsätzlich unterscheidbar. Damit fallen alle Eigenschaften dahin, die das Werk als im voraus bestehende in Anspruch nimmt. Zu diesen Eigenschaften würde auch die Autonomie des Kunstwerks gehören, und so wird gerade in der Behauptung der Autonomie zugegeben, dass sie eine sprachliche Aussage, eine Fiktion ist.

Indem sie sprachlich sind, haben Weiners Werke vorerst die Eigenschaft, keine Eigenschaft zu besitzen. Sie können nicht umschrieben werden, denn es handelt sich stets um einzelne sprachliche Formulierungen, meist Aussagen ohne Subjekt und konjugierte Verben. Man kann wohl behaupten, dass Weiner einen besonderen Sprachstil, eine Stilisierung durchwegs vermieden hat. Weiners Werke sind vorerst kaum zu lokalisieren, denn sie unterscheiden sich formal nicht von anderen sprachlichen Sequenzen, die im Umlauf sind. Sie sind beinahe nichts neben allen anderen Sätzen einer Sprache – aber ist eine Skulptur aus Holz oder Stahl mehr als fast nichts neben der bestehenden Menge von verarbeitetem Holz oder Stahl? Sie ist es wohl nicht in quantitativem, sondern in qualitativem Sinn. Der Unterschied liegt aber darin, dass ein Werk aus dem Material der Sprache, das sich notwendigerweise in dem allen zugänglichen Sprachraum aufhält, dieses Beinahe-Nichts stets thematisiert. Ob es den von Weiner formulierten Satz schon einmal gegeben hat oder ob er jetzt erfunden wurde, ist nebensächlich. Dies im Gegensatz zur Beschaffenheit einer Skulptur, die sich aus ihrer Einzigartigkeit definiert, daraus, dass ein Material in einer bestimmten Bearbeitung und in einer bestimmten Plazierung so noch nicht zu sehen war, daraus, dass eine Menge von Eigenschaften für dieses Material einmalig festgelegt wird. Die Eigenschaftslosigkeit von Weiners Werken wird anhand der Frage des Massstabs deutlich, die für die meisten öffentlichen Skulpturen schon den Schritt ins Verderben bedeutet. Eine überaus stark vergrösserte Typographie wie beispielsweise in Weiners Rotterdamer Arbeit

AS LONG AS IT LASTS

1993 auf Höhe des Euromastes installiert, leistet nur Übermittlung; das Werk selber ist nicht monumentaler als die kleine Blechtafel

COVERED BY CLOUDS

am Furkapass insofern als ihm die Schriftfassung äusserlich bleibt. Weil das Werk keine inhärente Massstäblichkeit besitzt – und dafür würde es eine feste Konsistenz, vorgegebene Eigenschaften benötigen –, kann es in einer Realisation die Proportionen nie verfehlen.

Das Beinahe-Nichts der sprachlichen Sequenz verlangt nach dem Präsentationsmoment, nach einer bestimmten Installation, in der die Skulptur dem Publikum offeriert wird. Weiner hat diesen Übergabemoment verlängert, indem er mittels der Bezeichnung «Public Freehold» einzelne Werke zum öffentlichen Eigentum erklärte und damit darauf verzichtete, sie zu verkaufen. So ist

BROKEN OFF

beispielsweise endgültig der Öffentlichkeit anvertraut. Mit dieser Erklärung der Eigentumsübertragung unterstreicht Weiner, dass er seine Sätze nicht spricht, sondern dass er sie anderen überlässt. Ein Werk muss nicht in einem öffentlichen Raum gebaut werden, es genügt, dass es übergeben wird: die Übergabe des Werks macht es zu einem kulturellen Faktum, das möglicherweise von da an über das Beinahe-Nichts eines Satzes hinausleuchtet.

1) Zitiert in Lucy R. Lippard, *Six Years: The Dematerialization of the Art Object from 1966 to 1972* [...]. New York: Praeger Publishers, 1973, S. 48.
2) Arthur R. Rose [=Joseph Kosuth], Four Interviews with Barry, Huebler, Kosuth, Weiner, *Arts Magazine*, Vol. 43, No. 4 (Februar 1969), S. 23.

DIETER SCHWARZ

Public Freehold

Much has been heard in recent years of what has come to be called "art in public spaces" and some artists, among them Lawrence Weiner, have designed works specifically for such spaces. But how is that possible? Depending on the way you look at it, there is something tautological or contradictory about the idea that works of art should be intended particularly for public spaces. After all, it is impossible to conceive of an artwork without a public arena, that is, outside of a structure that includes author, object, and beholder. By defining a work of art as such, it is drawn into the world of utterances and thus reveals its linguistic qualities. Even where privacy is targeted, it is still enmeshed in a social and cultural network that makes the work possible and legitimizes it. Galleries and museums, by definition open to the public, are simply more protected than other spaces, being subject to a special consensus; and there is no denying that the private home of the collector is entirely infiltrated by public connotations and contingencies. It follows that a culture cannot be divided into private and public realms. On the other hand, the concept of art for public spaces implies a specific function and purpose that is extremely difficult to reconcile with the afunctionality and purposelessness of the modernist work of art. That does not mean that art is meaningless, but rather, that it deals exclusively with artistic concerns and not with anything else. If it addresses a task, then it functions as a helpful device and becomes, for example, a design or a document.

DIETER SCHWARZ is director of the Kunstmuseum Winterthur and editor of *Katalog Raisonné, Bücher Lawrence Weiner,* Cologne, 1989.

This situation is brought to a head in Lawrence Weiner's work, which consists of language and the materials referred to. A work of this kind can never occupy a fixed place in a specific space because it is based on the fact that the linguistic statement has no final outward form. The work is, of course, confined to a particular formulation within one language and is recorded as such in the English catalogue raisonné. But given the way Weiner defines his work, it does not have a fixed place in one language but can be transferred at will from one language to another. However, every site within any given language is public because it is impossible to reserve a particular portion of a language as private. Lawrence Weiner's linguistic works are public by definition, that is, they inhabit space in general; they are part of the linguistic community on which a culture is based. In fact, Weiner already referred to space in general in the early sculptures which he physically made himself. As he stated in 1968, "The piece would have existed wherever it was put; it was in relationship to an outdoor space, as opposed to a specific outdoor space."[1] But what his work signifies in this general space is a question that cannot be answered by the artist alone.

Weiner reformulates the question of a work's functional use or its autonomy, as demonstrated by his conviction that the work is translatable. This pragmatic approach claims to deploy the medium of language functionally: The outward form of the work is irrelevant if the content, that is, the described materials, remain the same. In other words, material reference as a constant is opposed to exchangeable linguistic sequences. Can this functional concept be applied to the placement of Weiner's works? Once installed, does the work serve the architecture, the client, an issue? Let us assume that language is merely the instrument that establishes a direct relationship to materials, and that it is also freely exchangeable. Then the utterance moves unhindered from one language to another. Then it eludes our grasp even when it is painted on the wall or engraved on a plaque. Then a sentence can indeed be here today and somewhere else tomorrow:

BROKEN OFF

on a postcard, on a broken tile, stenciled onto a surface, a mosaic made of stones... And even if the lettering remains (*scripta manent*...), it is always in the hands of the person who reads it; it never belongs to the architecture, to a client, to an issue, that is, to its carrier or producer. Material reference—and Weiner banks on it—is of course not an object but rather material that has acquired semantic density through long-term use in a variety of contexts. The original reference is transformed, in a work by Weiner, into an incalculable set of linguistic statements.

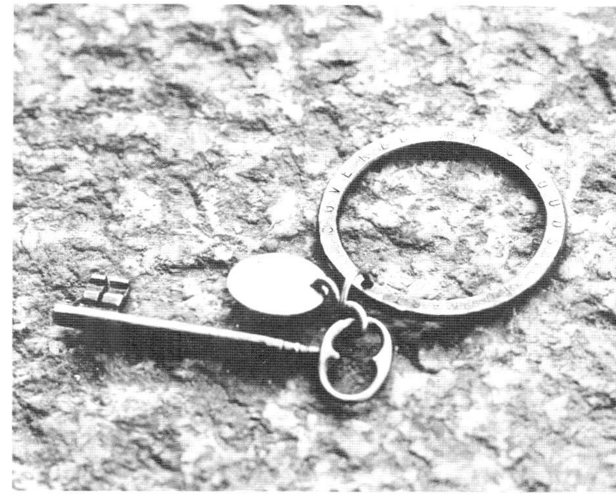

LAWRENCE WEINER, COVERED BY CLOUDS, 1989, multiple, here with the key of the Hotel Furkablick on the Furkapasshöhe, Switzerland. (PHOTO: CLAUDE JORAY)

If functionality falters in work that consists of language, the autonomy of the work is also called into question. In his early works Weiner always foregrounded the making of the artwork; nothing could distract him from this single-minded purpose, neither the process nor the physical appearance of the presentation. "Materialist implies a primary involvement with materials, but I am primarily concerned with art. One could say the subject matter is materials, but its reason to be goes way beyond materials to something else, that something else being art."[2] Weiner resolved this problem by giving his works a linguistic turn. The work still has a material setting, but the material does not detract from the fact that the work refers to more than just itself. Being linguistic, it cannot do otherwise; it inevitably refers to something else. But whether Weiner's "something else," namely art, is identical to the something else of language must remain a moot question. In any case, language goes further; it shifts away from direct representation, away from unambiguous reference as, for instance, to the idea of art. The idealistic pretension of Weiner's statement—of his reference to art as an abstract—is canceled out by the fact that he entrusts his works to a medium that does not yet possess certainty but first has to establish it. Thus if a linguistic work purports to deal with "art," then it is the task of that work's medium to construct the concept of art to begin with. Art does not exist before language; it does not exist before the work formulated by Weiner. Determining statement and determined statement are basically indistinguishable. This eliminates all the properties appropriated by the work as already given. One of these properties would be the autonomy of the artwork, so that the very claim to autonomy in itself concedes that it is a linguistic statement, a fiction.

By being linguistic, Weiner's works have the property, above all, of having no properties. They cannot be circumscribed because they are, for the most part, isolated linguistic formulations, usually statements with neither subject nor conjugated verb. One can certainly say that Weiner consistently avoids a specific linguistic style or stylization. In fact, the works initially elude localization because they are formally indistinguishable from other linguistic sequences in circulation. They are almost nothing next to all the other sentences of a language—but is a sculpture of wood or steel more than almost nothing next to the existing quantities of worked wood or steel? It probably is, although not in terms of quantity but rather of quality. The difference lies in the fact that a work made of the material of language, which necessarily inhabits a linguistic space that is accessible to everyone, has this "almost-nothing" as its subject matter. Whether the sentence articulated by Weiner already existed or has just been invented is irrelevant. In contrast, the quality of a sculpture is defined by its singularity, by the fact that a material is treated and placed in a way that has never been seen before, by the fact that this material has been invested with a unique set of properties. A look at the scale that is the downfall of most public sculptures underscores the absence of properties in Lawrence Weiner's works. A vastly enlarged typography as in

AS LONG AS IT LASTS

installed at the height of the Euromast in Rotterdam in 1993, still serves only to transmit; the work itself is no more monumental than the small tin plaque

COVERED BY CLOUDS

on the Furka mountain pass in Switzerland. Since the work possesses no inherent scale, which would necessarily entail predetermined properties, the proportions of any given realization can never be amiss.

The almost-nothing of a linguistic sequence demands a presentation, a specific installation in which the sculpture is offered to the public. Weiner has extended this moment of presentation by declaring certain of his pieces as "public freehold" and therefore waiving their sale. Thus

BROKEN OFF

has been entrusted to the public. By officially bequeathing his property to the public, Weiner underscores the fact that he does not speak through his sentences but rather leaves them to others. A work does not have to be constructed in a public space; it need only be handed over; the act of handing it over makes it a cultural fact that could, from then on, possibly shine beyond the almost-nothing of a sentence. *(Translation: Catherine Schelbert)*

1) In Lucy R. Lippard, *Six Years: The Dematerialization of the Art Object from 1966 to 1972.* (New York: Praeger Publishers, 1973), 48.

2) Arthur R. Rose [=Joseph Kosuth], "Four Interviews with Barry, Huebler, Kosuth, Weiner," in *Arts Magazine,* vol. 43, no. 4 (February 1969), 23

LAWRENCE WEINER, AS LONG AS IT LASTS / SOLANGE ES HÄLT, 1993, Euromast, Rotterdam.

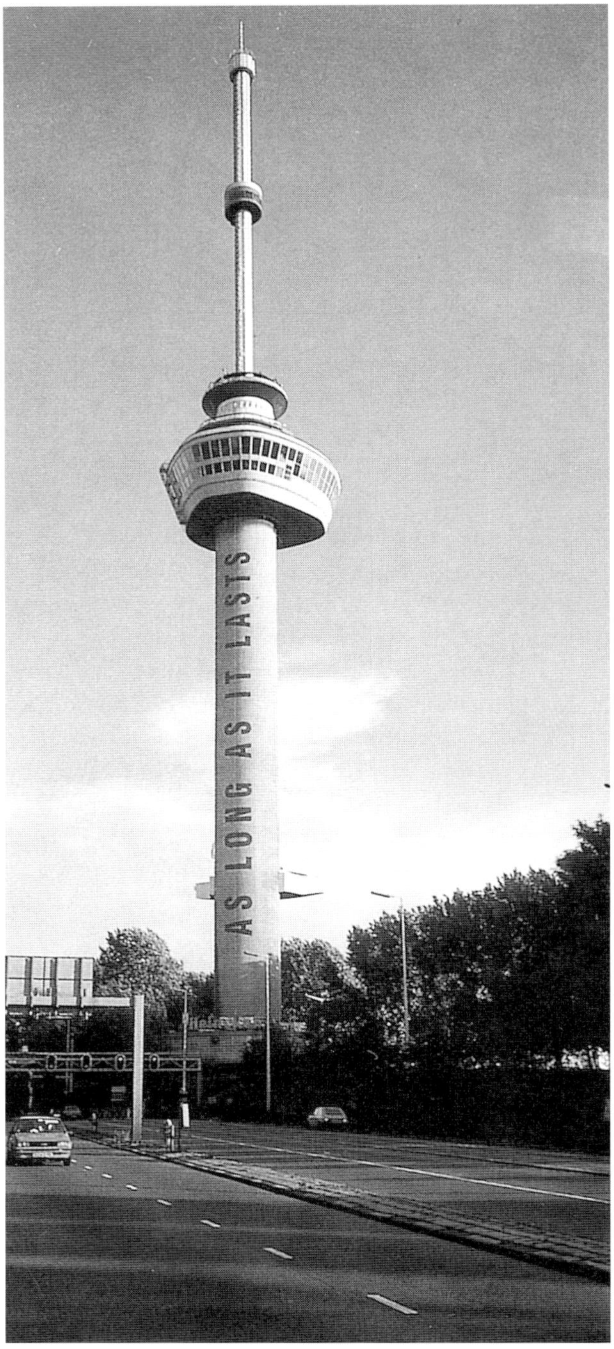

LAWRENCE WEINER, A RUBBER BALL THROWN INTO THE AMERICAN FALLS NIAGARA FALLS A RUBBER BALL THROWN INTO THE CANADIAN FALLS NIAGARA FALLS, 1969. A series of film frames by Hollis Frampton.

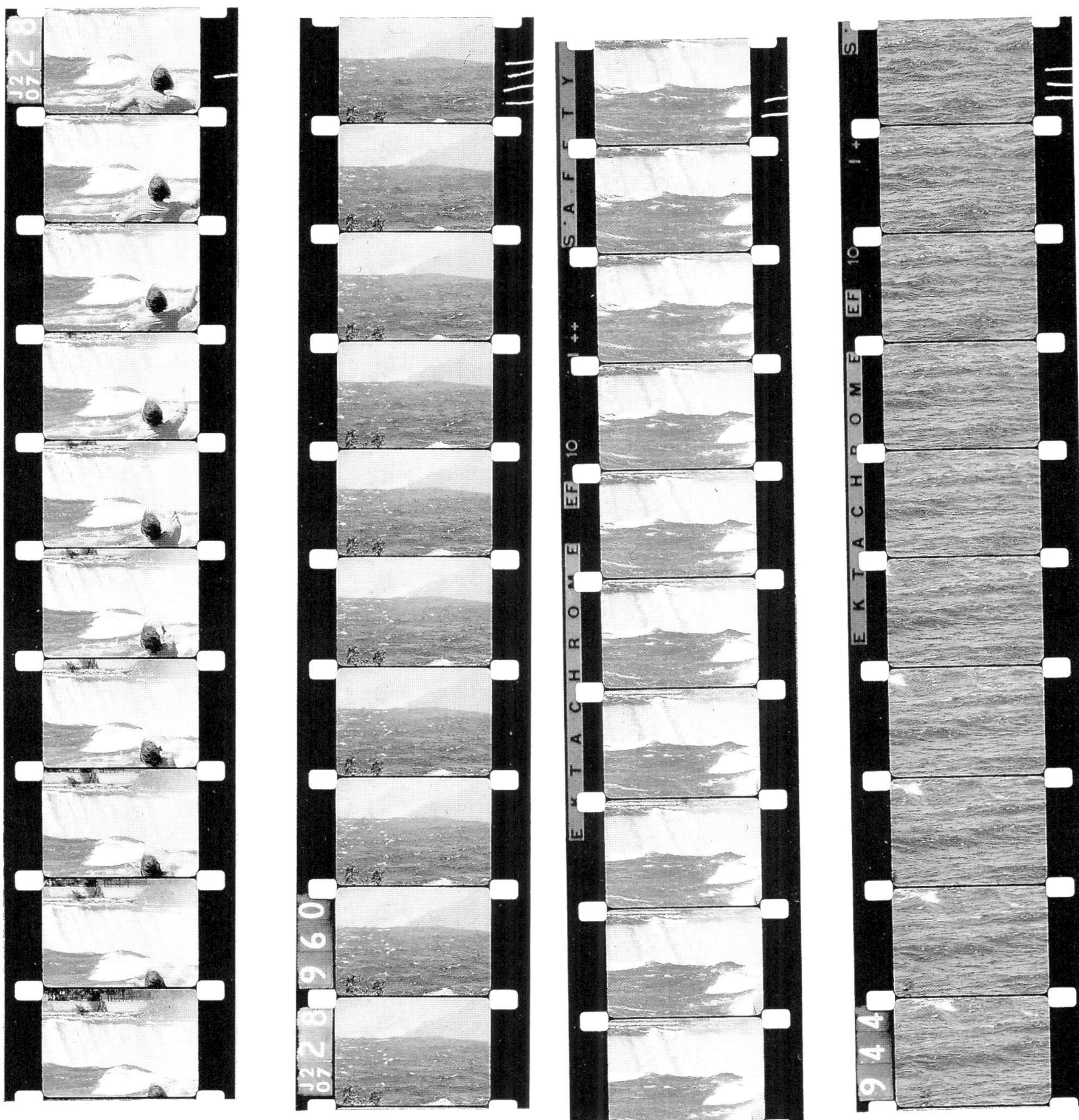

DANIELA SALVIONI

The Meaning that Comes Away from the Work of Art

One adjective that broadly characterizes modern art of the twentieth century is "self-reflective." Some of the most avant-garde movements in this vein have been about the context of art. Duchamp explored the context of art in several directions, by placing a bottle rack in an exhibition space, a moustache on a reproduction of the Mona Lisa, and so on. In contemporary art, through theatricality, Minimalism stressed the viewer's presence as an integral component of the context of art. Conceptualism took context to be a variety of structures that subtend art—institutions, language, abstract systems. The investigation of art's context at each point gave rise to art which expanded the limits of acceptable forms. One of the most salient ways to describe this development was the de-materialization of art—a notion which is too homogenizing and too often inaccurate, but which, however, underscores the extreme experimentation to which the presentation of art has been subjected in recent times.

Lawrence Weiner's work fits comfortably within the avant-garde trajectory thus cursorily summarized. His original statement of intent is worth reiterating in its entirety as it is virtually a manifesto for the most provocative avant-garde position—

1. The artist may construct the piece.
2. The piece may be fabricated.
3. The piece need not be built.

Each being equal and consistent with the intent of the artist the decision as to the condition rests with the receiver upon the occasion of receivership.

The first point simply states that the traditional way of making art (that is, that the artist fabricates it) is an option. The second point says that the artist may have the work fabricated by others. The third point makes explicit the idea that the art work does not reside exclusively, or even principally, in its material incarnation. While this is an extreme position associated most closely with conceptual art, the concluding remark is perhaps his most radical. It states that the condition of the work of art depends on the interaction between the work and the viewer. In the case of Weiner's work, this claim to an open work (in the sense originally outlined by Umberto Eco) has significant repercussions. In particular, it means that the discrete instances of his work may differ considerably in appearance and import. It also means for him that the work can exist in more than one place at the same time.

DANIELA SALVIONI is a writer who lives in San Francisco.

These aspects of Weiner's work seem to be consonant with the avant-garde investigation of the context of art. It is therefore puzzling to encounter statements by the artist in which he explicitly distances himself from context-oriented art and the Duchampian tradition. Here are some examples:

"I don't find Duchamp an interesting artist:
all he was interested in were the opinions of his elders,
only in the context."

"Art about context is art that uses either the negation of an accepted premise in art history, or the negation of a pat or standard form of art, or the acceptance of art history as its bolstering and bulwark and that's all it does. Art about materials, art about content, fits within the context of history (it might negate, or shore up, or whatever) but that's not the subject matter of the work."

"... art is about material objects."

"... when you see a photograph of an installation of mine, essentially all you have to remember is the meaning of the words. You don't have to remember the architecture."[1)]

Examining Lawrence Weiner's public sculptures may disentangle the apparent conundrum between his self-proclaimed distance from context-oriented art and what he seems to share with it. There is nothing inherently different between his public sculptures and the presentation of the work in private and/or commercial settings. After all, for him the work is composed of text and the materials therein designated. The presentation of the work and its support structure (what surface carries the text, what color the text is, how big the letters are, and so on), all the aesthetic and material factors that make up the way the text is presented are incidental to the essence of the work. However, because of the overload of references that impinge on a sculpture set in a public space, Weiner's public works, in a sense, test the role of context and content in his work.

ZERSCHMETTERT IN STÜCKE
(IM FRIEDEN DER NACHT)

is a public work in Vienna dating from 1991. The text sprawls across the upper portion of three anti-aircraft defense towers adjacent to bustling commercial districts of the city. The letters are two meters high, painted silver outlined in black, hovering high above the casual passerby, their color suggesting the silver of bomber planes. The huge, fifty meter tall towers, which were meant to function also as air-raid shelters, are remnants of World War II—they are not ruins, properly speaking, because they are structurally intact—which are left standing because it is simply too costly to tear them down. Therefore, there is an ironic relationship between the first part of the text—"smashed to pieces"—and the edifice it is written on: The bunker cannot be smashed to pieces; it was built to protect people from being blown apart. The foreboding subtext of the second part of the text—"in the still of the night"—is enhanced here as air-raids would typically occur in the night, thereby breaking the still of the night. This contrasts sharply with the placid, cocooning sense of the dominant significance of "in the still of the night." In German, the text and its internal juxtaposition go through another twist of meaning as the translation of "still of the night" is "peace of the night." Double entendres unfurl into a multiplicity of evocations centering on war and peace, immutability and the ephemeral, purposelessness and commercialism.

As dense and evocative a set of associations as these may be, this is but one presentation of the work which can contain a very different reading when it is presented differently. Indeed,

SMASHED TO PIECES
(IN THE STILL OF THE NIGHT)

is a work which precedes the Viennese commission and that therefore has an independent existence from the particular reading suggested by the Viennese installation. Without the bellicose towers as its support structure, other sets of meanings easily come into play. More specifically, reading the text in isolation or envisioning it in a more natural setting opens up and even destabilizes its meaning. The sense of the phrase appears more enigmatic and the viewer is called upon to fill in the blanks more aggressively.

There are simply fewer crutches upon which to base one's interpretation, leaving more to the viewer's discretion. Of course, the viewer also participates in the construction of meaning in the public installation of the piece, but there are more clues to work with. Or perhaps we should say that the viewer can create more clues upon which to base her/his interpretation in a setting that is itself replete with references.

SOME LIMESTONE SOME SANDSTONE
ENCLOSED FOR SOME REASON
SOME LIMESTONE SOME SANDSTONE
INCLOSED FOR SOME REASON

is a public work which Weiner created expressly for the Henry Moore Sculpture Trust in 1993. Situated in Halifax, a de-industrialized area of England, the work is in forged iron recast from an obsolete weighbridge and reset in the largest carpet factory in the world. The letters are raised and, as the plaque is set in the ground, it can be walked on, not unlike medieval or Renaissance tombs. The words "sandstone" and "limestone" are uncoupled, so that sand, lime, and stone are materials also overtly denoted in the text. The textual staccato reinforces the sonorous rhythm of the text that echoes the chug-chug of the trains which once traveled these rails so industriously. The latter half of the text—enclosed for some reason—could refer back to the amalgamation of words (sandstone, limestone) so as to make new words and, by extension, to the geological processes that forged the earthly matter in the first instance. But, enclosed also suggests enclosures, the device by which British landowners ran farmers off the land so that it could be devoted exclusively to raising sheep. This socio-economic shift—when, it has been said, sheep ate men—brutally and permanently altered the relations of production and created the first mass of workers who had only their labor to sell. Enclosures constituted a transformation that made the industrial revolution possible. The final note of the text—"... for some reason"—hints, perhaps, at the absurdity of this transformation once one refuses to accept the logic of capital which underlies it.

But, this cursory interpretation may just be an instance of Weiner's sculpture providing for, as the artist has put it, "other people's metaphor needs" (mine, in this case). For, as he has pointed out on several occasions, it is not his intention to make metaphors himself. Indeed, it is easy to imagine the Halifax work as a wall-piece, such as one may view in a gallery, with very different connotations. Weiner gives us no reason to think that it would have less integrity as an artwork. It is this elastic attitude towards the content of the work which is behind certain extreme positions enunciated by the artist. For instance, he has said, "Anyone making a reproduction of my art is making art just as valid as art as if I had made it."[2)]

At the same time, however, the importance of content over context remains paramount—recall his snide comment to the effect: "... when you see a photograph of an installation of mine, essentially all you have to remember is the meaning of the words. You don't have to remember the architecture."

Art that thematizes context, Weiner seems to be suggesting, risks relying for its meaning excessively on the actual, immediate context of the artwork. If this is the case, paradoxically it shares with painting the pitfall of being illusionistic. Just as painting traditionally functions by illustration, so can excessively context-driven art degenerate into illustration when, for instance, the institutional context is collapsed into the architecture in which the artwork is situated.

In the late 1960s, Weiner repudiated painting on the grounds that it functioned via illusion. He describes his own works as sculpture, relating to his belief that art should be deeply materialist, that is, that it should be about the relations between objects and people. It is in light of this Marxian sense of the term "materialism" that one should read the oft-quoted comment by Rudi Fuchs that Weiner's work "... is no solemn form, but rather a nimble, dialectical argument." The dialectical beauty of Weiner's work is its extreme freedom of meaning coupled with fundamentally being about what it says it's about.

By looking at Lawrence Weiner's public commissions, we see that the meaning of his work may be affected by its situation but is not reliant upon it. Privileging content, however, has not led him to a retrograde position where meaning is impervious to art's surroundings. In particular, the viewer can

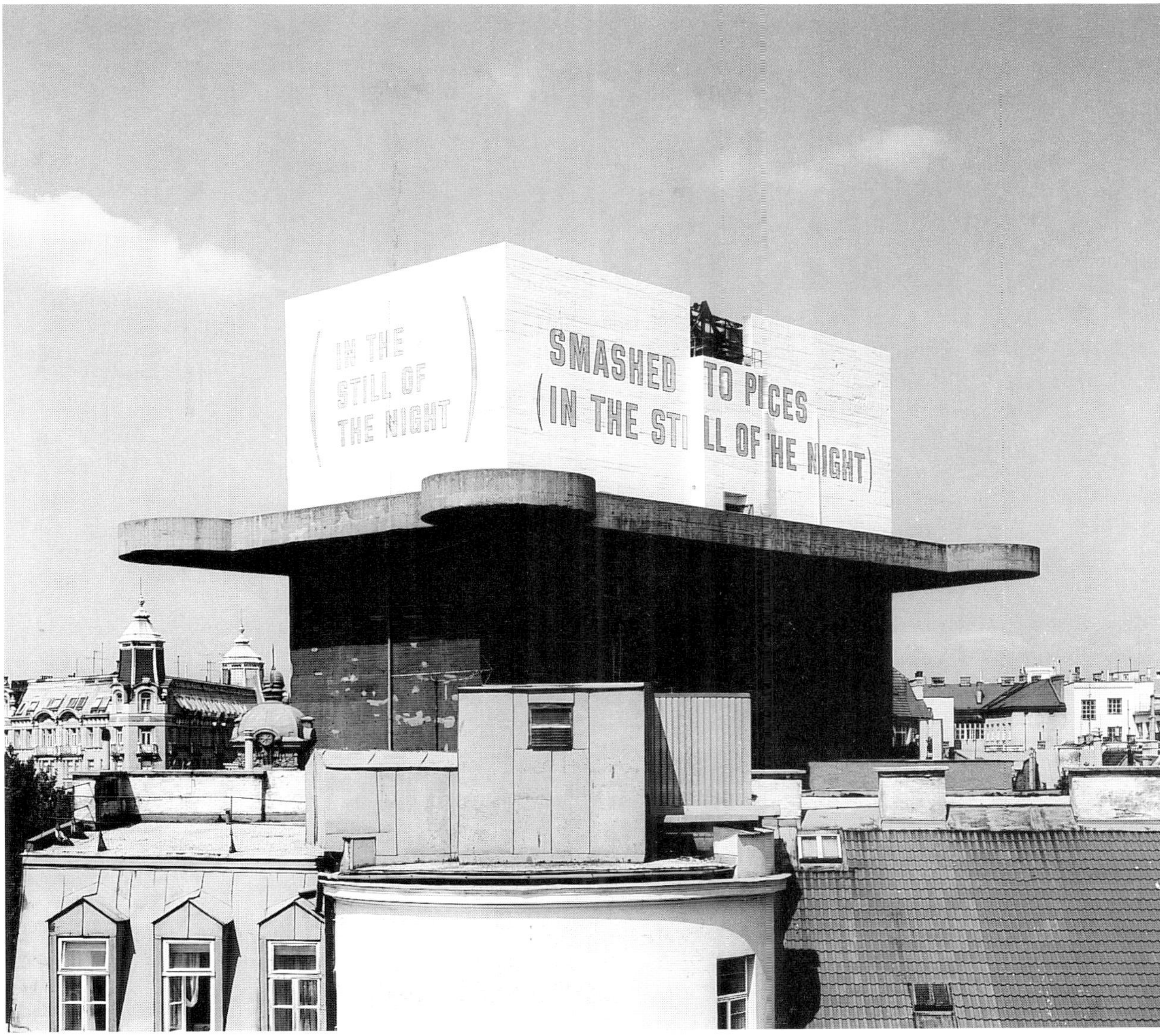

LAWRENCE WEINER, SMASHED TO PIECES (IN THE STILL OF THE NIGHT) / ZERSCHMETTERT IN STÜCKE (IM FRIEDEN DER NACHT), 1991, Flakturm / anti-aircraft defense tower, Esterházypark, Wien / Vienna. (PHOTO: CHRISTIAN WACHTER)

actively participate in the construction of meaning. Nor does this mean that the work is simply an empty vessel waiting to be filled. The play of meaning in Weiner's work is built upon a solid material foundation—after all, the medium of the work is language and the materials referred to in the text. Finally, the work is not context-driven, nor deconstructive, but rather its principal mode is additive. Art critics have correctly noted the non-authoritarian voice in Weiner's work, but this does not go far enough. In the dialectical play between what is and what can be, Weiner opens up an intrinsically liberatory space.

1) All quotes from David Batchelor, *"I Am Not Content,"* interview with Lawrence Weiner, *Artscribe*, March/April, 1989.
2) Lawrence Weiner, "October 12, 1969," in Ursula Meyer, ed., *Conceptual Art* (New York: E.P. Dutton, 1972), p. 21.

DANIELA SALVIONI

Die Bedeutung, die sich vom Werk löst

Ein Adjektiv, das die moderne Kunst des 20. Jahrhunderts allgemein charakterisiert, ist «selbstbezüglich». Einige der avantgardistischsten Strömungen in dieser Richtung befassten sich mit dem Kontext der Kunst. Duchamp untersuchte den Kontext von Kunstwerken in verschiedener Hinsicht, indem er etwa einen Flaschentrockner in einem Ausstellungsraum plazierte, indem er einer Reproduktion der Mona Lisa einen Schnurrbart verpasste, usw. In der zeitgenössischen Kunst betonte der Minimalismus die Anwesenheit des Betrachters als integralen Bestandteil des Kontexts von Kunstwerken mit Mitteln des Theaters. Die Konzeptkunst verstand Kontext als eine Vielfalt von Strukturen, die aller Kunst zugrunde liegen – Institutionen, Sprache, abstrakte Systeme. Die Untersuchung des Kontexts liess in jedem Fall Kunst entstehen, welche die Grenzen der anerkannten Ausdrucksformen erweiterte. Die auffälligste Art und Weise der Beschreibung dieser Entwicklung war die Entmaterialisierung der Kunst – ein Begriff, der zu wenig differenziert und oft nicht genau trifft, der jedoch den hochgradigen Experimentcharakter unterstreicht, dem die Präsentation von Kunst in jüngster Zeit unterliegt.

Lawrence Weiners Arbeit passt sehr gut in dieses zusammenfassend skizzierte Bild der Avantgarde. Es lohnt sich jedoch, seine ursprüngliche Aussage über seine Intention noch einmal genau anzusehen, da sie auf ein Manifest für einen äusserst provokativen avantgardistischen Standpunkt hinausläuft –

1. Der Künstler kann das Werk bauen.
2. Das Werk kann angefertigt werden.
3. Das Werk muss nicht gebaut werden.

Je gleichwertig und übereinstimmend mit der Intention des Künstlers, bleibt die Entscheidung über den eintretenden Umstand dem Empfänger in seiner jeweiligen Empfangssituation überlassen.

Der erste Satz sagt lediglich, dass die hergebrachte Art, Kunst zu machen (also, dass der Künstler Kunst macht), eine Möglichkeit unter anderen ist. Der zweite Satz sagt, dass der Künstler das Werk durch andere herstellen lassen kann. Der dritte Satz macht deutlich, dass das Kunstwerk nicht ausschliesslich oder gar in erster Linie in der materiellen Verkörperung besteht. Während dies eine extreme Position ist, die der Konzeptkunst sehr nahe steht, ist Weiners abschliessende Bemerkung vielleicht seine radikalste. Sie stellt fest, dass die Bedingung der Entstehung eines Kunstwerks von der Interaktion zwischen Werk und Betrachter abhängt. Im Fall von Weiners Arbeit hat dieser Anspruch auf ein offenes Kunstwerk (wie es Umberto Eco in seinem gleichnamigen Buch definiert hat) bedeutsame Rückwirkungen. Insbe-

DANIELA SALVIONI schreibt und lebt in San Francisco.

sondere heisst dies, dass seine Arbeiten sich in unterschiedlichen Situationen hinsichtlich Erscheinungsbild und Bedeutung beträchtlich unterscheiden können. Es heisst auch, dass sein Werk an mehreren Orten gleichzeitig existieren kann.

Diese Aspekte von Weiners Werk scheinen zur avantgardistischen Untersuchung des Kontexts von Kunst zu passen. Es ist deshalb verwirrend, auf Äusserungen des Künstlers zu stossen, in welchen er sich ausdrücklich von der kontextorientierten Kunst und von der Duchampschen Tradition distanziert. Dafür einige Beispiele:

«Ich halte Duchamp nicht für einen interessanten Künstler; alles, was ihn interessierte, waren die Meinungen seiner Vorgänger, lediglich im Kontext betrachtet.»

«Kunst über Kontext ist Kunst, die entweder mit der Ablehnung eines anerkannten Grundsatzes der Kunstgeschichte arbeitet, oder mit der Ablehnung einer gekonnten oder gängigen Kunstform, oder aber die Kunstgeschichte als Polster und Schutz für sich akzeptiert, das ist auch schon alles. Kunst, die Werkstoffe und Materialien oder Inhalte thematisiert, bewegt sich innerhalb des geschichtlichen Kontexts (ob sie diesen nun verneint, stützt oder was auch immer), aber das ist nicht das Wesentliche an einem Kunstwerk.»

«... in der Kunst geht es um materielle Gegenstände.»

«... wenn man die Photographie einer meiner Installationen sieht, genügt es, sich an die Bedeutung der Wörter zu erinnern. An die Architektur braucht man sich nicht zu erinnern.»[1)]

Vielleicht kann eine Betrachtung der öffentlichen Skulpturen Weiners den zutage getretenen Widerspruch zwischen seiner erklärten Distanz zur kontextorientierten Kunst und den scheinbar vorhandenen Gemeinsamkeiten auflösen. Es gibt keinen wesentlichen Unterschied zwischen seinen Skulpturen im öffentlichen Raum und der Präsentation seiner Arbeiten in privater Umgebung und/oder im Kunsthandel. Schliesslich setzt sich sein Werk aus dem Text und aus den darin bezeichneten Gegenständen zusammen. Die Präsentation des Werks und seiner Trägerstruktur (die Oberfläche, die den Text trägt, die Farbe des Textes, die Grösse der Buchstaben usw.), alle ästhetischen und materiellen Faktoren, die die Art und Weise der Textdarstellung bestimmen, sind dem Wesen des Werks äusserlich. Doch wegen der Überfülle von Sinnbezügen, die auf eine im öffentlichen Raum plazierte Skulptur einstürzen, unterziehen Weiners öffentliche Arbeiten sozusagen die Funktion von Kontext und Inhalt in seinem Werk einer Prüfung.

SMASHED TO PIECES (IN THE STILL OF THE NIGHT)

ist eine öffentliche Arbeit in Wien, aus dem Jahr 1991. Der Text zieht sich über den oberen Teil von drei Luftabwehrtürmen, in nächster Nähe zu den hektischen Geschäftsvierteln der Stadt. Die Buchstaben sind zwei Meter hoch, silbern, mit schwarzem Rand, und schweben hoch in der Luft über allfälligen Passanten. Ihr Silber erinnert an die Farbe von Jagdbombern. Die gigantischen 50 Meter hohen Türme, die auch als Luftschutzbunker dienten, sind ein Relikt aus dem zweiten Weltkrieg – es sind nicht eigentlich Ruinen, denn sie sind baulich unbeschädigt –, man hat sie einfach stehenlassen, weil das Abreissen zu teuer ist. Deshalb entsteht eine ironische Beziehung zwischen dem ersten Teil des Textes – «smashed to pieces» – und dem Gebäude, auf dem er geschrieben steht: Der Bunker kann nicht in Stücke zerschmettert werden; er wurde gebaut, um Leute vor Bomben zu schützen. Der warnende Unterton der zweiten Texthälfte – «in the still of the night» – wird an dieser Stelle verstärkt, da Luftangriffe gewöhnlich nachts stattfinden und deshalb den nächtlichen Frieden stören. Diese Aussage steht in starkem Gegensatz zum beschaulichen, Geborgenheit vermittelnden Sinn der Hauptbedeutung von «in the still of the night». Im Deutschen erhält die Bedeutung des Texts und der in ihm enthaltenen Entgegensetzung einen zusätzlichen Dreh, weil der Ausdruck «still of the night» mit «Frieden der Nacht» übersetzt wird. Doppeldeutigkeiten beschwören eine

Vielfalt von Assoziationen rund um Krieg und Frieden herauf, Unveränderliches und Flüchtiges, Zweckfreiheit und Profitinteresse.

So dicht und beschwörend solche Assoziationen sein mögen, dies ist nur eine Darstellungsvariante dieses Werks, das ganz anders gelesen werden kann, wenn es anders präsentiert wird. Tatsächlich ist

ZERSCHMETTERT IN STÜCKE
(IM FRIEDEN DER NACHT)

ein Werk, das vor dem Wiener Auftrag entstanden ist. Es hat deshalb eine von der besonderen, durch die Wiener Installation hervorgerufenen Lesart unabhängige Existenz. Ohne die kriegerischen Türme als Trägerelement kommen sofort andere Bedeutungsfelder ins Spiel. Genauer: Liest man den Text für sich oder stellt ihn sich in einer natürlicheren Umgebung vor, so wird seine Bedeutung weiter und kommt ins Wanken. Der Sinn des Satzes wird rätselhafter, und der Betrachter ist heftiger dazu aufgerufen, die Sinnlücken zu füllen. Es gibt einfach weniger Krücken, auf denen sich eine Interpretation abstützen liesse, um so mehr bleibt der Entscheidung des Betrachters überlassen. Natürlich ist der Betrachter auch im Fall der öffentlichen Werkinstallation an der Konstruktion der Bedeutung beteiligt, aber es gibt dort von Anfang an mehr Anhaltspunkte. Man könnte vielleicht auch sagen, dass der Betrachter selbst mehr Anhaltspunkte schaffen kann, auf denen er seine Interpretation aufzubauen vermag, in einem Umfeld, das in sich gesättigt ist mit Sinnbezügen.

SOME LIMESTONE SOME SANDSTONE
ENCLOSED FOR SOME REASON
SOME LIMESTONE SOME SANDSTONE
INCLOSED FOR SOME REASON

ist eine öffentliche Arbeit, die Weiner 1993 speziell für den Henry Moore Sculpture Trust geschaffen hat. In Halifax, einer entindustrialisierten Gegend Englands angesiedelt, ist diese Arbeit in Stahl gefertigt, der aus einer nicht mehr benützten Brückenwaage wiedergewonnen wurde, und wurde auf dem Gelände der grössten Teppichfabrik der Welt wieder aufgestellt. Die Buchstaben sind erhaben, und die Stahlplatte ist im Boden eingelassen, so dass sie begehbar ist, mittelalterlichen oder Renaissance-Gräbern nicht unähnlich. Die Wörter «sandstone» und «limestone» sind nicht zusammengeschrieben, so dass, «sand», «lime» und «stone» (Sand, Kalk und Stein) im Text als Material ebenfalls direkt bezeichnet werden. Dieses Staccato des Textes unterstreicht den eindrücklichen Textrhythmus, der an das tschu-tschu der Züge erinnert, die einst in grosser Zahl über diese früheren Schienen rollten. Die zweite Hälfte des Textes – «enclosed for some reason» – könnte sich zurückbeziehen auf die Vermengung von Wörtern (sandstone, limestone) zur Erzeugung neuer Wörter und, im erweiterten Sinn, auf die geologischen Prozesse, die alle irdische Materie ursprünglich formten. Aber «enclosed» lässt auch an «enclosures» (Einzäunungen) denken, an das Mittel, durch das die britischen Grundbesitzer die Pachtbauern von ihrem Land verdrängten, so dass es ausschliesslich für die Aufzucht von Schafen genutzt werden konnte. Diese sozioökonomische Verlagerung – als, wie man sagt, Schafe Menschen frassen – veränderte die Produktionsverhältnisse rücksichtslos und dauerhaft und schuf die erste Masse von Arbeitern, die nichts als ihre Arbeitskraft zum Kauf anbieten konnten. Die Einzäunungen bewirkten eine Veränderung, welche die industrielle Revolution erst ermöglichte. Die letzte Bemerkung des Texts – «for some reason» – deutet vielleicht auf die Absurdität dieser Veränderung hin, die jedem bewusst wird, der sich weigert, die dem Vorgang zugrundeliegende Logik des Kapitals anzunehmen.

Aber dieser Interpretationsversuch ist vielleicht nur ein Beispiel dafür, welchen Bedürfnissen Weiners Skulpturen Rechnung tragen, wie er selbst gesagt hat, «anderer Leute Bedürfnisse nach Metaphern» (meinem, in diesem Fall). Denn, wie er bei verschiedenen Gelegenheiten betont hat, es ist nicht seine Absicht, selbst Metaphern zu schaffen. In der Tat ist es nicht schwer, sich die Halifax-Arbeit als Wandrelief vorzustellen, wie man ihm in einer Galerie begegnen könnte, mit ganz anderen Konnotationen. Weiner gibt uns keinen Grund zu denken, dass es als Kunstwerk dadurch verlieren könnte. Es ist diese Beweglichkeit im Umgang mit dem Inhalt seiner Werke, die hinter gewissen extremen Äusse-

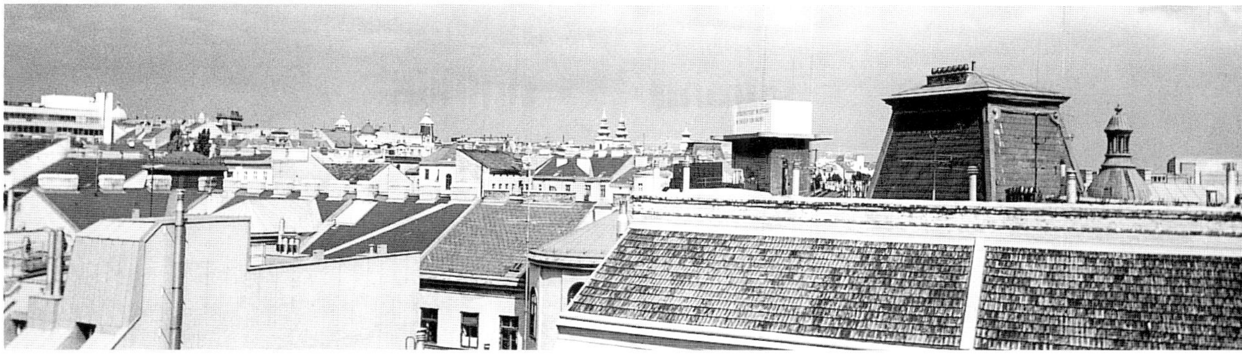

Der Flakturm über den Dächern Wiens / The anti-aircraft defense tower over the rooftops of Vienna. (PHOTO: BIRGIT JÜRGENSSEN)

rungen des Künstlers steht. Zum Beispiel sagte er: «Jeder, der eines meiner Kunstwerke reproduziert, macht Kunst, die als Kunst genauso gültig ist, wie wenn ich es gemacht hätte.»[2]

Aber gleichzeitig bleibt der Vorrang von Inhalt vor Kontext unübersehbar – man rufe sich seine schillernde Bemerkung dazu in Erinnerung: «... wenn man die Photographie einer meiner Installationen sieht, genügt es, sich an die Bedeutung der Wörter zu erinnern. An die Architektur braucht man sich nicht zu erinnern.»

Kunst, die Kontext thematisiert, scheint Weiner anzudeuten, geht das Risiko ein, hinsichtlich ihrer Bedeutung weitgehend vom aktuellen und unmittelbaren Kontext des Kunstwerks abhängig zu sein. Ist dies der Fall, so tappt sie paradoxerweise gemeinsam mit der Malerei in die Falle des Illusionismus. Genauso wie die Malerei traditionell durch Illustration wirkt, so kann extrem kontextbestimmte Kunst zur Illustration verkommen, wenn, zum Beispiel, der herkömmliche Kontext in der Architektur verlorengeht, in der das Werk plaziert wird.

In den späten 60er Jahren lehnte Weiner die Malerei ab, mit der Begründung, sie wirke über die Illusion. Er beschreibt seine eigenen Werke als Skulptur, aufgrund seiner Überzeugung, dass Kunst zutiefst materialistisch sein solle, das heisst, dass sie von der Beziehung zwischen Objekten und Menschen handeln solle. Im Lichte dieser Marxschen Bedeutung des Begriffs «Materialismus» sollte man die häufig zitierte Bemerkung von Rudi Fuchs verstehen, Weiners Werk sei «... keine strenge Form, sondern eher ein gewandtes dialektisches Argument». Die dialektische Schönheit von Weiners Kunst ist ihre äusserste Bedeutungsfreiheit, verbunden mit der Tatsache, dass sie wirklich zutiefst von dem handelt, wovon sie zu handeln verspricht.

Wenn wir Lawrence Weiners öffentliche Auftragsarbeiten betrachten, sehen wir, dass die Bedeutung seiner Werke vom jeweiligen Umfeld beeinflusst wird, aber letztlich nicht davon abhängig ist. Die Gewichtung des Inhalts hat den Künstler jedoch nicht zu einem überholten Standpunkt geführt, wo die Bedeutung nicht berührt würde von der Werkumgebung. Insbesondere kann der Betrachter an der Herstellung von Bedeutung aktiv teilnehmen. Das heisst aber nicht, dass das Werk lediglich ein leeres Gefäss wäre, das darauf wartete, gefüllt zu werden. Das Spiel der Bedeutungen in Weiners Arbeiten hat eine solide materielle Grundlage – immerhin, das Medium seiner Arbeit ist die Sprache und sind die konkreten Gegenstände, auf die der Text verweist. Schliesslich ist seine Arbeit weder kontextbestimmt noch dekonstruktiv, sondern seine Grundmethode ist additiv. Kunstkritiker haben zu Recht auf die nicht-autoritäre Stimme in Weiners Werk hingewiesen, aber das geht noch nicht weit genug. Im dialektischen Spiel zwischen dem, was ist, und dem, was sein könnte, eröffnet Weiner einen in sich Freiheit erzeugenden Raum. *(Übersetzung: Susanne Schmidt)*

1) Alle Zitate aus David Batchelor, *I Am Not Content*, Interview mit Lawrence Weiner, *Artscribe*, März/April 1989.
2) Lawrence Weiner, October 12, 1969, in Ursula Meyer, Hrsg., *Conceptual Art* (New York: E.P. Dutton, 1972), S. 21.

Lawrence Weiner

Strassenbefragung zu

ZERSCHMETTERT IN STÜCKE (IM FRIEDEN DER NACHT)

Mann: «Relativ kontrastreiche Worte. Deutet auf Kraft hin. Kraftvolle Sprache. Frieden deutet auf Ruhe, Rast und Harmonie. Ich stelle mir Fragen: Geht die Zerschmetterung vom Flakturm aus? In der Nacht leuchtet er und glänzt er. Es schaut phosphorisierend aus. Es gefällt mir gut. Mehr Kunst auf den Flakturm! Man soll die Hoffnung nicht aufgeben, ein paar Leute werden sicher darüber nachdenken. Es kann etwas bewegen.»

Alte Frau: «Gute Idee. Muss heim.»

Künstlerin: «Niemand ist der Arbeit von Lawrence Weiner so nah' wie ich. Ich habe sie täglich von meinem Atelierfenster aus *face to face*. Manchmal beleuchte ich sie nächtens heimlich. Auch in der Morgendämmerung mag ich sie sehr.»

Zwei Jugendliche: «1991 waren wir noch nicht auf der Welt. Wir denken, wenn wir es lesen, an Tiere. Wir schlafen alle in Frieden in der Nacht, was bedeutet das? Ist das von Leonardo da Vinci?»

Junge Frau: «Der Hundertwasser malt seine Sachen, und hier ist halt das drauf.»

Frau: «Nichtssagend.»

Junger Mann: «Es ist wichtig, dass Kunst öffentlich zugänglich ist. Die Arbeit speziell ist mir aufgefallen, hat mich jedoch nicht so aufgewühlt wie andere Kunst im öffentlichen Raum; lieber hätte ich eine Diashow.»

Junge Frau: «Ich war verwundert, wie ich's zum ersten Mal gesehen habe. Es ist mir sofort aufgefallen. In Englisch gefällt es mir besser. Ich denke, dass es viel Arbeit war. Man geht so durch die Gegend, man ist oft abgelenkt, aber ich finde es wichtig, dass es stehenbleibt. Ganz genau verstehe ich allerdings nicht, was das heissen soll. Ich finde es aber toll, denn der Turm ist sowieso so hässlich.»

Frau: «Das ist mir schon oft aufgefallen, und ich wünsche mir, dass man's zerschmettern sollte, das scheussliche Ding. Man sollte eine Diskothek machen, weil das total lärmgeschützt wäre.»

Mann im mittleren Alter: «Ist mir aufgefallen; find' es nicht schlecht; weiss nicht, was oben steht.» Nachdem es ihm gesagt wird: «Klingt gut.»

Junge Frau: «Mir ist das wurscht.»

Chinesin: «Weiss ich nicht, was ist das, verstehe ich nicht. Das ist doch das ‹Haus des Meeres› (ein Aquarium). Ich weiss nicht, was das bedeuten soll, vielleicht wissen es ältere Menschen, die die Geschichte kennen. Ich denke an Frieden, Frieden in der Nacht. Die Zeiten werden immer schlimmer, und die Menschen sollen mehr an Frieden denken.»

Ältere Frau: «Also den Flakturm soll man zerschmettern im Frieden der Nacht?» Sie geht kopfschüttelnd.

Frau: «Habe an Krieg gedacht, an eine Bombe, die den Turm zerfetzt.»

Zwei Ausländerinnen: «Ist ein Bunker vom zweiten Weltkrieg, mehr weiss ich nicht. Fragen Sie einen Österreicher, fragen Sie die Frau da drüben.»

Junger Ausländer: «Das ist Kunst und schaut sehr schön aus, wenn man hinaufschaut. Von wem ist das? Sie können ihm ausrichten, dass es wunderbar ist.»

Mutter mit Kind: «Am Anfang habe ich mir gedacht: beachtlich, wie die das geschafft haben. Ich erinnere mich immer an die Nazizeit. Wenn's bunter wäre, würde es mehr auffallen. Schlecht wäre es, wenn der Turm nicht mehr da wäre. Man darf den Turm unter gar keinen Umständen für Werbezwecke verwenden. Kunst und Flakturm sind eine Kombination, die mir zu ernst ist. Gerade in unseren Zeiten des Erstarkens des Rechtsradikalismus ist es wichtig, dass der Turm da ist.»

Frau: «Eigentlich verstehe ich den Inhalt nicht. Was soll das bedeuten, ‹zerschmettert›? Ich kann mir nichts darunter vorstellen. Ich möchte so gerne, dass man das begrünt mit Kletterpflanzen. Ich seh' es immer, jeden Tag. Vielleicht kann man's begrünen.»

Mann: «Als Mahnobjekt ist es sinnvoll. Der Turm ist so hässlich, er hat eine abschreckende Funktion. Die Schrift ist gut, weil man vielleicht doch auf wichtige Gedanken kommt und sich die Menschen auf den Frieden besinnen sollen und nachdenken sollen.»

Mann: «Positiv, die Arbeit. Das ist das Beste, was man aus dem Flakturm machen kann.»

Ungar: «Stört mich überhaupt nicht, ist nicht schlecht.»

Junges Mädchen: «Kann nichts damit anfangen. Ist das ein Kunstwerk? Ich sehe das zum ersten Mal. Ich finde das gut. Eindrucksvoll. Hab mir's bisher nicht angeschaut. Seit drei Jahren ist das da? Ist mir noch nie aufgefallen. Das wurde in einem Krieg erbaut, zur Abwehr oder so. Ich würd's mit dem Krieg verbinden, aber das ist sicher nicht nur auf den Krieg bezogen. Ich muss jetzt darüber nachdenken.»

LAWRENCE WEINER, ZERSCHMETTERT IN STÜCKE (IM FRIEDEN DER NACHT), 1991 / SMASHED TO PIECES (IN THE STILL OF THE NIGHT), Flakturm / anti-aircraft defense tower, Esterházypark, Wien / Vienna. (PHOTO: CHRISTIAN WACHTER)

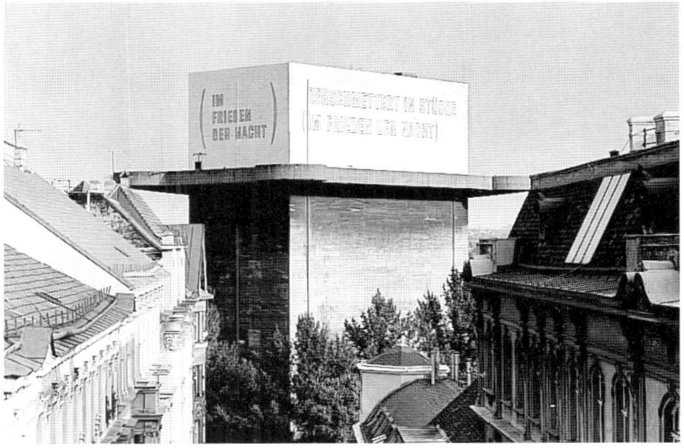

Junge Mutter: «Das war eine Veranstaltung, damals, als sie die Schrift gemacht haben. Vielleicht sollte noch mehr drauf sein, der Flakturm ist ja so hässlich. Ich finde die Arbeit aber ästhetisch.»

Junger Ausländer: «Es hat sicher einen Sinn, aber wer hat das geschrieben? Kannst du mir das erklären? Den Satz merke ich mir aber, vielleicht kann ich ihn einmal gebrauchen.»

Jugendliche, Schulkinder: «Wir haben das Klassenzimmer gegenüber. Das war schon vor der Wahl. Naja. Der gehört geändert, Reklame muss drauf. Cola-Werbung wäre toll.» Frage: «Habt ihr schon einmal darüber in der Schule geredet, mit den Lehrern?» «Nein, wir haben noch nie darüber geredet.»

Obdachloser Mann: «Keine Ahnung, keine Ahnung, ehrlich net.»

Ältere Frau: «Na freilich hab ich's schon gsehn. Das ham die Amerikaner gmacht. Mein Gott, was soll ma da scho gfalln? Das Sprücherl da oben ist wahrscheinlich im Bezug auf die Fliegerangriffe. Ich war ja selber da drinnen, wenn Fliegeralarm war, im Dunkel der Nacht passt guat. Kletterpflanzen sind nicht gegangen, jetzt ist er halt so geblieben, wie er ist.»

Junge Frau: «Ist mir schon lange aufgefallen. Gefällt mir gut. Ich kenne den Satz auswendig. Es geht um Frieden, Freundschaft. Der Mond scheint hell. Gemeinschaft. Schaut nicht aus wie eine Werbung, es passt zu diesem Haus. In diesem Haus ist nicht sehr viel Liebe.»

Die Umfrage entstand in Zusammenarbeit mit der Galerie Winter in Wien.

SMASHED TO PIECES (IN THE STILL OF THE NIGHT)

The Public Reacts*

Man: "Relatively contradictory words. Indicates strength. Forceful language. Peace indicates stillness, rest and harmony. I ask myself questions: Does the anti-aircraft tower do the smashing? At night it radiates and shines. It looks phosphorescent. I like it a lot. More art on the tower! You shouldn't give up hope; it will certainly make a few people think. It can start something."

Woman: "I've often noticed it and I wish they would smash it up, that horrible thing. They should put a disco in there because it would be completely noise proof."

Woman: "It brings back hard times; it's depressing."

Older woman: "So, they're supposed to smash the anti-aircraft tower in the peace of the night?" Walks away shaking her head.

Woman, artist: "No one is as close to Lawrence Weiner's work as I am. I see it *face to face* from my studio window everyday. Sometimes I secretly light it up at night. I like it very much at daybreak, too."

Two youths: "We weren't around in 1991. It makes us think of animals when we read that. We all sleep in the still of the night; what does that mean? Did Leonardo da Vinci make that?"

Man: "It's meaningful as a reminder. The tower is so ugly it acts as a deterrent. The lettering is good because it makes you aware of important things and people should remember peace and think about it."

Old woman: "Good idea. Have to go home."

Hungarian man: "Doesn't bother me at all, it's not bad."

Young woman: "It seemed strange when I saw it the first time. It struck me right away. I like it better in English. I thought of all the work it took to make it. You just walk not paying attention, but I think it's important for it to stay there. I can't say I really understand what it means. But I think it's great because the tower is so ugly anyway."

Woman: "Actually, I don't understand the content. What do they mean by 'smashed'? I don't know what the point is. I wish so much they would plant creepers. I see it all the time, everyday. Maybe they could add some greenery."

Young Man: "It is important for art to be accessible to the public. The work caught my eye but it didn't stir me up as much as other art in public spaces; I would prefer a slide show."

Homeless man: "No idea, no idea, honestly ..."

Girl: "Doesn't mean anything to me. Is that a work of art? I never saw it before. I think it's good. Impressive. Never noticed it before. It's been there for three years? The tower was built during a war, for defense or something. I would relate it to the war but that's certainly not the only connection. I have to think about it."

Mother with child: "At first I thought it was pretty good the way they managed that. It reminds me of Nazi times. It would be more noticeable if it were more colorful. But it would be a bad idea to take the tower down. It certainly shouldn't be used for advertising. Art and anti-aircraft tower is a combination that is too serious for me. It is important for the tower to be there, now especially, because of the resurgence of the extreme Right."

Woman from the SPCA: "Should be outlawed."

School children: "Our school is across the street. It was already there before the elections. Oh well. They should change it, put advertisements on it. Coke-ads would be great." Question: "Have you talked about it in school, with your teachers?" "No, never."

Woman: "Reminds me of war, of a bomb shattering the tower."

Older woman: "Sure I've noticed it. Some Americans did it. I should like that? That little saying up there? Probably to do with air raids. I was in there myself during air raid alarms; in the darkness of night—that fits. Creepers didn't work, so now they've just left it the way it was."

Man, drunk: "Tear it down, tear it down, that shit."

Young woman: "Who did that? Is the sentence by him, only the sentence? I need to think about it. How long has that been up there, that sentence? Maybe they could make it more colorful, the sentence, that would be nice."

Young foreigner: "It must mean something but who wrote it? Can you explain it to me? I'm going to remember that sentence, maybe I can use it someday."

Middle-aged man: "I've seen it; not bad; don't know what it says at the top." Reaction on being told: "Sounds good."

Young woman: "I couldn't care less."

Woman: "Meaningless."

Young foreigner: "That's art and looks beautiful when you look up at it. Who is it by? You can tell him it's wonderful."

Young woman: "It was a special event when they painted the letters. Maybe there should be more on it; the tower is so terribly ugly. But I think the work is aesthetic."

Two foreign women: "Is a bunker from the 2nd World War, that's all I know. Ask Austrians, ask that woman over there."

Young woman: "I live here but the piece doesn't say anything to me. The anti-aircraft tower is there; you have to live with it, but it's not a thing of beauty. Hundertwasser paints his things and here they've painted this. That's the way it goes"

Man: "Positive, the work. The best you can do with an anti-aircraft tower."

Chinese woman: "Don't know what it is, don't understand. That's the House of the Sea (ein Aquarium), isn't it? I don't know what it's supposed to mean. Maybe older people know, people who know history. I think of peace, peace at night. Times are getting worse and people should think more about peace."

Young man: "To be honest, it doesn't send me. I noticed it and I think the connection with art is good, but you could do it differently—for example, you could paint the tower."

Young woman: "I noticed it a long time ago. I really like it. I know the sentence by heart. It's about peace. Friendship. The moon shining bright. Community. Doesn't look like advertising. It suits the structure. There's not much love in that building."

* This inquiry was conducted in Vienna in collaboration with the Winter Gallery. Since the *Still of the Night* has been rendered in German as the *Peace of the Night* many people addressed this issue in their responses. *(Translation: Catherine Schelbert)*

LANE RELYEA

But Can She Bake a Cherry Pie?

UNTITLED, 1991, the last work Lawrence Weiner exhibited in Los Angeles, reads from left to right as follows:

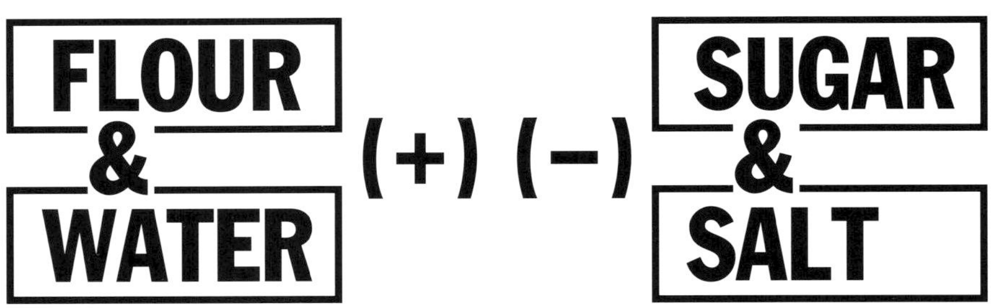

Forget about the esoterics of art appreciation; some schooling in the three R's is all that's needed here. Despite his radically untraditional approach, Weiner at base seems to hold modest aspirations for his art. He doesn't demand that it be admired, if that means our simply gawking at it passively; nor does he seem intent on crusading, on having us get with or behind his oratory. He just wants us to get it, period. And he takes great pains to help us along—isn't that why he literally spells it out, tells it straight, tries so hard to make it as plain as day? (Think of it: When was the last time one of his language murals included a word with more than three syllables?)

So call me dense, but I still don't get it.

FLOUR & WATER (+)(–) SUGAR & SALT

Though the meaning of each particular unit in the equation is clear, how they add up is anything but.

LANE RELYEA is a writer who lives in Los Angeles.

Typical for Weiner, his words and symbols seem carefully chosen for their referential and functional precision—they can only be taken at their word. Not that this insistence on descriptive rigor has remained absolute over the years: On occasion the artist has indulged double entendres—a 1982 work scolding neo-expressionism's self-aggrandizement opens with the pun— "I am not content" as well as metaphor—a wall piece from 1987 waxes poetic about

SOME OBJECTS TAKING THE PLACE IN THE SUN OF SOME OTHER OBJECTS

Also there's the confusion over which direction his statements indicate—do they summarize prior events or do they anticipate them, awaiting to be assigned relationships by the viewer? According to Weiner, both: In interviews he remarks impatiently that "Duchamp insists that his rebuses refer beyond the context of art, that they depict existing empirical facts," and at the same time that "presentation is part of the production" of his work.

Such an outline erases any difference between representation and presentation, as if Weiner's working process included no starting and end points, only points where the art begins again. Unanchored to a single interpretation, a specific "for instance," all his language reads as dislocated, whether it's his seemingly timeless, self-enclosed tautologies or his orphaned, fragmentary dependent clauses and prepositional phrases. Maybe that's why, regardless of the format of its display, Weiner's work always appears both intransigent and evanescent, resembling at once frescoes and xeroxes.

Floating outside time and place, at home nowhere, here free speech assumes the guise of a fugitive, a cryptogram.

FLOUR & WATER (+)(–) SUGAR & SALT

Many of the formula's integers—the sugar and salt, the corner of the room that splits the math between the parenthetical plus and minus—have appeared before, in

**SALT + SUGAR
IN A LUMP
IN A CORNER
OF THE EARTH**

from 1987. The newer version cuts the number of lexical nouns from five to four, yet manages to generate much more activity: The earth is dispersed into combinatory elements, minerals and nonminerals, natural beds and plants, three solubles and a base. The corner vaporizes as a word only to rematerialize as a physical inflection; the lump is mobilized from an object into a force. On the diagram's left there emerges a tasteless glue like the wheatpaste used to post broadsides; on the right, the additives used in cooking to draw out flavor. Facing each other they suggest a colorless flow, a pulse between adhesion and extraction. And this reorients the plus and minus signs at the equation's crux, no longer implying self-cancellation but rather combustion, like the opposing poles of an electrical current, a system that maintains energy by constantly reversing its direction.

On second thought, all this could be just Weiner's recipe for unleavened bread. He virtually says as much: In a corner of a preparatory drawing exhibited at the same time, there's written the question "But can she bake a cherry pie?" The line is lifted from an old American folk song, the lyrics of which are split into a dialog between a character named Billy and an anonymous interrogator who prods the boy about his ill-fated, tireless search for a wife. "She can bake a cherry pie," Billy responds to Weiner's question, "quick as you can blink an eye." Then, according to the song, Weiner asks another question, then another, and through this process he and his audience come up with answers that bring them no closer to the object of desire but do provide insight into, as Weiner puts it in his own, very unmusical words, "relationships of human beings to objects and objects to objects in relation to human beings." Here again is a recipe with four ingredients—the artist, the viewer, the artwork that betokens their shared desire for knowledge, and the world of experience such desire plunges them into.

LANE RELYEA

Aber kann sie einen Kirschkuchen backen?

UNTITLED, 1991, die letzte Arbeit, die Lawrence Weiner in Los Angeles zeigte, liest sich von links nach rechts folgendermassen:

FLOUR & WATER (+) (–) SUGAR & SALT

Vergessen Sie den ganzen esoterischen Kunstverstand; ein paar Grundkenntnisse in den drei Hauptfächern sind alles, was Sie brauchen. Trotz seines radikal untraditionellen Ansatzes scheint Weiner im Grunde einen sehr bescheidenen Anspruch mit seiner Kunst zu verbinden. Er erwartet keine Bewunderung, sofern diese sich in passiv ergebenem Glotzen äussert. Auch scheint er keinen Kreuzzug anzustreben, um uns in die Geheimnisse seiner Rhetorik einzuweihen. Sie soll einfach bei uns ankommen, basta. Und er nimmt eine Menge auf sich, um uns auf die Sprünge zu helfen; warum sonst buchstabiert er uns vor, ohne drumherum zu reden, warum sonst würde er alles daransetzen, um die Sache sonnenklar zu machen? (Überlegen Sie mal: Wann kam in einer seiner Wandschriften zum letzten Mal ein Wort mit mehr als drei Silben vor?)

Halten Sie mich für beschränkt, aber ich versteh's immer noch nicht.

MEHL & WASSER (+)(–) ZUCKER & SALZ

Wenn auch die Bedeutung jedes einzelnen Gliedes in der Gleichung klar ist – was sie zusammen ergeben, ist alles andere als klar. Es ist typisch für Weiner, dass er Wörter und Symbole nach ihrer referentiellen und funktionalen Präzision auswählt – man kann sie nur wörtlich nehmen. Nicht dass dieses Beharren auf streng deskriptivem Charakter über die Jahre keine Ausnahmen zugelassen hätte: Gelegentlich hat der Künstler sich auch Doppeldeutiges gegönnt – eine Arbeit von 1982, die die Selbstüberhöhung der Neo-Expressionisten geisselt, beginnt mit dem Wortspiel «I am not content» (ich bin nicht zufrieden / ich bin

LANE RELYEA ist Autor und lebt in Los Angeles.

nicht Inhalt)oder auch Metaphorisches – ein Wandstück von 1987 schwelgt poetisch:

EINIGE OBJEKTE, DIE DEN PLATZ AN DER SONNE EINIGER ANDERER OBJEKTE EINNEHMEN

Ausserdem herrscht Verwirrung darüber, wohin seine Statements weisen – fassen sie frühere Ereignisse zusammen, oder nehmen sie sie vorweg, indem sie davon ausgehen, dass der Betrachter die Bezüge herstellt? Nach Weiners Willen beides: In Interviews sagt er ungeduldig, «Duchamp besteht darauf, dass seine Bilderrätsel sich auf etwas jenseits vom Kunst-Kontext beziehen, dass sie bestehende empirische Fakten wiedergeben und dass zugleich ‹die Präsentation Teil der Produktion› seiner Arbeit ist.»

Eine solche Regel eliminiert den Unterschied zwischen Darstellung und Dargestelltem, so als gäbe es in Weiners Arbeits-Prozess keinerlei Anfang oder Ende, nur Punkte, an denen die Kunst wieder einsetzt. Nicht gesichert durch eine bestimmte Interpretation, ein spezielles «zum Beispiel», liest seine gesamte Sprache sich wie etwas aus dem Zusammenhang Gerissenes, seien es nun seine scheinbar zeitlosen, in sich selbst verkapselten Tautologien oder seine verwaisten, bruchstückhaften Nebensätze oder präpositionalen Redewendungen. Vielleicht erscheint Weiners Arbeit deshalb auch, unabhängig von der Form ihrer Präsentation, immer zugleich radikal und von flüchtiger Konsistenz, gleichzeitig an Freskos und an Photokopien erinnernd.

Freie Sprache – schwebend, ausserhalb von Zeit und Raum, nirgends zu Hause – zeigt sich hier als Ungreifbares, als Kryptogramm.

MEHL & WASSER (+)(–) ZUCKER & SALZ

Manche Bestandteile dieser Formel – Zucker und Salz, die Raumecke, die die Rechnung zwischen dem parenthetischen Plus und Minus aufspaltet – tauchten schon 1987 auf in

SALZ + ZUCKER
AM STÜCK
IN EINEM WINKEL
DER ERDE

Die jüngere Version reduziert die Zahl der Hauptwörter von fünf auf vier und schafft doch viel mehr Aktivität: Die Erde ist aufgelöst in Kombinations-Elemente, Mineralien und Nicht-Mineralien, natürliche Reagenzien und Pflanzen, drei lösliche Elemente und eine Base. Die Ecke verdampft als Wort, um als physikalische Abwandlung wieder Gestalt anzunehmen. Das Stück hat sich vom Gegenstand in eine Kraft gewandelt. Auf der linken Seite des Diagramms taucht der Gedanke an geschmacklosen Kleister auf, an jene Weizenpaste etwa, wie man sie zum Ankleben von Plakaten verwendet; die rechte Seite nennt die Zutaten, mit denen man Geschmack ans Essen bringt. Wenn sie sich gegenüberstehen, suggerieren sie einen farblosen Fluss, eine Pendelbewegung zwischen Anziehung und Abstossung. Und das verleiht den Plus- und Minus-Zeichen im Mittelpunkt der Gleichung neuen Sinn; statt sich selbst aufzuheben, geraten sie in Bewegung, wie die gegensätzlichen Pole eines Stromkreislaufs bilden sie ein System, das seine Energie daraus bezieht, dass es ständig die Richtung wechselt.

Auf den zweiten Blick könnte das alles aber auch Weiners Rezept für ungesäuertes Brot sein. Das sagt er im Prinzip selbst: Auf einer Entwurfzeichnung, die zur gleichen Zeit ausgestellt wurde, vermerkt Weiner in einer Ecke die Frage: «Kann sie einen Kirschkuchen backen?» Die Zeile stammt aus einem alten Volkslied, dessen Text aus einem Dialog besteht zwischen einem Typen namens Billy und einem anonymen Fragesteller, der den Jungen bei seiner ebenso erfolglosen wie unermüdlichen Suche nach einer Frau anspornt. «Sie kann einen Kirschkuchen backen», antwortet Billy auf Weiners Frage, «schneller, als du gucken kannst.» Wie in diesem Lied stellt Weiner dann eine andere Frage, und dann noch eine, und durch diesen Vorgang kommen er und sein Publikum auf Antworten, die sie dem Objekt der Begierde zwar nicht näherbringen, die aber dafür Einsicht gewähren in – wie Weiner es mit seinen eigenen unmusikalischen Worten ausdrückt – «Beziehungen zwischen Menschen und Gegenständen, sowie zwischen Gegenständen in bezug auf Menschen». Da haben wir also wieder ein Rezept mit vier Zutaten – Künstler, Betrachter, das Kunstwerk, das ihrer beider Wunsch nach Wissen zeigt, und die Welt der Erfahrung, in die solches Wünschen sie stürzt.

(Übersetzung: Nansen)

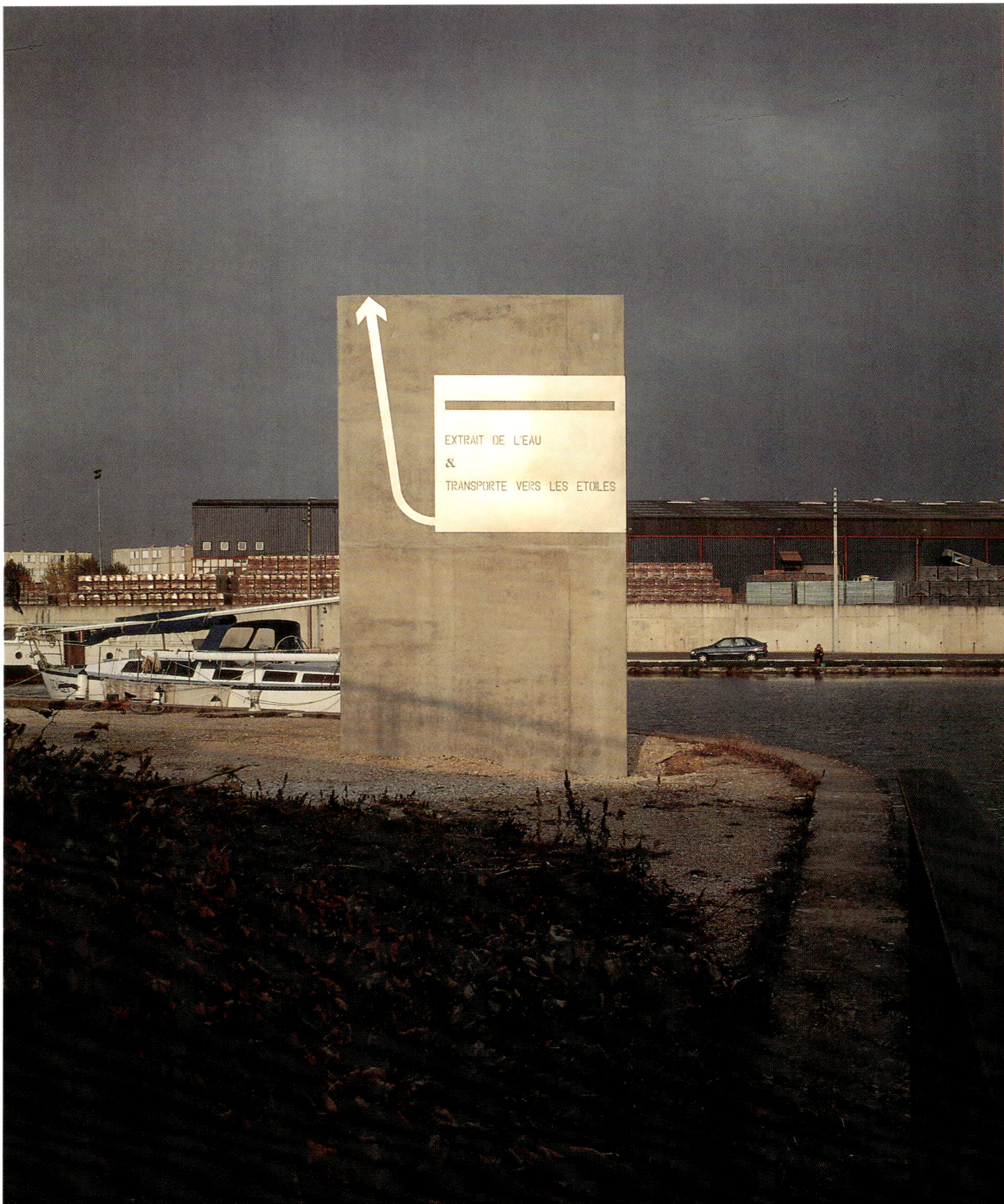

LAWRENCE WEINER, 1990, Port du Canal de Chagny, France.

EDWARD LEFFINGWELL

& VERS LES ÉTOILES

In *Querelle de Brest,* Jean Genet describes a cannon's barrel stripped from its carriage and turned upright in the middle of a prison courtyard, marking a site where inmates were once assigned to service on the sea.[1] For Genet, these impressed sailors become the personification of certain stars (the Great Bear, the Pole Star, the Southern Cross) as they move across the waters. He characterizes the sea as the sailor's girl, and the port his anchor, wherever the sailor, wherever the ship. To the criminal poet Genet, who loved these sailors, and to the murderer Querelle that Genet conceived, Lawrence Weiner erects a work in France above the waters where the Canal de Centre enters the Port of Chagny.

Chagny, in the Bourgogne, is an inland port near the principal watershed of France, just west of the Jura. Part of an extensive system of ports, canals, rivers, and aqueducts, Chagny services a great trade route that links the heartland of vineyards, fields, orchards and industries, to the English Channel and the ports of France, Belgium, and Holland, to the north, and by deep locks to the Saône, south to Lyon, to the Rhône, and to the Mediterranean ports of the south. The Canal, begun on the eve of the Revolution, cuts away from the Dheune at Chagny, ten miles south of Beaune. Here, Weiner's work is "hung, mounted, laced on a concrete slab," five meters high by three meters by one, facing the harbor.[2] The slab is "sheathed/embraced by the work cut out of stainless steel." The work is:

EXTRAIT DE L'EAU
& TRANSPORTÉ VERS LES ÉTOILES

(TAKEN FROM THE WATER
& CARRIED TO THE STARS)

MIS SUR L'EAU
EN DESSOUS DES ÉTOILES

(PLACED UPON THE WATER
UNDERNEATH THE STARS)

Since the work for Chagny is dedicated to *Querelle de "Genet"/Brest* (Querelle's northern port of call, Brest, built on rock, site of the crimes that ennoble Genet's sailor), Weiner has determined to commemorate the event of its completion with the fabrication of pom-pomed caps like those worn by French sailors, and hara-kiri knives inscribed, like the work itself,

& VERS LES ÉTOILES

Querelle sports his cap at a singular angle, part of the reassuring armor of his uniform, and "decks" a sailor who dares to ape his fashion. A girl touches Querelle's pom-pom for good luck, and Querelle

EDWARD LEFFINGWELL is a Los Angeles-based curator and writer.

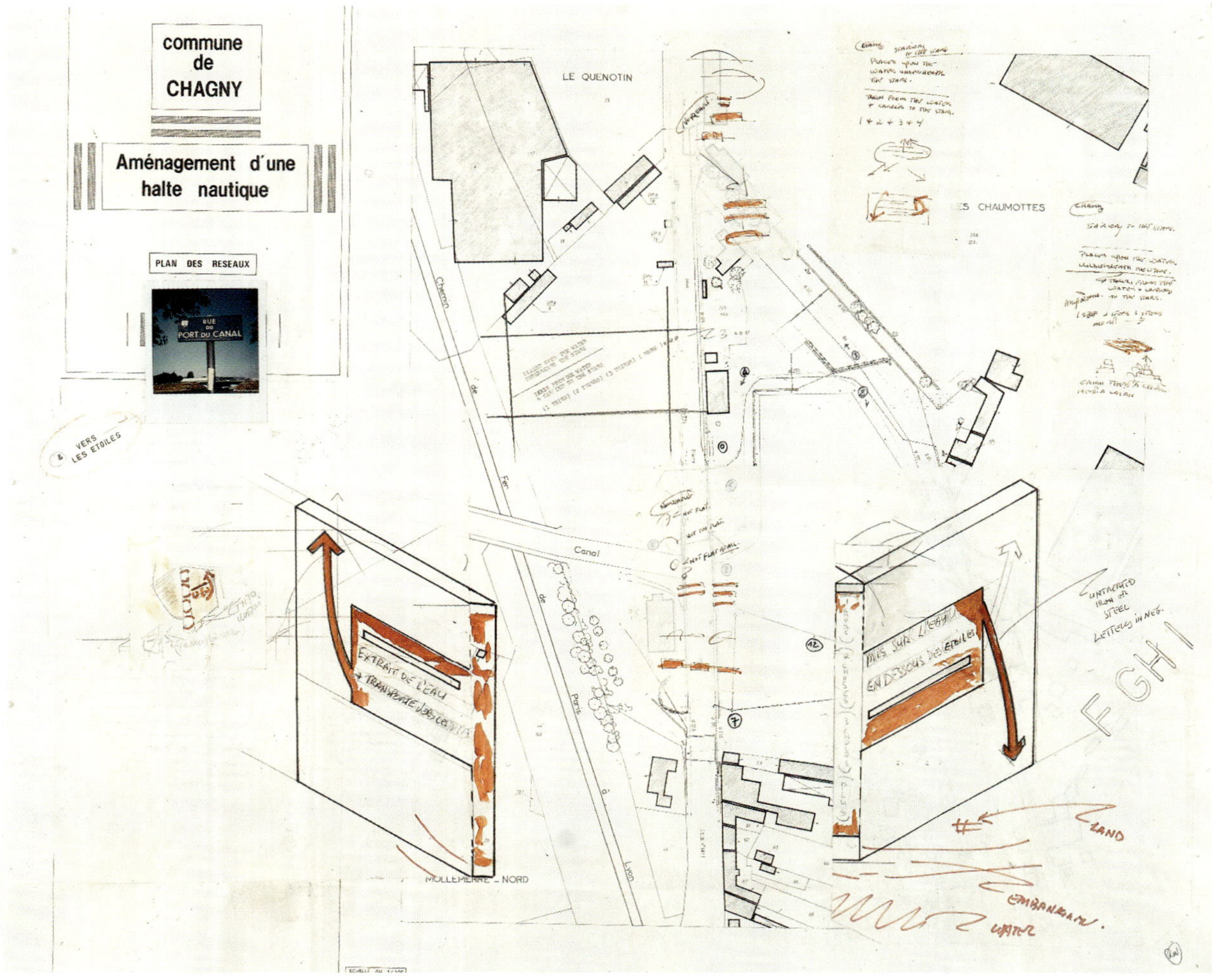

LAWRENCE WEINER, 1990, drawing for / Entwurf für Port du Canal de Chagny, France.

slaps her in return. A violent man, his knife appears in moments of anger, an instrument in the dance of dominance and subjugation. After murdering a mate, Querelle "... put the knife back in his pocket. His beret he was holding in front of him, with both hands, at the level of his belt, the pom-pom against his belly. The smile was gone." Weiner chooses these things, the cap, the knife, because they are wholly emblematic of Querelle who is, as Genet remarks, "a happy moral suicide." Weiner writes by way of comment, "Either you treat the world as a sailor or they force you into hara-kiri." The condition of the artist, among others, in the conduct of life. Do it or be done.

Weiner's work is something to reckon by, at a junction of the water and the sky. When a young man, he went to sea as a merchant marine, and in subsequent years has lived aboard a ship, working, making films, and other things, in the port of Amsterdam.

1) Jean Genet, *Querelle,* New York, 1974. Translated from the French by Anselm Holo. Originally published in French as *Querelle de Brest,* Paris, 1953.
2) The work is a co-production of Pietro Sparta and the City of Chagny.

EDWARD LEFFINGWELL

& VERS LES ÉTOILES

In *Querelle de Brest* beschreibt Jean Genet ein von seiner Lafette abmontiertes und in der Mitte eines Gefängnishofes aufrecht gestelltes Kanonenrohr, das die Stelle markierte, an der Gefangene einst dem Dienst auf See zugeteilt worden waren.[1] Für Genet werden diese unter Zwang angeworbenen Seeleute in ihrer Fahrt quer über die Meere zur Personifikation bestimmter Sterne (der Grosse Bär, der Polarstern, das Kreuz des Südens). Die See selbst beschreibt er als das Mädchen des Matrosen und den Hafen, wo auch immer der Seemann, wo auch immer das Schiff, als seinen Ankerplatz. Dem kriminellen Poeten Genet, der diese Seeleute liebte, und dem von Genet ersonnenen Mörder Querelle setzt Lawrence Weiner ein Denkmal; in Frankreich, über dem Wasser, dort, wo der Canal du Centre die Hafenstadt Chagny erreicht.

Das in der Bourgogne gelegene Chagny ist ein Binnenhafen nahe der Hauptwasserscheide Frankreichs, unmittelbar westlich des Jura. Als Teil eines ausgedehnten Systems von Häfen, Kanälen, Flüssen und Aquädukten unterhält Chagny eine grosse Handelsroute, die das Herzland der Weinberge, Äcker, Obstgärten und Industriebetriebe nach Norden mit dem Ärmelkanal und mit den Häfen Frankreichs, Belgiens und Hollands sowie nach Süden durch die über tiefe Schleusenkammern führende Anbindung an die Saône mit Lyon, der Rhône und den Mittelmeerhäfen im Süden verbindet. Der Canal du Centre, mit dessen Bau am Vorabend der Revolution begonnen wurde, zweigt in Chagny, etwa 15 km südlich von Beaune, von der Dheune ab.

Hier ist Weiners Arbeit «aufgehängt, montiert, angebracht auf einer Betonplatte», fünf Meter hoch, drei Meter breit und einen Meter dick, die dem Hafen zugewandt ist.[2] Die Platte ist «beschlagen/überzogen mit dem aus rostfreiem Stahl herausgeschnittenen Werk». Dies ist das Werk:

EXTRAIT DE L'EAU
& TRANSPORTÉ VERS LES ÉTOILES

(DEM WASSER ENTNOMMEN
& ZU DEN STERNEN GETRAGEN

MIS SUR L'EAU
EN DESSOUS DES ÉTOILES

(ANGEBRACHT ÜBER DEM WASSER
UNTER DEN STERNEN)

EDWARD LEFFINGWELL ist Ausstellungsorganisator und Schriftsteller und lebt überwiegend in Los Angeles.

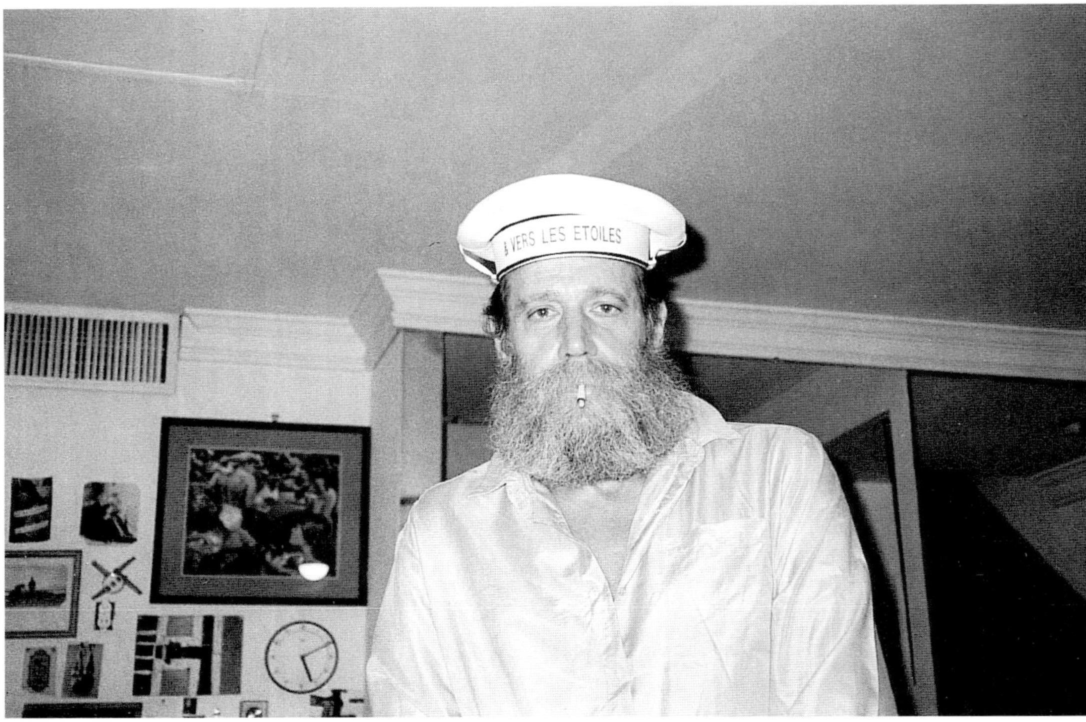

LAWRENCE WEINER. (PHOTO: FLAVIA VOGEL)

Da das Werk für Chagny *Querelle de «Genet»/Brest* gewidmet ist (Querelles nördlicher Anlaufhafen, Brest, auf Felsen errichtet, Schauplatz der Verbrechen, die Genets Matrosen adeln), hat Weiner anlässlich seiner Fertigstellung blaue Kappen mit Pompons, wie sie von französischen Matrosen getragen wurden, sowie Harakiri-Messer anfertigen lassen und jede Edition wie das Werk selbst beschriftet mit den Worten

& VERS LES ÉTOILES

Querelle trägt seine Kappe verwegen gekippt – Teil des beruhigenden Panzers seiner Uniform – und «vertrimmt» einen Matrosen, der es wagt, seinen Stil nachzuahmen. Ein Mädchen berührt den Pompon der Kappe als Glücksbringer, woraufhin er sie ohrfeigt. Er ist ein gewalttätiger Mensch, dessen Messer in Augenblicken der Gewalt zum Vorschein kommt, ein Instrument im Spiel von Macht und Unterjochung. Nachdem er einen Kumpel ermordet hat, steckt Querelle «das Messer wieder in seine Tasche. Seine Kappe hielt er mit beiden Händen in Gürtelhöhe, den Pompon gegen den Bauch gedrückt. Das Lächeln war verschwunden.» Weiner wählt diese Dinge – die Kappe, das Messer – aus, weil sie Embleme schlechthin für Querelle sind, der, wie Genet sagt, «ein glücklicher moralischer Selbstmörder» ist. Weiner schreibt, gewissermassen als Kommentar: «Entweder man betrachtet die Welt wie ein Matrose, oder sie zwingen dich zum Harakiri.» Die Lage, in die das Leben auch den Künstler bringt. Erledige es selbst, oder du wirst erledigt.

Weiners Arbeit ist ein Orientierungspunkt an einer Schnittstelle von Wasser und Himmel. Als junger Mann ging er in der Handelsmarine zur See, und später hat er jahrelang auf einem Boot im Hafen von Amsterdam gelebt, gearbeitet und Filme sowie andere Dinge gemacht.

(Übersetzung: Magda Moses, Bram Opstelten)

1) Jean Genet, *Querelle*, aus dem Französischen von Ruth Uecker-Lutz, Reinbek 1974. Die Originalausgabe mit dem Titel *Querelle de Brest* erschien 1953 in Paris bei Editions Gallimard.
2) Die Arbeit ist eine Koproduktion von Pietro Sparta und der Stadt Chagny.

LAWRENCE WEINER, WIR SIND SCHIFFE AUF DEM MEER KEINE ENTEN AUF DEM TEICH / WE ARE SHIPS AT SEA NOT DUCKS ON A POND, Hamburg, 1989. (PHOTO: WOLFGANG NEEB)

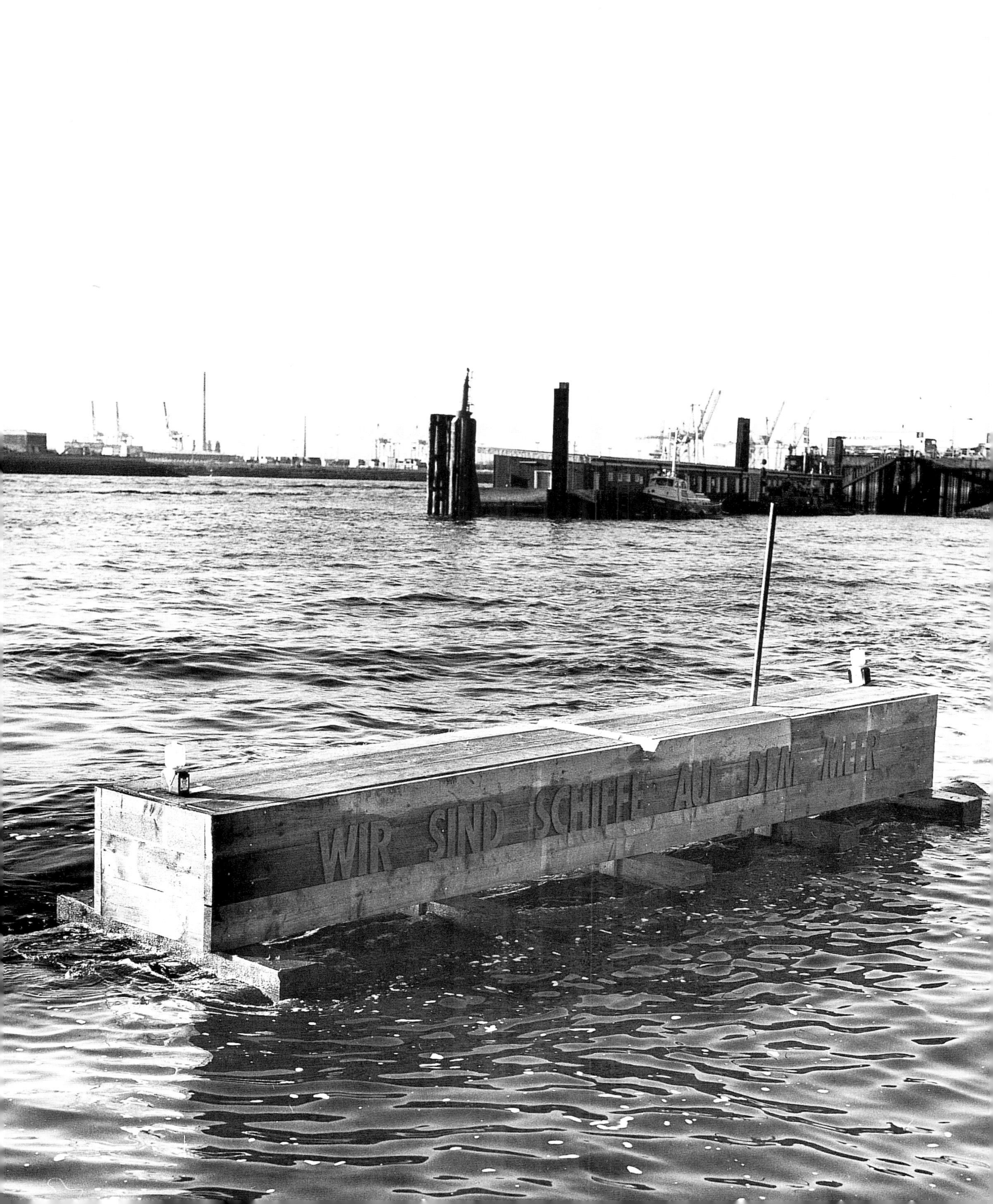
WIR SIND SCHIFFE AUF DEM MEER

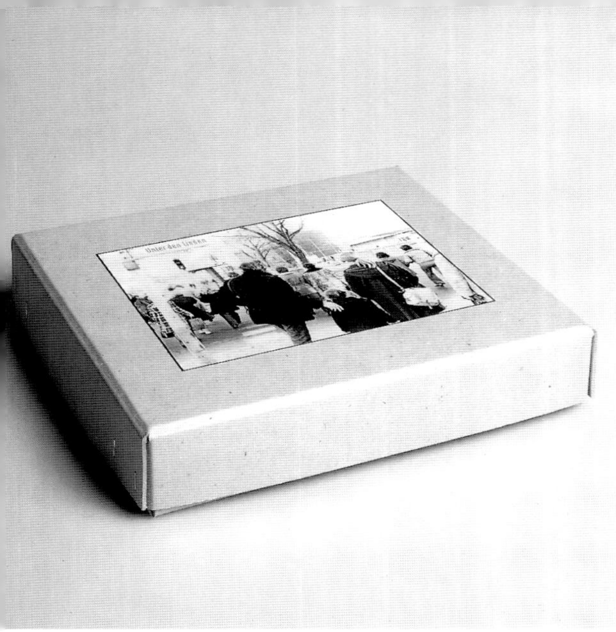

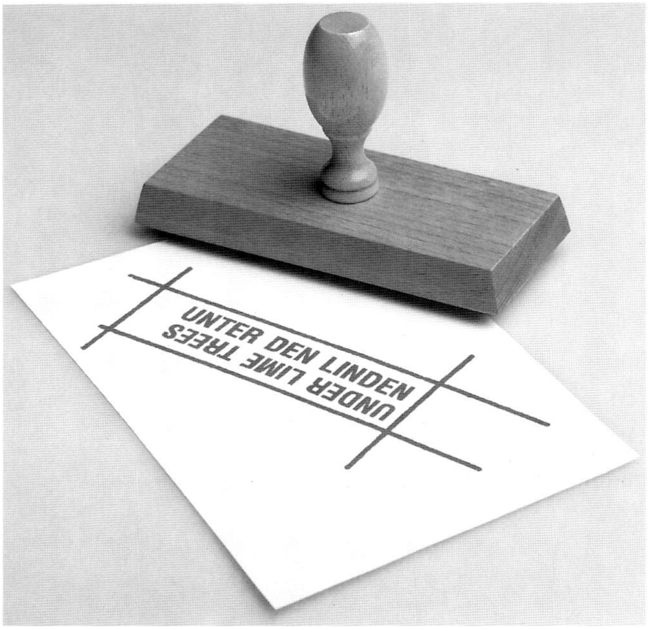

EDITION FOR PARKETT

LAWRENCE WEINER

UNTER DEN LINDEN – UNDER LIME TREES, 1994

Stamp approx. 7½ x 3¾ x 3½" with red ink pad

in silkscreened cardboard box.

Edition of 80, signed and numbered

UNTER DEN LINDEN – UNDER LIME TREES, 1994

Stempel ca. 19 x 9,5 x 9 cm mit

rotem Stempelkissen in Kartonschachtel,

Feinrastersiebdruck.

Auflage: 80, signiert und numeriert

PHOTO: MANCIA/BODMER

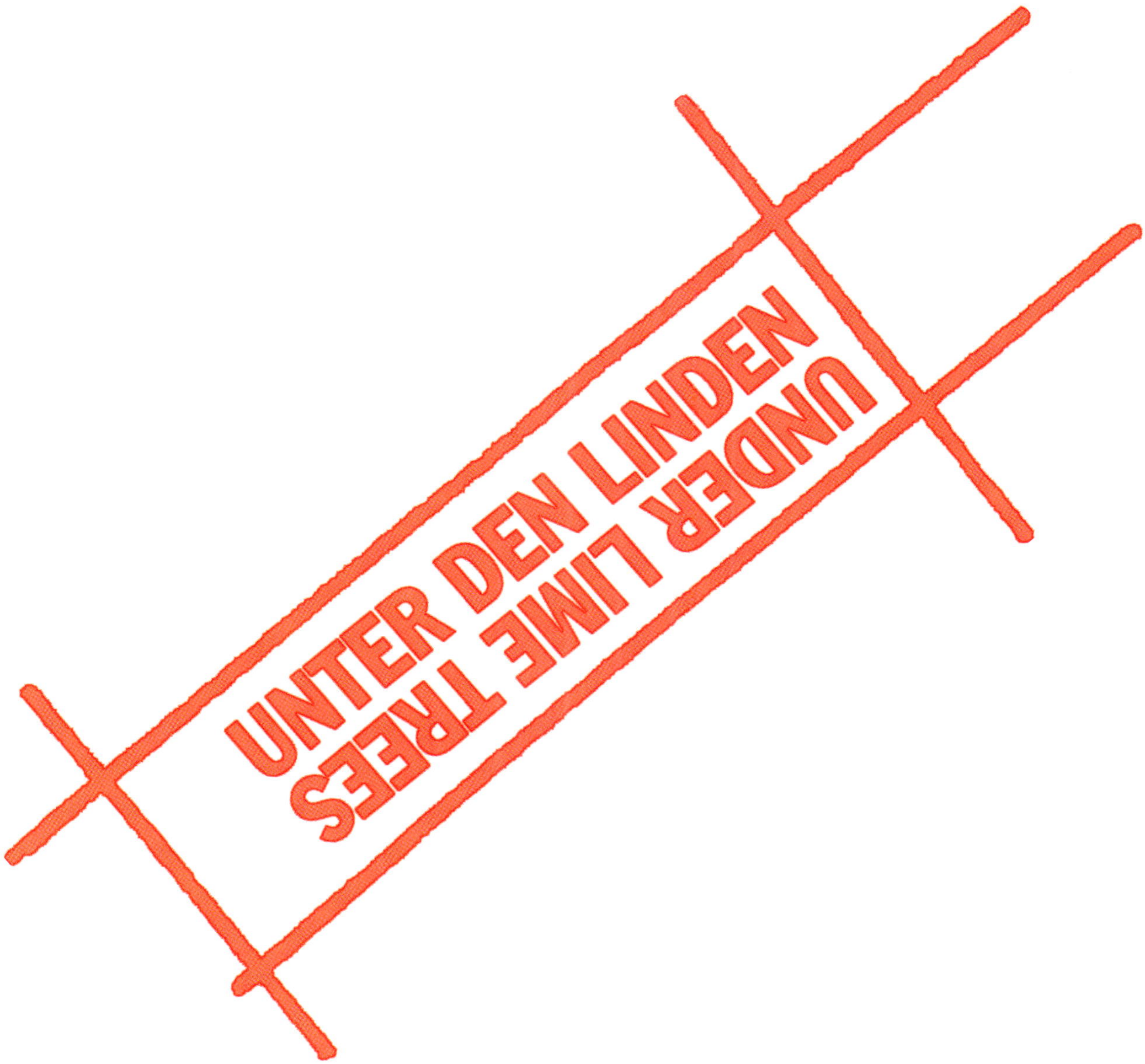
UNTER DEN LINDEN
UNDER LIME TREES

NEVILLE WAKEFIELD

Rachel Whiteread:

Separation Anxiety and the Art of Release

Within the abstract and speculative zone that might be termed the ontology of sculpture, the cast object occupies a curious position. Generally it exists only as a reproduction of a reality to which it is related metonymically. This is the object whose lineage can be traced through a series of negative and positive incarnations—feints and reversals which result in solid form and mimetic likeness. Alongside this process is another type of casting more often associated with mould-making which arrests the dialectic, refusing synthesis and the final resolution of the object, presenting instead a negative impression related to the original at just one remove. The process is simple: Liquid material is poured into a cavity or void surrounding the object being cast; the contours, boundaries, and geographies of the object are exactly modelled, its surface topography becoming one with that of the casting material, its reality being inscribed upon this shared surface. United along this fine border, the cast and the object from which the cast is taken form a physical continuum, an apparently indivisible entity without edge or surface. As with the well-known Borgesian allegory in which the cartographers of the Empire draw up a map so detailed as to be co-extensive with the territory that it seeks to describe, the material indivisibility of the object and the cast, the contiguity of reality and its inscription, is a rock upon which the whole representational metaphysics of presence and absence founders. Only when the two entities are separated, when the primal division into positive and negative forms is effected, is the impossible space broken.

Negotiating this border from which are sprung the dialectics not only of sculptural presence but also, in the grander metaphorical sense, the whole humanist edifice of spatial awareness, is an agent of release or separation. Sculpturally invisible, and to all intents and purposes two-dimensional, sophisticated silicon releases can be measured in microns; topographically, the space that it describes is neither positive or negative since it is both. Simultaneously interior and exterior, mould and moulded, container

NEVILLE WAKEFIELD is a writer who lives in New York.

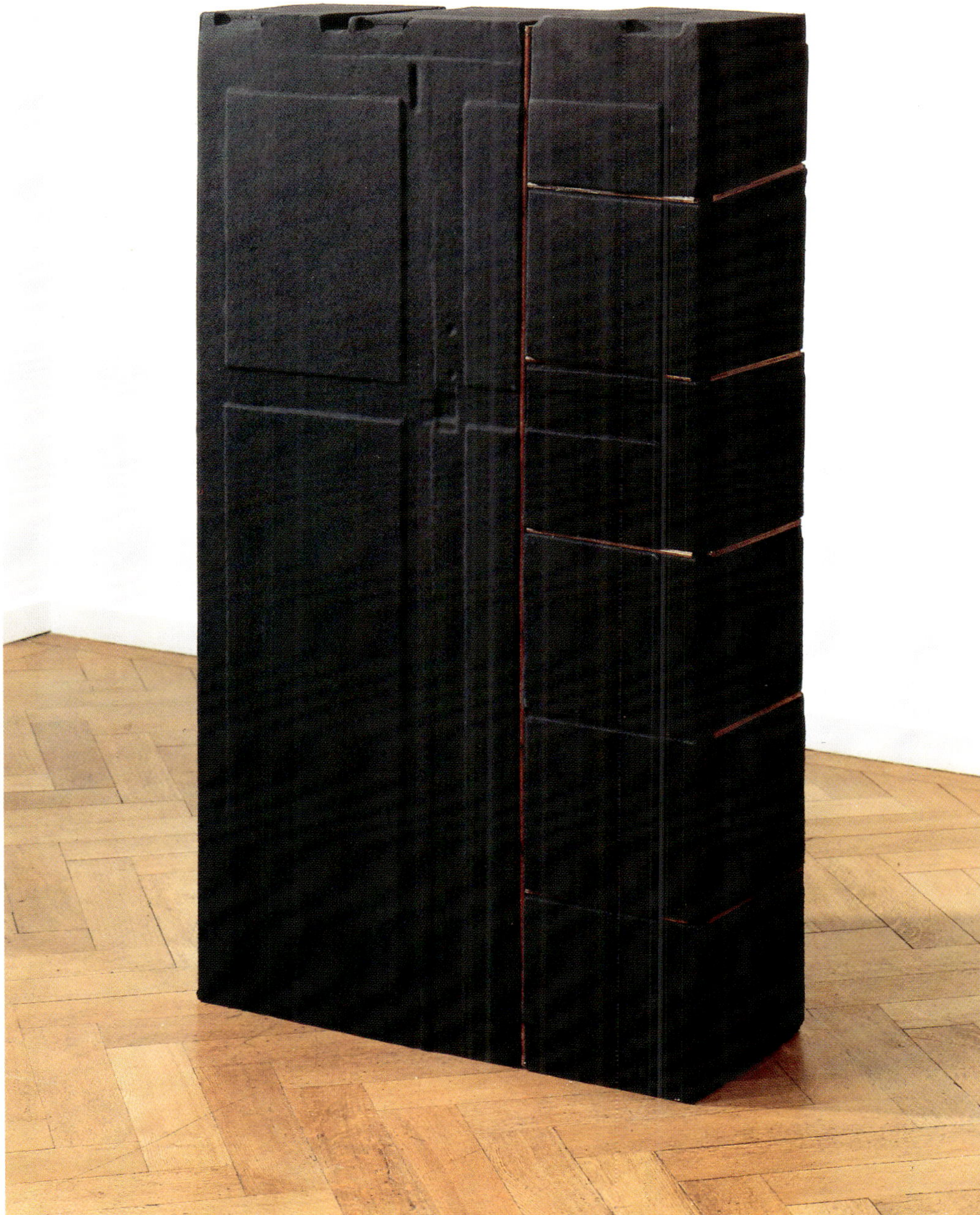

RACHEL WHITEREAD, CLOSET, 1988, wood, felt and plaster, 63 x 34⅝ x 14½" /
SCHRANK, Holz, Filz und Gips, 160 x 88 x 37 cm.

RACHEL WHITEREAD, YELLOW LEAF, 1989, plaster, Formica and wood, 59 x 29 x 37" / GELBES BLATT, Gips, Resopal und Holz, 150 x 74 x 94 cm. (PHOTO: SUSAN ORMEROD)

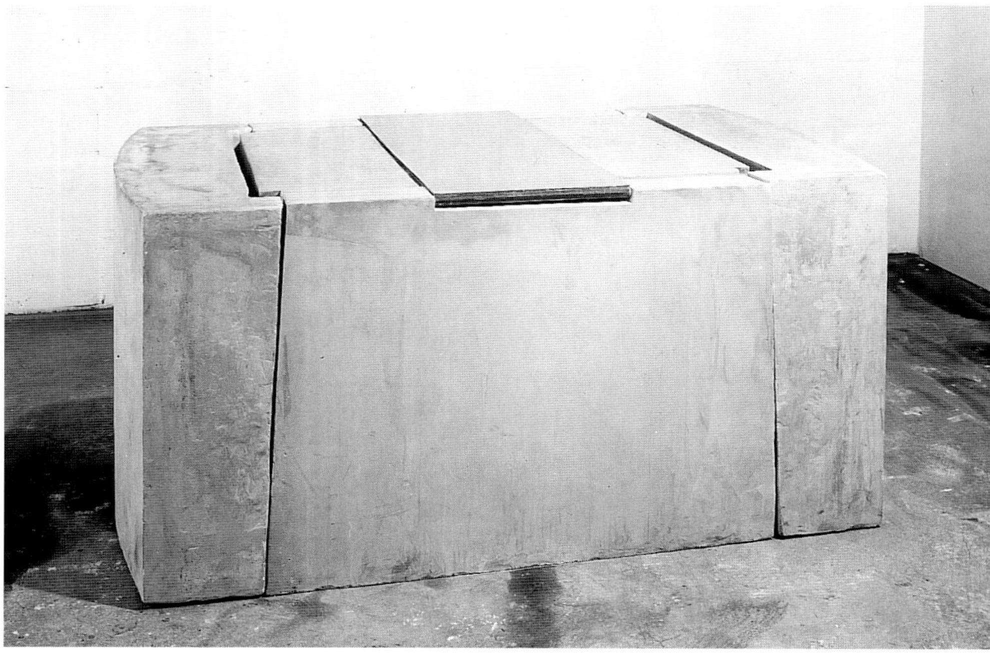

and contained, it is like the continuous one-sided surface of a Möbius strip. Forcing doubt upon the certainty of inside and the distinctness of outside, the metaphorical space of release threatens to upset not just the old Euclidean homelands of relational geometry but also the sense in which it has penetrated our own bodies. As Elaine Scarry puts it, "The interchange of inside and outside surfaces requires not the literal reversal of bodily linings but the making of what is originally interior and private into something exterior and shareable, and, conversely, the reabsorption of what is now exterior and shareable into the intimate recesses of individual consciousness."[1)] Sculpturally, all casting procedures follow the interchange attributed by Scarry to the body. Extroverted from an impossible space, the cast form enters the world as a set of boundary conditions—boundaries which, whether renegotiated within the body or in the space around it, trace their origins to the simultaneity of contact and detachment implicit in release.

Rachel Whiteread's casts of domestic and architectural voids, impressions of relief surfaces and solid objects, embody these tensions while activating the synaptic space between the object and the world. Dispensing with the intermediary processes that characterize "lost form" casting, Whiteread reasserts the cast's one-to-one relation with the original by presenting the negative form as the object itself. The materials are also suggestive of this inversion. Wax, the medium of loss in "lost form" normally displaced by substances of greater permanence and worth, is here presented as a material in its own right. Plaster, concrete, rubber, and polyester resins—materials more often associated with the production of the mould than of the cast—are used to describe directly the absented object from which they have been formed. By arresting a process that normally proceeds through subsequent generations, Whiteread trades the literal presence of reproduction for a conceptual and spatially ambiguous presence of deduction. Withholding the transformation offered by the mould—of negative space into positive form—we are invited to construct presence out of absence, solidity out of the void. Bewitched by the spell of the missing dimension, we conceptually recast the object in the non-space of the imagination. ("To make inside concrete and outside vast is the first problem, it would seem," claims Bachelard, "of an anthology of the imagination.")[2] For the space that we are presented with is an impossible space, viewed from a position we could never assume: the space between the object and the cast, the space of release.

Belying the spatial and ultimately psychological complexity of the sculptures is the apparently quotidian subject and simplicity of form. CLOSET (1988) adopts the appearance of monolithic minimalism. Obdurate and vaguely menacing, it describes the interior space of a wardrobe, as solid void from which the exterior has been stripped. Divided into four relief panels corresponding to the construction of the door, the face of the CLOSET is broken asymmetrically by a vertical partition from which are sprung five shelves, still visibly embedded within the cast. Descriptively, the piece seems to solicit discussion within the formal vocabulary of Minimalism. CLOSET like one of Judd's plexi and steel boxes from the mid-sixties plays off suggestions of volume (the horizontal shelves) against those of shape (the relief mouldings), whilst maintaining the whole as a unitary gestalt. Later work, which has tended to dispense with or circumvent the formal issues raised by the incorporation of the object in the casting—a feature not just of CLOSET (1988) but also of YELLOW LEAF, FORT, LEDGER, and FLAP (all 1989), as well as being a necessary condition in the casting of HOUSE (1993–1994)—has nonetheless maintained the appearance of Minimalism whilst inverting its main tenet. Substituting the phenomenology of absence for that of presence, Whiteread's resonant voids activate not just the (minimalist) space of object-relations but also that of memory.

The figural allusions relayed by the minimal work into the presence of the beholder are here reverted to the beheld: the mnemonic body inscribed within domestic architecture. "I use furniture as a metaphor for human beings,"[3] says Whiteread. But as well as metaphor it is extension. Etymologically derived from *furnir,* meaning to further or to forward, furniture is a prosthesis of the body that determines in its absence not just posture and deportment but interior structure—its very osteomorphology. As if in recognition of this, Whiteread's casts of sinks, baths, and mattresses make poetic play of the introversions and extroversions of the body they propose. They are bodies which are both hard and soft, plaster as well as rubber. Eviscerating the dwelling, Whiteread exposes the soft interior and non-spaces normally sheltered behind the conceptual and architectural rigidity of the frame. Soft emotional spaces heavily impregnated with memory, bodily fluids, and fluid desires are found slumped against hard walls. Architectures of inside and outside are confused and exchanged. "My body is everywhere," says Sartre, "the bomb which destroys my house also destroys my body insofar as my house was already an indication of my body."[4]

Three plaster casts taken from the underside of cast-iron Victorian bathtubs (ETHER, VALLEY, and UNTITLED, all 1990) suggest the body in repose or death. The interior enamel linings that once contained the amniotic envelope of bath water have here become etiolated and porous. Drainholes penetrate the lower volume of the sculptures. Both are positioned at a height precluding normal usage. Access to the interior of UNTITLED is denied by the presence of a sheet of glass punctured at two points corresponding to the hot- and cold-water taps. Monumentalising the absented body in its rituals of ablution and death, these negative spaces have been variously described as sarcophagi and graves. But the evocation of death goes beyond simple allusion to the cadaver—allusions played out to the full in SLAB (PLUG) (1994)—suggesting perhaps the more disturbing proximity of life and death held in the mortal and precarious equilibrium of the flesh. Connected to the world around it by drains and apertures, VALLEY posits the absented body as extending into a domestic arterial and venous system similar to, and indeed connected to, its own. The architectural shell that encases and protects life contains within it the premonition of death; the body's exhalations of dead skin, spent mucous, fecal matter, hair, and toenails are ever-present, trapped in the U-bend under the bath or circulating around us in waste pipes and plumbing secreted in wall cavities and running along floor joists. (It comes as no surprise that Whiteread associates UNTITLED (FLOOR) (1992), as much with the masturbatory space of Vito Acconci's SEEDBED as with the formalism of, for instance, Carl Andre.) Significantly, in J. G. Ballard's novel *High-Rise*, the pulse of the monolithic building—the central metaphor for the social body and its divisions—is taken through its internal canals, the secret spaces of its circulatory system. Gossip, the atmosphere of hostility and collision, passes like Legionnaires' Disease through the elevator shafts and air-conditioning systems. Like the body, the building's ability to distance itself from, and expel, its own waste becomes the index of its well-being.

Like Ballard's vision, Whiteread's archeology of the present suggests the psychic landscapes formalised in space and time. The leitmotifs of psychological enclosure—the high-rise, motorway embankment, and automobile—are rediscovered in the most quotidian signifiers of life in not-so-great Britain. GHOST, a cast taken from the interior of a small room in Highgate, London, magnifies in its reversals the conditions that pose comfort and confinement as interdependents within the contracting spatial economy of the city. Doors and windows, "crude versions of the senses" in the room described by Scarry as simultaneously a "magnification of the body" and a

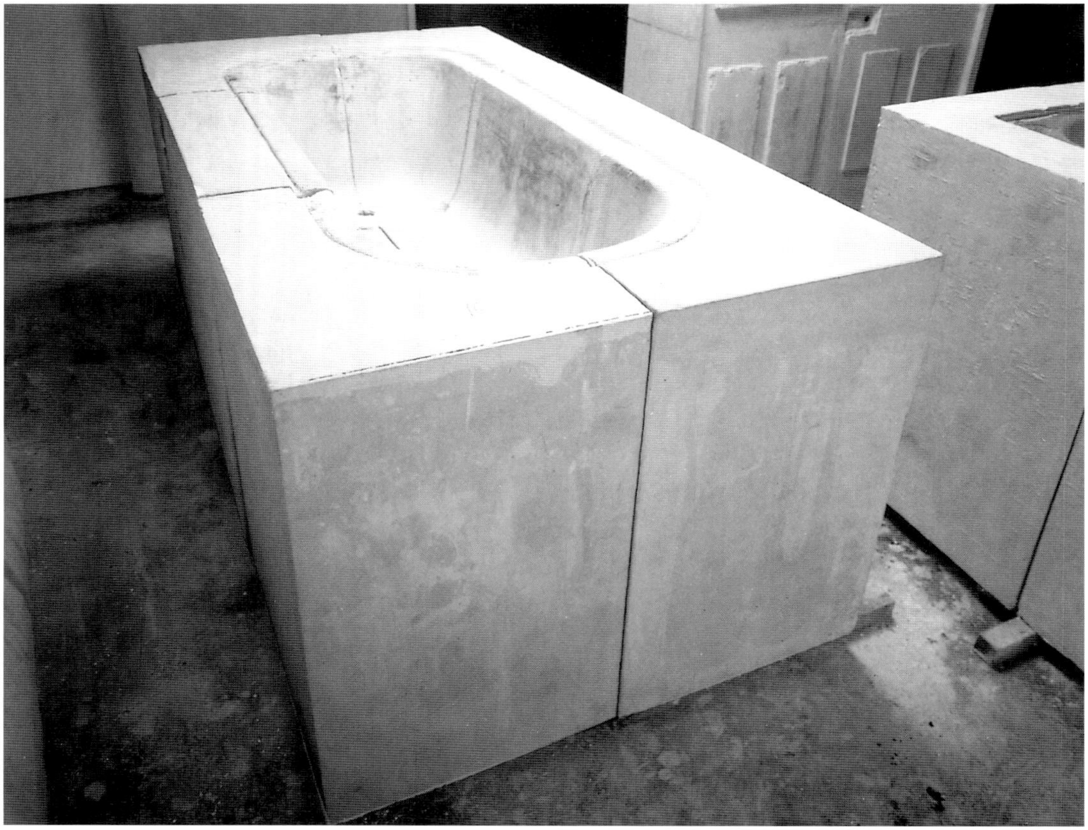

"miniaturization of the world,"[5] are here nothing more than blank inscrutable projections in a plaster cast. The invitation to entry has become a rebuttal, the house itself an oneiric space all but closed to the outside world. More like a bunker than a dwelling, it has become the vault or repository for images of protected intimacy. A monument to all that has been dismantled and lost in the rush to disown the welfare state's responsibility to ordinary lives, GHOST—like HOUSE, which stood alone in a street in Bow as if a solitary tooth waiting to be pulled from a gum scarred by the marks of all previous extractions—suggested the dereliction of memory and the passing of the everyday into a more hostile world. Both structures seem to mark the passage of interior life, its flight from the bareness of the present into the nooks, crannies, and secret places of the past—harbours for repressed dreams of sex and death.

Underwriting the collective psyche of the nineteenth century as much as they do that of today, these are dreams unearthed as if by archaeology. "What had formerly been the city of Pompeii assumed an entirely changed appearance, but not a living one; it now appeared rather to become completely petrified in dead immobility. Yet out of it stirred a feeling that death was beginning to talk."[6] For Freud, in his 1919 essay, "The Uncanny," Jensen's celebrated account of the discovery of the past locked permanently into the present provided both spatial and archaeological analogies for the procedures of psychoanalysis itself. The entombed city represented the suspension of history and the revelation

RACHEL WHITEREAD, ETHER, 1990, plaster, 43 x 34½ x 80" / ÄTHER, Gips, 109 x 88 x 203 cm. (PHOTO: EDWARD WOODMAN)

RACHEL WHITEREAD, UNTITLED (TORSO), 1992, dental plaster, 3 x 9 x 6½" / OHNE TITEL (TORSO), zahntechnischer Gips, 8 x 23 x 16,5 cm. (PHOTO: SUSAN ORMEROD)

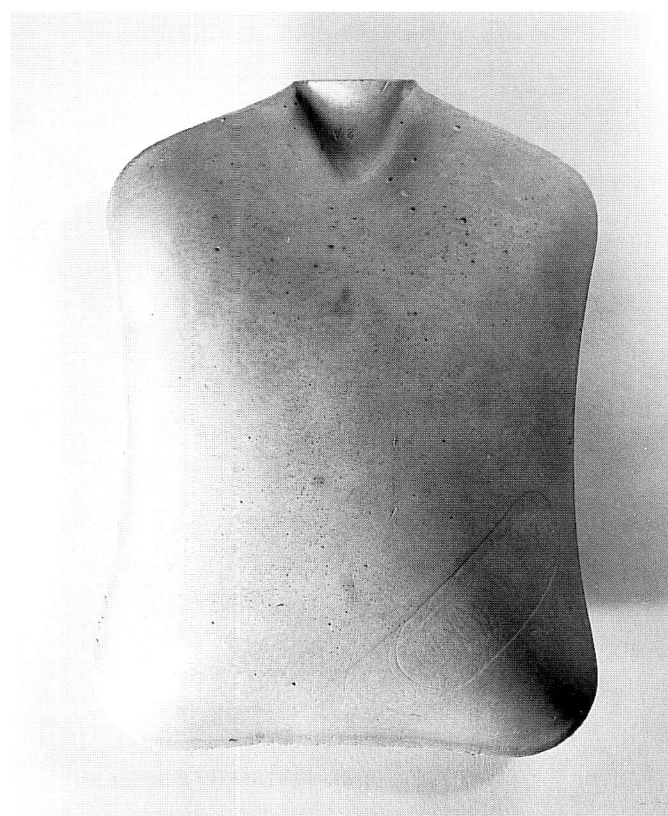

of the invisible; significantly for Chateaubriand and subsequent commentators, it was the trace of a woman's breast visible as a negative impression left in the ash, a macabre *nature morte* that provided the erotic subtext to a meditation on the suspension of life in the ruins of the present. The eroticism of these archaeological "impressions" has been replayed in the late twentieth century as a confrontation not between man and nature but between man and technology. Chateaubriand's fascination with the sculpted death of Pompeii perfectly parallels that of the protagonist in J. G. Ballard's seminal novel *Crash*. Here the erotic of indentation is mapped not onto volcanic ash but directly onto the flesh, a sinister portent of the marriage of sex and technology: "For Vaughan, each crashed car set off a tremor of excitement, in the complex geometries of a dented fender, in the unexpected variations of crushed radiator grilles, in the grotesque overhang of an instrument panel forced onto a driver's crotch as if in some calibrated act of machine fellatio. The intimate time and space of a single human being had been fossilized forever in this web of chromium knives and frosted glass."[7] At the conjunction of materials—the collision of textual surfaces where the organic meets the inorganic, where liquidity meets solidity, where the soft interior meets the hard exterior—this is the site of record, the fossilised moment in which the fluid geometry of pliant desire is captured momentarily in arrested time.

Stalking the psychological borders of Whiteread's cast objects, a similar necrophile erotic signals the residency of death. Rooted in the commemoration of the past, casting, like photography, was in its historical nascency a means of invoking the deceased, early photography being used to render in two dimensions what the death mask had made plastic. Both served to preserve the memory of the past as a chemical trace, the imprint of light or substance on another material. The moment of release—like the closing of the shutter—is the release from time and worldly immanence, the moment at which reality is detached from itself. A fossil trace of life turned mineral, the cast, like the photograph, becomes a certificate of detachment. In both we have what Roland Barthes has termed a "superimposition of reality and past" from which the viewer has been all but excluded. Only the purchase of memory can restore the missing dimension for "the life of someone whose existence has somewhat preceded our own encloses in its particularity the very tension of History, its division. History is hysterical: it is constituted only if we consider it, only if we look at it, and in order to look at it we must be excluded from it."[8] For Barthes, Gallic and bourgeois to the end, the meditation upon the photograph of his dead mother comes to rest not in the image itself but in anamnesis, the photograph awakening in him the rumpled softness of her crepe de Chine and the perfume of rice powder. For Whiteread, veteran of Thatcher's Britain, the evocation of the past lives has a different call—in the rank mustiness of Salvation Army clothes, the residues of semen and urine still clinging to old mattresses.

Embodying the "tension of History," Whiteread's cast sculptures are also hysterical. It is a hysteria manifest as exclusion in the impossible space of volumetric dyslexia, in the sculptures' catatonic refusal to speak in the spatial discourse of the world that encloses us. The division that is built into these works, in the way in which they have been made, in the way that they meditate upon the past, belongs to that curious gap in experience, a gap which is the interstitial space between life and death—psychologically as well as sculpturally, the moment of release.

1) Elaine Scarry, *The Body in Pain: The Making and Unmaking of the World*, London: Oxford University Press, 1985, p. 284.
2) Gaston Bachelard, *The Poetics of Space*, Boston: Beacon Press, 1994, p. 215.
3) Quoted in Jan Debbaut and Selma Klein Essink, *Rachel Whiteread*, Eindhoven: Stedelijk Van Abbemuseum, 1992–93, p. 3.
4) Jean-Paul Sartre, *Being and Nothingness*, New York: New York Philosophical Library, 1956, p. 325.
5) Scarry, p. 38.
6) Wilhelm Jensen, *Gradiva: A Pompeiian Fancy* (1903), trans. Helen M. Downey, quoted in Sigmund Freud, *Delusion and Dream*, ed. Philip Reiff, Boston: Beacon Press, 1956, pp. 175–176.
7) J. G. Ballard, *Crash*, New York: Vintage, 1985, p. 12.
8) Roland Barthes, *Camera Lucida*, trans. Richard Howard, London: Fontana Paperbacks, 1984, p. 65.

NEVILLE WAKEFIELD

Rachel Whiteread:

Trennungsangst und die Kunst der Ablösung

Innerhalb des abstrakt-spekulativen Bereichs, den man als Ontologie der Skulptur bezeichnen könnte, nimmt das gegossene Objekt eine eigenartige Stellung ein. Im allgemeinen existiert es nur als Reproduktion einer Wirklichkeit, zu der es einen metonymischen Bezug hat. Es ist ein Objekt, dessen Entstehung sich durch eine Reihe negativer und positiver Inkarnationen und Umkehrungen zurückverfolgen lässt und sich am Ende in fester Form und mimetischer Ähnlichkeit manifestiert. Daneben gibt es noch eine andere Form des Giessens, für die häufiger der Begriff «Formguss» verwendet wird; sie bannt die Dialektik, weil sie auf Synthese und schliessliche Ablösung des Objekts verzichtet. Statt dessen entsteht ein Negativ-Abdruck, der vom Original nur einen Schritt entfernt ist. Der Vorgang ist einfach; in einen Hohlraum rund um das abzugiessende Objekt wird Flüssigkeit gegossen. Konturen, Grenzen und Ausformungen des Gegenstands bilden sich exakt ab, die Topographie der Oberfläche deckt sich mit der des Gussmaterials, ihre Realität wird dieser gemeinsamen Oberfläche einbeschrieben. Geeint entlang dieser schmalen Grenze, bilden die Form und ihr Abguss ein physisches Kontinuum, ein scheinbar untrennbares Ganzes, ohne Rand und Oberfläche. Wie in der bekannten Allegorie von Borges, bei der die Kartographen des Reiches eine Landkarte so detailliert zeichnen, dass sie genauso gross wird wie das Gebiet, das sie beschreibt, ist die materielle Untrennbarkeit von Gegenstand und Abguss, die Nähe zwischen Realität und Abdruck ein Widerstand, an dem die ganze Darstellungs-Metaphysik von Präsenz und Absenz scheitert. Erst wenn die beiden Gebilde voneinander getrennt werden, ergibt sich die ursprüngliche Unterteilung in positive und negative Formen, wird der undenkbare Raum aufgebrochen.

Die Überwindung der Grenze, aus der alle Dialektik hervorgeht, nicht nur die der skulpturalen Präsenz, sondern, im weiteren Sinne, auch das ganze humanistische Gedankengebäude vom räumlichen

NEVILLE WAKEFIELD ist Publizist und lebt in New York.

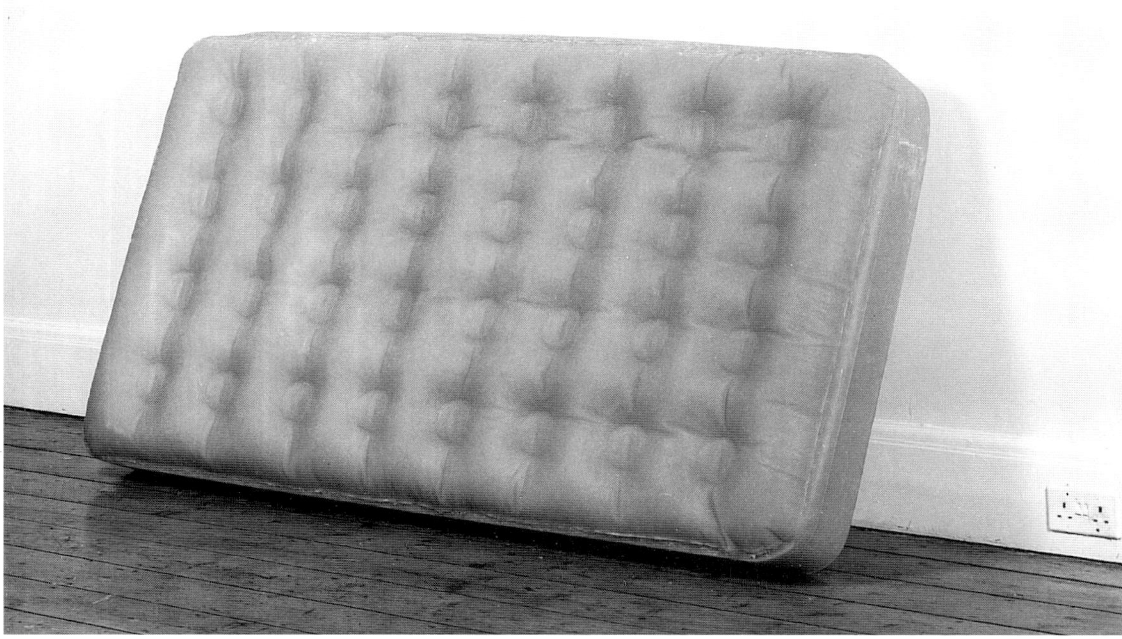

RACHEL WHITEREAD, UNTITLED (CONVEX), 1993, rubber and high-density foam, 39½ x 77 x 13" / OHNE TITEL (KONVEX), Gummi und hochdichter Schaumstoff, 100 x 196 x 33 cm. (PHOTO: PREDENCE CUMMING ASSOCIATES)

Bewusstsein, bedeutet Ablösung und Trennung. An der Skulptur unsichtbar, weil eigentlich zweidimensional, sind raffinierte Silikon-Abdrücke in Mikronen messbar. Topographisch gesprochen, ist der damit beschriebene Raum weder positiv noch negativ, das heisst beides. Innen und Aussen zugleich, Objekt und Abguss, Behälter und Inhalt, gleicht er der endlos-einseitigen Oberfläche eines Möbius-Bandes. Zweifel kommen auf, dass innen wirklich innen ist und aussen wirklich aussen, und so droht der metaphorische Raum des Abdrucks nicht nur die alten euklidischen Gewissheiten der relationalen Geometrie über den Haufen zu werfen, sondern auch unser davon geprägtes eigenes Körpergefühl. Elaine Scarry formuliert das so: «Der Austausch von Innen- und Aussenflächen erfordert nicht die tatsächliche Umkehrung von Körperflächen, sondern die Umwandlung des ursprünglich Inneren und Privaten in etwas Äusseres und Teilbares und umgekehrt die Zurücknahme des jetzt Äusseren und Teilbaren in die intime Abgeschlossenheit des individuellen Bewusstseins.»[1] Bei der Skulptur folgen alle Gussvorgänge jenem Wechselspiel, das Scarry in bezug auf den Körper beschreibt. Aus einem undenkbaren Raum nach aussen gekehrt, produziert die gegossene Form ein Bündel von Grenzbedingungen – von Grenzen, die, gleichviel ob sie innerhalb des Körpers oder in dem Raum, der ihn umgibt, aufs neue überwunden werden, ihren Ursprung in der Gleichzeitigkeit von Kontakt und Trennung beim Ablösen verraten.

Rachel Whitereads Abgüsse von häuslichen und architektonischen Hohlräumen, Abdrücke von plastischen Oberflächen und festen Objekten, bergen ebendiese Spannungen in sich und aktivieren zugleich den synaptischen Raum zwischen Objekt und Welt. Sie verzichtet auf jenen Vermittlungsprozess, der typisch ist für den Guss der «verlorenen Form» und rückt statt dessen das Eins-zu-eins-Verhältnis von Abguss und Original in den Vordergrund, indem sie die Negativform selbst als Objekt präsentiert. Auch die Materialien legen eine solche Umkehrung nahe. Wachs, der bei der «verlorenen Form» später nicht mehr gebraucht wird und normalerweise durch dauerhaftere und wertvollere Materialien ersetzt wird, ist hier ein eigenständiges Medium. Gips, Beton, Gummi und Polyesterharz – Materialien, die man eher mit der Herstellung der Gussform als mit dem Abguss selbst in Verbindung bringt – beschreiben hier unmittelbar den abwesenden Gegenstand, nach dem sie geformt sind. Jenen Vorgang, der normalerweise mehrere Stadien durchläuft, unterbricht Whiteread und tauscht damit die buchstäbliche Präsenz der Reproduktion gegen eine konzeptuelle und räumlich-ambivalente Präsenz der Deduktion ein. Der in der Gussform angelegte Wandel – vom Negativ-Raum zur Positiv-Form – wird nicht vollzogen; statt dessen sind wir aufgefordert, aus der Abwesenheit Präsenz zu konstruieren, aus dem Hohlraum einen Körper. Gebannt vom Zauber der fehlenden Dimension, formen wir auf begrifflicher Ebene das Objekt im Nicht-Raum der Vorstellung. («Das Innen fest zu machen und das Aussen weit», sagt Bachelard, «das scheint mir das erste Problem einer Anthologie der Vorstellungskraft zu sein.»[2]) Denn der Raum, mit dem wir es zu tun haben, ist ein undenkbarer Raum, betrachtet aus einer uneinnehmbaren Position: der Raum zwischen Gegenstand und Abguss, der Raum der Auslösung.

Die Verleugnung der räumlichen und letztendlich auch psychologischen Komplexität von Skulpturen macht die scheinbar alltägliche Thematik und Einfachheit der Form aus. CLOSET (1988) präsentiert sich als monolithischer Minimalismus. Sperrig und irgendwie bedrohlich, beschreibt das Stück den Innenraum eines Kleiderschranks als ausgefüllten Hohlraum, von dem die äussere Hülle entfernt wurde. Die Oberfläche des Schrankes ist – entsprechend der Türkonstruktion – in vier asymmetrisch-vertikale Relief-Flächen unterteilt; im Abdruck erkennt man die Spur von fünf Regalbrettern. Vordergründig scheint das Stück eine Diskussion innerhalb des formalen Vokabulars des Minimalismus zu führen. Ähnlich wie Judds Plexi- und Stahlboxen aus der Mitte der 60er Jahre spielt CLOSET Volumen (die horizontalen Bretter) gegen Form (die Relief-Abdrücke) aus, während das Ganze als einheitliche Gestalt erhalten bleibt. Spätere Arbeiten, die dazu neigten, jene formalen Fragen, die sich aus der Verkörperung des Objekts im Guss ergaben – ein Element nicht nur in CLOSET (1988), sondern auch in YELLOW LEAF, FORT, LEDGER und FLAP (alle 1989) sowie notwendige Bedingung beim Guss von HOUSE (1993/94) –, auszuklammern oder zu umgehen, haben dennoch ihr minimalistisches Erscheinungsbild beibehalten, zugleich aber ein anderes Ziel verfolgt. Whitereads resonante Hohlräume ersetzen die Phänomenologie der Absenz durch die der Präsenz und aktivieren nicht nur den (minimalistischen) Raum der Objekt-Beziehungen, sondern auch den der Erinnerung.

Jene figürlichen Anspielungen, die die minimalistische Arbeit in die Gegenwart des Betrachters verlagert, werden hier in den Gegenstand der Betrachtung zurückverlegt: der mnemonische Körper ist häuslicher Architektur einbeschrieben. «Ich verwende Möbel als Metapher für Menschen», sagt Whiteread.[3] Doch als Metapher sind sie auch Erweiterung. Etymologisch stammt das Wort «Möbel» von «funir», was soviel heisst wie «fördern» oder «befördern»; es ist eine Prothese für den Körper, die in ihrem Fehlen nicht nur eine Stellung oder Haltung festlegt, sondern eine innere Struktur, exakt die Form der Knochenstellung. Als wollten sie genau darauf verweisen, treiben Whitereads Abgüsse von Waschbecken, Badewannen und Matratzen ein poetisches Spiel mit der Introversion und Extroversion des jeweiligen Körpers. Als Körper sind sie sowohl weich als auch hart, sowohl Gips wie Gummi. Whiteread weidet das Haus aus und führt jene unmateriellen Innen- und Nicht-Räume vor, die normalerweise hinter der konzeptuellen und architektonischen Rigidität des Rahmens verborgen bleiben. Labile Gefühls-Räume, gesättigt mit Erinnerung, Körper-Flüssigkeiten und fliessendem Begehren, prallen gegen harte Wände. Innen- und Aussen-Architekturen geraten durcheinander, sind vertauscht. «Mein Körper ist überall», sagt Sartre, «die Bombe, die mein Haus zerstört, zerstört insofern auch meinen Körper, als mein Haus bereits ein Zeichen meines Körpers war.»[4]

Drei Gipsabgüsse von der Unterseite gusseiserner Badewannen aus viktorianischer Zeit (ETHER, VALLEY und UNTITLED, alle 1990) beschwören die Form eines ruhenden oder toten Körpers. Die innere Email-Schicht, die einst als dünne Haut das Badewas-

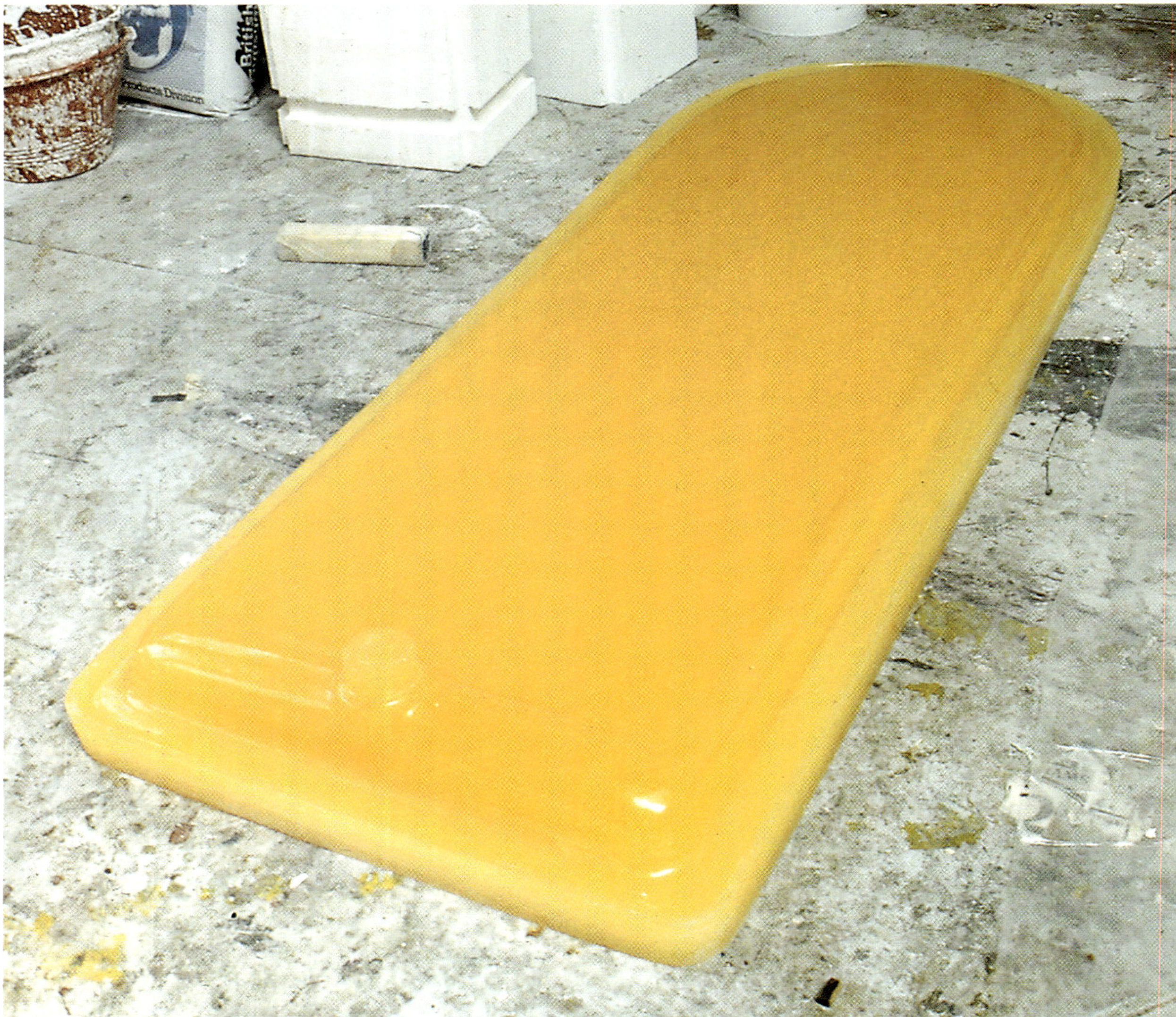

RACHEL WHITEREAD, SLAB (PLUG), 1994, rubber, 8 x 30 x 79" /
PLATTE (STÖPSEL), Gummi, 20 x 76 x 200 cm.

ser hielt, wirkt hier ausgelaugt und porös. Im unteren Teil der Skulpturen befinden sich Abflusslöcher. Sie sind beide in einer Höhe angebracht, dass sie einen normalen Gebrauch von vornherein ausschliessen. Den Zugang zum Inneren von UNTITLED verwehrt eine Glasscheibe, die an den Heiss- und Kaltwasserhähnen durchbohrt ist. Diese Negativ-Räume sind eine Art Monument des nicht vorhandenen Körpers in seinen Reinigungs- und Todes-Ritualen, und so wurden sie denn auch immer wieder als Särge oder Gräber beschrieben. Doch die Todes-Assoziation geht über die einfachen Anspielungen auf den Leichnam hinaus, Anspielungen, die in SLAB (PLUG) (1994) erst richtig zum Tragen kommen. Vielmehr wird auch die irritierende Nähe von Tod und Leben deutlich, wie sie in der sterblich-labilen Balance des Fleisches angelegt ist. VALLEY verzweigt den nicht vorhandenen Körper in ein häusliches System aus Arterien und Venen, das dem seinen ähnlich, ja in der Tat verbunden ist. Die architektonische Hülle, die das Leben schützend umgibt, birgt zugleich die Vorahnung des Todes. Die Ausdünstungen des Körpers im Tod, Haut, Schleim, Fäkalien, Haare und Zehennägel sind allgegenwärtig, eingefangen im Knie-Rohr unter der Badewanne, oder sie zirkulieren in grossen Rohren und Leitungen um uns herum, die in Wänden verborgen oder auf Bodendielen verlegt sind. (Es nimmt keineswegs wunder, dass Whiteread bei UNTITLED [FLOOR] von 1992 einerseits an den Masturbationsraum in Acconcis SEEDBED denkt und andererseits an den beispielsweise von Carl Andre vertretenen Formalismus.) Bezeichnenderweise wird in J. G. Ballards Roman *High-Rise* der Pulsschlag des monolithischen Gebäudes – zentrale Metapher für den Körper der Gesellschaft und seine Verzweigungen – durch die inneren Kanäle geleitet, jene geheimen Räume seines Blutkreislaufs. Tratsch, eine Atmosphäre von Feindseligkeit und Konfrontation streicht wie die Legionärskrankheit durch die Aufzugschächte und Leitungen der Klimaanlagen. Wie auch beim menschlichen Körper ist die Fähigkeit des Hauses, den eigenen Müll auszustossen und loszuwerden, ein Zeichen für seine Intaktheit.

Ähnlich wie bei Ballard suggeriert Whitereads Archäologie der Gegenwart psychische Landschaften, formal gefasst in Raum und Zeit. Die Leitmotive der psychologischen Eingeschlossenheit – Aufzug, Hochhaus und Autobahn – werden in den Alltäglichkeiten von Nicht-so-gross-Britannien aufgespürt. GHOST, ein Abguss vom Inneren eines kleinen Raums im Londoner Highgate, vergrössert in seinen Umkehrungen jene Bedingungen, die Komfort und Einengung innerhalb der immer enger werdenden städtischen Raum-Ökonomie untrennbar miteinander verbinden. Türen und Fenster, «grobe Versionen der Sinne» in jenem Raum, den Scarry zugleich als «Vergrösserung des Körpers» und «Verkleinerung der Welt»[5] beschreibt, sind hier nichts anderes als blosse und doch geheimnisvolle Projektionen eines

RACHEL WHITEREAD, UNTITLED, (AMBER SLAB), 1991, rubber and high-density foam, 81 x 31 x 4½" / OHNE TITEL (BERNSTEIN-PLATTE), Gummi und hochdichter Schaumstoff, 206 x 79 x 11 cm.

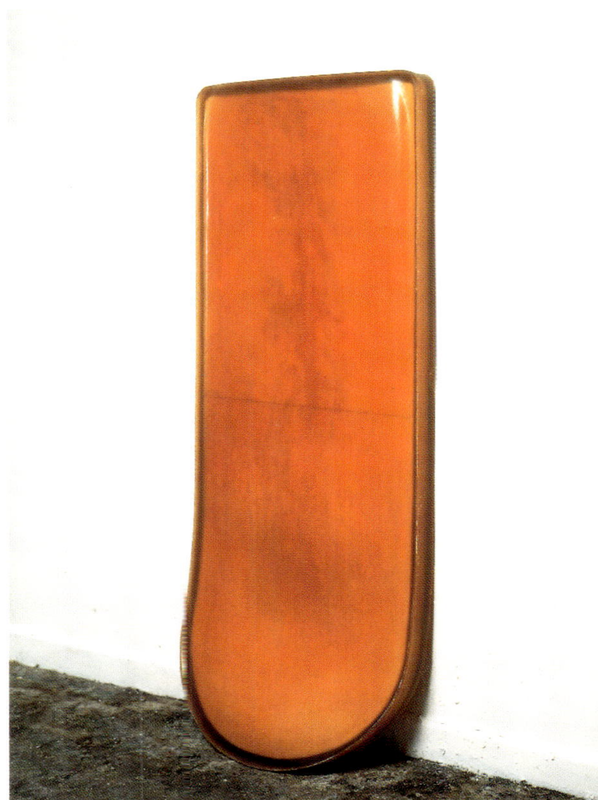

Gipsabgusses. Die Aufforderung einzutreten ist ins Gegenteil verkehrt, das Haus selbst ein Phantasie-Raum, der sich der Aussenwelt verwehrt. Mehr Bunker als Behausung, ist er zum Speicher oder Behälter für Phantasien von geschützter Intimität geworden. GHOST ist ein Monument für alles, was preisgegeben wurde und verlorenging im Streben, die Verantwortlichkeit des Wohlfahrtsstaats für die Existenzgrundlage zu verleugnen. Und wie HOUSE, das allein in einer Strasse in Bow stand, gleich einem einsamen Zahn, der darauf wartet, aus einem Kaugummi gezogen zu werden, in dem die Abdrücke der vorher schon gezogenen Zähne noch zu sehen sind, gemahnte dieses Stück an sträflich vernachlässigte Erinnerung und den Übergang von der Alltäglichkeit zur Feindseligkeit. Beide Strukturen scheinen die Flüchtigkeit des Innenlebens zu signalisieren, die Flucht von der Ausgesetztheit der Gegenwart in die Schlupfwinkel, Ritzen und geheimen Orte der Vergangenheit – Häfen unterdrückter Träume von Sex und Tod.

Diese Träume, die die kollektive Psyche des 19. Jahrhunderts ebenso prägten wie die unserer heutigen Zeit, sind hier auf fast archäologische Weise ans Licht geholt. «Was früher einmal Pompeji war, kam nun in ganz anderer – doch nicht in lebendiger – Form daher; vielmehr schien es nun vollständig versteinert in totengleicher Starre. Doch daraus erhob sich ein Gefühl, als begänne der Tod zu sprechen.»[6] In seinem Aufsatz «Das Unheimliche» von 1919 stellt Freud Jensens berühmten Bericht über die Entdeckung, dass die Vergangenheit permanent in die Gegenwart hineinwirkt, als räumliche und archäologische Analogie zu den psychoanalytischen Vorgängen dar. Die versunkene Stadt stand für die Aussetzung der Geschichte und die Enthüllung des Unsichtbaren. Für Chateaubriand und spätere Kommentatoren war es bezeichnenderweise der Abdruck einer weiblichen Brust in der Asche, ein makabres Stilleben, das dem Bild des jäh geendeten Lebens in den Ruinen der Gegenwart seinen erotischen Beiklang verlieh. Diese Erotik des archäologischen «Abdrucks» taucht am Ende des 20. Jahrhunderts als Konfrontation nicht zwischen Mensch und Natur, sondern zwischen Mensch und Technik wieder auf. Chateaubriands Faszíniertheit vom Skulptur gewordenen Tod in Pompeji entspricht haargenau der des Protagonisten in J. G. Ballards wegweisendem Roman *Crash*. Die Erotik des Abdrucks ist hier nicht der Vulkanasche aufgedrückt, sondern unmittelbar dem Fleisch – unheilvolles Vorzeichen für die Verbindung von Sex und Technik: «Bei Vaughan löst jeder verunglückte Wagen ein erregtes Zittern aus, in der komplexen Geometrie eines verbeulten Kotflügels, in den überraschenden Varianten zerquetschter Kühlergitter, im grotesken Überhang eines Armaturenbretts, das von der Lenkstange aufgespiesst wird, als handelte es sich um eine technisch-exakte Form von Maschinen-Fellatio. Die Intimität von Raum und Zeit eines einzelnen Menschen ist für immer erstarrt in diesem Netz aus Chromleisten und geborstenem Glas.»[7] An der Verbindungsstelle der Materialien – jener Kollision von Oberflächen, bei der Organisches auf Anorganisches trifft, Flüssiges auf Festes, das weiche Innere auf die harte Aussenschale – liegt der Ort des Festhaltens, der zum Fossil erstarrte Augenblick, in dem die fliessende Geometrie des im Fluss befindlichen Begehrens vorübergehend in der angehaltenen Zeit eingefangen ist.

Nähert man sich den psychologischen Grenzen von Whitereads gegossenen Objekten, so signalisiert eine ähnlich nekrophile Erotik den ihnen innewohnenden Tod. Ursprünglich diente der Abguss, ähnlich wie die Photographie, der Beschwörung der Vergangenheit, dem Andenken eines Toten; und so gab die anfängliche Photographie in zwei Dimensionen wieder, was die Totenmaske plastisch dargestellt hatte. Beide konservierten sie die Erinnerung an die Vergangenheit in chemischen Rückständen, als Spur von Licht oder Materie in einem anderen Material. Der Augenblick der Ablösung ist – wie das Auslösen beim Photographieren – die Ablösung von Zeit und In-der-Welt-Sein, der Augenblick, in dem die Realität von sich selbst erlöst wird. Fossile Spur im Mineral, wird Abguss wie Photo zum sicheren Hinweis, dass die Ablösung stattgefunden hat. In beiden Fällen haben wir es mit einer – wie Roland Barthes es nennt – «Überlagerung von Realität und Vergangenheit» zu tun, aus der der Betrachter nahezu ausgeschlossen ist. Nur wer der Spur der Erinnerung folgt, kann die fehlende Dimension rekonstruieren, denn «das

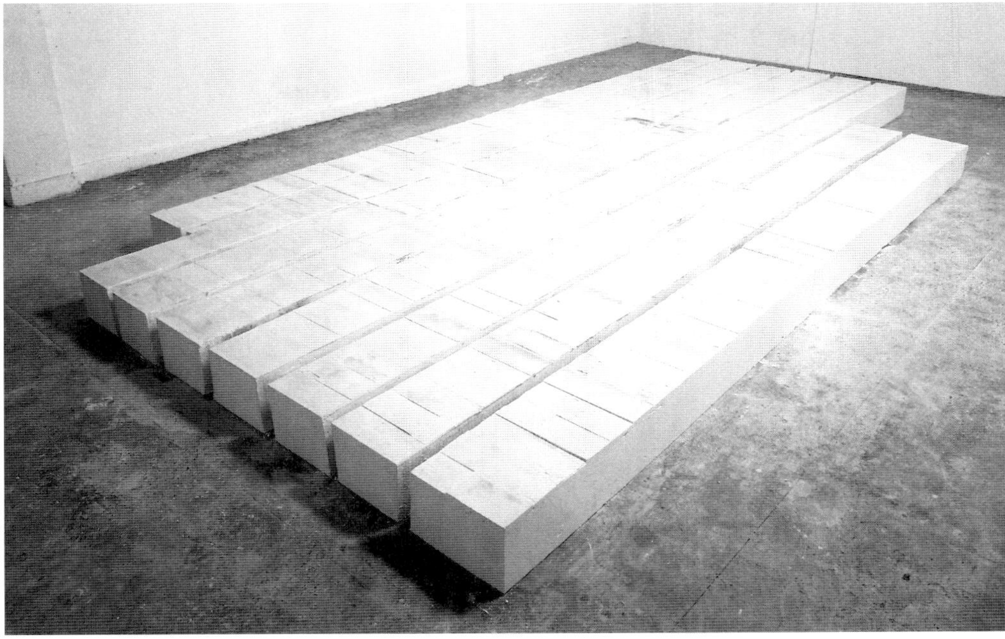

RACHEL WHITEREAD, UNTITLED (FLOOR), 1992, plaster, 9½ x 110¼ x 245" / OHNE TITEL (BODEN), Gips, 24 x 280 x 622 cm.

Leben eines Menschen, der einige Zeit vor uns existiert hat, umschliesst in seiner Einmaligkeit eben jene Spannung der Geschichte, ihre Abgeschlossenheit. Geschichte ist hysterisch: es gibt sie nur, wenn wir uns ihr zuwenden, wenn wir sie betrachten, und um sie betrachten zu können, müssen wir von ihr ausgeschlossen sein.»[8] Für Barthes – ein Gallier und bis ins letzte bourgeois – kommt die Meditation über die Photographie von seiner toten Mutter nicht im Bild selbst zur Ruhe, sondern in der Rückerinnerung: das Photo weckt in ihm die Erinnerung an ihren knittrig-weichen Chinakrepp und den Geruch von Reispulver. Für Whiteread, eine Veteranin aus dem Grossbritannien Margret Thatchers, hat die Beschwörung der Vergangenheit einen anderen Beiklang: den stechend-muffigen Geruch von Heilsarmee-Kleidern, die Reste von Samen und Urin, die an alten Matratzen haften.

Auch Whitereads gegossene Skulpturen sind hysterisch, denn sie verkörpern die «Spannung der Geschichte». Es handelt sich um eine Hysterie, die sich als Ausgeschlossenheit im undenkbaren Raum volumetrischer Dyslexie manifestiert, in der Weigerung der Skulpturen, im räumlichen Diskurs jener Welt zu sprechen, die uns umgibt. Die Abgeschlossenheit, die diesen Werken eigen ist, in der Art ihrer Herstellung ebenso wie in der Art ihrer Reflexion auf die Vergangenheit, gehört zu jener seltsamen Kluft in der Erfahrung, jenem Raum zwischen Leben und Tod, im psychologischen wie im skulpturalen Sinn, zum Augenblick des Lösens.

(Übersetzung: Nansen)

1) Elaine Scarry, *The Body in Pain: The Making and Unmaking of the World*, London 1985, S. 284.
2) Gaston Bachelard, *The Poetics of Space*, Boston 1994, S. 215.
3) Zitiert in Jan Debbaut und Selma Klein Essink, *Rachel Whiteread*, Eindhoven: Stedelijk Van Abbemuseum, 1992–93, S. 3.
4) Jean-Paul Sartre, *Being and Nothingness*, New York: New York Philosophical Library, 1956, S. 325.
5) Scarry, S. 38.
6) Wilhelm Jensen, *Gradiva: A Pompeiian Fancy* (1903), trans. Helen M. Downey, zitiert in Sigmund Freud, *Delusion and Dream*, ed. Philip Reiff, Boston 1956, S. 175–176.
7) J. G. Ballard, *Crash*, New York 1985, S. 12.
8) Roland Barthes, *Camera Lucida*, Übersetzung: Richard Howard, London 1984, S. 65.

Whiteread's GHOST

TREVOR FAIRBROTHER

In her early casts Rachel Whiteread gave solid form to intangible, unremarked places to elicit childhood memories, for example, the spaces beneath tables or beds, and the interior cavities of wardrobes and hot-water bottles. She often used plaster, a "low" material that is more commonly associated today with medicine and archeology than finished works of art. Critics agreed that these enigmatic cast forms hinted at things unknown within the landscape of human domesticity. Whiteread's first architectural project, GHOST (1990), marked an ambitious development in her work, for it shifted attention from individual household items to the larger unit of a domestic room. She wanted to visualize the envelope constituted by four walls, "mummifying," as she remarked, the air within.[1] Whiteread worked in an abandoned building at 486 Archway Road, North London, a modest row house, typical of the city's vast spread of late Victorian middle- and working-class dwellings. She did the casting in a parlor, a room she had stripped down to its bare architectural decor. After gridding each wall into units that could be easily cast, she made a multi-partite plaster mold, proceeding with one unit at a time. Since the plaster blocks are only about five inches thick, Whiteread did not damage the walls or the room when she removed the sections. But this is probably a minor point since the whole building was derelict, corpse-like, and slated to disappear in the process of urban change.

TREVOR FAIRBROTHER works at the Museum of Fine Arts, Boston, where he is Beal Curator of Contemporary Art.

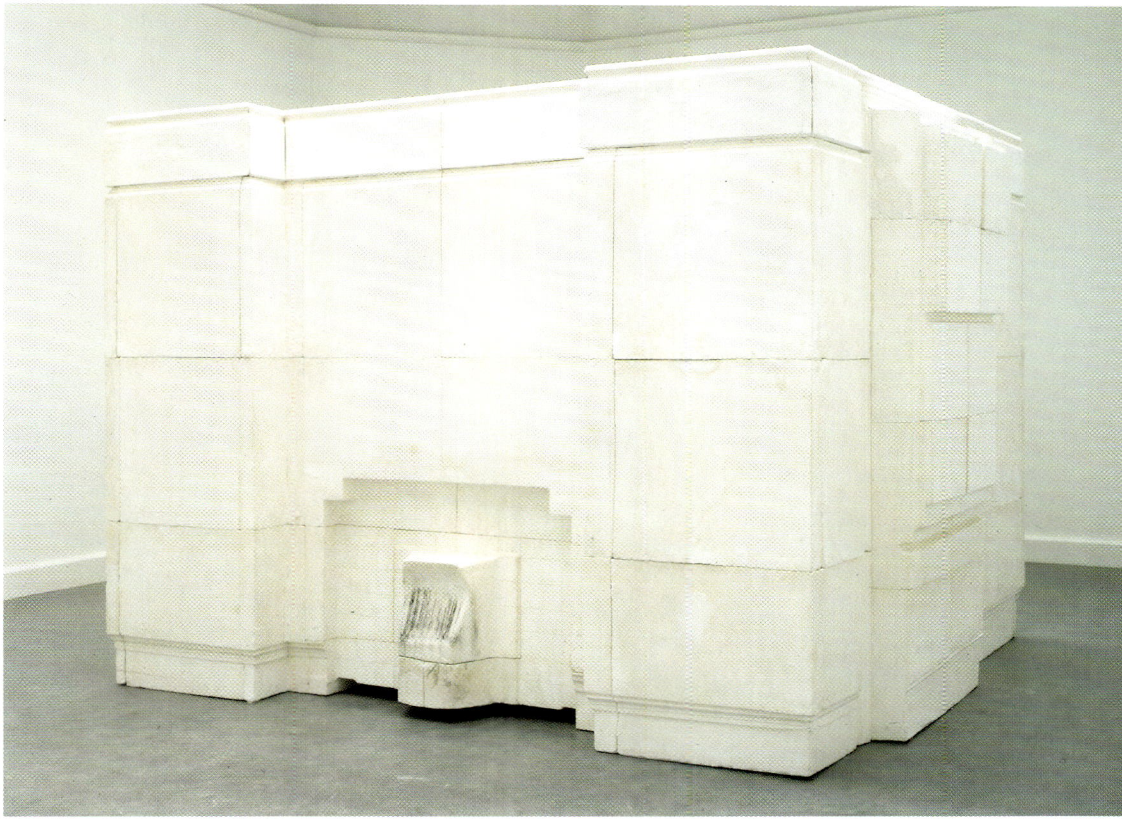

RACHEL WHITEREAD, GHOST, 1990, plaster on steel frame, 106¼ x 125⅛ x 143¾" / GEIST, Gips auf Stahlgerüst, 270 x 318 x 365 cm.

When the units of GHOST are reassembled in the gallery in their original configuration they make what appears to be a solid, freestanding monument with no means of physical entry. The sculpture confronts the viewer with a disorienting inversion of a room, for the facade it presents was molded from the inner lining of a room. The exterior of GHOST bears the negative imprints of a door, a window, a fireplace, and various decorative moldings; there are also more subtle traces left by the embossed texture of wallpaper and specks of soot and ash transferred from the hearth. The piece does not hide the fact that it is hollow and open at the top, for cracks between the plaster blocks allow glimpses of the interior space containing the metal armature that stabilizes the walls.

This sculpture is aptly titled: It is the abstracted and disembodied spirit of something dead, a pale, ethereal apparition. It fuses contradictory sensations and associations, and unsettles the viewer by reversing notions of positive and negative. For example, from close quarters I found it difficult to be certain whether I was looking at a cast replica of a door (no) or a molded imprint taken from the surface of a door (yes). GHOST summons up the peculiar feeling of looking at, as if for the first time, what was assumed to be known. It elicits opposing emotional responses, inducing viewers to vacillate between comforting and sinister thoughts. To the nostalgic it suggests the bare trimmings of a cozy, old-fashioned room, and serves as a screen onto which to project memories of old domestic rituals. Alternatively, and more bleakly, GHOST may appear oppressive, airless, dingy, and macabre. Viewed in a large open space it is easily taken for a Victorian mausoleum. There is cruel

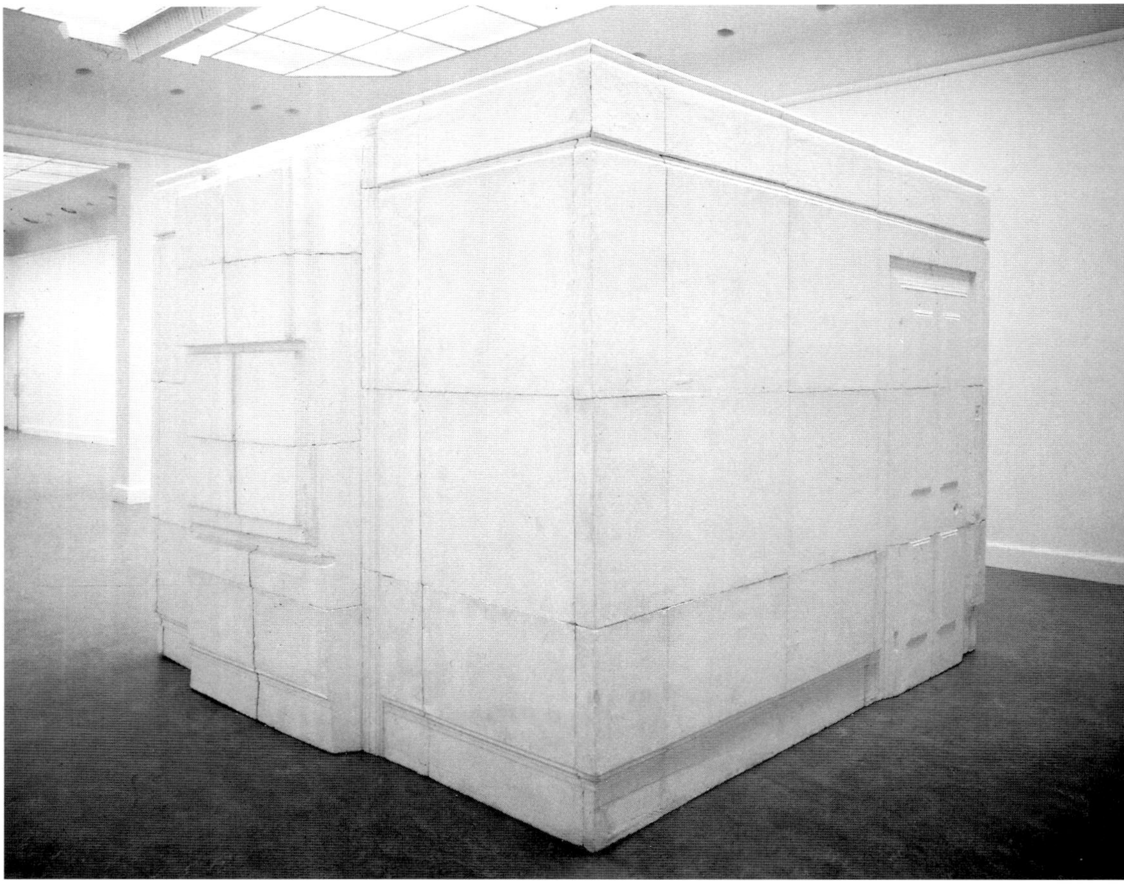

Double page / Doppelseite:
RACHEL WHITEREAD, GHOST, 1990, plaster on steel frame, 106¼ x 125⅛ x 143¾" /
GEIST, Gips auf Stahlgerüst, 270 x 318 x 365 cm.

irony in the fact that the remains of a wealthy individual might spend "eternity" in the same amount of space as the Archway parlor where generations of poorer folk passed their lives. On the other hand, GHOST itself demands to be housed within the institutional shelter of a gallery or museum, for despite its fortress-like stance, it is a fragile work of art. Although it speaks another language, this piece claims kinship with the relics of ancient temples and the cosmetically enhanced "period rooms" that live in the museological limbo. Whiteread's piece also has a rapport with the architectural plaster casts that were educational mainstays in nineteenth-century museums; but they were made in the most straightforward sense as records and replicas, whereas GHOST seeks to move and transform viewers in unpredictable ways.

Whiteread grew up in London in a house similar to the one that was the site for GHOST. She worked for a while on the grounds crew at Highgate Cemetery, where she was fascinated by the graves and crypts in disrepair. "Although I didn't want to look, I was curious. Peeling through the cracks was, and remains, so compelling."[2] It is logical to make a biographical and/or London-based reading of GHOST, for Victorian cemeteries and derelict Victorian buildings abound in the neighborhood. Whiteread herself acknowledges that her work is informed in some way by the social deprivations initiated in the 1980s by the Thatcher government. Nonetheless, the artist resists old,

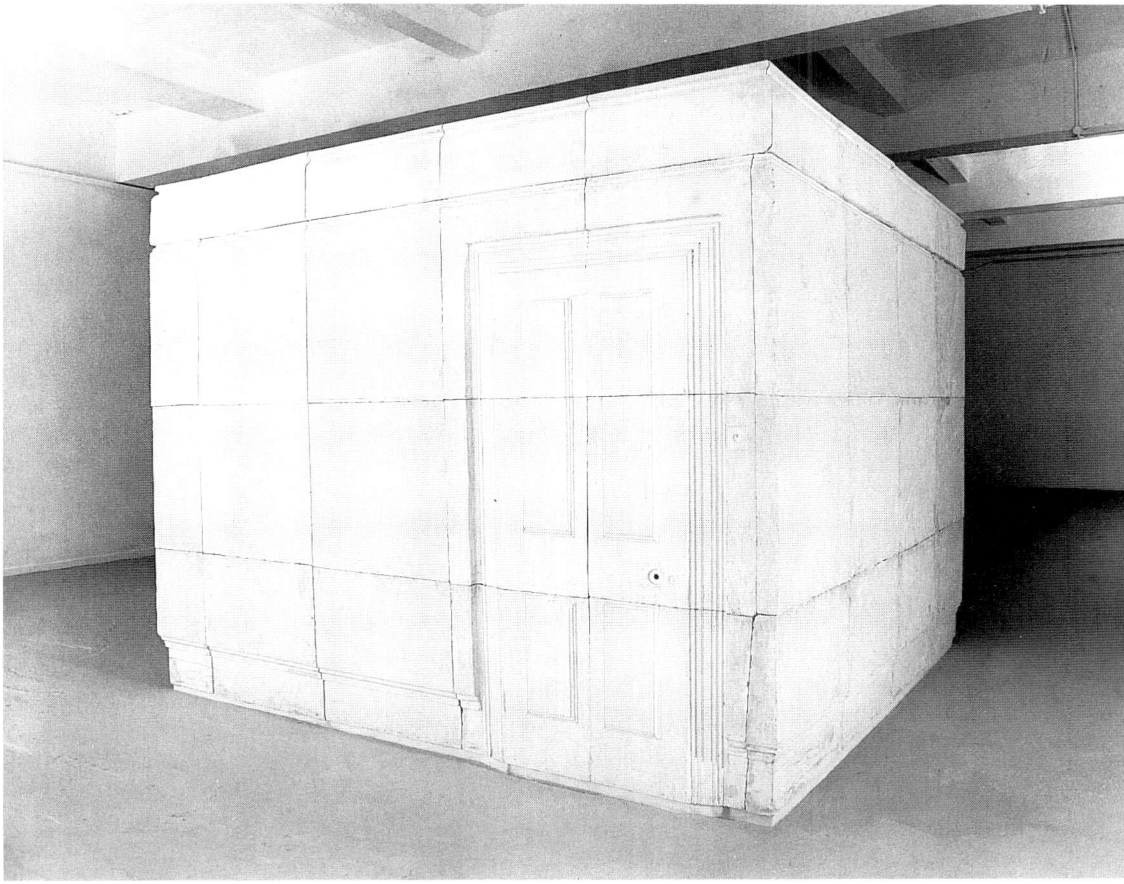

worn-out things and details that might encourage a blatantly sentimental or narrative response from viewers. GHOST, however, cannot avoid this kind of responsex despite its abstract, monochromatic formal aspect. The local and personal inflections of GHOST may explain why the artist later felt the need to make a similar piece representing a fictitious, newer-looking, and even more generically anonymous space: ROOM (1993) was cast from elements assembled in her studio during a residency in Berlin.

When GHOST was on view at the Museum of Modern Art in New York in 1994, I overheard visitors speculating that it was a cast replica of a mausoleum in New Orleans. It seemed appropriate that recollections of a country's famous cemeteries would crowd first impressions of this piece; presumably, many people from France would think of *Père Lachaise*. GHOST is a site that can flood us with thoughts about lives as they are lived, places that shelter lives, and places that are intended to memorialize the dead. It is remarkable that Whiteread unleashed such a wealth of visual experience and feeling through the simple yet arduous task of making a plaster mold of a small room.

1) Whiteread quoted by Beryl Wright, in *Options 46: Rachel Whiteread*, Chicago: Museum of Contemporary Art, 1993, p. 3.
2) Whiteread quoted by Iwona Blazwick, in *Rachel Whiteread*, Eindhoven: Van Abbemuseum, 1992, p. 10.

Whitereads GEIST

TREVOR FAIRBROTHER

Mit ihren frühen Guss-Plastiken verlieh Rachel Whiteread körperlosen, unbemerkten Orten eine feste Form; diese Orte konnten Kindheitserinnerungen wecken, an Räume zwischen Tischen oder Betten beispielsweise, an das Innere von Kleiderschränken und Wärmflaschen. Oft verwendete sie dabei Gips, ein «minderwertiges» Material, das man heute eher mit Medizin und Archäologie denn mit einem fertigen Kunstwerk in Verbindung bringt. Die Kritiker waren sich darin einig, dass diese rätselhaften Guss-Formen auf Dinge verweisen, die in unserem häuslichen Leben eher unbekannt sind. Whitereads erstes Architektur-Projekt mit dem Titel GHOST (1990) markierte einen entscheidenden Schritt in ihrer Arbeit, weil sich der Blick nun vom individuellen Haushalt auf die häusliche Umgebung im weiteren Sinn verlagerte. Sie wollte jene Hülle aus vier Wänden sichtbar machen, die – wie sie sagt – die Luft darin «mumifiziert».[1] Whiteread arbeitete mit einem leerstehenden Haus in 486 Archway Road, Nord-London, einem bescheidenen Reihenhaus, das typisch ist für ein Stadtbild mit vielen viktorianischen Mittel- und Arbeiterklasse-Häusern. Den Abguss nahm sie vom Wohnzimmer, einem Raum, den sie bis auf die reine architektonische Form entkleidet hatte. Nachdem jede Wand in Einheiten aufgeteilt war, von denen sich leicht ein Abguss herstellen liess, fertigte sie eine mehrteilige Gipsform an und goss eine Einheit nach der anderen ab. Da die Gipsblöcke nur etwa dreizehn Zentimeter dick sind, brauchte Whiteread die Wände bzw. den Raum beim Abnehmen der einzelnen Teile nicht zu zerstören. Das spielte aber wohl keine grosse Rolle, weil das Haus fast geisterhaft verlassen dastand und im Rahmen des urbanen Wandlungsprozesses ohnehin verschwinden sollte.

Wenn die Einzelteile von GHOST in der Galerie zu ihrer ursprünglichen Form zusammengesetzt sind, wirken sie wie ein solides, freistehendes Monument, zu dem es keinen realen Zutritt gibt. Die Skulptur konfrontiert den Betrachter mit einer irritierenden Raum-Umkehrung; denn sie präsentiert eine Fassade, die vom Inneren eines Raums abgegossen wurde. Die Aussenseite von GHOST weist die Negativ-Abdrücke von einer Tür, einem Fenster, einem Kamin und zahlreichen Dekorationen auf. Darüber hinaus entdecken wir feinere Spuren, eingeprägt von Tapeten sowie Russ- und Asche-Partikeln aus dem Kamin. Das Stück verbirgt nicht, dass es hohl ist; Spalten zwischen den Gipsblöcken geben den Blick auf das Innere frei, wo ein Metallgerüst die Wände stabilisiert.

Der Titel der Skulptur trifft den Nagel auf den Kopf: es ist der abstrakte und entkörperte Geist von etwas Totem, eine fahle, geisterhafte Erscheinung. Es verbindet widersprüchliche Gefühle und Assoziationen miteinander und irritiert den Betrachter durch die Umkehrung von Positiv und Negativ. Wenn ich nah davor stand, war ich mir zum Beispiel nicht sicher, ob ich es mit der gegossenen

---

TREVOR FAIRBROTHER arbeitet am Museum of Fine Arts in Boston als Kurator für zeitgenössische Kunst.

Replik einer Tür zu tun hatte (nein) oder mit einem Oberflächen-Abguss von der Tür (ja). GHOST provoziert das eigenartige Gefühl, etwas, das man zu kennen glaubte, zum ersten Mal zu sehen. Es weckt widersprüchliche emotionale Reaktionen, indem es den Betrachter zwischen angenehmen und düsteren Gedanken hin und her pendeln lässt. Geradezu nostalgisch beschwört es die schlichten Elemente eines heimeligen, altmodischen Zimmers und bietet eine Projektionsfläche für die Erinnerung an alte häusliche Rituale. Man kann GHOST aber auch in einem weniger freundlichen Licht sehen: bedrückend, düster, schäbig und makaber. Wie es da so allein auf weiter Flur steht, kann man es fälschlicherweise auch für ein viktorianisches Mausoleum halten. Eine grausame Ironie liegt in der Tatsache, dass die sterblichen Überreste eines einzigen Reichen auf ebensoviel Raum in die «Ewigkeit» eingehen wie das Wohnzimmer, in dem ganze Generationen ärmerer Leute ihr Leben fristeten. Andererseits verlangt das Werk selbst, im institutionellen Schutzraum einer Galerie oder eines Museums untergebracht zu werden, weil es trotz seines festunghaften Aussehens ein fragiles Kunstwerk ist. Auch wenn dieses Stück eine andere Sprache spricht, weist es doch eine gewisse Verwandtschaft mit den Überresten antiker Tempel auf sowie mit den kosmetisch aufbereiteten «historischen Räumen», die in der musealen Vorhölle existieren. Whitereads Arbeit hat darüber hinaus auch einen Bezug zu den architektonischen Gipsabgüssen, die in den Museen des 19. Jahrhunderts die pädagogischen Grundpfeiler bildeten. Diese waren jedoch als eindeutige Darstellung bzw. Replik gedacht, während GHOST die Betrachter auf unbekannte Pfade lockt.

Whiteread wuchs in einem Londoner Haus auf, das dem für GHOST verwendeten sehr ähnlich war. Sie arbeitete eine Zeitlang auf dem Highgate-Friedhof und war dort von den verfallenen Gräbern und Grabkammern fasziniert. «Ich wollte eigentlich gar nicht hinsehen, aber trotzdem war ich neugierig. Ich musste – und muss – einfach durch die Ritzen gucken.»[2] Es bietet sich an, GHOST in biographischem Licht und/oder in bezug auf London zu sehen, denn viktorianische Friedhöfe und leerstehende viktorianische Häuser gibt es dort im Überfluss. Whiteread selbst gibt zu, dass ihre Arbeit in gewisser Weise vom Sozialabbau geprägt ist, den die Thatcher-Regierung in den 80er Jahren betrieb. Dennoch widersteht die Künstlerin der Versuchung, alte, abgedroschene Dinge und Details zu verwenden, die dem Betrachter eine platt-sentimentale oder narrative Sichtweise erlauben würden. Doch kann GHOST – bei aller Abstraktheit und monochromatischen Formalität – diese Sichtweise andererseits auch nicht verhindern. Die lokalen und persönlichen Anklänge in GHOST mögen erklären, warum die Künstlerin es später für nötig hielt, ein ähnliches Stück mit einem fiktiven, neuartigeren und insgesamt auch anonymeren Raum herzustellen: ROOM (1993) entstand als Abguss von Elementen, die sie während eines Berlin-Aufenthaltes in ihrem Atelier zusammengetragen hatte. Als GHOST 1994 im New Yorker Museum of Modern Art gezeigt wurde, hörte ich Besucher darüber spekulieren, dass es sich vielleicht um den Abguss eines Mausoleums in New Orleans handeln könnte. Es schien mir naheliegend, dass der erste Eindruck dieses Werks Erinnerungen an bekannte Grabstätten heraufbeschwor; Franzosen dürften wahrscheinlich an *Père Lachaise* denken. GHOST ist ein Ort, der Gedanken an gelebtes Leben aufsteigen lässt, an Räume, die Leben schützen und an Räume zum Gedächtnis an Tote. Bemerkenswert ist, dass Whiteread einen derart reichen Strom von visuellen Erfahrungen und Gefühlen auslöst, durch das simple aber aufwendige Abformen eines kleinen Raumes in Gips. *(Übersetzung: Nansen)*

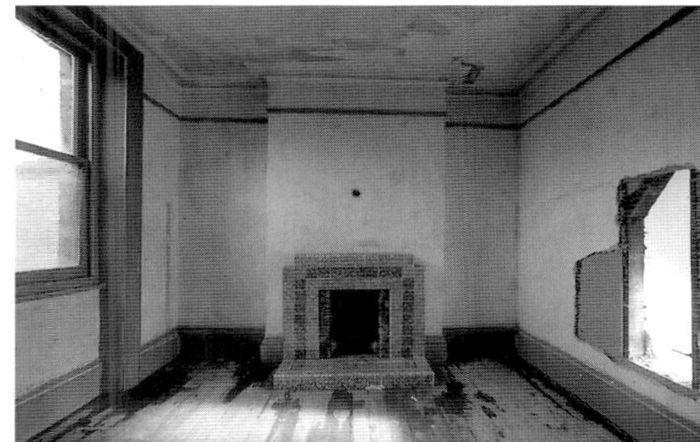

RACHEL WHITEREAD, GHOST, actual room / GEIST, ursprünglicher Raum.

1) Whiteread zitiert nach Beryl Wright, in *Options 46: Rachel Whiteread*, Chicago, Museum of Contemporary Art, 1993, S. 3.

2) Whiteread zitiert nach Iwona Blazwick, in *Rachel Whiteread*, Van Abbemuseum, Eindhoven 1992, S. 10.

RUDOLF SCHMITZ

DIE GEBREMSTE MONUMENTALITÄT DES UNSICHTBAREN

«Könige fassen Türen nicht an», schreibt Francis Ponge. «Sie kennen dies Glück nicht: sanft oder heftig eine dieser vertrauten Füllungen vor sich her zu schieben, dann sich umzudrehen nach ihr, um sie wieder zurechtzurücken – eine Tür in den Armen zu halten... Das Glück, eins dieser hohen Hindernisse eines Zimmers bei seinem Porzellanknopf am Bauch zu packen; dies unverhoffte Leib-an-Leib, wenn der Schritt einen Takt verhält, das Auge sich öffnet und der ganze Körper sich an seine neue Behausung gewöhnt.»[1)]

Kennt Rachel Whiteread dieses Glück? Ich bin mir dessen sicher, obwohl es in ihrem Fall nicht die bestimmende Art von Glück ist. Aber was Francis Ponge versuchte – nicht von den Dingen zu schreiben, sondern aus den Dingen heraus, «die Dinge zu schreiben» –, das gelingt ihr auf anderem Terrain. In einer Form, die ebenfalls anthropomorphe Rückstände zu tilgen beschlossen hat. Und so fühlt sich der Betrachter, der durch ihre Ausstellung geht, leicht selbst wie ein Fossil: Abkömmling einer Welt in Bewegung, der Rachel Whitereads honigfarbenen Fliegenfängern auszuweichen versucht. Es sind geronnene Fliegenfänger, die den Blick ins diffuse Innere locken, obwohl ihre äussere Grenze scharfgeschnitten und eindeutig ist.

Rachel Whitereads Skulpturen gestatten diese Möglichkeit des Eindringens. Selbst wenn sie sich als verdichteter Zeit- und Raumkern darstellen. Doch «Kern» ist natürlich nicht der angemessene Ausdruck: es geht nicht um Qualität und Definition, sondern um das Herstellen unterschiedsloser Dichte, entstanden durch gleichmässiges und gleichmütiges Auffüllen. Kein Zweifel allerdings, dass genau darin die künstlerische Haltung sich präzisiert.

Der Vorgang der akkumulierenden Herstellung haftet Whitereads Skulpturen an und wirkt als ständiges Korrektiv und prozessuale Unterfütterung dessen, was die Augen wahrnehmen.

Selbst in ihren wirklich grossen Skulpturen wie ROOM (1993), die in der Kunsthalle Basel im grossen Saal gezeigt wurde und die Abformung eines archetypischen Raumes ist, den die Künstlerin während ihres Berlin-Aufenthaltes eigens konstruiert hatte, gibt es so etwas wie gebremste Monumentalität. Das liegt an den Schnitten, die durchs Gipsmaterial gehen. Sie verbreiten kolonialistische Aura und erinnern an die ägyptischen Götterbilder in Abu Simbel, die man zersägt hat, um sie an sicherer Stelle wieder aufzubauen. Und das macht das Ganze – bei aller Lakonie – zu einem Bauklötz-

RUDOLF SCHMITZ ist freiberuflicher Kunstkritiker. Er lebt in Frankfurt.

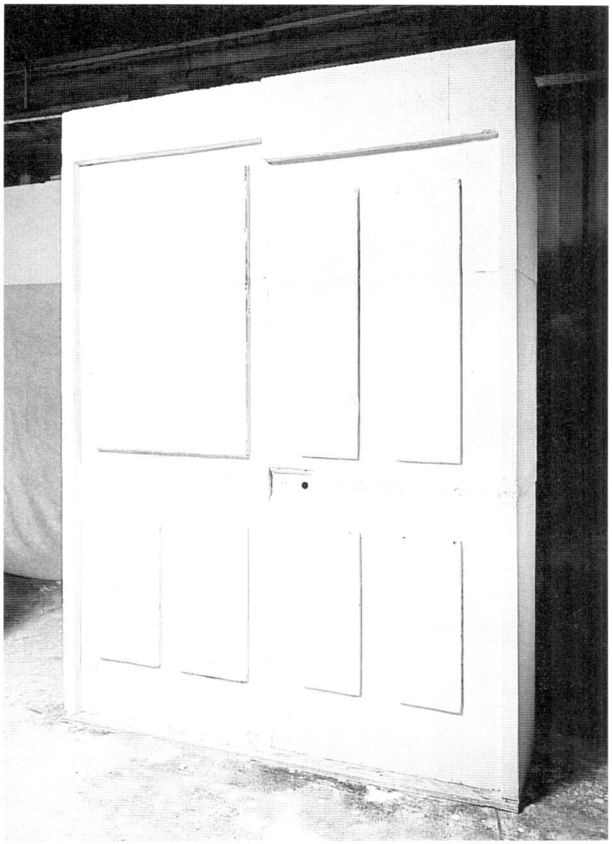

RACHEL WHITEREAD, FALSE DOOR (BACK), 1991, plaster, 84½ x 60 x 16" / FALSCHE TÜR (RÜCKSEITE) Gips, 215 x 152 x 41 cm. (PHOTO: EDWARD WOODMAN)

chenspiel, bei dem auch andere, «falsche» Kombinationen möglich sind.

In Richtung dieser falschen Kombinationen – also zur eigentlichen Kombinatorik – scheint es bei Rachel Whitereads jüngsten Arbeiten zu gehen. TABLE AND CHAIR in Polyesterharz bzw. Gummi und Polystyrol lassen an die Schleifspuren der Dinge, an Nachbilder von Bewegung denken, wie sie sich in einer geblendeten Videokamera abzeichnen. Dass Whitereads Werk irgend etwas mit Blendung zu tun hat, ist unabweisbar. Es handelt sich um eine Art von Blendung, die im Gegenzug und als Kompensation eine ungeheure Steigerung des Haptischen mit sich bringt. Das Unsichtbare eines Raums, in dem man sich befindet, wird ganz und gar abgeformt, so dass man es betasten kann. Offensichtlich also gibt es das Bedürfnis und die Möglichkeit, diesem Raum, der uns als Fluidum umgibt, zu entwischen. Und weil man diesem Raum so existentiell verhaftet war, ist das Triumphgefühl angesichts einer solchen formalen Lösung so gross.

Rachel Whiteread reagiert mit zeitgenössischer Strategie auf einen klassischen Wunschtraum: in einer «grossen» Form die Fülle zu bewältigen. Zeitgenössisch ist daran, dass die Verwirklichung dieses Traums mit Ereignisnivellierung verbunden ist. Vorkommnisse, Bewegungen, Emotionen, Biographien, die man unwillkürlich mit den von ihr ausgewählten Räumen, Behältern, architektonischen Fragmenten verbindet, sind aufgesaugt in einem homogenisierenden Abformungsverfahren. Es scheint bei Rachel Whiteread Abscheu vor einer gewissen Art von Artikuliertheit zu geben. Als wolle sie zu einem Allgemeinen, zu einer Ursubstanz zurück. Das hat nichts mit Nostalgie zu tun. Ihr Werk erscheint pauschalisierend und ist trotzdem in die Zukunft gerichtet. Als wolle Rachel Whiteread, nicht ohne unvermeidbares Mitläufertum, unsere modischen Obsessionen von Räumen, Körpern, Ereignissen, Choreographien, spezifischen Objekten endgültig abwehren.

Aber wenn man so redet, ist immer die Qualität der Differenz zu beachten, die Rachel Whiteread hartnäckig wahrt. Sie geht nicht aus sich heraus, sondern lässt die Dinge zu sich kommen. Sie geht in sich, indem sie «über-geht». Sie bleibt vor Ort und investiert hier in ihre weltumspannenden Unterneh-

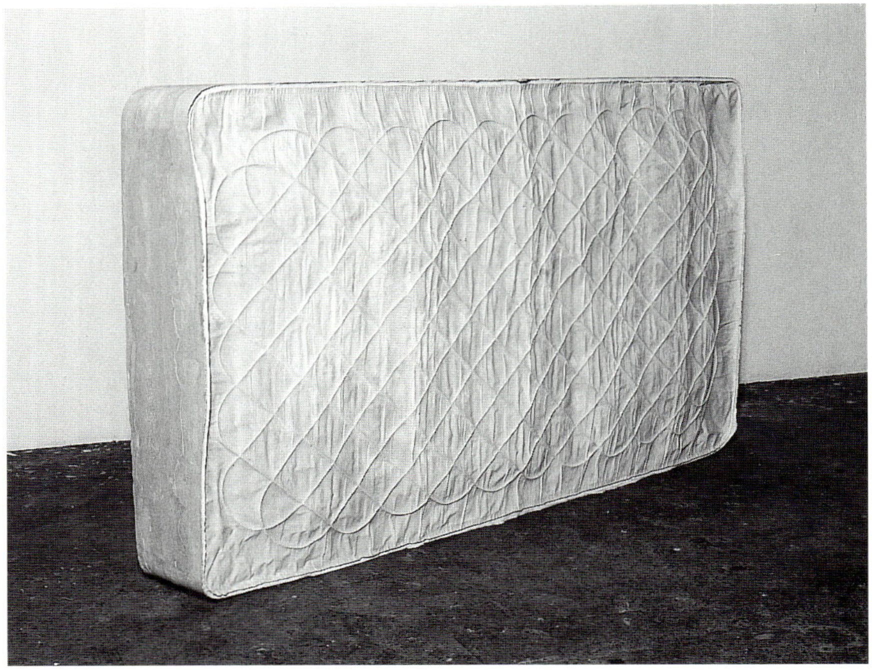

RACHEL WHITEREAD, UNTITLED (FREESTANDING BED), *1991, dental plaster and polystyrene, 41 x 72 x 9" /* OHNE TITEL (FREISTEHENDES BETT), *zahntechnischer Gips und Polystyrol, 104 x 183 x 23 cm.* (PHOTO: ALEX HARTLEY)

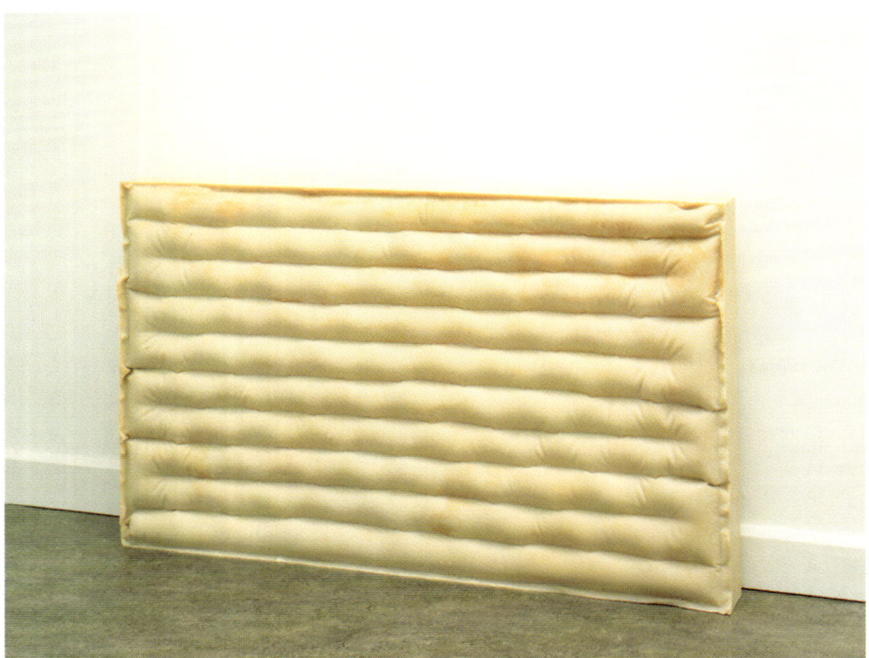

RACHEL WHITEREAD, UNTITLED (LILO), *1992, rubber and neoprene, 9 x 47 x 76 3/8" /* OHNE TITEL (LILO), *Gummi und Neopren, 22 x 120 x 194 cm.* (PHOTO: PETER COX)

mungen. Ihr Kosmos ist kaum auszuschöpfen, selbst wenn sie sich nicht vom Fleck rührt. Die Künstlerin widmet sich unverdrossen dem, was anliegt, und scheut dabei keine Verausgabung.

Für die Abformung eines viktorianischen Arbeiterreihenhauses im Londoner East End, ein Projekt, das in Zusammenarbeit mit den Artangel Trust entstand, beschäftigte Rachel Whiteread ein Team von Ingenieuren und Bauarbeitern. «Wenn das Kunst ist, bin ich Leonardo da Vinci», soll ein Anwohner aus der Nachbarschaft gesagt haben. So viel Aufwand, um Leben und Alltag in Entropie zu überführen. Kein Wunder, dass der Werftarbeiter sich dagegen wie der verkörperte Erfinder von Flugmaschinen vorkam.

Als Bertrand Lavier das Kajütboot *Argo* mit Acrylfarbe bedeckte und die Wirklichkeit eines Schiffes in die Wirklichkeit der Malerei verwandelte, hatte er einen Realitätskern «weggeschafft» und zugleich ins Fundament der Wahrnehmung verwandelt. Und deshalb traf ein Schreiner, der mit *Argo* konfrontiert wurde, den Nagel auf den Kopf, als er bemerkte: «Ich wollte nicht glauben, dass ein Schiff so aussieht.»

Die Dimension von Handgreiflichkeit, die Rachel Whiteread sich zutraut, ist nicht geringer als die von Bertrand Lavier oder Gordon Matta-Clark. Während letzterer in die Häuser eindrang, weil er sie als kompakte zerstörbare Einheit begriff, vollzieht sich der Zugriff bei Rachel Whiteread heimtückischer. Zäh und leise fliessend nämlich, aber nicht minder überwältigend und Tatsachen schaffend. Die Künstlerin präsentiert Abstraktionen, die unmittelbar berühren. Weil lebensweltliche Empathie sich nicht abstellen lässt. Rachel Whiteread bedient sich dieses Reflexes, um ihr plastisches Gemisch porös zu halten. Der Raum wird in seiner Besonderheit darstellbar, gerade weil er von menschlichen Spuren durchzogen und Medium eines Durchgangsgeschehens ist. Da sind tausend Leichen, die in diesen Wannen gewaschen wurden, da hat man selbst auf diesen Matratzen gelegen und ist mit seinen Sprechblasen in einem Eiswürfel gefangen. Und trotzdem interessiert das alles nur am Rande.

Dass es die menschliche Figur nicht braucht, um über den Menschen zu sprechen, ist ein alter Topos unseres Jahrhunderts. Hatte Giacometti noch mittels einer Auszehrung der Körper und Raumdimensionen ein vibrierendes Vorstellungsbild erzeugt, hatte Bruce Nauman noch eine Pseudogeometrisierung von Körperfragmenten vorgeführt und auf diesem Weg die anwesende Abwesenheit des Menschen inszeniert, so vermittelt uns Rachel Whiteread bereits eine Dummie-Erfahrung. Da wird ein grosser imaginärer und zugleich äusserst realer Körper erzeugt, dessen innere Struktur aus Gleichbehandlung besteht und dessen äussere Grenze den Rand unserer Befindlichkeit streift. Den Moment allerdings auch, wo wir aus Nähten platzen und aus Fenstern stürzen.

Hinterhältig ist auch die Haut dieser Skulpturen. Sie schreit nach Berührung, lässt aber Finger oder Hand augenblicklich stocken. Der eindringende Blick stösst auf die Provokation einer allmählich zunehmenden Dichte. – Die Arbeiten aus Gips oder opakem Material verkörpern lediglich das Extrem dieses Prinzips.

Der Prozess des Aufschichtens von Sichtbarkeit schlägt um ins Undurchdringliche. Was aber sichtbar bleibt, ist die Entstehungstiefe dieser Erfahrung. Es scheint so, als möchte Rachel Whiteread den Augapfel herausnehmen und von aussen betrachten. Was dann zu sehen wäre? Keine traurige, aber eine träge Gallerte.

Auch hier soll das letzte Wort Francis Ponge gehören, der aus guten Gründen weniger an einer Geschichte des Auges als vielmehr an einer Geschichte des Kieselsteins interessiert war: «Seit der langsamen Katastrophe des Erkaltens ist die Geschichte dieses Körpers, der mit der Fähigkeit, sich zu erregen, ein für allemal auch jene verloren hat, erneut zu einer einheitlichen Gestalt einzuschmelzen, nur noch die eines steten Zerfalls. Doch in diesem Augenblick tritt etwas anderes ein: kaum ist die Grösse verblichen, beweist das Leben auch schon, dass es nichts mit ihr gemein hat. Sogleich, mit tausend Hilfsmitteln.»[2]

1) Francis Ponge. *Einführung in den Kieselstein und andere Texte.* Fischer-Verlag. Frankfurt 1986. «Das Vergnügen mit der Tür», S. 53.
2) Ibid. S. 79.

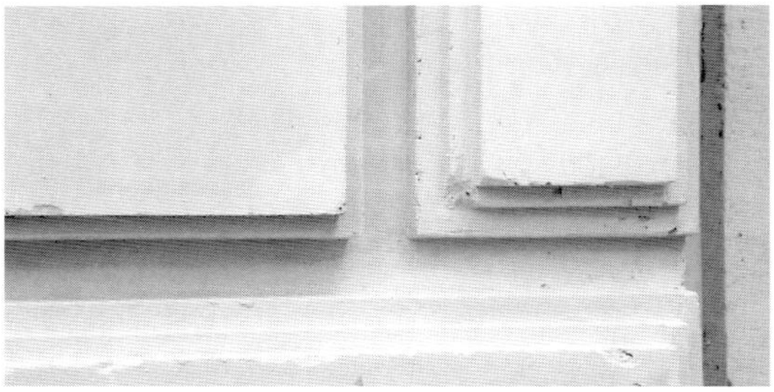

RUDOLF SCHMITZ

THE CURBED MONUMENTALITY OF THE INVISIBLE

"Kings do not touch doors," Francis Ponge writes. "They do not know the joy of giving one of those familiar fillings a gentle or violent shove, then turning around to put it in place again—of holding a door in one's arms... The joy of grabbing the porcelain knob on the belly of one of those tall obstructions to a room; this unexpected body-to-body contact when one takes a measured step, opens one's eyes, and one's entire body adjusts to its new habitat."[1])

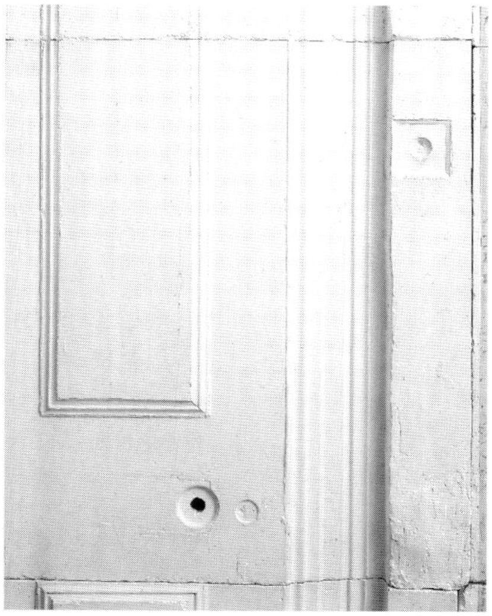

Has Rachel Whiteread felt this joy? Most certainly, although, in her case, it is not a definitive kind of joy. Nonetheless, although her terrain is different, she has succeeded in doing what Francis Ponge tried to do: not to write about things but rather through them, to let them write themselves. The form she has chosen eliminates anthropomorphic residue so that viewers walking through her shows feel slightly fossilized themselves: descendants of a world in movement, trying to sidestep the artist's honey-colored fly catchers, clotted fly catchers that lure the gaze into a diffuse interior despite its clear-cut, sharply delineated contours.

Rachel Whiteread's sculptures permit this kind of entry, even as compressed cores of time and space. "Core" is, of course, not the most suitable word: it is not a question of quality and definition but rather of producing a uniform density of even and indifferent fillings that paradoxically define the artist's attitude with great precision. Whiteread's sculptures incorporate the process of accumulative production, which acts as a constant corrective and processual lining for what the eyes perceive.

RUDOLF SCHMITZ is a freelance art critic living in Frankfurt.

Even her extremely large sculptures like ROOM (1993), a cast of an archetypal room built by the artist during a residency in Berlin, convey a sense of curbed monumentality. This lies in the incisions through the plaster. They transmit a colonialist aura; one is reminded of the Egyptian statues of the gods in Abu Simbel, which were sawed apart for reconstruction on safe, high ground. This lends the whole—despite its terseness—a flavor of playing with building blocks and risking the possibility of other "wrong" combinations.

The potential of wrong combinations, or rather, combination as a device, seems to be targeted in Rachel Whiteread's latest works. TABLE AND CHAIR, made of polyester, rubber, and polystyrene, evokes the drag marks, the afterimages of movement, similar to those registered by a video camera in blinding light. That her work has something to do with blinding is indisputable. It is a blinding compensated by an overwhelmingly haptic counterweight. The invisibility of the space in which we find ourselves has been cast in its entirety so that we can touch and feel it. We have not only the need but also the chance to escape this space whose aura envelops us. Our ties to this space are so existential that we wax triumphant in the face of such a formal solution.

Rachel Whiteread applies a contemporary strategy to the classical dream of mastering fullness on a "grand" scale. It is contemporary because the fulfillment of this dream entails a leveling of events. The occurrences, movements, emotions, biographies that we inevitably associate with her selection of spaces, containers, architectural fragments are sucked into a homogenizing mold. It would seem that Whiteread has a distinct aversion to a certain kind of articulation—as if she were seeking a return to the general, to a primal substance. This has nothing to do with nostalgia. Although her work appears to make sweeping statements, it is still future-oriented. It is as if—despite unavoidable concurrence—she were fending

RACHEL WHITEREAD, UNTITLED (ROOM), detail / OHNE TITEL (RAUM), Detail

RACHEL WHITEREAD, GHOST, Detail / GEIST, Detail

RACHEL WHITEREAD, UNTITLED (ROOM), 1993, plaster, 108¼ x 118 x 137¾" / OHNE TITEL (RAUM), Gips, 275 x 300 x 350 cm. (PHOTO: TATE GALLERY PHOTOGRAPHY DEPARTMENT)

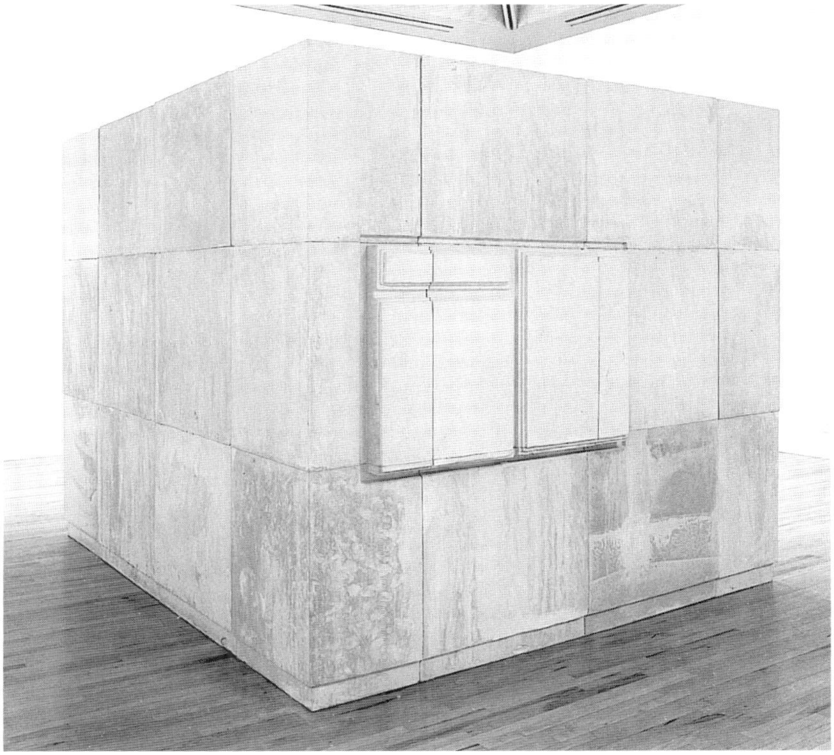

off our fashionable obsessions with spaces, bodies, events, choreographies, specific objects with unmistakable finality.

In the wake of such reflections, we must not underestimate the quality of difference that stubbornly persists in Whiteread's oeuvre. The artist does not reach out; she waits for things to come to her. She withdraws by "drawing in." Her position is stationary, and from there she invests in global enterprises. She stays put to explore her near-inexhaustible universe. The artist goes to infinite lengths in her indefatigable devotion to what is at hand.

To make a cast of a Victorian terrace house in London's East End (a project conceived and carried out in collaboration with Artangel Trust), a team of engineers and construction workers was recruited. "If this is art, then I'm Leonardo da Vinci," a local resident is supposed to have said. Such a great effort to translate life and the everyday into entropy. No wonder the dockworker saw himself as the inventor incarnate of flying machines.

When Bertrand Lavier covered a yacht, the *Argo*, with acrylic paint and transformed the reality of the boat into the reality of painting, he "eliminated" and immediately transformed a core of reality into the fundament of perception. A carpenter's reaction on seeing the *Argo* hits the nail on the head: "I couldn't believe a boat could look like that."

Rachel Whiteread's work is as forcefully haptic as Bertrand Lavier's or Gordon Matta-Clark's. Matta-Clark broke into houses because he read them as compact, destructible units. Whiteread takes a more devious approach: viscous and gently flowing, but no less overwhelming and fabricated. The artist presents abstractions of immediate impact: attendant empathy cannot be tuned out. She avails herself of this reflex to retain the porosity of her sculptural mix. The specific character of space is brought to the fore precisely because human traces have been left behind, and it functions as a medium of transitional events. Thousands of bodies have been washed in these tubs; we have lain on those mattresses ourselves and been frozen in an ice cube, along with our balloons of words. Devices all, and all of only marginal interest.

It is an old topos of our century that we do not need the human figure in order to talk about people. Giacometti was still able to generate his vibrant imagery by means of emaciated figures and spatial dimensions; Bruce Nauman still draws on pseudo-geometrical body fragments to signal the presence of human absence; and now Rachel Whiteread imparts a dummy experience. An enormous, imaginary and yet extremely real body is evoked whose inner structure consists of uniform treatment and whose exterior seems to sideswipe the edge of our state of mind, while zeroing in on the moment when we are about to explode and jump out of windows.

The skin of these sculptures is also insidious. It screams to be touched but instantly halts the movement of fingers or hands. Our penetrating gaze is confronted with the provocation of a gradually increasing density. The pieces made of plaster or opaque material merely incorporate this principle in the extreme.

The process of stratified visibility flips over into impenetrability. What remains visible, however, is the depth at which this experience occurs. It would seem that Rachel Whiteread wants to remove her eyes and observe from outside. And then what would she see? Not sorrowful but lethargic jelly.

The last word shall belong to Francis Ponge again, who had good reason to be more interested in the history of the pebble than of the eye. "Since the slow catastrophe of cooling off, the history of this body—which has forever lost along with the capacity to get excited, the ability to coalesce back into a unified form—can only be the history of inexorable decay. But at that moment something else happens: hardly has greatness faded when life proves that it has nothing in common with greatness. And by means of a thousand devices."[2)]

(Translation: Catherine Schelbert)

1) Francis Ponge, "Das Vergnügen mit der Tür," in *Einführung in den Kieselstein und andere Texte* (Frankfurt: Fischer Verlag), 1986, p. 53.
2) Ibid., p. 79.

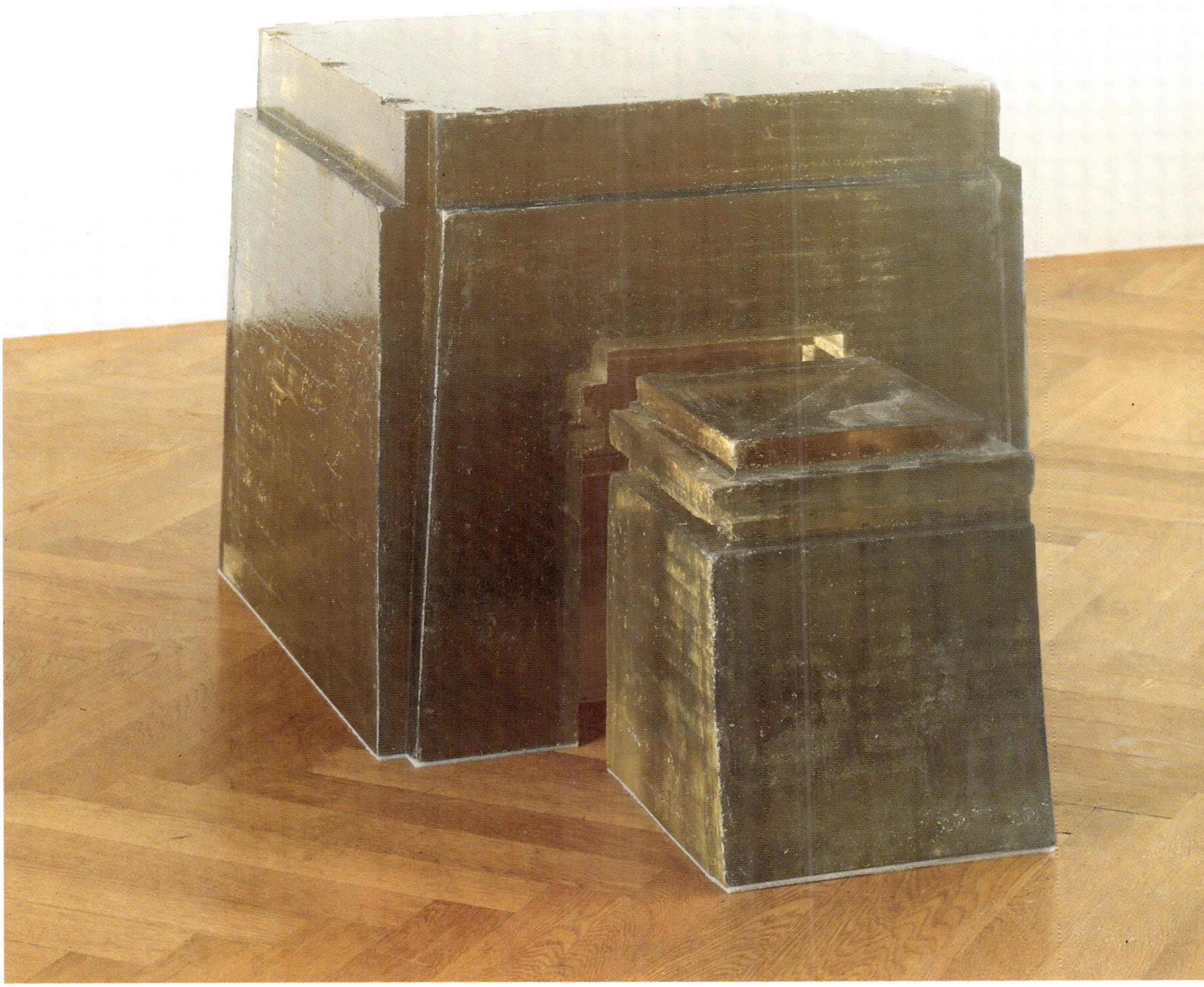

RACHEL WHITEREAD, TABLE AND CHAIR (CLEAR), 1994, resin, 26½ x 47¼ x 29½" /
TISCH UND STUHL (KLAR), Polyesterharz, 67 x 120 x 75 cm. (PHOTO: VOLKER NAUMANN)

About the HOUSE

SIMON WATNEY

PROLOGUE

"The concept is interesting—the idea of something from the inside out."
Jim Dann, local resident, quoted by Ulla Kloster, "If this is art then I'm Leonardo da Vinci," *East London Advertiser,* 4 November, 1993, p. 15.

"They make way for the Queen Elizabeth Gate, a tinselly kitsch embarrassment nailed forever into the heart of London, but see HOUSE *destroyed without a blink, righteously declaring, if asked, that green spaces must be saved from artistic defilement."*
Hugo Young, journalist, "Politicians who give no room to art," *The Guardian,* London, 25 November, 1993, p. 24.

"A surreal whimsy that grows thin with repetition and meagre with increasing scale."
Brian Sewell, art critic, "Ballyhoo and the glittering Prize," *Evening Standard,* London, 4 November, 1993, p. 29.

"As far as I'm concerned, any of the 'thousands of towns and cities across Europe' that Mr. Neilson feels would love to have HOUSE *are welcome to it."*
Counselor Eric Flanders, Chair, Bow Parks Board, letter, *The Independent,* 17 November, 1993, n.p.

"It angered me that Mr. Graham-Dixon's patronising tone made the assumption that the meaning attached to the sculpture was lost on these east Londoners. Why should they give a monkey's about a two-storey block of concrete just because of its 'merits' as a piece of modern art?"
Richard Jackman, letter, *The Independent,* 14 January, 1994, p. 16.

"The hunger to erase HOUSE *so quickly masks an insecurity about the potential for art to communicate in ways which are unheralded and unpredictable."*
James Lingwood, art critic/curator, "Our house is a very nice house," *The Times,* London, 27 November, 1993, n.p.

"A strange and fantastical object which also amounts to one of the most extraordinary public sculptures created by an English artist this century."
Andrew Graham-Dixon, art critic, "This is the house that Rachel built," *The Independent,* London, 2 November, 1993, p. 25.

"It's an amazing piece; a real achievement (...) The whole house could've fallen apart. Concrete is warm and can explode. It's a great feat of engineering."
Al Maltby, builder, "Opinions," *Independent on Sunday,* London, 31 October, 1993, n.p.

"In Bow, neighbours of the ghost house only want to see the back of it—so to speak. Mrs. Gulsun Bodur, from across the road, described it as 'a pain.' She wants, she adds, 'to get rid of it.'"
Dalya Alberge, journalist, "HOUSE of ghostly memory," *The Independent,* London, 26 October, 1993, n.p.

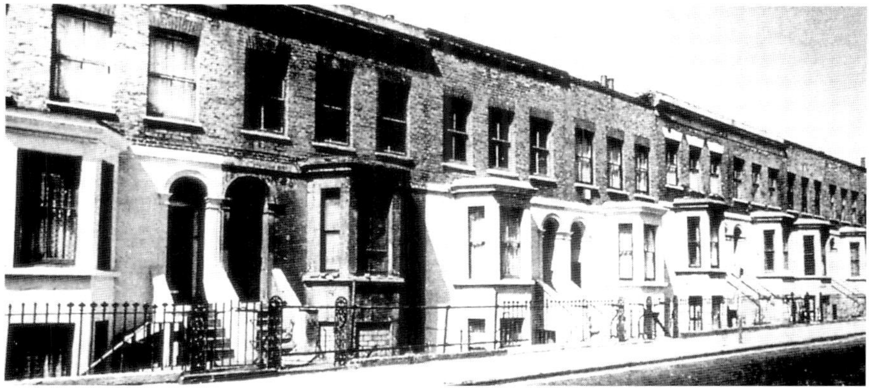

Grove Road early 1980s / Grove Road in den frühen 80er Jahren. (PHOTO: ARTANGEL)

Much of the success of Rachel Whiteread's extraordinary HOUSE resides in its effective resistance of any single, fixed, dominant meaning, or single cluster of meanings. For HOUSE continues to function as a kind of prism which reflects back to us whatever we bring to it, filtered through its own site-specific field of cultural and historical associations. Thus, by subject and technique, HOUSE brings together and aligns questions of house-construction and of housing; our deep ambivalence about domesticity and "family values"; parenting; the relation of the "public" to the "private"; the effects of World War II in British popular memory; the relationship between art criticism and commercial journalism; notions of "neighbourhood"; and so on. Physically demolished, HOUSE remains nonetheless located at a complex intersection between different and frequently conflicting sets of collective memories (and forgettings)—about the gulf between the ideal, imaginary worlds of "childhood" and "home," and our actual remembered (and forgotten) childhoods and homes. And much more besides.

One powerful strand of British public discourse on HOUSE insisted predictably enough—"If this is art then I'm Leonardo da Vinci."[1] Thus tabloid and other journalists laboured mightily to demonstrate that HOUSE was not locally popular in London's East End, in tandem with the political claims to "public opinion" mobilised by some (but not all) elected local government officials. Yet as one group of eighteen local Bow residents explained in a letter to *The Independent:*

"Nobody knows exactly what the balance of local feeling is towards HOUSE *at this juncture. Opinion is divided in Bow as it is nationally (...) response to the work's challenging presence is strong, and its power and validity are hotly debated."*[2]

Such an alignment of the local to the national is important, for HOUSE draws at least as much upon a national history and iconography of terraced housing as it does on the named streets of the East End of London. Commenting on the Turner Prize awarded to Whiteread last year, newspaper art critic Andrew Graham-Dixon argued that the Prize has a useful function insofar as it:

"Focuses attention on how almost primevally backward, how dull, how embarrassingly narrow-minded and ill-informed most discussion of contemporary art in this country remains."[3]

Writing the day after HOUSE's demolition, Graham-Dixon described the baffled response of non-British journalists to "the destruction of a major work by a nationally honoured artist":

"But perhaps they are unaware that there is a venerable history of this sort of thing in England, an old tradition of iconoclasm that stretches back to the days of the Reformation, when religious zealots (...) systematically destroyed the sculpture and painting of the Middle Ages. And perhaps

---

SIMON WATNEY is a London-based writer and critic.

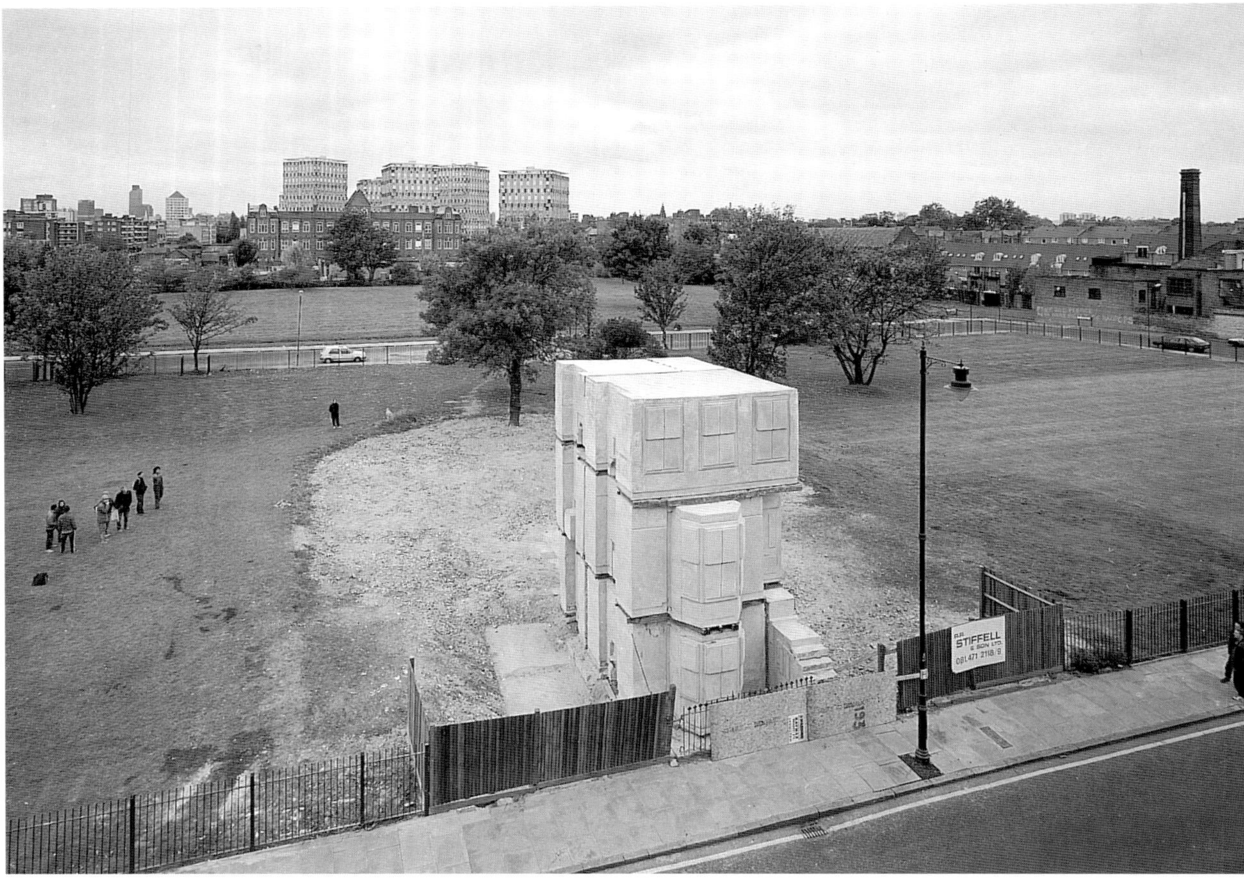

RACHEL WHITEREAD, HOUSE,
Grove Road, London, October 1993–January 1994.
(PHOTO: JOHN DAVIES)

the wreck that was HOUSE *itself amounts to a monument of a peculiarly English kind: a monument to an abiding and virtually fanatical distrust of visual art rooted deep within the British psyche."*[4)]

Unfortunately such a simple explanation cannot account for how Britain managed to produce a complex cultural heritage in the first place, prior to the Reformation, let alone how HOUSE itself came into being, commissioned by the London-based agency, the Artangel Trust, and realised with the assistance of Tarmac Structural Repairs, Beck's Brewery, the Arts Council of Great Britain, the London Arts Board, and The Henry Moore Foundation. Paradoxically, it is as difficult to imagine HOUSE being originally constructed in any other comparable European city as it is to imagine its destruction elsewhere in Europe.

Perhaps not enough attention has been paid to the inside-outness of HOUSE. If they could open, its concrete doors would swing outwards, not inwards, releasing us from our confinement, while simultaneously giving us access from the outside where we stand. While the volumes of the rooms that constitute HOUSE are physically clear, they are psychologically impossible. HOUSE places us in two places at once, in two dimensions—inside and outside. We gaze at its exterior, composed of interior walls, trapped forever outside and inside. HOUSE is an ensemble of rooms, a physical impress of their volume; thus it also carries with it a sense of privacy exposed, of intimate domestic life suddenly open to the world. HOUSE has no secrets. Always we are on the outside, locked out, rejected, shown the door. Always we are also locked inside, unable to escape, cut off, alone. It is this physical and psychic conflation of our senses of inside and outside that is the sculptural ground of HOUSE, its fundamentally uninhabitable character. HOUSE makes no comment whatsoever. The "excessive" responses it has stimulated only serve to demonstrate the power of the themes of ambivalence and conflict with which it engages. Not least of these was its devastating aloneness, signified in only too crumblingly material concrete—like any other bunker; and finally in its absence, its own removal into the wider conflicting field of popular memory.

The discourse of vandalism surrounding the HOUSE project, while interesting, was largely predictable, as previously conflicting lobbies sought to "claim" it—either as "masterpiece," or as "eyesore/spoof." The "HOUSE affair" teaches us many things, not least the inadequacy of political claims concerning the supposed value of works of art according to their "accessibility" or their supposed "elitism." A minority is not necessarily an elite. Nor is "accessibility" an intrinsic universal aesthetic value. HOUSE continues to engage the spectator with powerful feelings of both exclusion and entrapment. Taken in the context of all that houses may signify, from longing for past happiness to panic-memories of childhood hell, from questions of homelessness to the "conservation" of houses as museums, HOUSE could not have been uncontroversial. Its triumph as a work of art, however, lies not in the index of attendant controversy, but in the confident eloquence of its refusal to take sides.

I would like to thank James Lingwood and the staff of the Artangel Trust, London for providing me with access to press cuttings concerning HOUSE.

1) Ulla Kloster, "If this is art then I'm Leonardo da Vinci," *East London Advertiser,* 4 November, 1993, p. 15.
2) Nigel Glendinning et. al., *The Independent,* London, 20 November, 1993, n.p.
3) Andrew Graham-Dixon, "I don't know much about art, but I know what I hate," *The Independent,* London, 24 November, 1993, p. 26.
4) Andrew Graham-Dixon, "Artless earthmover finally brings 'House' down," *The Independent,* London, 12 January, 1994, n.p.

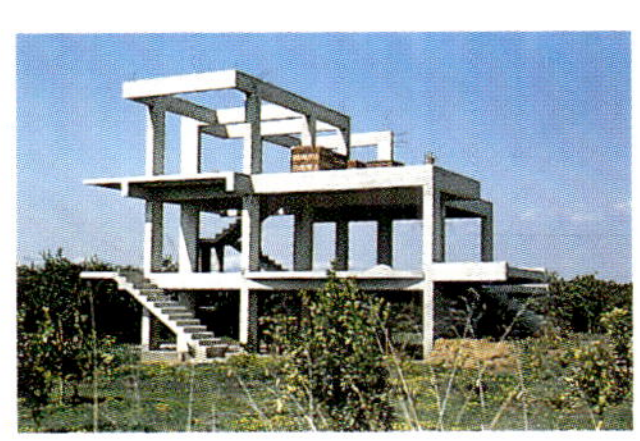

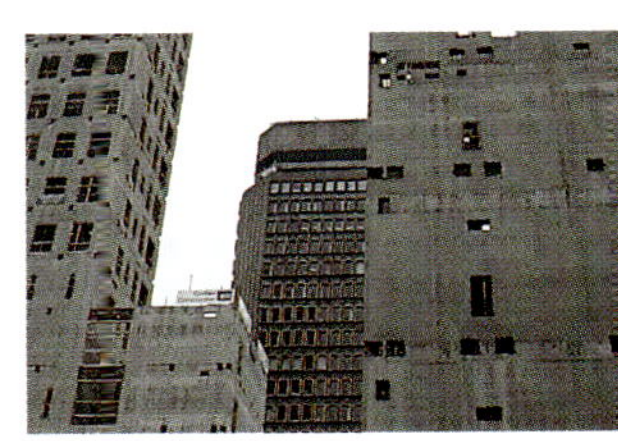

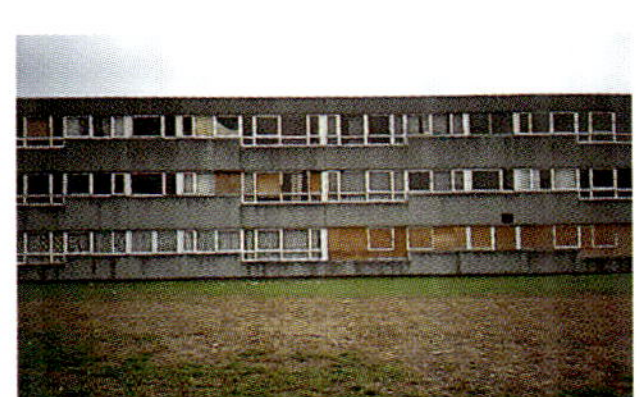

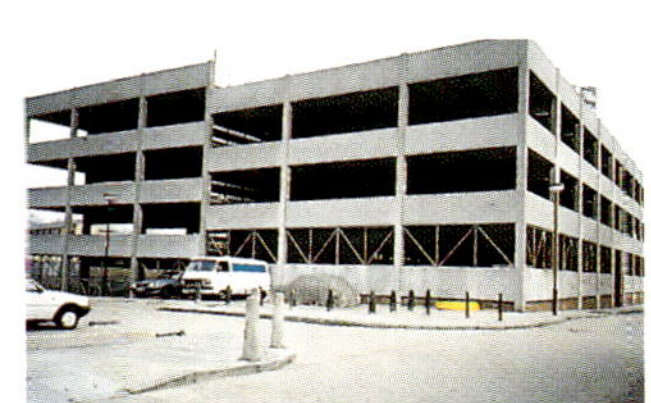

Construction, Greece, 1993 / Baukonstruktion, Griechenland.

Liverpool Street, London, 1990.

Hackney, East London, 1991.

Hackney, East London, 1990.

(PHOTOS: RACHEL WHITEREAD)

Über HOUSE

SIMON WATNEY

PROLOG

«Die Idee ist interessant – etwas von innen nach aussen Gekehrtes.»
Jim Dann, Anwohner, zitiert nach Ulla Kloster, «If this is art then I'm Leonardo da Vinci», *East London Advertiser,* 4. November 1993, S. 15.

«Für das Queen Elizabeth Gate, einen aufgemotzten, peinlichen Kitsch, der sich für immer ins Herz von London bohrt, machen sie Platz; aber HOUSE *lassen sie ohne mit der Wimper zu zucken zerstören und erklären selbstgerecht auf Anfrage auch noch, dass man Grünflächen vor künstlerischer Verschandelung bewahren muss.»*
Hugo Young, Journalist, «Politicians who give no room to art», *The Guardian,* London, 25. November 1993, S. 24.

«Eine surreale Absonderlichkeit, die durch die Wiederholung an Substanz verliert und mit wachsender Grösse eher weniger wird.»
Brian Sewell, Kunstkritiker, «Ballyhoo and the glittering Prize», *Evening Standard,* London, 4. November 1993, S. 29.

«Es ärgert mich, dass Mr. Graham-Dixon mit seinem gönnerhaften Ton so tut, als seien die Ost-Londoner zu blöd, die Bedeutung der Skulptur zu verstehen. Warum sollen sie sich um einen zweistöckigen Betonklotz scheren, bloss weil es sich angeblich um moderne Kunst handelt?»
Richard Jackman, Brief, *The Independent,* 14. Januar 1994, S. 16.

«Es ist ein erstaunliches Stück, eine richtige Errungenschaft (...) Das ganze Haus hätte auseinanderfallen können. Beton ist warm und kann bersten. Es ist eine technische Meisterleistung.»
Al Maltby, Baumeister, «Opinions», *Independent on Sunday,* London, 31. Oktober 1993, o. S.

«Hinter dem Drang, HOUSE *so schnell abzureissen, verbirgt sich eine Unsicherheit, ausgelöst durch die Möglichkeit der Kunst, auf ungewohnten und unvorhersehbaren Wegen zu kommunizieren.»*
James Lingwood, Kunstkritiker/Kurator, «Our house is a very nice house», *The Times,* London, 27. November 1993, o. S.

«Ein ebenso seltsames wie phantastisches Objekt, das sich als eine der aussergewöhnlichsten öffentlichen Skulpturen erweist, die in diesem Jahrhundert von englischen Künstlern geschaffen wurden.»
Andrew Graham-Dixon, Kunstkritiker, «This is the house that Rachel built», *The Independent,* London, 2. November 1993, S. 25.

«Wenn es nach mir geht, können die ‹Tausende von Städten und Orten in ganz Europa›, von denen Mr. Neilson meint, dass sie HOUSE *gern bei sich sähen, es gern haben.»*
Ratsmitglied Eric Flanders, Vorsitzender des Bow Parks Board, Brief, *The Independent,* 17. November 1993, o. S.

«In Bow sähen die Nachbarn das Geisterhaus am liebsten von hinten – sozusagen. Mrs. Gulsun Bodur, die auf der anderen Strassenseite wohnt, nennt es ‹eine Qual›. Und sie möchte, sagt sie, ‹es loswerden›.»
Dalya Alberge, Journalistin, «HOUSE of ghostly memory», *The Independent,* London, 26. Oktober 1993, o. S.

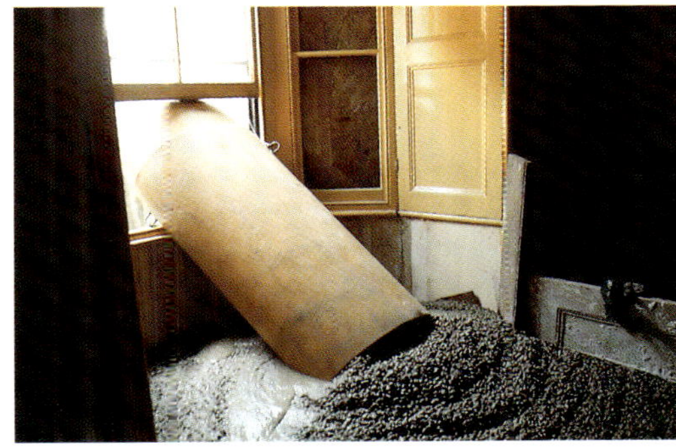

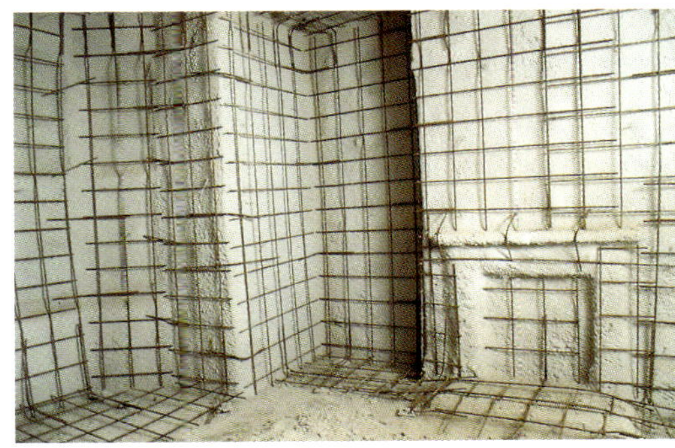

(PHOTOS: RACHEL WHITEREAD)

HOUSE, in progress / während der Arbeit.

HOUSE, in construction / im Bau, 1993.

Der Erfolg von Rachel Whitereads aussergewöhnlichem HOUSE beruht zum grössten Teil darauf, dass sich das Stück jedweder ausschliesslichen, festgelegten, dominanten Bedeutung bzw. einer bestimmten Interpretation verweigert, denn es funktioniert wie eine Art Prisma, das uns widerspiegelt, was immer wir an Bedeutung hineinlegen, gefiltert durch seine eigene Situationsspezifik der kulturellen und historischen Assoziationen. So wirft HOUSE in Thema und Technik Fragen zum Hausbau und zum Wohnen an sich auf; es verweist auf unsere tiefe Ambivalenz gegenüber Häuslichkeit und «familiären Werten»; auf Elternschaft; auf die Beziehung zwischen «Öffentlichem» und «Privatem»; auf die Spuren des Zweiten Weltkriegs im Gedächtnis der britischen Öffentlichkeit; auf die Beziehung zwischen Kunstkritik und kommerziellem Journalismus; auf Vorstellungen von «Nachbarschaft» und so weiter. Auch wenn HOUSE inzwischen physisch nicht mehr existiert, markiert es doch weiterhin eine komplexe Überschneidung unterschiedlicher und häufig widersprüchlicher Ebenen von kollektivem Gedächtnis (und Vergessen) – jene Kluft zwischen den idealimaginären Welten von «Kindheit» und «Zuhause» einerseits und jener Kindheit, jenem Zuhause, wie wir es tatsächlich erinnern (und vergessen haben) andererseits. Und noch viel mehr.

Wie nicht anders zu erwarten, machte sich eine Fraktion im Diskurs der britischen Öffentlichkeit besonders laut bemerkbar: «Wenn das Kunst ist, bin ich Leonardo da Vinci.»[1)] Die Boulevardpresse und andere Journalisten gaben sich also alle Mühe, zu zeigen, dass HOUSE im Londoner East End vollkommen unpopulär war, in schöner Eintracht übrigens mit dem politischen Ruf nach «Volkes Stimme», den einige örtliche Regierungsbeamte (allerdings nicht alle) erhoben. Immerhin erklärte aber auch eine Gruppe von 18 Bow-Anwohnern in einem Brief an *The Independent*.

«Niemand weiss genau, wie die Stimmung gegenüber HOUSE *im Moment eigentlich wirklich ist. Die Meinungen sind geteilt, in Bow ebenso wie im ganzen Land (...) die Reaktion auf die provokante Präsenz der Arbeit ist stark, seine Ausstrahlungskraft und sein Wert sind heiss umstritten.»*[2)]

Diese Verknüpfung von Lokalem und Nationalem ist insofern wichtig, als HOUSE mit der nationalen Geschichte und Ikonographie von Reihenhäusern mindestens ebensoviel zu tun hat wie mit den betreffenden Strassen des Londoner East Ends. In seinem Kommentar zur Turner-Preis-Verleihung an Whiteread im letzten Jahr meint der Zeitungs-Kunstkri-

---

SIMON WATNEY lebt als Autor und Kritiker in London.

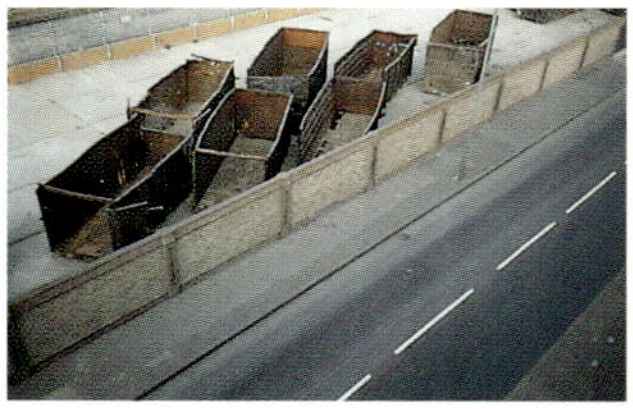

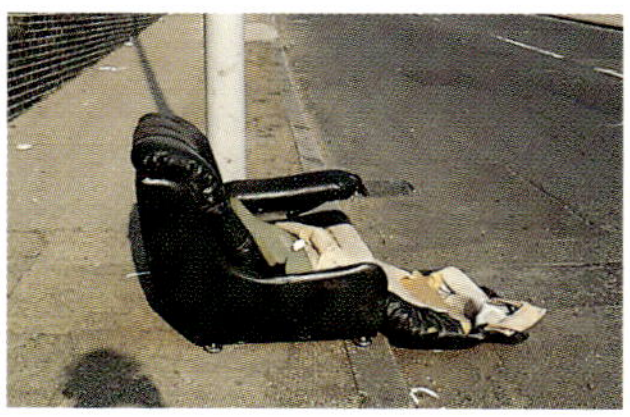

Hackney, East London, 1990.

Carpenter's Road, East London, 1989.

(PHOTOS: RACHEL WHITEREAD)

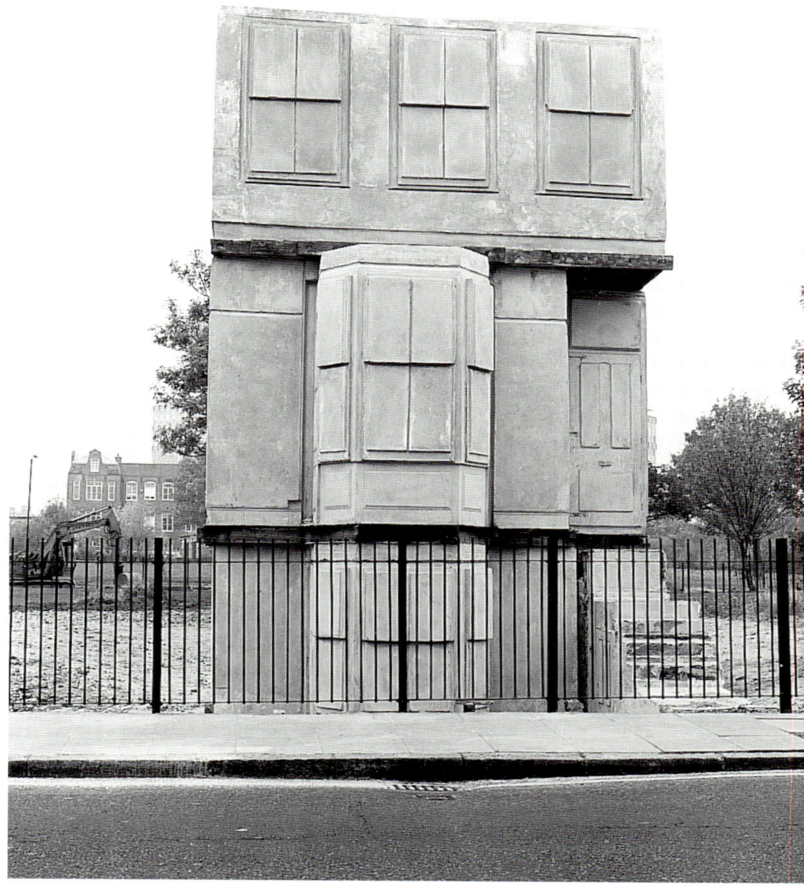

RACHEL WHITEREAD, HOUSE, Grove Road, London, 1993 (Vorderansicht / front view). (PHOTO: SUSAN ORMEROD)

tiker Andrew Graham-Dixon, dass der Preis insofern eine nützliche Funktion hat, als er:

«Ein Licht darauf wirft, wie schon fast steinzeitlich zurückgeblieben, wie stumpfsinnig, wie unglaublich engstirnig und uninformiert die Diskussion über zeitgenössische Kunst in diesem Land sich zeigt.»[3]

Am Tag nach der Zerstörung von HOUSE beschrieb Graham-Dixon das ungläubige Staunen ausländischer Journalisten über «die Zerstörung eines wichtigen Werks von einer im Lande hochangesehenen Künstlerin»:

«Aber vielleicht ist ihnen nicht klar, dass England in dieser Hinsicht bereits auf eine beachtliche Geschichte zurückblickt, auf eine alte Tradition des Ikonoklasmus, die bis in die Tage der Reformation zurückreicht, als religiöse (...) Eiferer systematisch die Skulptur und Bildhauerei des Mittelalters zerstörten. Und vielleicht stellt der Trümmerhaufen, der von HOUSE *übrigblieb, selbst ein Monument der besonderen englischen Art dar: ein Monument des anhaltenden und im Grunde fanatischen Argwohns gegenüber der bildenden Kunst, der tief in der britischen Psyche wurzelt.»*[4]

Ganz so einfach lässt sich leider nicht erklären, wie Grossbritannien überhaupt vor der Reformation ein so umfangreiches kulturelles Erbe zustande brachte, ganz zu schweigen davon, wie HOUSE – im Auftrag der Londoner Agentur Artangel Trust – entstehen und realisiert werden konnte mit Hilfe der Tarmac Structural Repairs, der Beck's-Brauerei, des Arts Council of Great Britain, des London Arts Board und der Henry Moore Foundation. Paradoxerweise lässt sich die Errichtung von HOUSE in irgendeiner anderen vergleichbaren europäischen Stadt ebensowenig vorstellen wie dessen Zerstörung andernorts in Europa.

Vielleicht ist der Umkehrung von Innen und Aussen bei HOUSE nicht genügend Aufmerksamkeit geschenkt worden. Wenn sich die Betontüren öffnen liessen, würden sie nach aussen schwingen, nicht nach innen, und uns aus unserer Eingeschränktheit erlösen, während wir zugleich von unserem aussen gelegenen Standpunkt ins Innere gelangten. Im physischen Sinne ist das Volumen der Räume von HOUSE klar, im psychologischen Sinn jedoch unmöglich. Das Stück versetzt uns an zwei Orte gleichzeitig, in zwei Dimensionen – nach innen und nach aussen. Unser Blick fällt auf die Aussenseite, die sich aus Innenwänden zusammensetzt, und bleibt so ständig im Innen und Aussen verhaftet. HOUSE ist ein Ensemble aus Räumen, ein physischer Abdruck ihres Inhalts; und darin liegt etwas von exponierter Privatheit, von intimem häuslichem Leben, das der Welt plötzlich zugänglich wird. HOUSE hat keine Geheimnisse. Immer sind wir draussen, ausgesperrt, zurückgewiesen, der Tür verwiesen. Und immer sind wir auch im Inneren eingeschlossen, unfähig zu entkommen, abgeschnitten, allein. Eben diese physische und psychische Verschmelzung von Innen und Aussen macht das skulpturale Fundament von HOUSE aus, seinen letztlich uneinnehmbaren Charakter. Nichtsdestoweniger gibt HOUSE selbst keine Deutung von irgend etwas. Die «übertriebenen» Reaktionen, die es auslöste, zeigen nur die Wucht der Ambivalenz und der Konflikte, um die es hier geht. Dazu gehörte nicht zuletzt die verheerende Vereinzelung, die auch in dem bröckeligen Beton zum Ausdruck kam – wie bei irgendeinem herumstehenden alten Bunker. Und jetzt, da das Objekt nicht mehr da ist, geht es in seiner Absenz ins erweiterte Konfliktfeld des öffentlichen Gedächtnisses ein.

Die Art von Diskurs, mit der sich die Leute über das HOUSE-Projekt hermachten, ist zwar interessant, war aber weitgehend vorhersehbar, da die streitenden Parteien es schon im Vorfeld entweder zum «Meisterwerk» «kürten» oder zum «Schandfleck» bzw. «Schwindel» erklärten. Die «HOUSE-Affäre» lehrt uns manches, nicht zuletzt, wie unangemessen es ist, wenn die Politik den angeblichen Wert eines Kunstwerks nach seiner «leichten Verständlichkeit» bzw. seinem angeblich «elitären Charakter» bemisst. Eine Minderheit ist nicht unbedingt eine Elite. Und «leichte Verständlichkeit» ist kein universal-ästhetischer Wert. HOUSE verwickelt den Betrachter auch weiterhin in starke Gefühle sowohl der Ausgeschlossenheit als auch des Gefangenseins. Wenn man das Stück im Kontext all dessen sieht, wofür Häuser stehen, von der Sehnsucht nach vergangenem Glück bis zu angstbesetzten Erinnerungen an die Hölle der Kindheit, von Problemen der Obdachlosigkeit bis zur «Konservierung» von Häusern als Museen, dann musste es einfach Kontroversen auslösen. Sein Triumph als Kunstwerk aber liegt nicht in der Zahl der provozierten Konflikte, sondern in der selbstbewussten Rhetorik seiner Weigerung, sich auf irgendeine Seite zu schlagen. *(Übersetzung: Nansen)*

Ich danke James Lingwood und den Mitarbeitern von Artangel Trust, London, für die Zurverfügungstellung der Presseartikel über HOUSE.

1) Ulla Kloster, «If this is art then I'm Leonardo da Vinci», *East London Advertiser*, 4. November 1993, S. 15.
2) Nigel Glendinning et. al., *The Independent*, London, 20. November 1993, o. S.
3) Andrew Graham-Dixon, «I don't know much about art, but I know what I hate», *The Independent*, London, 24. November 1993, S. 26.
4) Andrew Graham-Dixon, «Artless earthmover finally brings ‹House› down», *The Independent*, London, 12. Januar 1994.

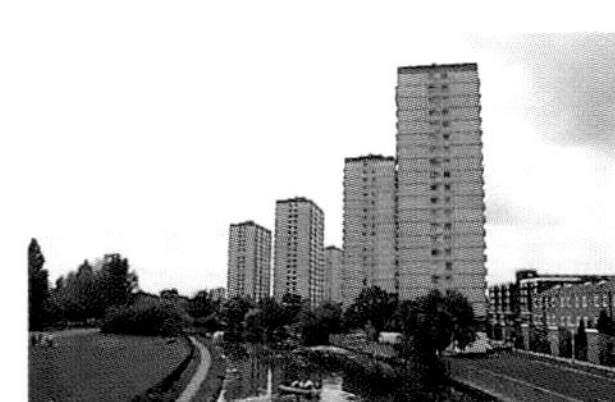

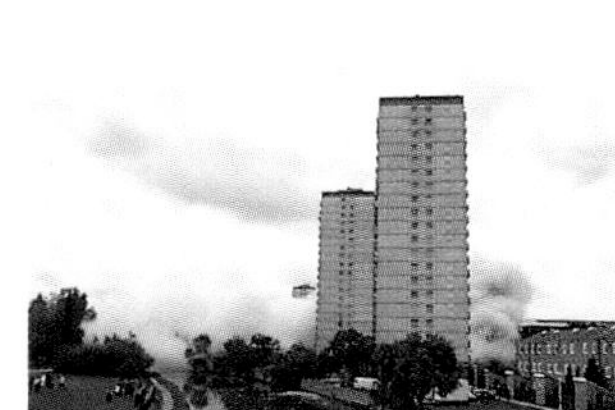

Hochhaussprengung, Hackney, East London 1993 / Towerblock destruction. (PHOTOS: RACHEL WHITEREAD)

EDITION FOR PARKETT

RACHEL WHITEREAD

SWITCH, 1994

object, plaster (prestia-ortho) and brass,

3½ x 3½ x 1⅛"

Edition of 60, signed and numbered

SCHALTER, 1994

Objekt, Gips (prestia ortho) und Messing

9 x 9 x 3 cm

Auflage: 60, signiert und numeriert

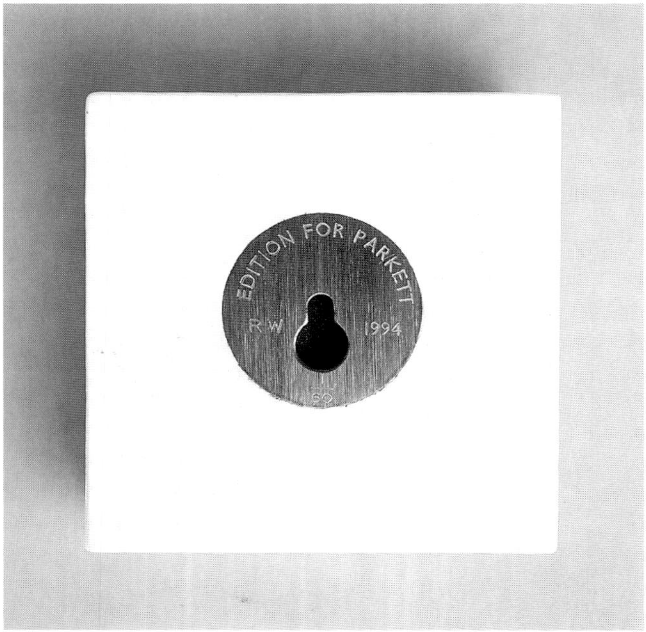

PHOTO: MANCIA/BODMER

INGRID SCHAFFNER

Cursive

There's an impulse at hand in contemporary art which one might call cursive. It comes out of the interstice between writing and drawing, amplifying images and gestures embedded in script to render writing impenetrably abstract or subversively graphic. Too undisciplined to be bound by any single style or approach—Florine Stettheimer's calligraphic painting and André Masson's spat-out ink-blots are equally cursive—it bridles against the strictures of style and stylization. And though many of its protagonists are painters, their work is based on lines, not brushstrokes. All the better to circumscribe the monoliths of art history and annotate its margins.

The cursive focuses on writing as a graphic practice. Sitting down to compose, author Roland Barthes paused over "a beautiful sheet of paper and a good pen..."

Although words may or may not be drawn into play, the impulse does seem to have gained a certain vitality in the wake of the text-driven art of the past decade. Appearing as an extension of the documentation of conceptual art, writing emerged as commonplace to art of the eighties. As unembellished as the voice of Joe Friday, block-lettered signs stated art's subject and content in the form of a clear and concrete message. However ironical, these authoritarian addresses apparently enjoyed the postmodern pleasure of the text quite literally. So that even in terms of this work's discourse, reading supplanted the visual activity of looking at art.

By contrast, the figments of language uncovered by the cursive sink pleasure back into the body of writing. An image of this body lies in the stuttering, uttering script of Cy Twombly's art. As his hand

"I feel my hand move, turn, join, dive and lift... delete or expand a line, taking the space right up to the margin, thus constructing from the apparently functional lines of the letter a space that is quite simply that of a work of art." [1)]

While of letters themselves, avatar of punk Vivienne Westwood recalls, "When I was five, I hated copying from the blackboard because I'd do my R's going round and round like snails because it looked prettier, yet I'd get a slap for it." [2)] An aficionado of bad behavior and abuse, Antonin Artaud admits that "since a certain day in October 1939 I have never again written without drawing." [3)]

moves, sometimes haltingly, other times with decisive speed, between actions of jotting, scribbling, scratching, sweeping, occluding, deleting, deliberating, and dotting, it renders marks which are legible—however impenetrable.[4)] The cursive impulse cultivates the same graphology, making it more or less abstract. In Donald Powley's paintings, the body of writing dissolves into a skeleton or ghost: a bit of found script, copied over and over again disappears in a surfeit of measured drips, leaving only the viscous traces of *Mrs. Sadie Henderson.* While in Jean-Michel Basquiat's

---

INGRID SCHAFFNER is a writer and curator who lives in New York.

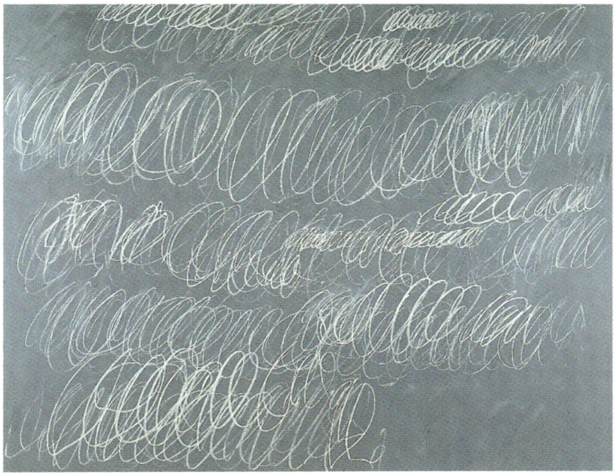

CY TWOMBLY, UNTITLED, NEW YORK CITY, 1967, crayon and oil on canvas, 58 x 70" / OHNE TITEL, NEW YORK CITY, Kreide und Öl auf Leinwand, 147,3 x 178 cm.

work, that body humps and squeals, along a graphic—almost audible—chain of signs linked through a traffic of unseen associations.

At its most non-representational, and impulsive, the cursive embodies an element of automatism. As practiced so diligently by the surrealists, this involved any number of expressive techniques meant to invoke, under trance-like conditions, "the actual functioning of thought."[5] However, in its cursive mode, stripped of any paranormal preoccupations, the automatic accounts for this art's simultaneously obsessive and detached quality of line. Mapping the terrain of his bubble-and-squeak landscapes, Carroll Dunham draws constantly, almost convulsively, though not unconsciously. "I'm very fussy about it..." he says, "I know when I'm in an area I don't want my work to be..."[6]

Surrendering her hand to chance, Elliott Puckette allows the luminous lines of her paintings to roil evenly and automatically, in and out of the medium space of their dark grounds. Like Twombly's blackboard paintings, these pictures contain a measure of unruliness, as if some student has taken off on a calligraphic spree, hell-bent on obliterating the handwriting model. These antisocial implications (remember what happened to Vivienne when she fiddled with her R's) fuel the cursive impulse.

"It must be conceded by everyone that any system of writing which does not lead to an automatic style embodying legibility, rapidity, ease and endurance is a failure."[7]

Prior to typewriters and word-processors, fine penmanship was once an enviable skill and expressive device. Social and business prospects were presumably dependant upon the quality of one's handwriting, which stood to be improved by applying oneself to drills in a copy book, which mercifully "kills individuality and makes freedom of movement possible."[8] In light of this creative euthanasia, it's not without irony to find the exercises of good style coopted by the cursive. Lari Pittman's use of calligraphic numbers, writing and silhouettes shows good penmanship deployed into describing a transgressive realm of homosexual innuendoes, memento mori attributes, and gothic decorations.

AMY SILLMAN, BIG MEAN MOM, 1993, gouache and ink on wood, 60 x 50" / DICKE BÖSE MUTTI, Gouache und Tinte auf Holz, 152,4 x 127 cm.

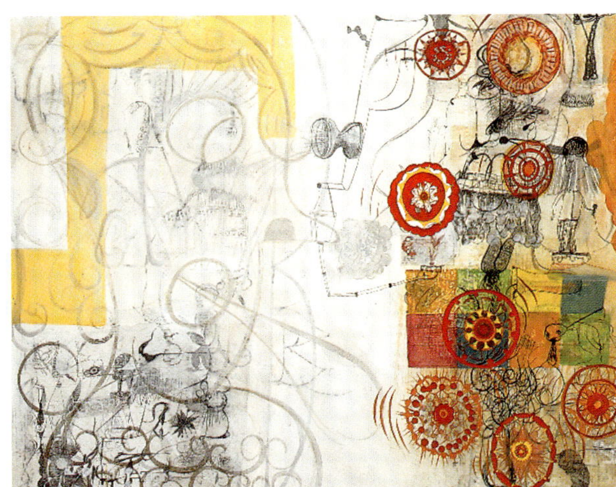

Almost esoteric, the art of writing seems to belong to past times and distant places: medieval monks bending over manuscripts, a Turk sending a message to god, a Chinese poet penning words inseparable from pictures, a real Lothario composing a sonnet, an art nouveau poster insinuating absinthe. The cur-

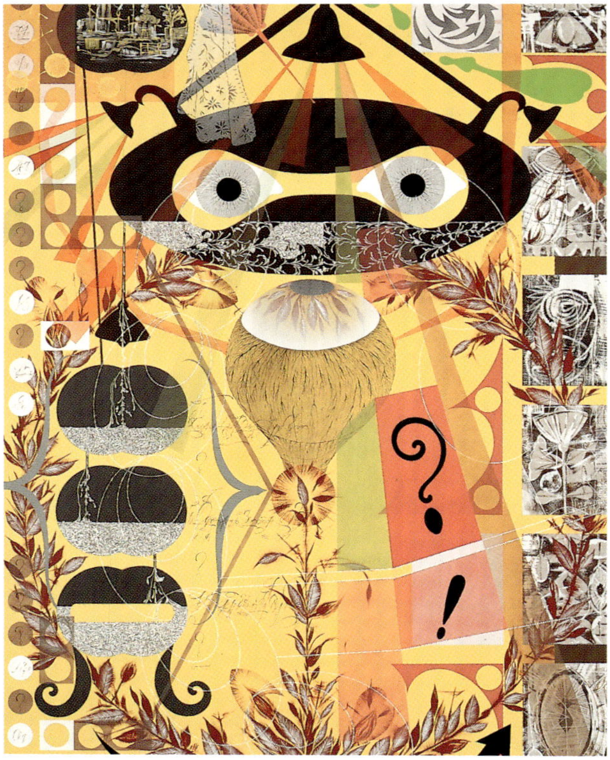

LARI PITTMAN, THE SOUNDS OF BELIEVE, TO AN ATHEIST, ARE VERY TOUCHING, 1988, acrylic on panel, 96 x 64" / DIE TÖNE DES GLAUBENS BERÜHREN EINEN ATHEISTEN SEHR, Acryl auf Holz, 244 x 162,5 cm.

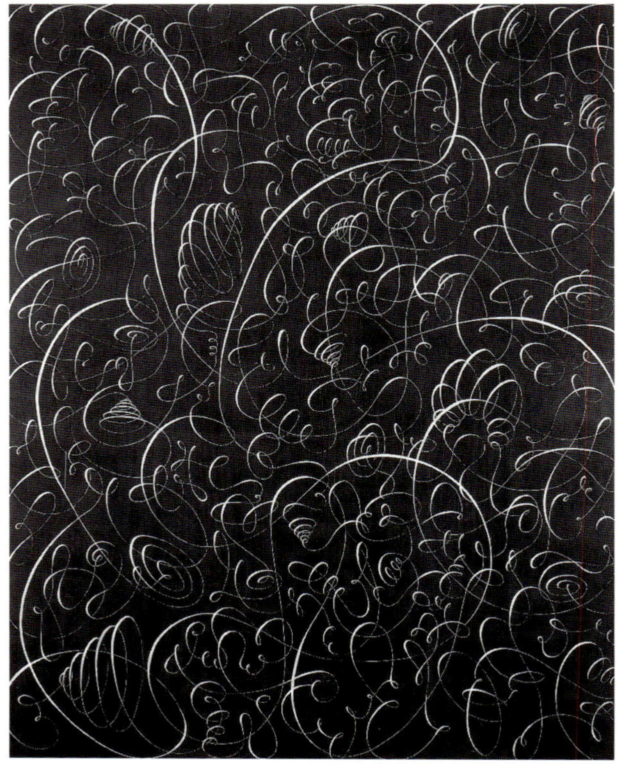

ELLIOTT PUCKETTE, MALEC, 1993, ink, gesso and kaolin on wood, 60 x 48" / Tinte, Kreide und Kaolin auf Holz, 152,4 x 122 cm.

sive exploits these associations, using calligraphy to conjure associations outside the designated territories of art and move into otherwise inaccessible ground. Pittman's post-pop calligraphy veers into the darkened niches of a nineteenth century salon. Amy Sillman's swooping lines and careful curves draw (in part) on Near Eastern scripts, constructing patterned scrims, like the latticed screens between harem and street, through which her paintings' drolleries are only partially disclosed.

Despite curiosity evinced in different cultures and histories, cursive never lingers or dwells so long as to become anachronistic or colonial. It's too eclectic. With the passion of a collector, the cursive is always on the look-out, rifling through wardrobes, film-stills, first-aid manuals, tattoo parlors, curiosity shops, rare books, comic books, bestiaries, beauty parlors, museums, and trash looking for whatever catches its eye. This is the aesthetic of the wunderkammer, cluttered with objects that verge on fetishes, from which are wrought idiosyncratic pictures of time and place based on the ephemeral. And as the wunderkammer is to a museum something of an arcade, the cursive is to the "masterpiece" something of a cartoon.

Cartoons play a particular role in relationship to paintings that has much to do with the privilege cursive confers on drawing. Originally *cartoons* were a method for transferring a sketch onto a surface prepared for fresco painting. Only their tracery survived, as the cartoons themselves were pricked with holes and subsequently destroyed to mark a picture's outlines.[9] Since slipping out from beneath painting's oppressive dominion, cartoons have assumed the identity of satiric drawings. Often calligraphic in style, annotated with words, aimed at undermining the status quo, it's now the cartoon that wounds.

By dint of their sly aversion to standards of good taste, cartoons make excellent vehicles for the cursive impulse. Elliott Green orchestrates a silly symphony of perverted bear, dog, and human hybrids into paintings that make an anxious and grotesque mockery of the medium's most sublime conceits. Nancy Spero and Sue Williams are two of a league of artists who have slipped into the arena of painting, with a cartoon weaponry aimed at overtaking a traditionally masculine domain with expressly feminine imageries and issues. Animating the classics, Megan Williams whips Mickey Mouse into a pornographic little beater.

Perhaps what endows cursive with its potential in terms of contemporary practice is its facility for folding the postmodern project of cultural revision in on itself. A critique aimed at reevaluating established canons and accommodating different readings has always been endemic to the cursive impulse. In that it takes delectation in difference, the cursive couples the erotic energy of copying, vested in writing and drawing, with the imaginative possibilities of illegibility. It gets the model wrong, in order to delineate its own desires in terms of an art which is willfully expressive and forcefully inchoate, in order to communicate some otherwise unspeakable impulse.

1) Roland Barthes (from his preface to R. Druet and H. Grégoire's *The Civilization of Writing*, 1976), quoted in Georges Jean, *Writing: The Story of Alphabets and Scripts*, Jenny Oates, trans. (New York, 1992), p. 196.
2) Vivienne Westwood quoted in Marion Hume: "Portrait of a Former Punk," *Vogue*, September, 1994, p. 208.
3) Antonin Artaud quoted in Jacques Derrida, "Maddening the Subjectile," reprinted in *Boundaries: Writing and Drawing*, Yale French Studies no. 84, (New Haven: Yale University, 1994), p. 160.
4) cf. Roland Barthes, *Cy Twombly: Works on Paper*, "The Responsibility of Forms," Richard Howard, trans., (Berkeley and Los Angeles: The University of California Press, 1985), pp. 157–176.
5) Making it nearly synonymous with automatism, André Breton defined "surrealism" as "pure psychic automatism by whose means it is intended to express verbally, or in writing, or in any other manner, the actual functioning of thought." In "Manifeste du surréalisme," (1924), quoted in Marcel Jean, ed., *The Autobiography of Surrealism*, New York, 1980, p. 123.
6) Artist interviewed by Carol Eckman, exhibition catalogue *Carroll Dunham: Drawings 1988–91*, (New York: David Nolan Gallery, 1992), p. 5.
7) A.N. Palmer, *The Palmer Method of Business Writing*, New York, 1992, p. 5.
8) ibid, p. 2.
9) The scarified surface of a spent cartoon creates an intriguing point of historical intersection between drawing and tattoos.

ANTONIN ARTAUD, AUTOPORTRAIT, 24 juin 1947.

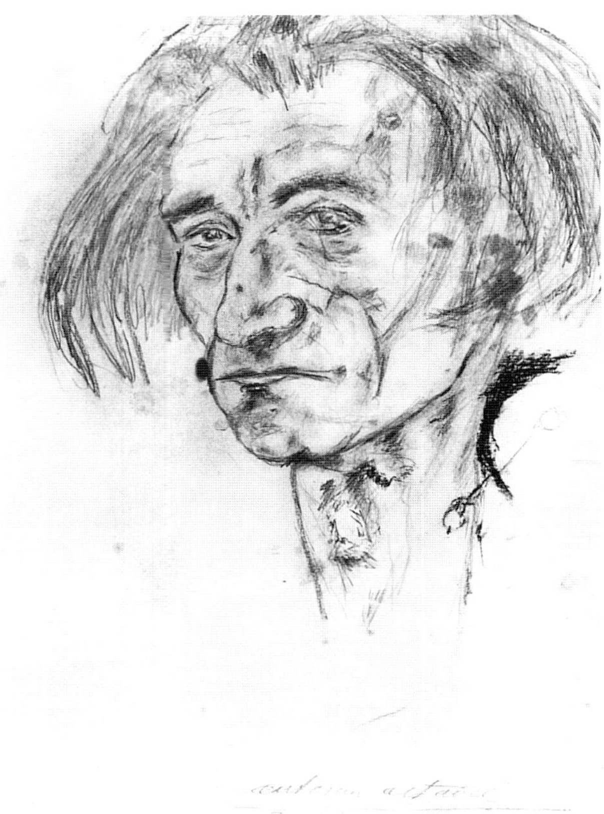

INGRID SCHAFFNER

Das Kursive

In der Kunst unserer Zeit ist eine Tendenz spürbar, die sich mit dem Begriff «kursiv» belegen liesse. Sie entspringt dem Grenzbereich zwischen Schreiben und Zeichnen: in der Schrift eingegrabene Bilder und Gesten werden übersteigert, so dass das Geschriebene unergründlich abstrakt oder subversiv bildhaft wird. Zu undiszipliniert, als dass sie sich in eine einzige Stilrichtung oder Methode hineinzwingen liesse – die kalligraphischen Malereien Florine Stettheimers sind ebenso kursiv wie André Massons gespritzte Tintenkleckse –, widersetzt sie sich jeglicher Einengung von Stil und Stilisierung. Und obgleich viele Protagonisten dieser Tendenz Maler sind, bilden Linien, nicht Pinselstriche das Grundgerüst ihres Werkes. Um so besser lassen sich die Monolithe der Kunstgeschichte eingrenzen und deren Ränder kommentieren.

Das Kursive konzentriert sich auf das Schreiben als eine Form des Zeichnens. Wenn er sich zum Schreiben niederliess, verweilte Roland Barthes über einem wunderschönen Blatt Papier und einem guten Federhalter...

> *«Ich spüre, wie sich meine Hand bewegt, dreht, schliesst, senkt und hebt... wie sie eine Zeile tilgt oder weiterführt und die beschriebene Fläche ganz bis an den Rand führt und so aus den scheinbar funktionalen Linien des Buchstabens einen Raum bildet, der ganz einfach der eines Kunstwerks ist.»*[1]

Die Ur-Inkarnation des Punk, Vivienne Westwood, wiederum erinnert sich: «Als ich fünf war, hasste ich es, von der schwarzen Tafel abzuschreiben, weil ich meine ‹Rs› immer mit lauter schneckenförmigen Schnörkeln verzierte. Ich fand, es sah schöner aus, und trotzdem bekam ich dafür eine verpasst.»[2] Antonin Artaud, der das Anstössige und Schroffe liebte, gestand, dass «ich seit einem bestimmten Tag im Oktober 1939 niemals mehr geschrieben habe, ohne zu zeichnen».[3]

Obgleich Wörter ins Spiel kommen können, aber nicht müssen, scheint diese Tendenz tatsächlich im Sog der textversessenen Kunst des vergangenen Jahrzehnts an Vitalität gewonnen zu haben. Weil es wie eine Weiterführung des Dokumentarischen der Konzeptkunst erschien, entwickelte sich das Geschriebene in der Kunst der 80er Jahre zum Gemeinplatz. Schmucklos wie die Stimme Joe Fridays brachten Zeichen in Blockschrift Gegenstand und Inhalt der Kunst in Form einer klaren, konkreten Botschaft auf den Begriff. Diese autoritären Reden schwelgten, auch wenn sie noch so ironisch waren, offenbar ganz wörtlich in der postmodernen Lust am Text, so dass selbst im Rahmen des Diskurses dieser spezifischen Kunst das Lesen an die Stelle der visuellen Betätigung der Kunstbetrachtung trat.

Im Gegensatz dazu lassen die Fiktionen der Sprache, die durch das Kursive freigelegt werden, die Lust wieder in den Körper des Geschriebenen sinken. Eine Erscheinungsform dieses Körpers findet

INGRID SCHAFFNER ist Publizistin und Ausstellungsorganisatorin und lebt in New York.

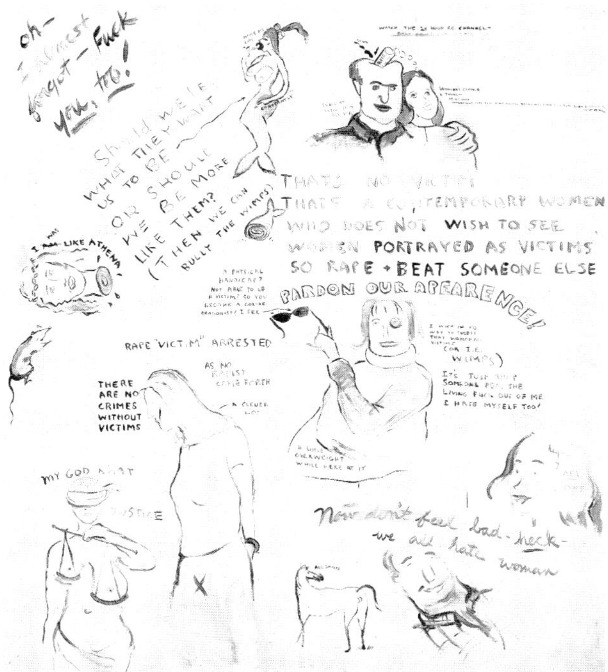

SUE WILLIAMS, TOBENDES OPFER, Acryl auf Leinwand, 162,5 x 137 cm / VICTIM RANTING, 1992, acrylic on canvas, 64 x 54".

sich in der sich stammelnd artikulierenden Schrift der Kunst Cy Twomblys. Wenn sich seine Hand bewegt, mal stockend, mal mit resolutem Tempo, und dabei abwechselt zwischen flüchtigem Notieren, Kritzeln, Kratzen, Peitschen, Verdichten, Tilgen, Innehalten und Tüpfeln, macht sie Zeichen, die, und seien sie auch noch so unergründlich, lesbar sind.[4)] Der kursive Impuls kultiviert, mehr oder weniger ins Abstrakte gewendet, eben diese Graphologie. In den Bildern von Donald Powley zersetzt sich der Körper des Geschriebenen in ein Gerippe oder Gespenst: ein immer wieder abgeschriebenes Fragment vorgefundener Schrift verliert sich in einer Überfülle abgemessener Tropfen, so dass nur die zähflüssigen Spuren des Namens *Mrs. Sadie Henderson* zurückbleiben. Bei Jean-Michel Basquiat dagegen kreischt und krümmt sich dieser Körper entlang einer lebendigen – fast hörbaren – Kette von Zeichen, die durch einen Austausch unsichtbarer Assoziationen zusammengehalten wird.

Wo es am wenigsten gegenständlich ist und am impulsivsten, birgt das Kursive ein Element des Automatismus in sich. In dem Eifer, mit dem die Surrealisten diesen Automatismus praktizierten, umfasste er jede Menge expressiver Techniken, die dazu dienten, unter tranceähnlichen Bedingungen den wirklichen Ablauf des Denkens «sich materialisieren zu lassen».[5)] Doch in seiner kursiven Form und frei von allen paranormalen Prätentionen erklärt das Automatische den zugleich obsessiven und distanzierten Charakter der Linie in dieser Kunst. Beim topographischen Vermessen seiner bizarren Landschaften zeichnet Carroll Dunham unentwegt, ja fast krampfhaft, jedoch nicht unbewusst. «Ich bin da sehr pingelig...», sagt er. «Ich weiss es, wenn ich in einem Bereich bin, von dem meine Arbeit nach meiner Vorstellung lieber fernbleiben sollte...»[6)]

Elliott Puckette überlässt ihre Hand dem Zufall und lässt die leuchtenden Linien ihrer Bilder gleichmässig und mechanisch in den mittleren Raum ihrer dunklen Gründe hinein- und wieder herauswirbeln. Wie Twomblys «Schultafelbilder» bergen diese Gemälde ein gewisses Mass an Aufsässigkeit in sich, so, als habe sich irgendein Student auf eine kalligraphische Spritztour gemacht, versessen darauf, dem

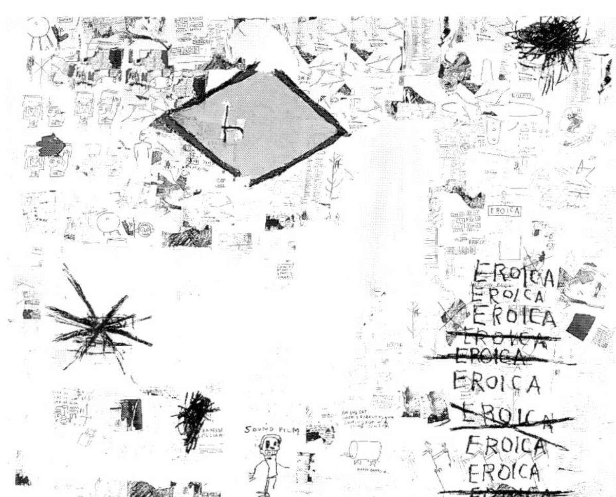

JEAN-MICHEL BASQUIAT, EROICA, 1987, Acryl, Fettkreide, Farbxerox, Papier-Collage auf Leinwand aufgezogen, 228,6 x 272 cm / acrylic, oilstick, color xerox, collage on paper mounted on canvas, 90 x 107". (PHOTO: THE ESTATE OF JEAN-MICHEL BASQUIAT, COURTESY ROBERT MILLER GALLERY, NEW YORK)

Modell der Handschrift den Garaus zu machen. Aus diesen unsozialen Implikationen (man bedenke, was mit Vivienne geschah, als sie mit ihren «Rs» herumspielte) nährt sich der kursive Impuls.

«Man wird zugeben müssen, dass jede Schreibmethode, die nicht zu einem automatischen Stil führt, der Lesbarkeit, Schnelligkeit, Mühelosigkeit und Ausdauer in sich vereint, verfehlt ist.»[7]

«Vor dem Aufkommen von Schreibmaschinen und Textverarbeitungsgeräten war eine schöne Schrift einmal eine beneidenswerte Fertigkeit und Form des Ausdrucks. Gesellschaftliche und berufliche Aussichten hingen vermutlich davon ab, wie sich die Handschrift darstellte, die zu verbessern war, indem man sich Übungen in einem Schönschreibheft unterzog, wodurch zum Glück ‹die Individualität ausgemerzt und Bewegungsfreiheit ermöglicht› wurde.»[8] Angesichts dieser Euthanasie des Schöpferischen entbehrt es nicht der Ironie, dass die Übungen des gepflegten Stils vom Kursiven vereinnahmt werden. Die kalligraphischen Ziffern, Schrift und Schattenrisse, derer sich Lari Pittman bedient, zeugen von einer trefflichen Schreibkunst, die dazu aufgeboten wird, eine anstössige Sphäre voller homosexueller Anzüglichkeiten, Memento-mori-Attributen und grotesker Ornamente zu beschreiben.

Fast esoterisch scheint die Kunst des Schreibens mit vergangenen Zeiten und fernen Orten assoziiert: mittelalterliche Mönche, die sich über Handschriften beugen, ein Türke, der Gott eine Botschaft schickt, ein chinesischer Dichter, der Wörter niederschreibt, die sich nicht von Bildern unterscheiden lassen, ein echter Don Juan, der ein Sonett dichtet, ein Art-nouveau-Plakat, das auf Absinth Geschmack machen soll. Das Kursive macht sich diese Assoziationen zunutze, bedient sich der Kalligraphie, um Assoziationen jenseits des abgesteckten Terrains der Kunst hervorzurufen und in ansonsten unzugängliches Gebiet vorzudringen. Pittmans Kalligraphie in der Nachfolge der Pop Art kehrt zurück in die dunklen Nischen eines Salons des 19. Jahrhunderts. Die stürzenden Linien und peniblen Kurven Amy Silmans schöpfen (zum Teil) aus Handschriften des Nahen Ostens, indem sie gemusterte Gewebe bilden,

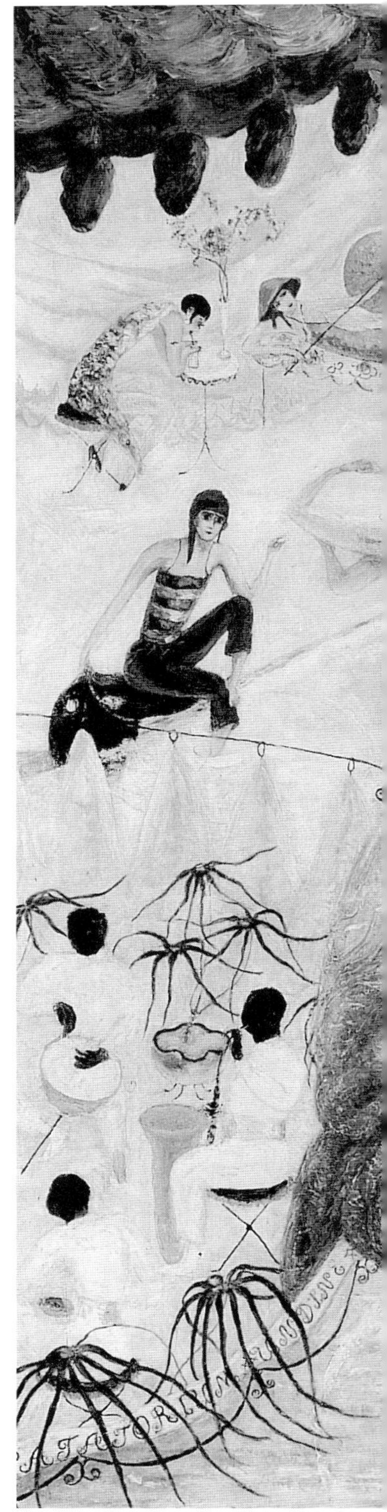

FLORINE STETTHEIMER, NATATORIUM UNDINE, 1927.
Öl und Enkaustik auf Leinwand, 128 x 152,5 cm / oil and encaustic on canvas 50½ x 60".

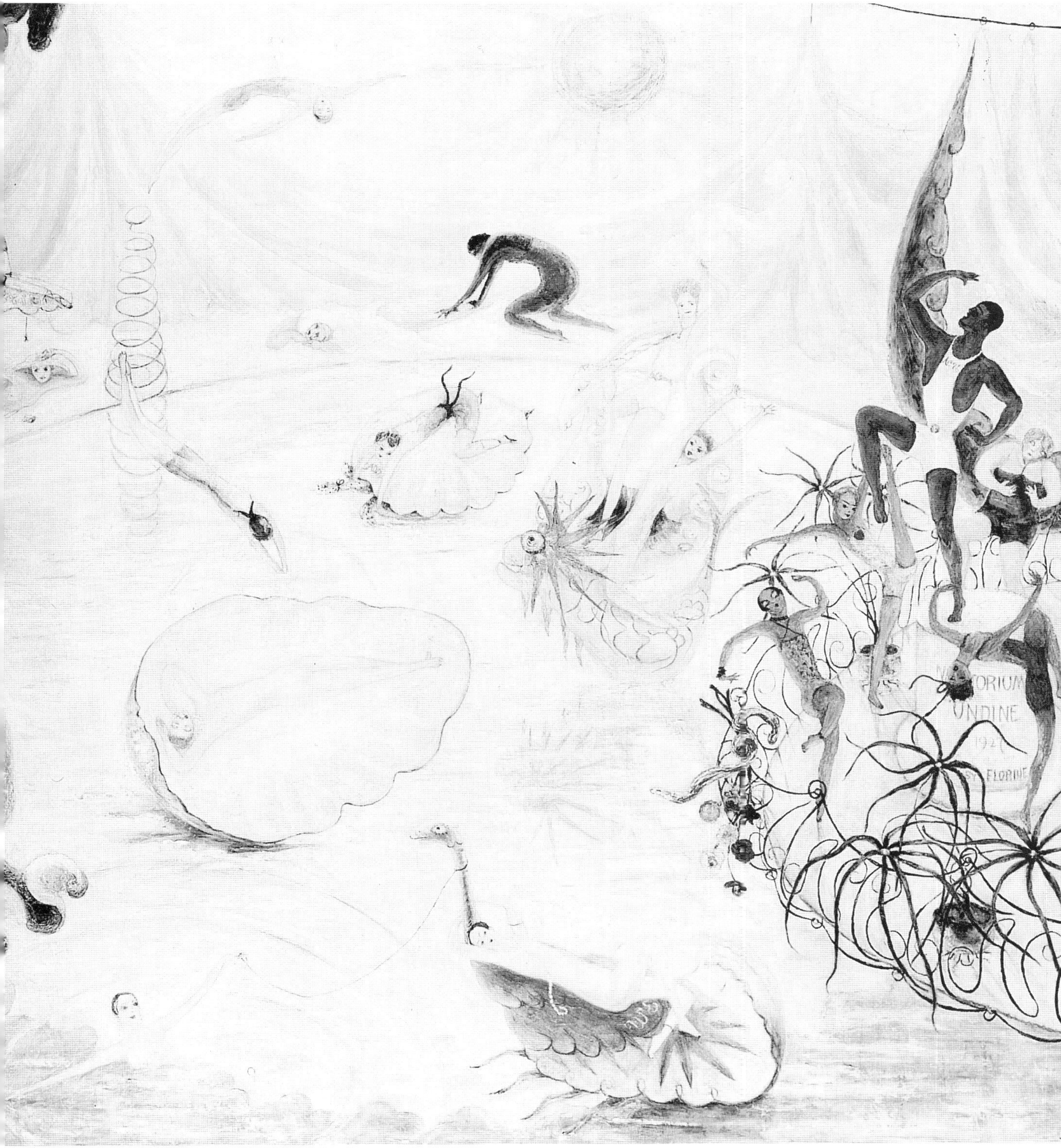
UNDINE
FLORINE

wie die Lattengitter zwischen Harem und Strasse, die nur teilweise den Blick auf die Drolerien ihrer Gemälde freigeben.

Trotz des bekundeten Interesses für andere Kulturen und Geschichten hält sich das Kursive nie so lange bei etwas auf, als dass es sich ins Anachronistische oder Kolonialistische wendete. Es ist zu eklektisch. Mit der Leidenschaft eines Sammlers hält das Kursive immer Ausschau, durchforstet Kleiderschränke, Filmbilder, Erste-Hilfe-Anleitungen, Tätowierungssalons, Raritätenläden, seltene Bücher, Comic-Hefte, Bestiarien, Schönheitssalons, Museen und Abfälle auf der Suche nach allem, was ins Auge fällt. Es ist die Ästhetik der Wunderkammer, angefüllt mit fetischhaften Gegenständen, denen auf der Grundlage des Ephemeren idiosynkratische Vorstellungen von Zeit und Ort abgerungen werden. Und so wie sich die Wunderkammer zu einem Museum wie eine Art Arkade verhält, verhält sich das Kursive zum Meisterwerk wie eine Art Cartoon.

Cartoons spielen in bezug auf gemalte Bilder eine besondere Rolle, die eng mit der Priorität zusammenhängt, die das Kursive der Zeichnung zuweist. Der Begriff *Cartoon* geht auf die Kartons zurück, mit deren Hilfe man ursprünglich eine Vorzeichnung für ein Fresko auf eine vorgrundierte Wandfläche zu übertragen pflegte. Nur ihre Linienzeichnung blieb erhalten, da die Kartons selbst zur Markierung der Umrisse des Bildes punktiert und anschliessend zerstört wurden.[9] Seitdem sie der tyrannischen Herrschaft der Malerei entschlüpft sind, haben Cartoons die Identität satirischer Zeichnungen angenommen. Vom Stil her oft kalligraphisch, mit kommentierenden Worten versehen und auf eine Unterhöhlung des Status quo abzielend, ist es jetzt der Cartoon, der stichelt.

Kraft ihrer verschmitzten Abkehr von den Normen des guten Geschmacks geben Cartoons ein vorzügliches Vehikel für den kursiven Impuls ab. Elliott Green orchestriert eine alberne Symphonie aus perversen Kreuzungen von Bären, Hunden und Menschen zu Bildern, die die hehrsten Prätentionen des Mediums in lüstern-grotesker Weise aufs Korn nehmen. Nancy Spero und Sue Williams zählen zu einem Kreis von Künstlerinnen, die sich in die Arena der Malerei eingeschlichen haben, und zwar mit der Waffe des Cartoons und mit dem Ziel, mit einer explizit weiblichen Bildersprache und Thematik in eine traditionell männliche Domäne einzubrechen. Megan Williams haucht den Klassikern des Comics neues Leben ein und nötigt Mickey Mouse in die Rolle eines pornographischen kleinen Rammlers.

Vielleicht ist das, was dem Kursiven im Rahmen heutiger künstlerischer Praxis Wirkungspotential verleiht, die Tatsache, dass es sich so opportun das postmoderne Projekt der kulturellen Revision überstülpen lässt. Eine auf eine Neubewertung etablierter Kanons und das Geltenlassen unterschiedlicher Sichtweisen abzielende Kritik war dem kursiven Impuls seit jeher inhärent. Indem es sich an der Verschiedenheit delektiert, koppelt das Kursive die ins Schreiben und Zeichnen einfliessende erotische Energie des Kopierens mit den imaginativen Möglichkeiten der Unlesbarkeit. Es pervertiert das Modell, um im Sinne einer bewusst expressiven und kraftvoll rudimentären Kunst seine eigenen Bedürfnisse aufzuzeichnen, um einem ansonsten unartikulierbaren Impuls Ausdruck zu verleihen.

(Übersetzung: Magda Moses, Bram Opstelten)

1) Roland Barthes (aus seinem Vorwort zu R. Druet und H. Grégoire, *The Civilization of Writing,* 1976), zit. bei Georges Jean, *Writing: The Story of Alphabets and Scripts,* New York 1992, S. 196.
2) Vivienne Westwood, zit. bei Marion Hume, «Portrait of a Former Punk», in *Vogue* (September 1994), S. 208.
3) Antonin Artaud, zit. bei Jacques Derrida, «Maddening the Subjectile», wiederabgedruckt in *Boundaries: Writing and Drawing,* Yale French Studies Nr. 84, Yale University, New Haven 1994, S. 160.
4) Vgl. Roland Barthes, «The Responsibility of Forms», in *Cy Twombly: Works on Paper,* The University of California Press, Berkeley und Los Angeles 1985, S. 157–176; vgl. auch Roland Barthes, *Cy Twombly,* Mervé Verlag, Berlin 1983.
5) Praktisch in Gleichsetzung mit Automatismus definierte André Breton Surrealismus als «reinen psychischen Automatismus, durch den man mündlich oder schriftlich oder auf jede andere Weise den wirklichen Ablauf des Denkens auszudrücken sucht»; André Breton, Erstes Manifest des Surrealismus, in ders., *Die Manifeste des Surrealismus,* Reinbek 1986, S. 26.
6) Der Künstler im Gespräch mit Carol Eckman, in *Carroll Dunham: Drawings 1988–91,* Ausst.-Kat., David Nolan Gallery, New York 1992, S. 5.
7) A.N. Palmer, *The Palmer Method of Business Writing,* New York 1928, S. 5.
8) ibid., S. 2.
9) Die punktierte Oberfläche eines gebrauchten Kartons bildet einen interessanten historischen Schnittpunkt zwischen Zeichnung und Tätowierung.

I N S E R T

N A N

G O L D I N

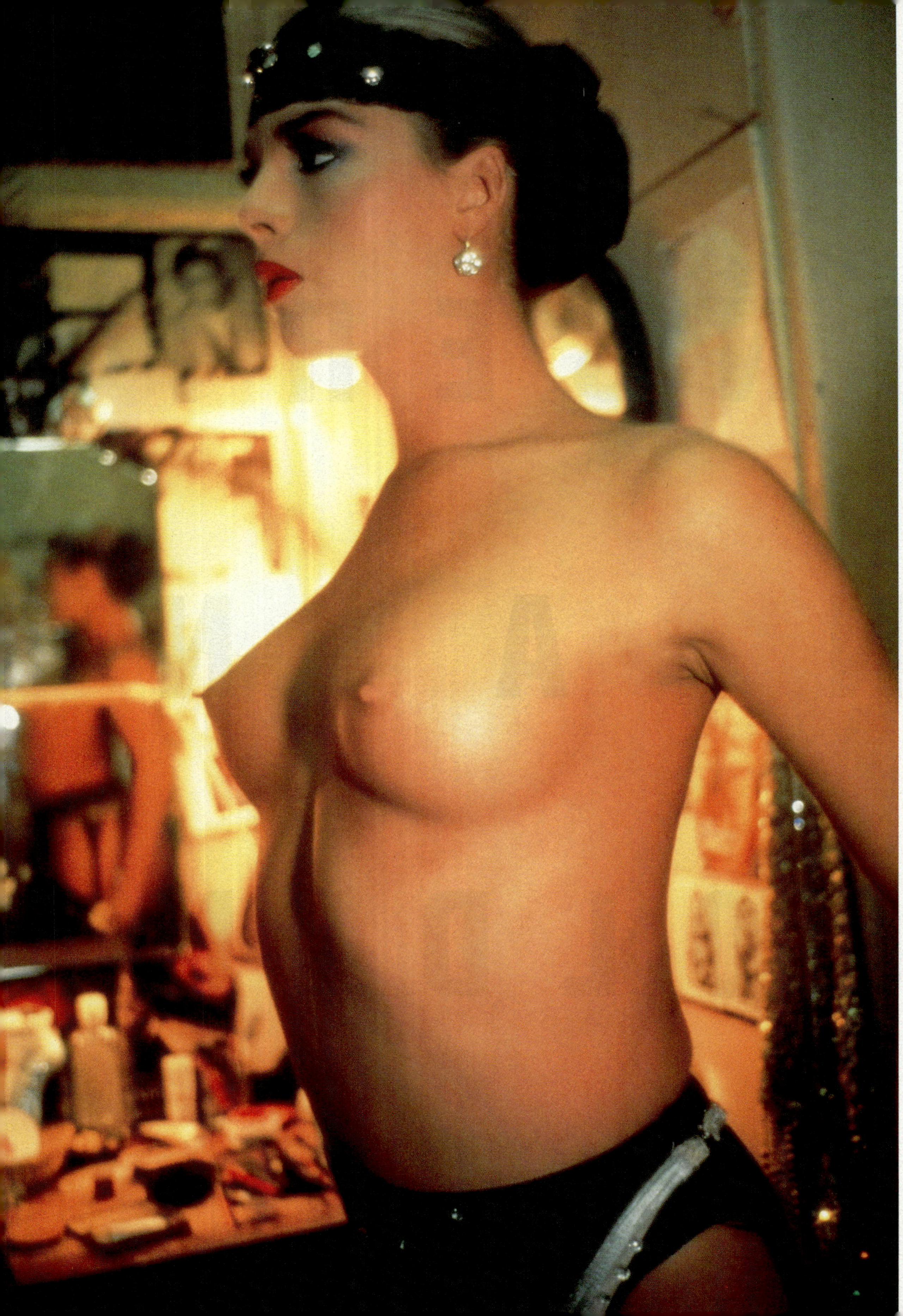

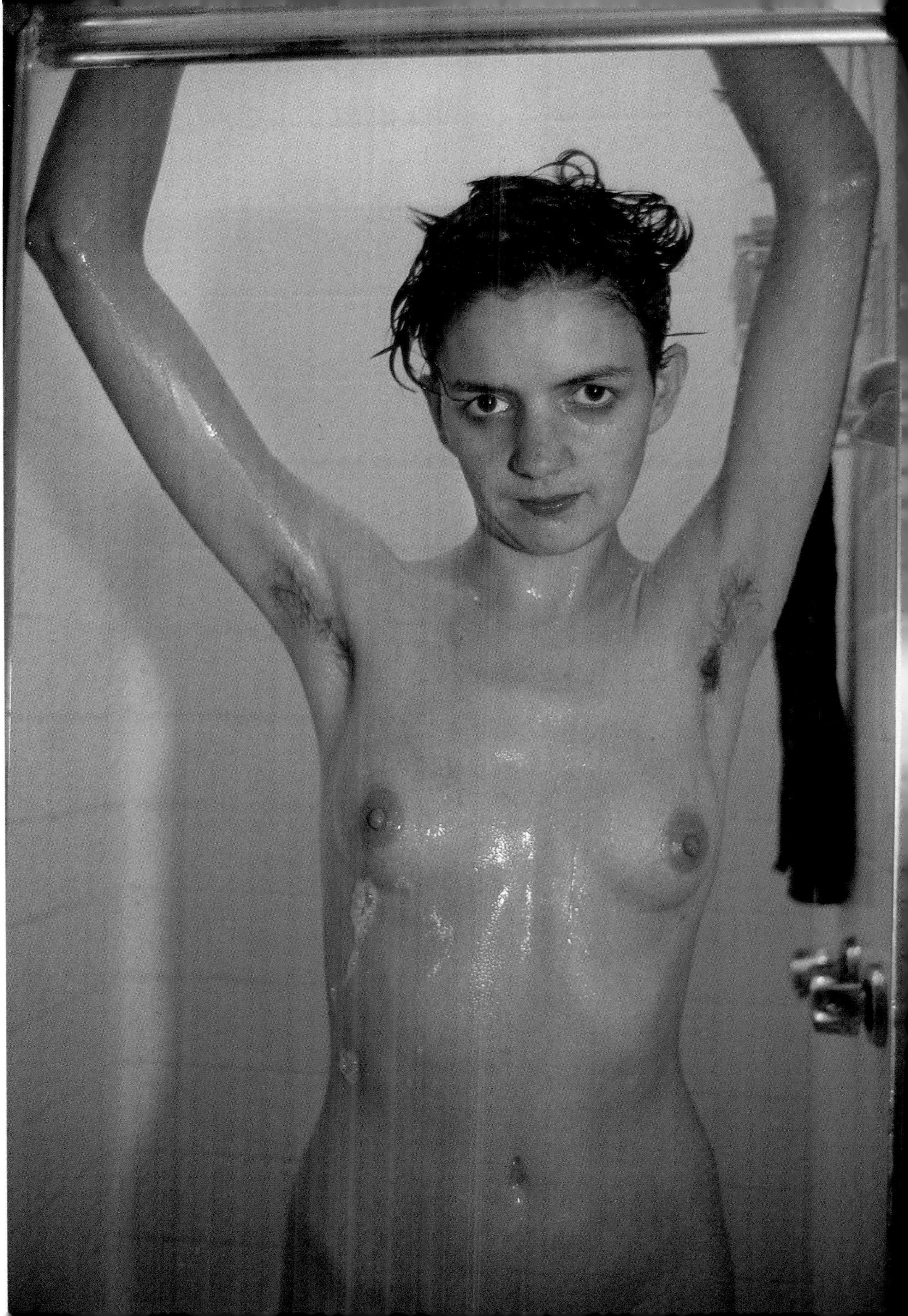

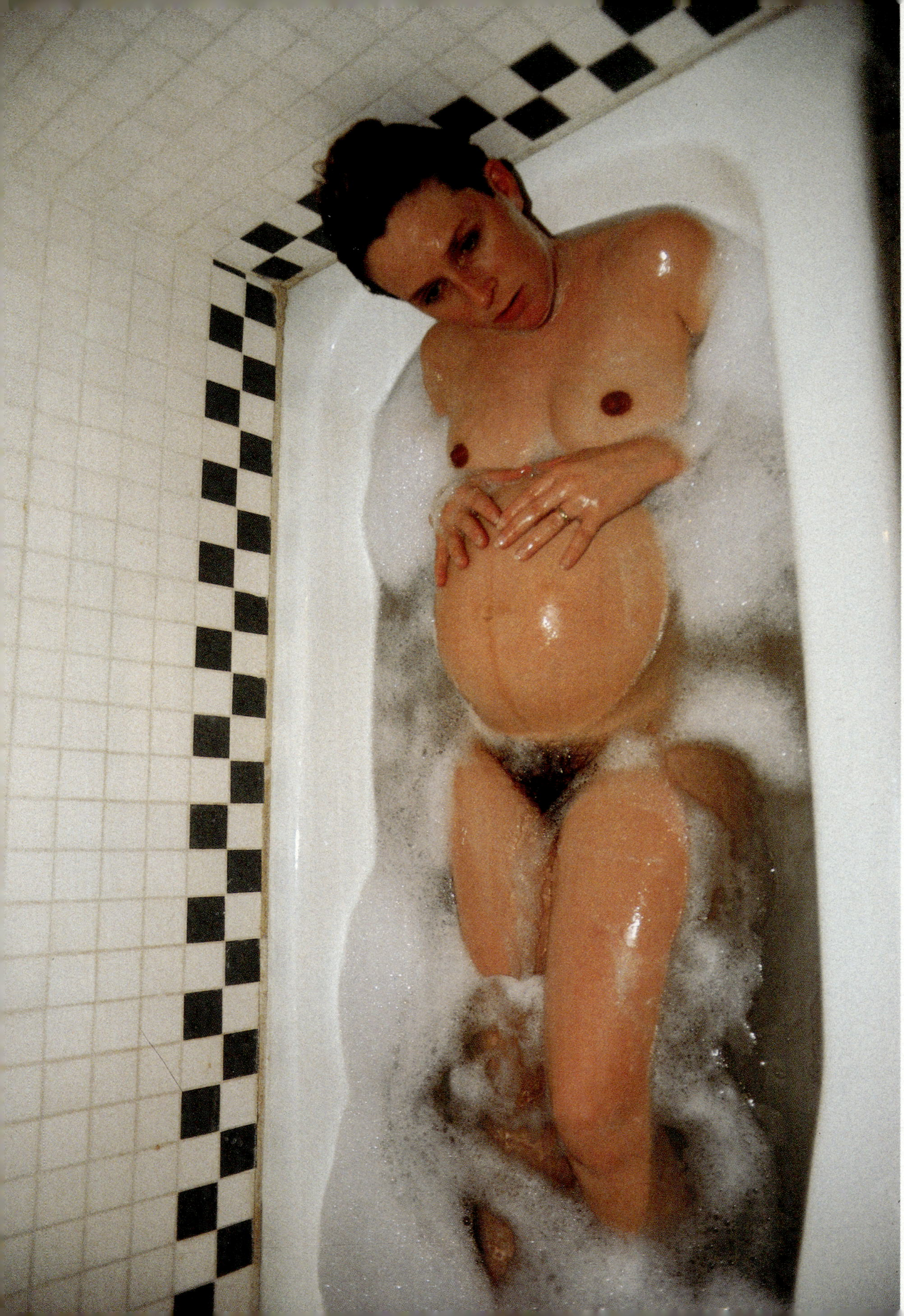

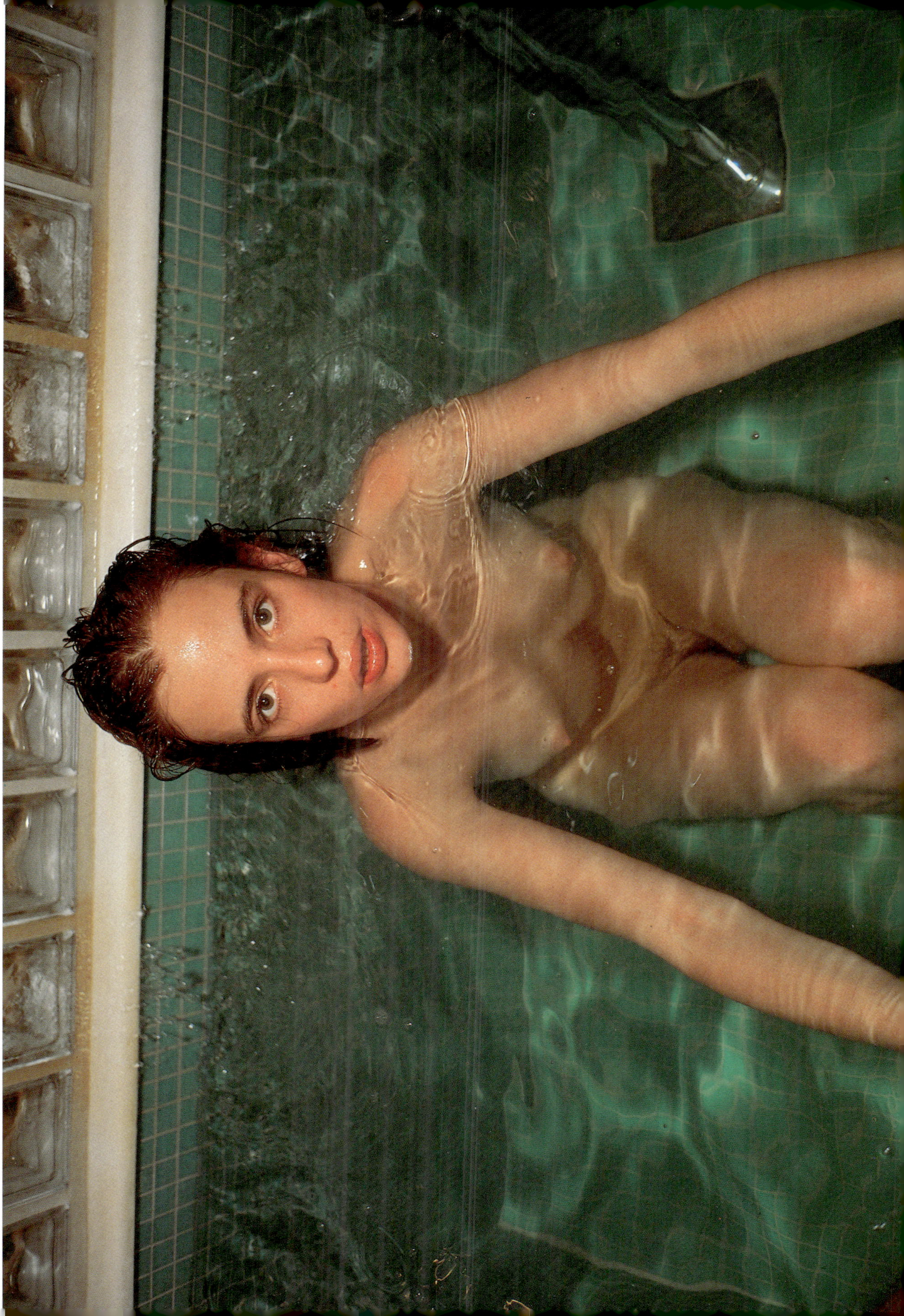

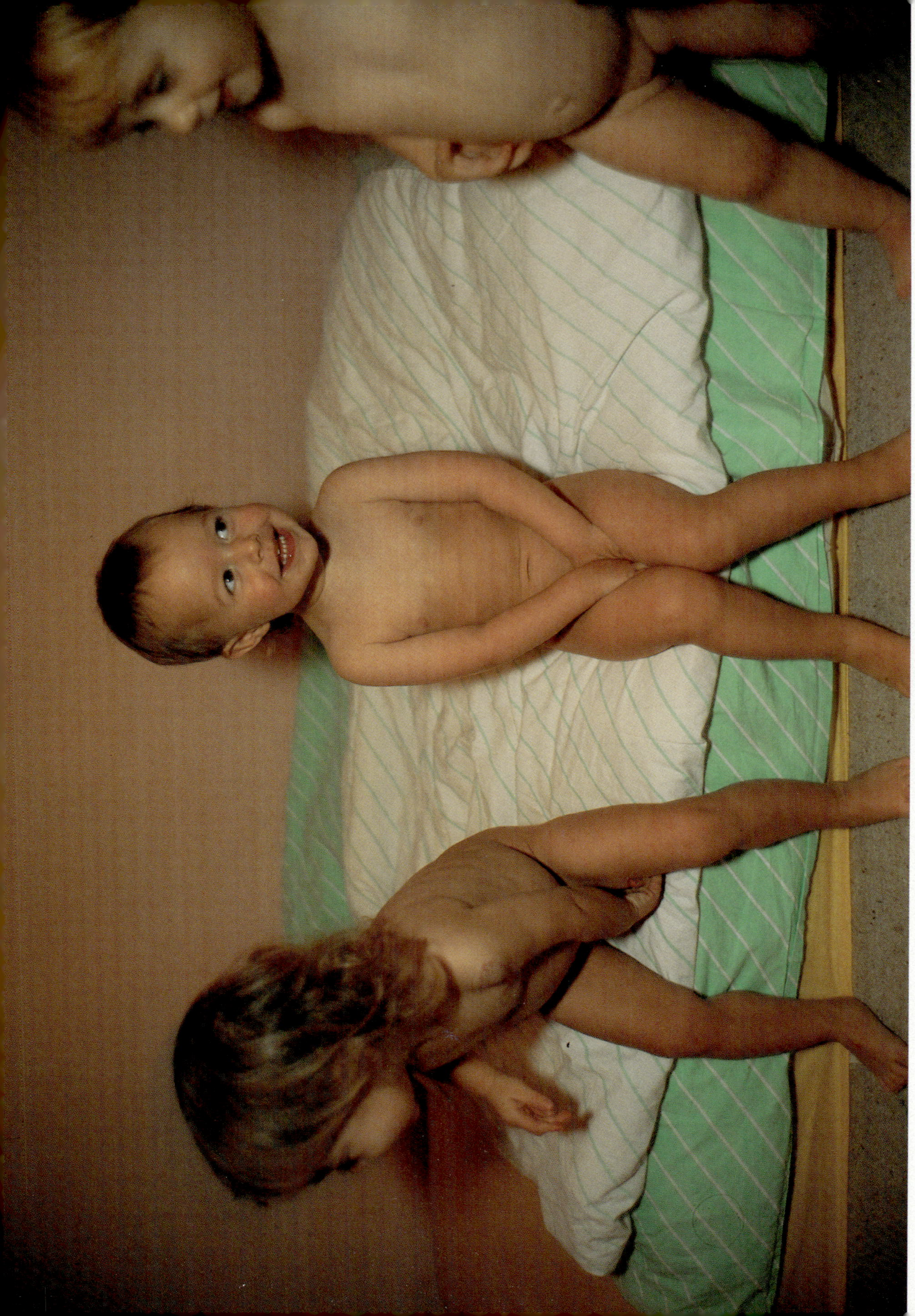

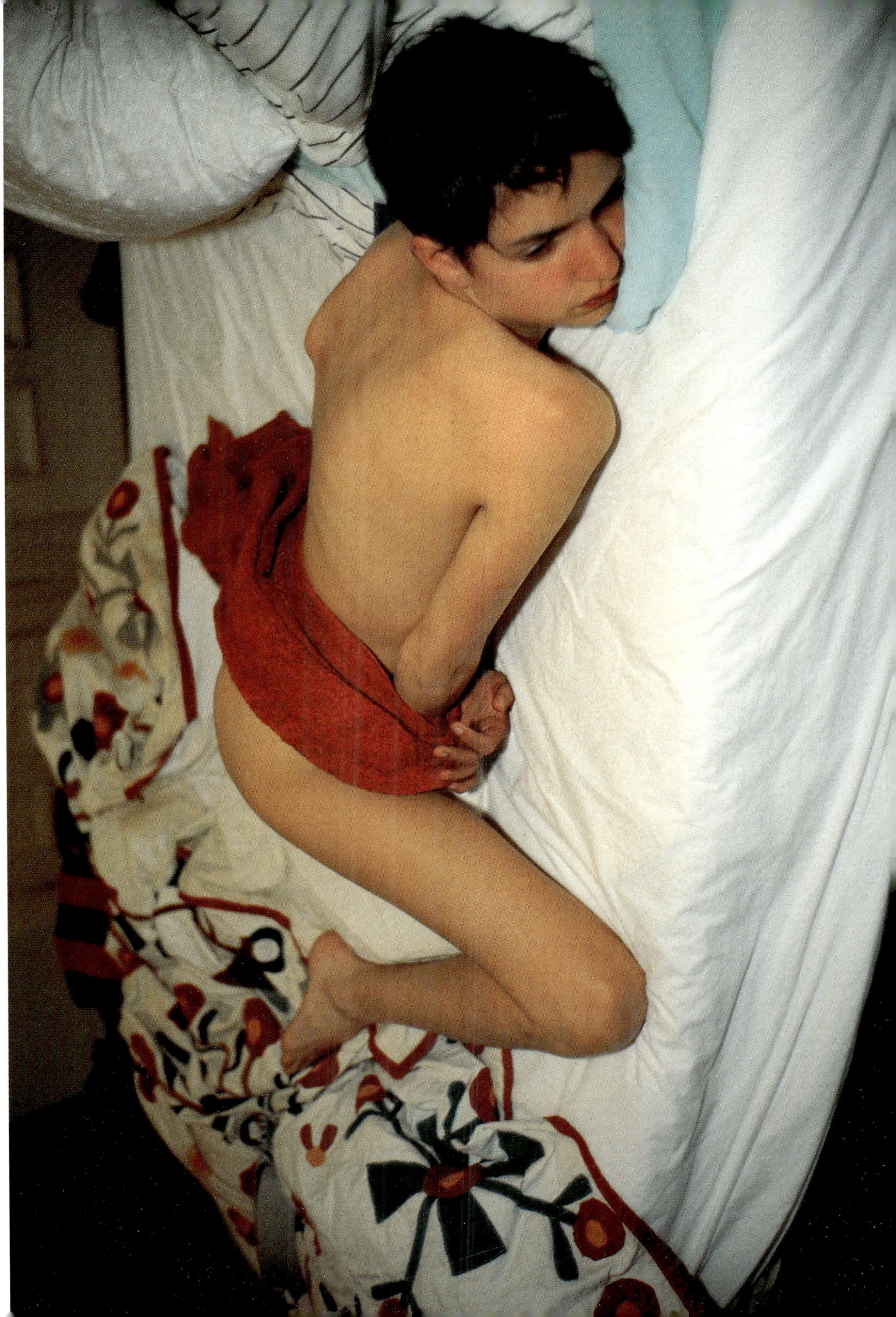

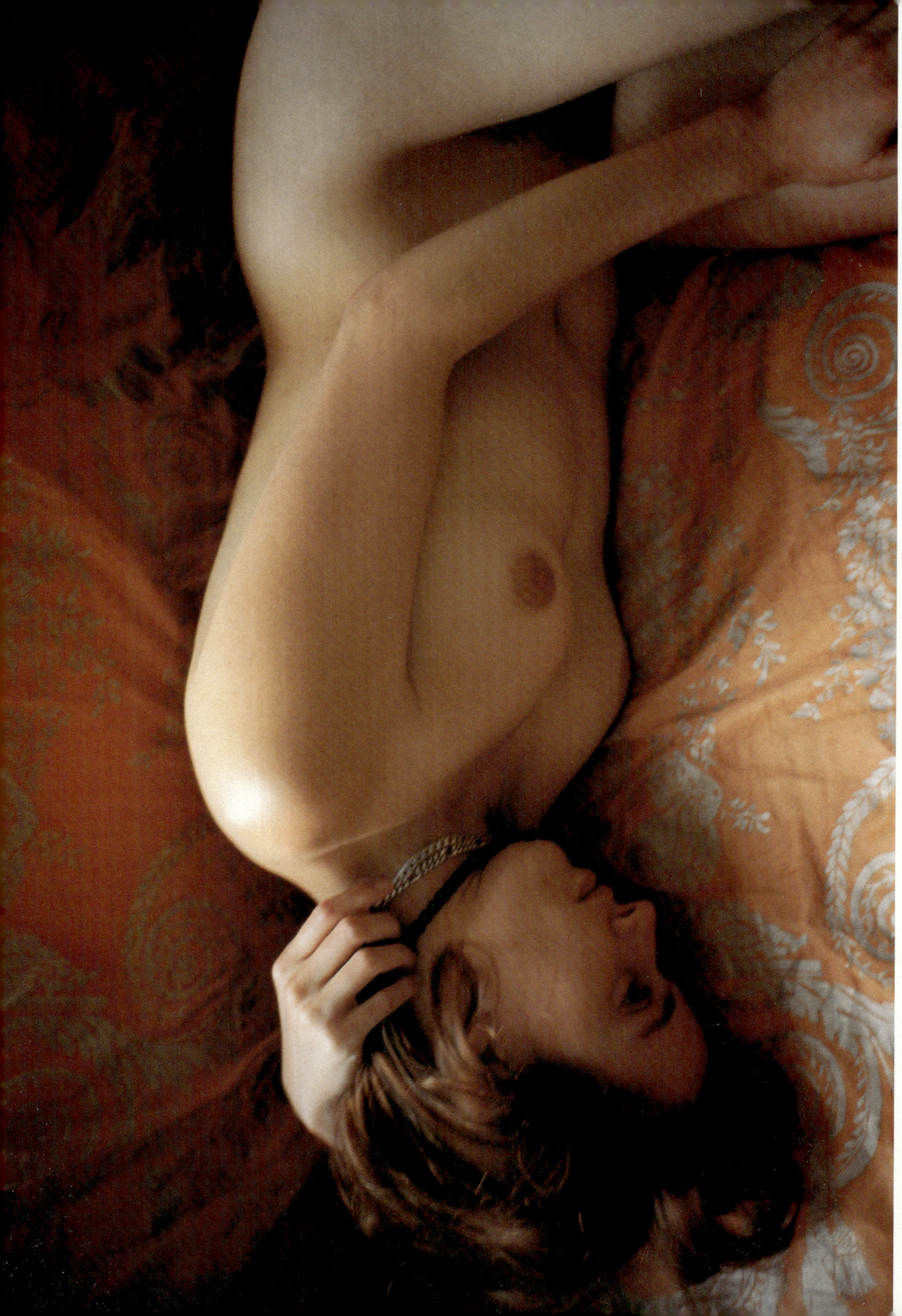

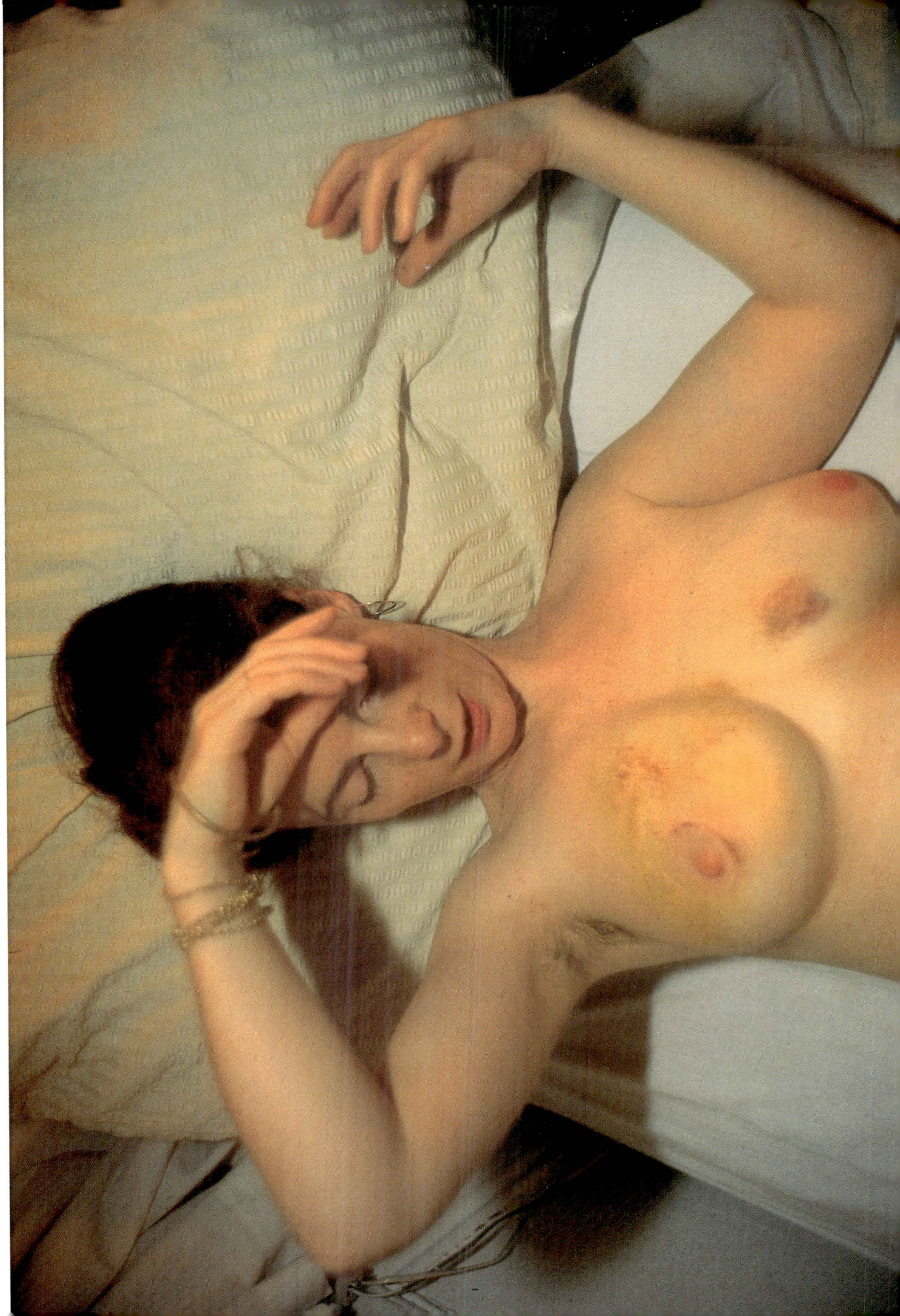

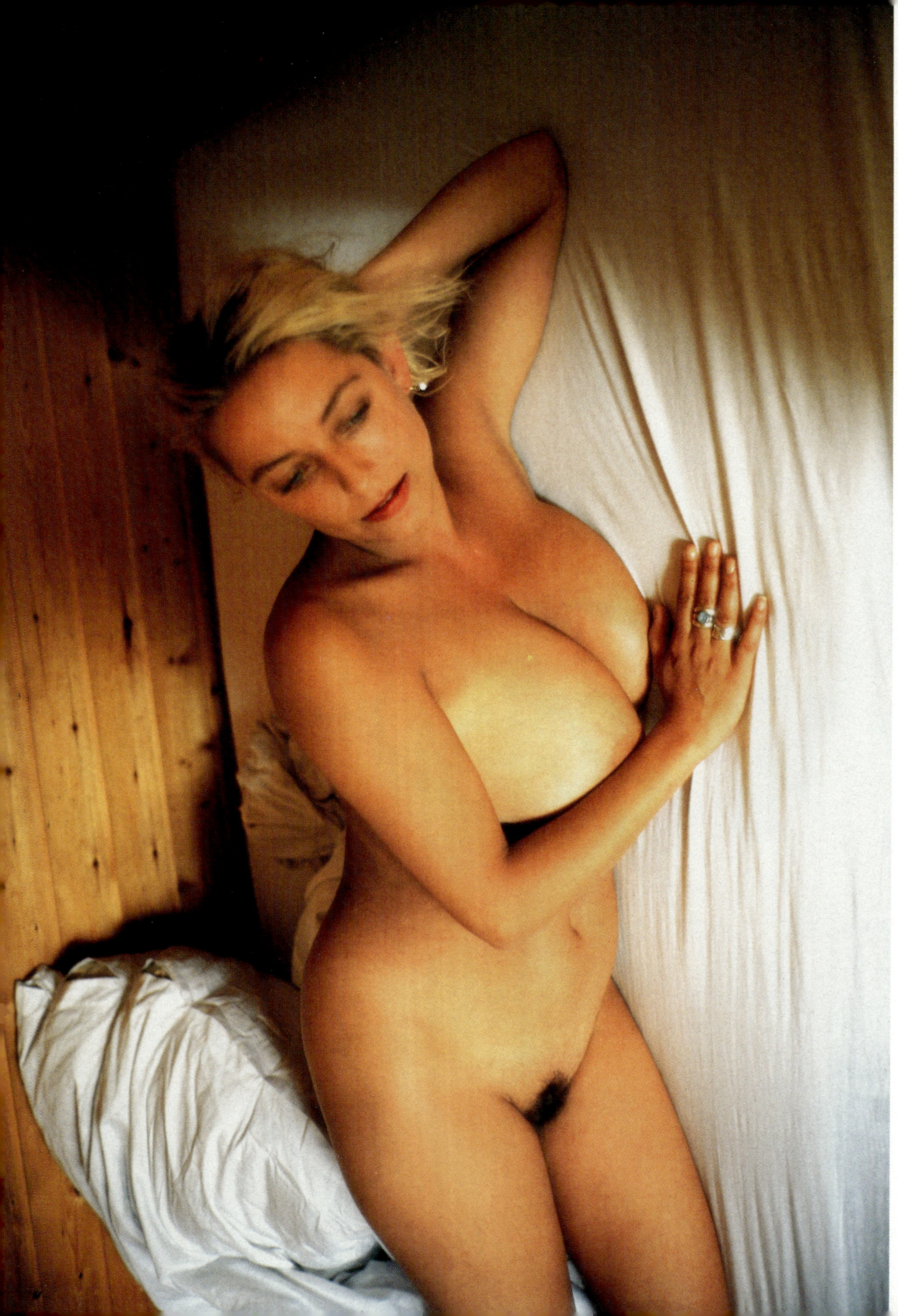

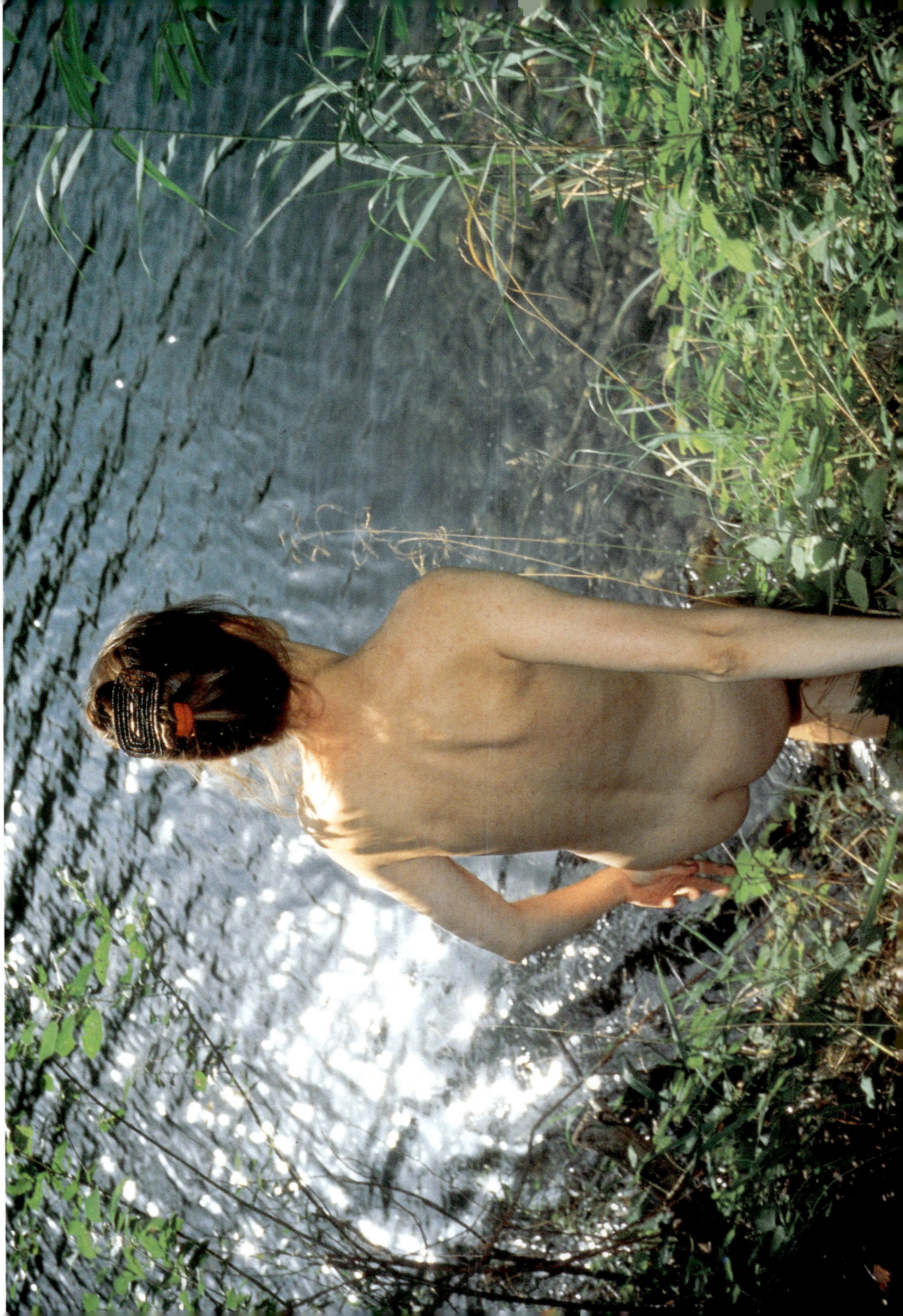

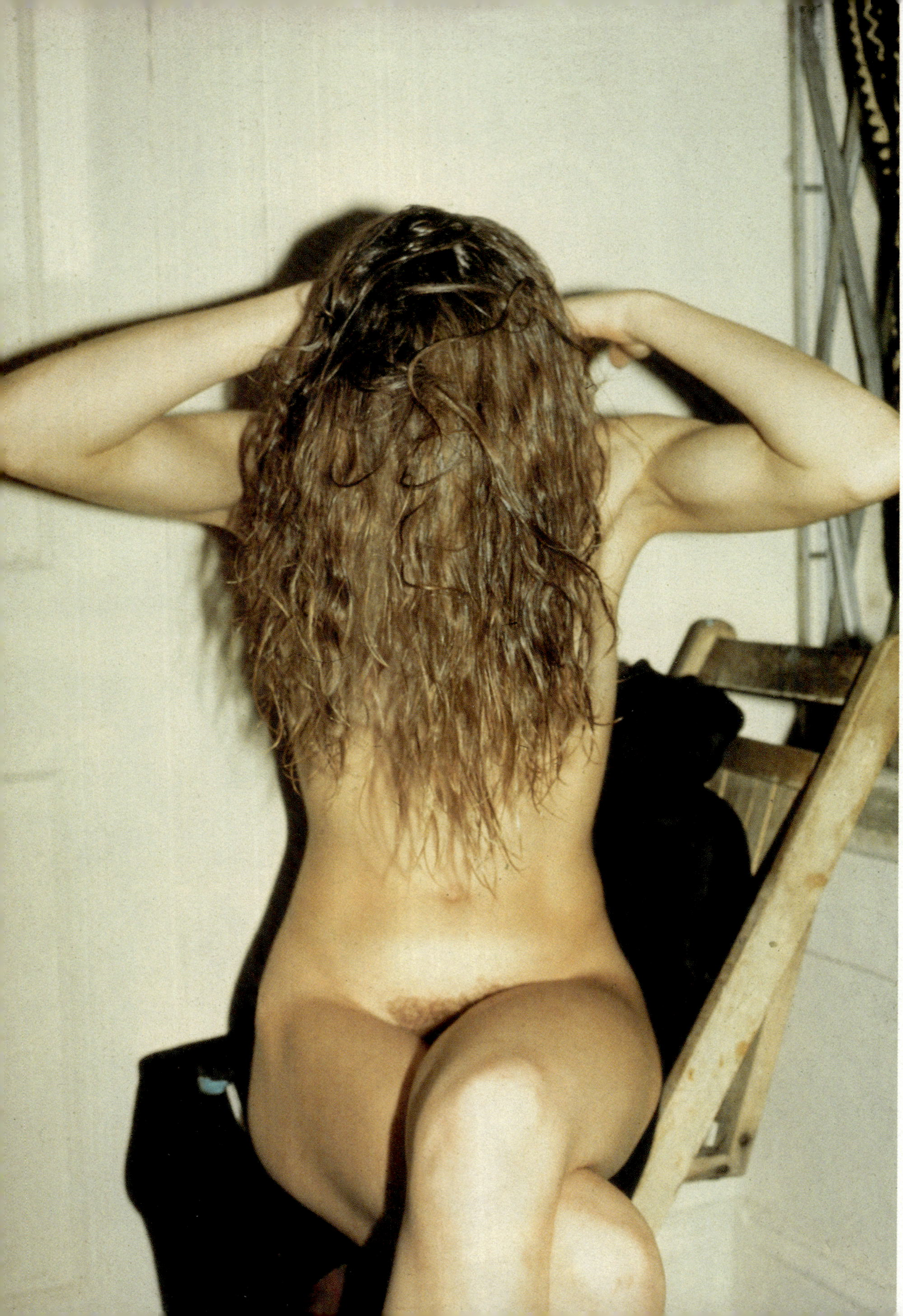

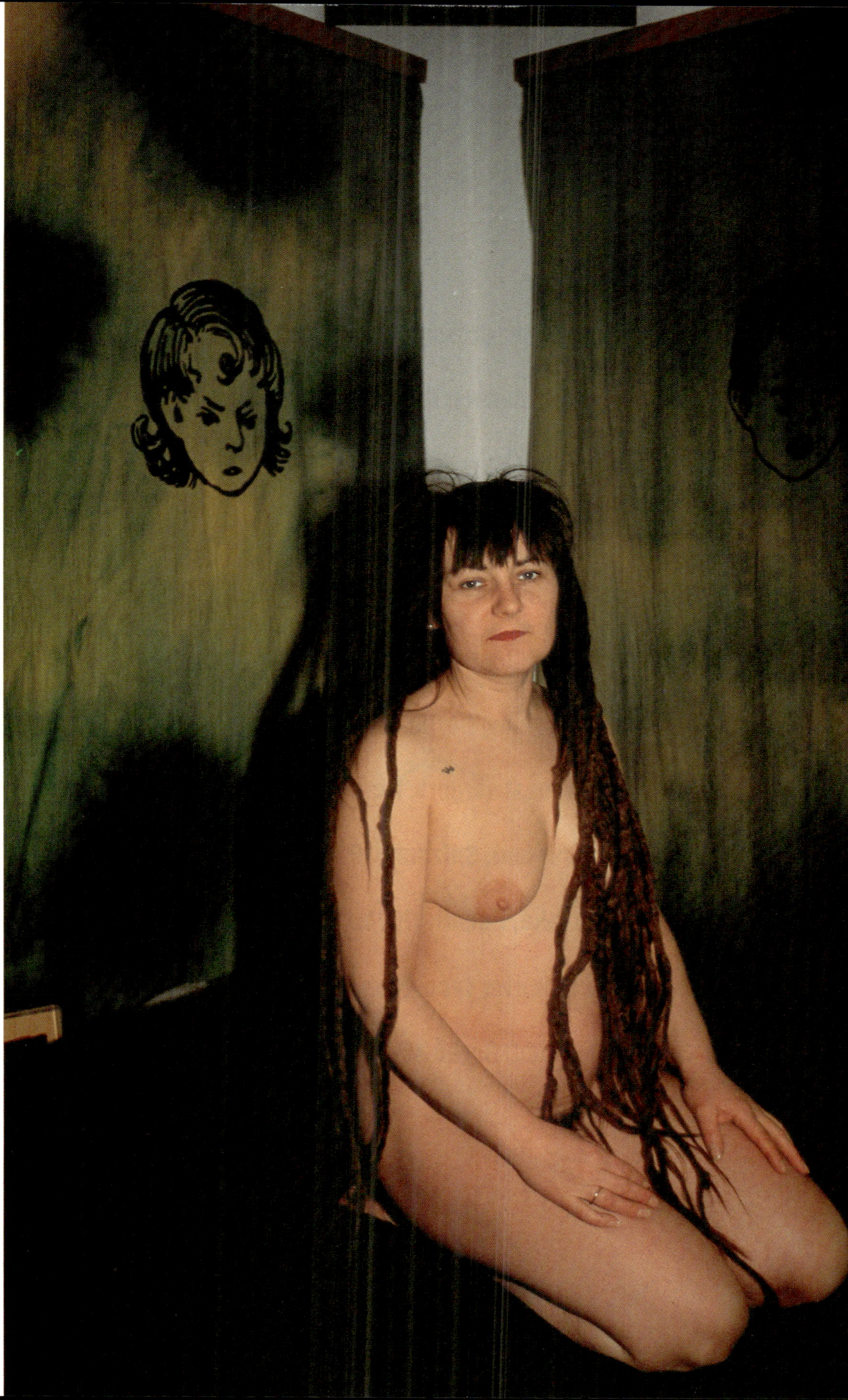

1. Kim Harlow in her dressing room, Paris 1991.
2. Siobhan in the shower, New York 1991.
3. Butch in the tub, New York 1988.
4. Amanda at the sauna, Berlin 1993.
5. Carmen's second birthday party, Berlin 1991.
6. Siobhan in bed, Boston 1991.
7. Amanda on Fortuny, Berlin 1993.
8. Fiona after breast surgery, New York 1991.
9. Monika on her bed, Salzburg 1994.
10. Gena in the lake, Bavaria 1994.
11. Greer with hair over face, New York 1983.
12. Käthe on her bed, Berlin 1994.

CLAUDE RITSCHARD

NEUERE SKULPTUREN VON MARKUS RAETZ ÜBER METAMORPHOSEN

Während der letzten Jahre hat Markus Raetz eine Folge von Rundplastiken mittlerer Grösse geschaffen, die das Phänomen der Metamorphose erkunden. Die zuerst entstandene METAMORPHOSE I (1990 für die Arbeit aus Gips, 1991 für den Guss) setzt, aus einem einzigen Stück, die Gegenüberstellung von Joseph Beuys und einem Hasen in Szene. Auf diesen ersten Zwitter folgen NICHTPFEIFE (Gips, 1990; Guss, 1992) und NICHTRAUCH (Gips, 1990), zwei Anspielungen auf Magrittes CECI N'EST PAS UNE PIPE, in denen, je nach Blickwinkel, die Pfeife oder deren Rauch umgekehrt erscheinen. 1991–92 nimmt Raetz eine zweite Fassung der Büste von Beuys mit Filzhut wieder auf, METAMORPHOSE II, und zitiert anschliessend, mit FORM IM RAUM (1991–92), in allgemeinerer Weise die formale Plastik. Hier verändert die Metamorphose das spiralförmige Gebilde zu einem Mickymaus-Kopf. Damit führt Markus Raetz einen zweiten Verweis auf eine eigene Arbeit vor; denn bereits in den 70er Jahren bediente er sich der Walt-Disney-Maus bei seinen Untersuchungen über die Anamorphose und die Verzerrung der Formen.

Im Jahr 1991 begann er mit den ersten Kopfstudien, aus denen sich entweder die Umkehrung des Gesichts von oben nach unten in SILHOUETTEN (1992) oder die Form eines JANUS (1991) mit doppeltem Profil ergeben.

Dieses Nachspüren wird durch zwei weitere Skulpturen vervollständigt; zum einen durch GROSS UND KLEIN (1992), eine Art Hommage an Morandi, bei der der Massstab eines Glases und einer Flasche, die nebeneinandergestellt sind, vom einen Gegenstand auf den anderen übergeht, zum anderen durch CECI-CELA (1992–93), einer Arbeit aus vier Bronze-Buchstaben (CECI), mit Stiften in die Wand fixiert, die übereck in einem Spiegel reflektiert als CELA zu lesen sind.

Die 1993–94 durchgeführte Wanderausstellung im *Ivam* in Valencia, später in der Londoner Serpentine Gallery, dann im Genfer Musée Rath (von der ein Teil im Herbst dieses Jahres in Helsinki im Nykytaiteen Museo zu sehen war), gewährte die Möglichkeit der Gegenüberstellung jener zwischen 1990 und 1993 geschaffenen Skulpturen. Diese Arbeiten bildeten den Ausgangs- und Bezugspunkt für die Werkauswahl, getroffen vom Initiator der Ausstellung «Retrospektive gegen den Strich», Ad Petersen, im Einverständnis mit Markus Raetz. Zudem boten die ungefähr 250 Werke – Zeichnungen, Reliefs und Skulpturen – aus den Jahren 1960 bis 1993 die Voraussetzung für einen aussergewöhnlich erhellenden Einblick in Markus Raetz' Recherche. Die verschiedenen Richtungen, die man ihn früher in seiner Arbeit hatte einschlagen sehen – verschieden vom Thema, von der Ausdrucksweise, von der Anlage her –, haben somit etwas von einem Bildrätsel angenommen und zeigen nicht nur ihren Sinn, sondern auch ihre Kohärenz.

Die Klarheit und Reichhaltigkeit dieser Ausstellung machten es mög-

CLAUDE RITSCHARD ist Kuratorin am Musée d'Art et d'Histoire in Genf.

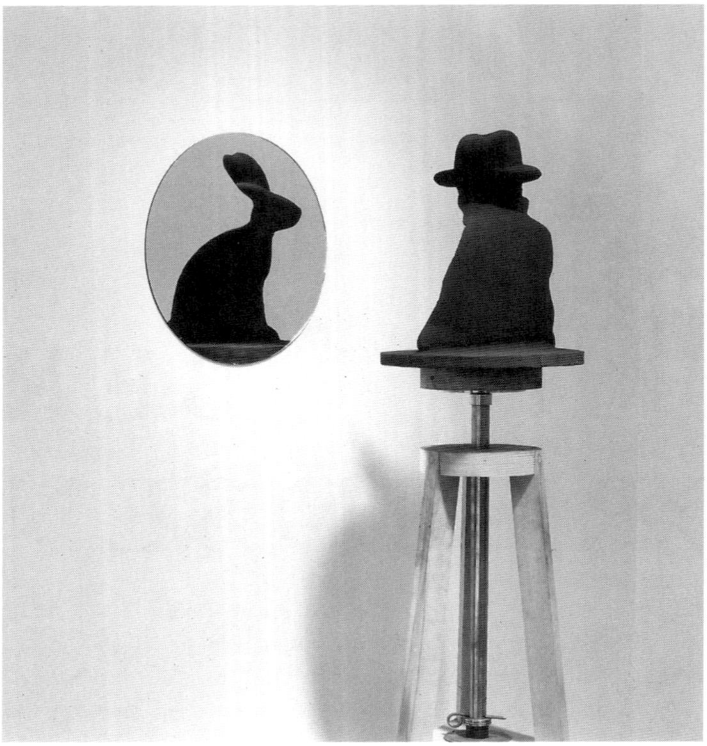

MARKUS RAETZ, METAMORPHOSE II, 1991–1992, Gusseisen und Spiegel, 40 x 33,5 x 33,5 cm / METAMORPHOSIS II, cast iron and mirror, 15¾ x 13⅛ x 13⅛".
(PHOTO: THOMAS WEY)

lich, Arbeiten in Beziehung zu setzen, deren Entstehung manchmal mehr als zwanzig Jahre auseinander liegt. So wurde ersichtlich, dass Markus Raetz' Thematik, die man für unüberschaubar hält, falls man sich nur auf die Erinnerung an einzelne Werke oder bescheidenere Ensembles stützt, die man in grösseren Zeitabständen hier oder da gesehen hatte, sich auf zwei vorherrschende Themen zusammenfassen lässt: Figur und Landschaft. Ebenfalls lässt sich feststellen, dass die Fülle von meist einfachen, wenn nicht gar schäbigen Materialien – die Objets trouvés reichen vom Pingpongball, vom Stück Eisendraht bis zum Eukalyptusblatt oder Treibholz – nicht auf Zersplitterung beruht, sondern in ganz enger Verbindung mit Raetz' Recherche zu sehen ist; nicht als Arbeitsverfahren, sondern als ein Prozess des Sehens. Auch die Vielzahl der Techniken hat ihren Grund; der Künstler wechselt von Zeichnung und Aquarell zum Relief und zur Skulptur[1)], und zwar aus einem anderen Bedürfnis heraus als demjenigen, sein Handwerk zu variieren: Jedes dieser Ausdrucksmittel stellt eine für das weitere Vorgehen notwendige Weise des Nachforschens dar und erfüllt, wie die von Markus Raetz ebenfalls verwendeten Polaroidaufnahmen, die Funktion eines Verifikationsprinzips.

Gegenstand dieser Verifikation ist die Beziehung zwischen konkreter Welt und der Ansicht, die das Auge von ihr vermittelt. In den Arbeiten von Markus Raetz, die das Bild verzerren, vervielfachen oder umwandeln, ereignet sich alles so, als sei das Gesehene nichts als Täuschung. Dies kann man zumindest in einer ersten Lesart postulieren, wenn man den Standpunkt einer Objektivität des Betrachters einnimmt. Unter Objektivität ist die dem Funktionieren des Auges zugesprochene Vertrauenswürdigkeit zu verstehen: «Ich glaube, was ich sehe.» Dabei wird vergessen, dass das Auge nur ein Objektiv ist, das die Sehlinien auf den Fleck der vom Gehirn lichtempfindlich gemachten Netzhaut lenkt. Das Bild entsteht in Verbindung mit Archetypen, die jedes Individuum schon von frühester Kindheit an gespeichert hat. Die Identifikation des Bildes, sein Wiedererkennen, ist ein Phänomen, das im Gehirn abläuft. Es besteht folglich keine «Objektivität» des Sehens, sondern im Gegenteil ein subjektives, individuell verschiedenes Sehen. Das Postulat einer Objektivität hat gleichwohl jahrhundertelang den Betrachter, also den Menschen, dazu ermächtigt, seiner Umwelt gegenüber die Vormachtstellung einzunehmen. Er sieht sie, bezeichnet sie, erkennt sie und eignet sie sich an. Dass es zur Zeit der Renaissance für notwendig gehalten wurde, die Regeln der Darstellung mittels der Theorie der visuellen Perspektive festzulegen, hat schon seine Bedeutung. Damit wurden gleichzeitig die Gesetze des Sehens und folglich die hierarchische Beziehung des Menschen zu seiner Umgebung festgelegt.

Seit den 60er Jahren spielt Markus Raetz mit einer nicht mathematischen, sondern pragmatischen und zugleich auf Intuition beruhenden Perspektive, was ihn dazu führt, Verformungen zu ergründen, die sich durch bestimmte, bis zur Anamorphose gesteigerte Überspitzungen der Perspektive ergeben. Solche Werke problematisieren die Funktion des Blicks, was die herkömm-

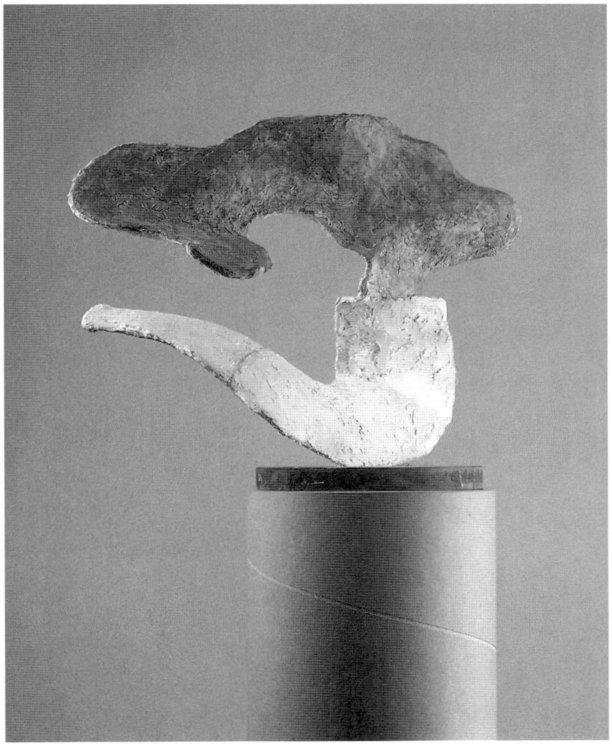

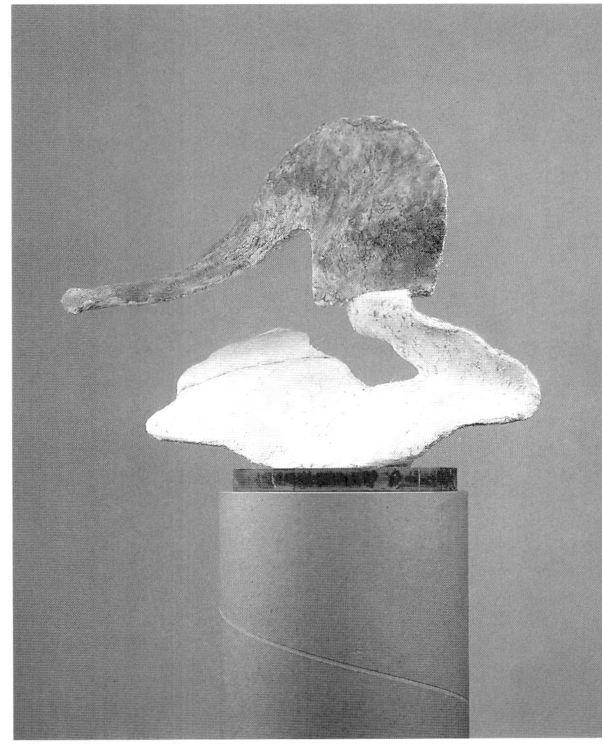

MARKUS RAETZ, NICHTRAUCH, 1990, Gips, teilweise bemalt, 34,3 x 45,7 x 24,2 cm / NONSMOKE, plaster, 13½ x 18 x 9½". (Zwei Ansichten / two views)

liche Hierarchie von Auge und Welt umstösst. SEEBLICK II (1981–85) zum Beispiel, das ein aus wenigen Zweigen gefertigtes Profil zeigt, von dem auf Augenhöhe eine Reihe von kleinen Seelandschaften wegführen, die auf mehrere, zu einem Dreieck angeordnete Stückchen Treibholz gemalt sind, offenbart eine zweifache Dynamik des Sehens: Das Relief lässt sich als vom Objektiv des Auges erfasster Blick aufs Meer lesen, aber auch, und zwar in untrennbarer Weise, als ins Auge eintretendes und sich der Netzhaut aktiv einprägendes Meer.

Für das Verständnis der neueren Skulpturen, in welchen Markus Raetz das Postulat einer aktiven und das Sehen steuernden Aussenwelt weiterführt, sind diese früheren Arbeiten notwendig. Bereits in den ersten Recherchen, die diese Vielschichtigkeit bezeugten, und insbesondere in den Anamorphosen, war der Betrachter aufgefordert, seinen Blickpunkt zu ändern, wollte er das Bild ganz erfassen. Um die letzten Skulpturen muss der Betrachter wahrhaftig herumgehen, will er die Metamorphose erleben. So ist die Hierarchie aufgehoben. Der visuellen Perspektive der Renaissance, die nur nach dem Leitprinzip eines festen Blickpunkts funktioniert, wird entgegengewirkt.

Aber die Metamorphosen beinhalten mehr als nur die streitbare Auseinandersetzung mit der Perspektive. Die eine Umformung oder einen Identitätswechsel vorgebende Metamorphose – Wandlung oder Inkarnation – entsteht aus einer brutal eintretenden Entwicklung, welche, auf der Ebene des Mythos, nur dem Willen der Götter folgt, die den Mutationen selbst unterworfen sind. Ob aufgrund einer Schicksalsprüfung oder einer Wiedergeburt, ein der Metamorphose unterworfenes Wesen ist, in seiner neuen Gestalt, nur noch eine Projektion dessen, was es einmal war. Es ist sowohl sich selbst als das andere, und die Unsichtbarkeit seines früheren Wesens macht, dass seine neue Gestalt ungewiss erscheint. Die Umwandlung dessen, was ein Körper, eine Materie, eine stoffliche Substanz gewesen ist, in etwas vollkommen anderes erschüttert von Grund auf jegliche Gewissheit sowohl über die Materie als auch über das Wirkliche.

Dem Beispiel der Mythologie folgend, zieht Markus Raetz Theorien und Systeme der Darstellung in Zweifel. Indem das Bild sich wandelt, entzieht es sich einer eindeutigen Benennung. Es ist nur als ein Trugbild wahrnehmbar, als ein sichtbarer Schein, der, für einen Augenblick, den Eindruck erweckt, als ob er wirklich wäre.

(Übersetzung aus dem Französischen: Thomas Aigner)

1) Den erwähnten Techniken ist noch die Graphik hinzuzufügen. Ad Petersen und Markus Raetz haben sich entschieden, sie nicht in diese Ausstellung aufzunehmen. Denn das graphische Werk war kürzlich in einer Retrospektive zu sehen, die 1991–1992 gemeinsam vom Kunstmuseum Bern und dem Cabinet des Estampes in Genf organisiert worden war und in verschiedene Städte Frankreichs reiste.

MARKUS RAETZ, CECI-CELA, 1992–1993, Gusseisen und Spiegel, Schrift: 8 cm hoch, Spiegel: 33 x 43,3 cm / cast iron and mirror, letters: 3⅛", mirror: 13 x 17". (PHOTO: PETER LAURI)

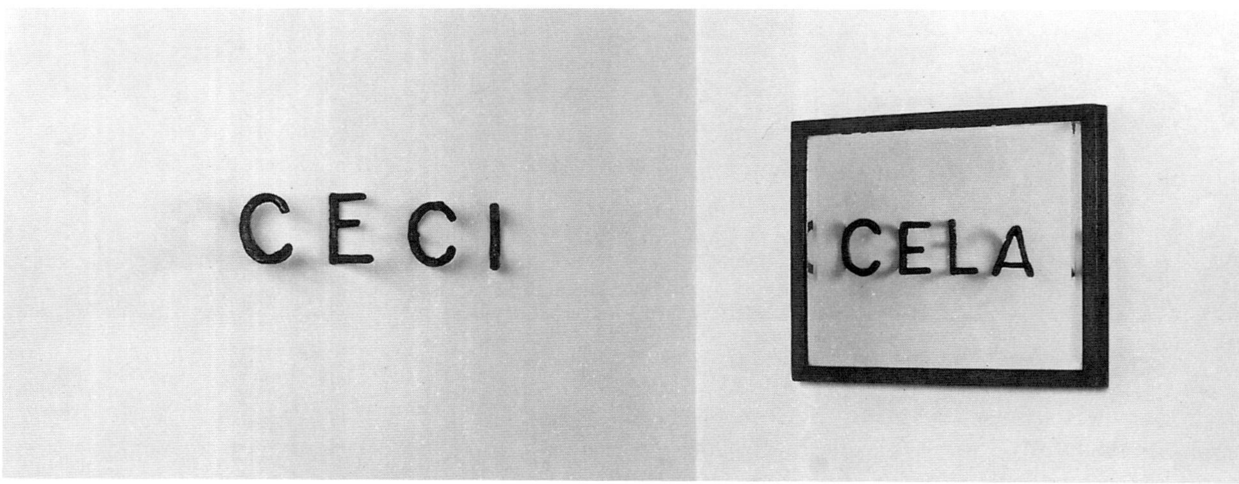

MARKUS RAETZ, SEEBLICK II, 1981–1985, 20 Teile (Heidekrautzweige und bemalte Holzstücke), 55 x 222 cm / SEAVIEW II, 20 pieces (heather and painted wood), 21⅞ x 87⅞".

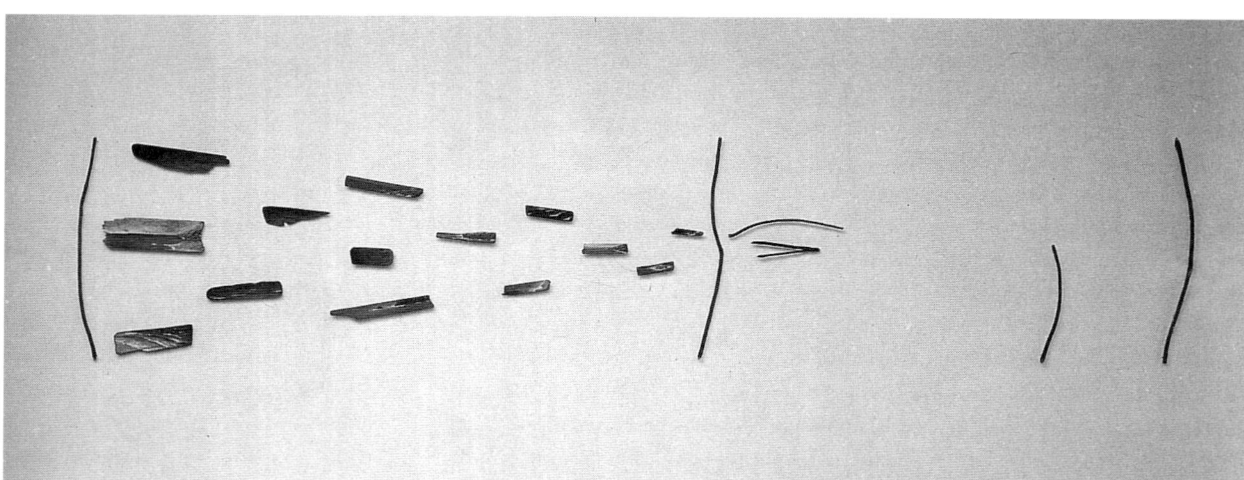

CLAUDE RITSCHARD

RECENT SCULPTURES OF MARKUS RAETZ ON THE SUBJECT OF METAMORPHOSES

Over the course of the last few years, Markus Raetz has produced a series of medium-sized sculptures in the round that explore the phenomenon of metamorphosis. The earliest of these, METAMORPHOSIS I (1990 for the plaster, 1991 for the casting), presents, in a single object, a face-to-face encounter between Joseph Beuys and a rabbit. This early hybrid is followed by NON-PIPE (1990, plaster, 1992, casting) and NON-SMOKE (1990, plaster), two allusions to Magritte's CECI N'EST PAS UNE PIPE, which invert, depending on one's perspective, the order of pipe and smoke. During 1991–92 Raetz began another version of the bust of Beuys wearing his felt hat, METAMORPHOSIS II, and created FORM IN SPACE, a more general citation of formal sculpture. The latter transforms the spiral form into a Mickey Mouse head, thus suggesting a second citation, this time of Markus Raetz's own work, which one will recognize if one recalls that, as early as the 1970s, the Disney mouse already served the artist as a pretext for experiments in the distortion of forms and anamorphosis. In 1991 he began his first studies of heads which would lead to both the permutation of the face from top to bottom (SILHOUETTES, 1992, and HEAD, 1992) and the two-profiled form of a JANUS (1991). Lastly, two other sculptures from this period complete his investigation: LARGE AND SMALL (1992), a kind of homage to Morandi that juxtaposes a glass and a bottle, inverting their respective scales, and CECI-CELA (1992–93), a bas-relief consisting of four bronze letters (CECI) attached with rods to one wall of a corner, and on the other wall, a mirror in which their reflection reads CELA.

The traveling exhibition organized in 1993–94, which was shown at the *Ivam* in Valencia, the Serpentine Gallery in London, and the Musée Rath in Geneva (and part of which is on exhibit this fall in Helsinki at the Nykytaiteen Museo) made it possible to confront all of Raetz's sculptures produced between 1990 and 1993. These recent works, moreover, served as the starting point and reference point for the choice of works selected for this "reverse retrospective" conceived by Ad Petersen and realized in collaboration with Markus Raetz himself. The 250 odd works—drawings, bas-reliefs and sculptures—dating from 1960 to 1993, aptly elucidate Markus Raetz's con-

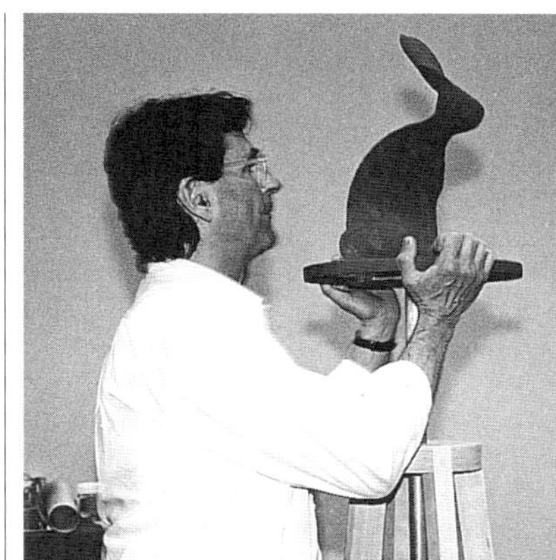

MARKUS RAETZ beim Aufbau seiner Ausstellung im Musée Rath (Juni 1994) / MARKUS RAETZ installing his exhibition in the Musée Rath.
(PHOTO: JACQUES BERTHET)

CLAUDE RITSCHARD is curator of the Musée d'Art et d'Histoire in Geneva.

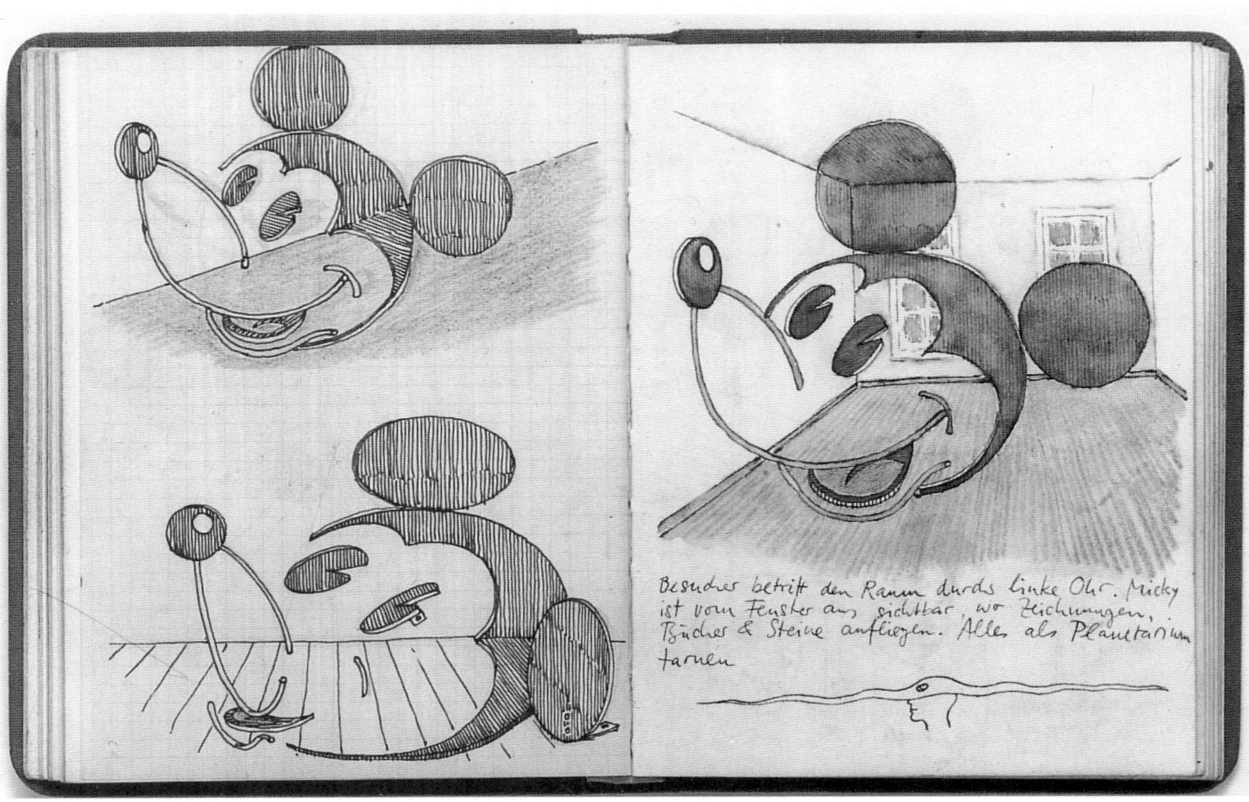

MARKUS RAETZ, DIE BÜCHER, 1972–1976, 10 Bände in Leinen gebunden / THE BOOKS, 10 volumes bound in cloth. (PHOTO: LUCIA DE GANDA)

cerns. The different directions that we have seen his works take in the past, with their different themes, languages and manners of execution, all fall into place like elements in a rebus, giving proof not only of their meaning but of their coherence as well.

The tremendous clarity and richness of this exhibition made it possible to discover connections between works separated by as much as twenty years. It becomes evident that the thematics of Markus Raetz— which seem to be innumerable when one has only a vague memory of individual pieces or modest ensembles seen with large intervals of the time between one show and the next—can be reduced to two predominant subjects: figure and landscape. One also notices that the diversity of the materials, which are usually very simple if not downright "poor"—found objects range from ping-pong balls and iron wire to eucalyptus leaves and driftwood—indicates not a dispersive approach, but rather falls strictly within Raetz's range of concerns as elements not of a work process, but of a process of vision. The variety of techniques also has its reason: the artist moves from drawing to watercolor to relief and to sculpture.[1] Each of these languages is a necessary mode of investigation in the development of his approach and functions, like the Polaroid snapshots Raetz also uses, as a principle of verification.

The object of this verification is the relationship between the concrete world and the vision that the eye presents of it. In the works of Markus Raetz that distort, multiply or transform the image, everything happens as though sight were just an illusion. This is the very least one can postulate upon a first reading, when one adopts the objective point of view of the observer. Here "objectivity" implies a reliability imputed to the functioning of the eye: "I believe what I see." What is forgotten is that the eye is but a lens directing the

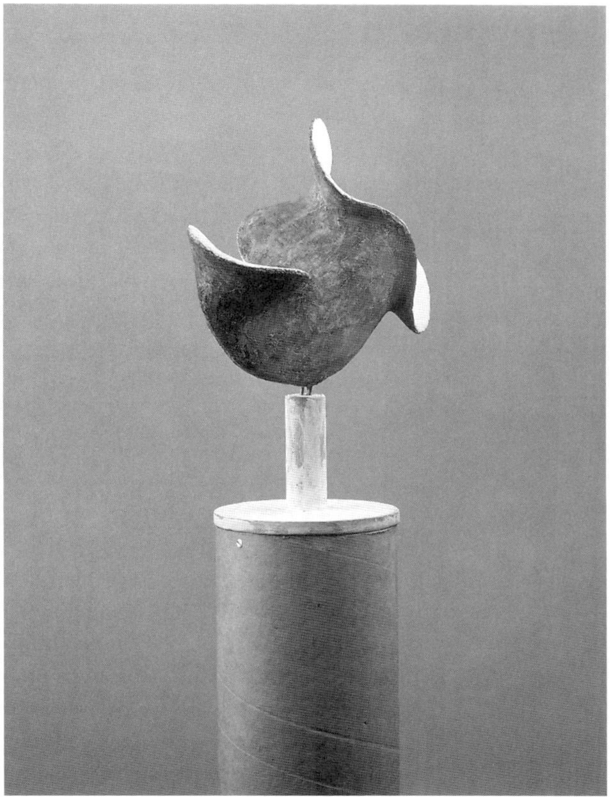

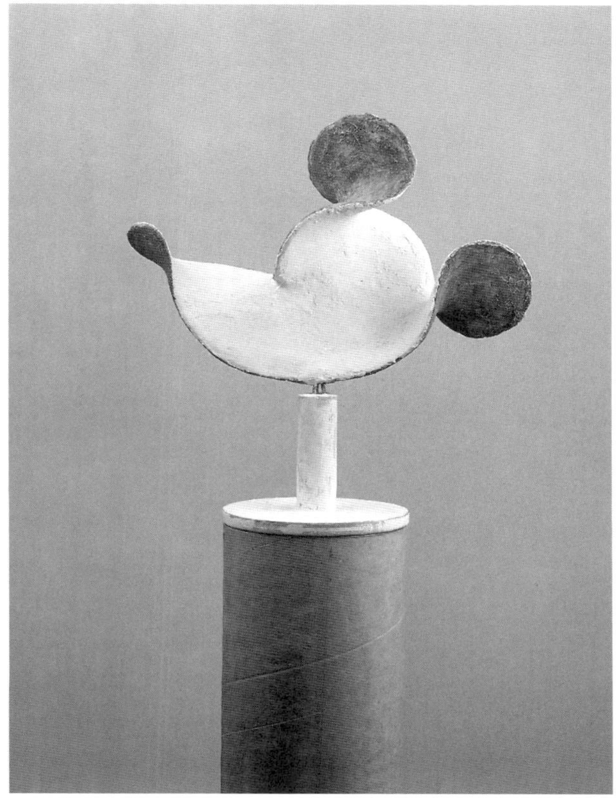

MARKUS RAETZ, FORM IM RAUM, 1991–1992, Gips, Holz, Kupferdraht und Hanf, 20,4 x 14 x 6,5 cm / FORM IN SPACE, plaster, wood, copper wire, and hemp, 8 x 5½ x 2½". (Zwei Ansichten / two views)
(PHOTO: PETER LAURI)

light rays on the plate of the photosensitive retina through the intermediary of the brain. The image takes form in relation to a reservoir of archetypes assembled by each individual from his very earliest childhood; the identification of the image, its recognition, is a cerebral phenomenon. There is therefore no "objectivity" of vision, but rather a subjective vision peculiar to each person. For centuries, however, the assumption of objectivity did have the power to situate the observer, man, in a position of dominance with respect to the world around him. He sees it, names it, recognizes it, and appropriates it. It is hardly naïve to recall that during the Renaissance one felt the need to define the rules of representation according to the theory of visual perspective. It was, at once, a definition of the rules of sight and therefore of the hierarchical relations between man and his environment.

Since the 1960s, Markus Raetz has been playing with a perspective that is not mathematical but at once pragmatic and intuitive. It leads him to explore distortions obtained by certain extravagances of perspective, sometimes pushed to the point of anamorphosis. Such works present a problematics of the function of sight, replacing the conventional hierarchy of the eye over the world. SEA VIEW II (1981–85), for example, which presents a face in profile made up of a few branches from which spring, at eye level, a series of little maritime landscapes painted on driftwood and arranged in a triangle, proposes a twofold dynamics of sight: one can read the bas-relief as the seaview framed by the lens of the eye, but also, and inseparably, as the sea entering the eye and impressed upon the retina.

These earlier works are necessary to an understanding of the recent sculptures, in which Markus Raetz prolongs this postulation of an active exterior world that is an agent of sight. In the

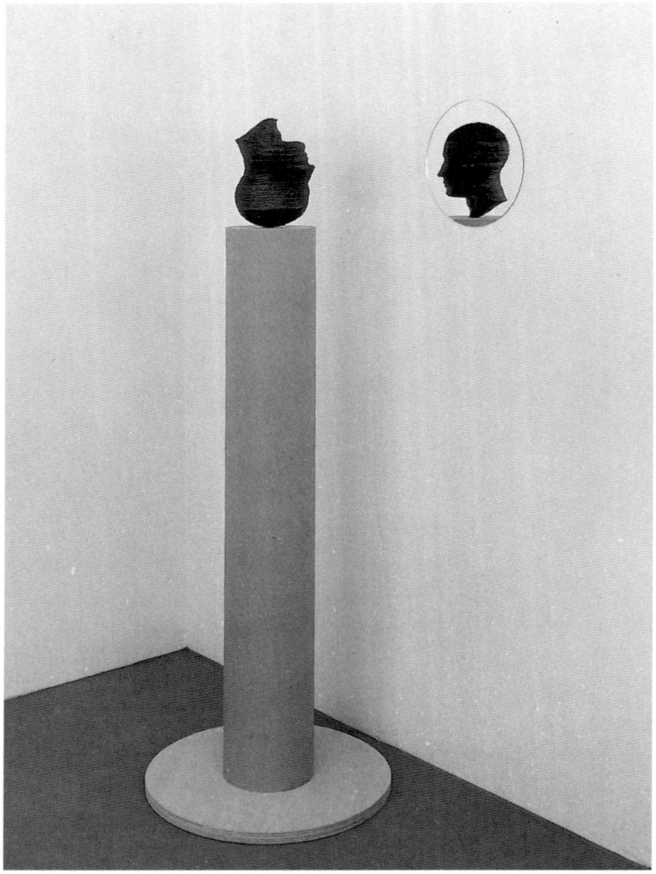

MARKUS RAETZ, SILHOUETTEN (FÜR ERNST MACH), 1992, Gusseisen und Spiegel, 27,8 x 20,4 x 20 cm, Spiegel: 32 cm / SILHOUETTES (FOR ERNST MACH), cast iron and mirror, 11 x 8 x 7⅞", mirror: 12⅝". (PHOTO: PETER LAURI)

early experiments displaying this complexity, especially in the anamorphoses, the observer was already invited to modify his point of view if he wanted to acquire vision. In the latest sculptures, the spectator must in fact walk around the works if s/he wants to witness their metamorphosis. Thus the hierarchy of positions is effaced, and Renaissance visual perspective is checkmated since it can only function on the guiding principle of a fixed point of a view.

Yet there is more in these metamorphoses than a simple dispute over perspective. Avatar or incarnation, metamorphosis, which implies a change of form or identity, is the result of a brutal evolution which, on the level of myth, can only occur by the will of the gods, who themselves are subject to such mutations. Whether the transformation is a trial or a rebirth, the being undergoing metamorphosis is no longer in his new form but a projection of what he was before. He is himself and another, and the invisibility of what his earlier essence was makes his new form precarious. The alteration of what was a body, a material, an identity, into something entirely other, shakes all certitudes about matter and reality to their very foundations.

Like mythology, Markus Raetz casts doubt on theories and systems of representation. In metamorphosing, the image escapes formulation. It is sensible only as a simulacrum, a perceptible appearance that presents itself, momentarily, as a reality.

(Translated from the French by Stephen Sartarelli)

1) To the techniques cited here, one should also add engraving. Ad Petersen and Markus Raetz chose not to include any works in that medium in this exhibition, given the fact that a retrospective of engraved works had been recently organized by the Kunstmuseum of Bern in conjunction with the Cabinet des Estampes in Geneva in 1991–92, a show that traveled through France as well.

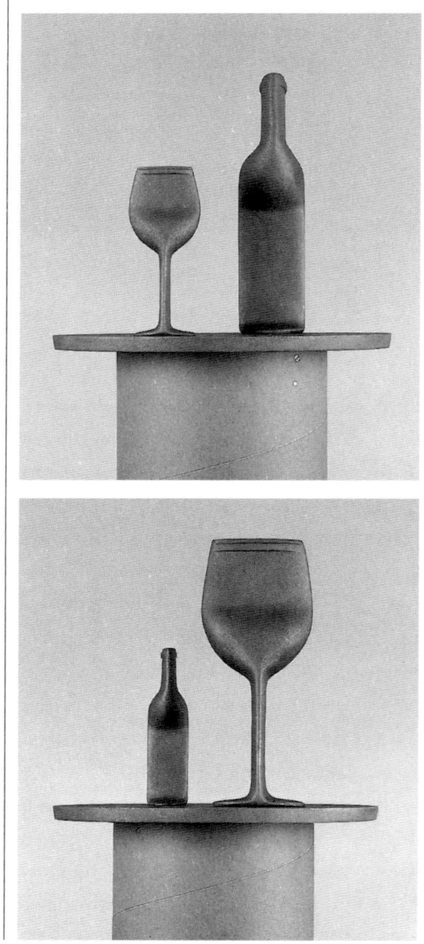

MARKUS RAETZ, GROSS UND KLEIN, 1992, Bronze, 30,3 x 36 x 36 cm / LARGE AND SMALL, bronze, 11⅞ x 14⅛ x 14⅛". (Zwei Ansichten / two views) (PHOTO: PETER LAURI)

CUMULUS

From Europe

IN EVERY EDITION OF PARKETT, TWO CUMULUS CLOUDS, ONE FROM AMERICA, THE OTHER FROM EUROPE, FLOAT OUT TO AN INTERESTED PUBLIC. THEY CONVEY INDIVIDUAL OPINIONS, ASSESSMENTS, AND MEMORABLE ENCOUNTERS—AS ENTIRELY PERSONAL PRESENTATIONS OF PROFESSIONAL ISSUES.

Our contributors to this issue are GUY BRETT, art critic and writer based in London, and MARTHA FLEMING, artist living in Montreal. Both texts were first written as lectures for the symposium Writing Art, organized in April 1994 by Rear Window London and the Kent Institute of Art and Design.

NEW MEASURES

GUY BRETT

I am driving my daughter to school. She picks up a miniature set of boxed books which have been lying around the interior of the car for years. Published by Puffin and called something like *Stupendous Facts.* While countless things have been put in and taken out of the car, the little box has stayed there, sinking lower and lower into the depths. "Can I read you a fact?" and she opens the book at random: If all the stars of the Milky Way had names and if someone were to say the names one after another, at the rate of one per second without stopping, it would take them 4,000 years. Earlier the same day while doing biology homework she told me that if all the blood vessels of the human body were laid end to end they would stretch twice round the earth. Something in the region of 96,000 kilometres.

How do words convey the immeasurable? How do words get the measure of anything? Beyond the use of pure numbers, language turns into metaphor. What it is, here, that words try to take the measure of could be called The Cosmic.

In these two random examples there is an interesting reversal in the choice of metaphor. The universe is brought close by the image of the person speaking names. The body is thrown back into distant space by the image of the earth's circumference.

I am returning from Bordeaux and decide to look up a friend in Paris. Somewhat incongruously, considering that he used to be a champion of kinetic and avant-garde art, he tells me of his current interest in the eighteenth century English genre of Conversation Pieces. When I get home I look up two old catalogues I have of English Conversation Pieces, by Zoffany and others, in order to send them to my friend and I notice nearby in the shelf David Dabydeen's book *Hogarth's Blacks.* It suddenly strikes me that this book is also about the same genre. It is for this reason that I begin to look at it. In his introduction Dabydeen says that of 18th century English artists William Hogarth was the most prolific painter and engraver of blacks, but that up until now, "no attempt has been made by art historians to place Hogarth's blacks in the narrative context in which they occur in his paintings." Dabydeen gives the example of Robert Cowley's "otherwise excellent" dissertation on Hogarth's MARRIAGE A LA MODE which, while examining each picture in minute detail "down to the 3 pins stuck in the broker's sleeve in frame 1 to the cobwebs in the window in frame 6 makes no mention whatsoever of the black man serving chocolate in frame 4, not even a token acknowledgment of his presence."

Exhibition and inhibition. Was the black servant invisible to Robert Cowley? It is more likely that he did not have the words, or did not trust himself to use the right words, to describe this aspect of the painting by Hogarth, even though Hogarth was an artist in whose pictures every detail has a precise meaning in a carefully conceived narrative. And so he passed over it. Could he say anything that would not betray his position as one of the inheritors? Not unless he were actually to acknowledge his predicament.

As Mikhail Bakhtin often pointed out, words cannot be just conveniently appropriated. Many stubbornly resist. They sound foreign in the mouth of the one who appropriated them. Someone eloquent and at ease in one branch of discourse is "reduced to silence or intervenes in a most awkward fashion" in others.

What it is that words try to take the measure of here could be called The Social.

These examples are meant to suggest three things which for me are important to the question of "writing art." First, do the words used have the measure of the thing described? Sec-

HELIO OITICIA, EDEN, 1969, installation, Jeu de Paume, Paris, 1992.

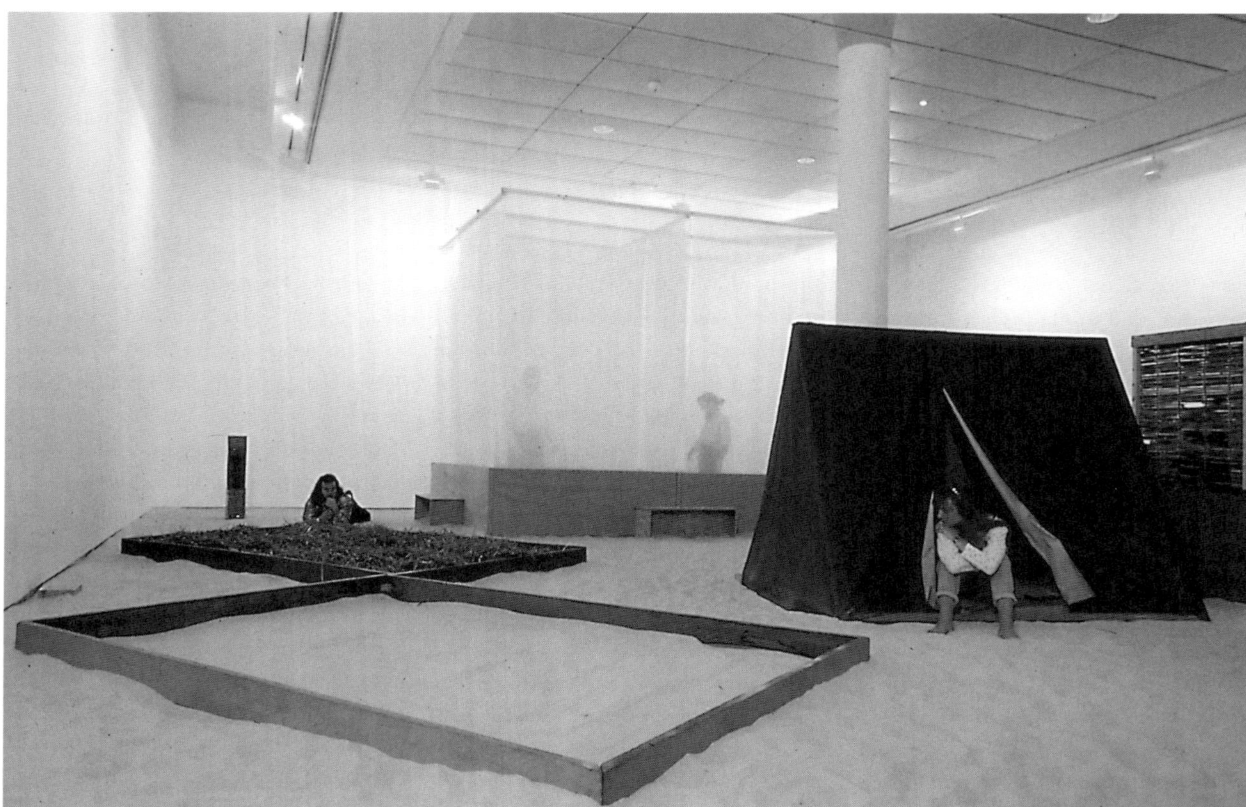

ond, no terms are absolute, no discourse can say everything, there are always protocols and proprieties. Writers' volubility in some areas is matched by their extreme reticence in others. Third, that experience, perception, insight come about in the immeasurable intricacy of the movements of everyday life. This affects all though. "Since consciousness goes on unceasingly, no one can stop it for inspection," as D. T. Suzuki, the Japanese writer on Zen, used to say.

In "writing art" the relationship between words and their object is a wide-open field. But at any given moment, in any given milieu, there's an acceptable or fashionable verbal structure, a buzzing of buzz words. They may not at all have the measure of the work described. The other day I received a catalogue of the work of a young painter living in Quito, Ecuador. To my eye the paintings strongly resembled John Piperish neo-romantic English semi-abstracts which could have been produced any time in the last forty years. I could imagine the kind of text which would have accompanied them in the 1960s, for example. It was strange, therefore, to learn from this 1990s catalogue that the paintings were concerned with "cultural nomadism," "artistic syncretism," "the discourse on the margin and the centre," "the interrogation of painting as a dominant language of modern art," "the subversion of the dominant discourse of modernism through an exploration of subjectivity..." and so on. The American filmmaker Maya Deren used to say that, in the experience of art, "the condition of receptivity is primary and must precede any analysis." In how many cases, I wonder, does analysis precede receptivity?

This phrase "condition of receptivity" seems to me to be a twin of the phrase about consciousness going on unceasingly. Both imply experience taking place in the stream of life, the lived experience of specific individuals, and an object which is capable of transformation, change, which has not been finished. Museums are places where certain analyses have settled around objects, isolating them and freezing their kinetic existence.

The Brazilian artist Helio Oiticica, when he came to describe his works in words, rarely referred to them as static, discrete objects but as part of a kind of ambulatory or bodily experience, as events. (It's interesting, incidentally, in this connection that much early art writing was a branch of travel writing: Fewer objects were collected in museums and were seen therefore as part of a whole exposure to another culture.)

Oiticica described his participatory environment, called EDEN, which he constructed at the Whitechapel Gallery in 1969, by the use of phrases such as "promenading through sites," "langour inside tents." "Continuing on over the sand," he wrote, "one comes across sand contained in an area, AREA BOLIDE 1 and upon hay, contained in AREA BOLIDE 2, and one lies down as if waiting for the internal sun, the non-repressive leisure..."

Oiticica had a concept he called creleisure, which many of his works were aspects of, or models for. Creleisure is a composite word combining creativity, leisure, pleasure, and probably also Creole. It was an attempt to see beyond the polarized modern concepts of work and leisure in the Westernized world, to "a world which creates itself through our leisure, around it, not as an escape, but as the apex of human desires."

The AREA BOLIDES Oiticica referred to in these phrases were simply rectangular enclosures bounded by low painted wooden borders. His description is pure imaginative projection, if you like, or a statement of possibilities. Is it therefore a fantasy or a mere expression of intention?

This question can be said to go to the heart of twentieth century art. It is a curious fact that in two of the famous court cases of the late nineteenth and early twentieth century, which were designed to test whether a modern work could be called art—those involving Whistler's paintings and Brancusi's sculpture—it was said by the conservatives in both cases that these works "left too much to the imagination." These court cases are fascinating because they represent the highly regulated form of a dispute taking place throughout society. They proceed from regulations and presumably lead to further regulations.

Although both the Whistler and the Brancusi works on trial alluded to empty space, the objections made to them were apparently of opposite kinds. It was the shadowy, formless, unfinished quality of Whistler's NOCTURNE IN BLACK AND GOLD (as well as its adoption of a musical title) which angered his attackers. In the Brancusi case, the dispute was over whether his polished bronze sculpture BIRD IN SPACE should be classified as a piece of manufactured material, a lump of metal—in which case it incurred an import tax—or a work of art, in which case it could enter the country freely. The original legislation had been designed to facilitate the circulation of art works as culture and separate them clearly from utilitarian artefacts. In the court, discourse tended to divide out between the poetic, the empathetic, the imaginative, and the rhapsodic on one hand, and the down-to-earth, pragmatic and materials-based on the other. This was despite the fact that the original legislation had attempted to draw a line between art and not-art based on distinctions between the artistic and the utilitarian use of materials. In the end, measurement was impossible and metaphor came in.

The Brancusi case was a sort of battle of metaphors. But there was, all along, a strong affinity between Brancusi's BIRD IN SPACE and a lump of matter. The original confusion, or ambiguity of signs, was itself significant.

I must admit to liking this confusion. In English writing I have always felt myself strongly drawn to two apparently opposed sides which have long been present: one which might be represented by the great cosmic, visionary, prophetic, bell-like tones and dialectical clarity of William Blake, and the other the scurrilous, anti-pretentious, mocking, self-mocking, nonchalant tone of a line of writers ending today in someone like Stephen Fry. I'm not sure which one I am: In other words I'm not sure if the sun is a silver disc about the size of a shilling or a choir of angels. So, not being able to resolve this dichotomy, I found myself drawn to another kind of writing which I thought, and still think, could serve as a model for the present-day genre, or sub-genre, of art writing, writing art or writing on art. This model was ancient and Renaissance prose discourse, and early scientific and technical treatise writing. Here are two examples:

"It seems to me to be of the greatest importance that anyone speaking of the science of medicine should confine himself to matters known to the general public, since the subject of inquiry and the discourse is none other than the maladies of which they themselves fall sick. Although it were no easy matter for common people to discover for themselves the nature of their own diseases and the causes why they get worse or get better, yet it is easy for them to follow when another makes the discoveries and explains the events to them. Then when a man hears about a disease he will only have to remember his own experience of it. But if anyone departs from what is popular knowledge and does not make himself intelligible to his own audience, he is not being practical."

from the *Penguin Book of Hippocratic Writings*

"If you find the leisure, it would please me if you should look again at this my little work On Painting *which I set into Tuscan for your renown... May it please you, then, to read me with diligence. If anything here seems to you to need emending, correct me. There was never a writer so learned to whom erudite friends were not useful. I in particular desire to be corrected by you in order not to be pecked at by detractors."* from Alberti's fifteenth century *Treatise on Painting*

There is a strong sense of the author as an ordinary person in the midst of life, whose ideas have been formed in the midst of life. And there is a very strong sense of the reader, the one addressed. The thing written is like a particle of on-going dialogues. "Knowledge" is presented with a sense of the thinking but fallible subject. There is also the enjoyable, perceptible tension in the writers themselves between the specialist and the ordinary person, one of the multitude, because specialization has not yet become the private profession, the "selfishness" as Tagore called it, which it later became.

The Socratic dialogue and the Buddhist dialogues could be taken as further examples of what I mean. Bakhtin has said two interesting things about this genre (for it was a genre of writing). First, he said that "In the Socratic dialogue the idea is organically connected with the image of a person, its carrier." And he also said that, at that time, the split that was to come later between the "abstractly scientific or philosophical concept and the artistic image" had not yet occurred.

I am not suggesting that this genre be imitated, or cultivated as a self-conscious style, especially in a nostalgic sense. This is for the very reason that it is not susceptible to mechanical copying but is capable of endless renewal. What is appealing, I think, in this manner or tone, is that it makes us feel our own actual contemporaneity.

This text was originally given as a contribution to a symposium, "Writing Art," organized by Rear Window, London, and the Kent Institute of Art and Design, in April 1994.

NEUE MASSSTÄBE

GUY BRETT

Ich fahre meine Tochter zur Schule. Sie entdeckt einen Schuber mit Miniaturbüchern, der seit Jahren im Wagen herumliegt. Die Bücher sind im Verlag Puffin erschienen, und ihr Titel lautet so ähnlich wie *Verblüffende Tatsachen*. Während unzählige Sachen im Wagen verstaut und wieder herausgenommen wurden, war der kleine Schuber dort liegengeblieben und immer weiter in die Tiefen hinabgesunken. «Darf ich dir eine Tatsache vorlesen?» und sie öffnet ein Buch an einer beliebigen Stelle: «Wenn alle Sterne der Milchstrasse einen Namen hätten und jemand diese Namen einen nach dem anderen aufsagen würde, und zwar einen pro Sekunde, ohne zu unterbrechen, bräuchte er dazu 4000 Jahre.» Am gleichen Tag hatte sie mir, während sie ihre Biologie-Hausarbeit machte, bereits erzählt, dass, würde man alle Blutgefässe des menschlichen Körpers mit ihren Enden aneinanderlegen, diese zweimal um die Erde herumreichen würden. Etwa 96 000 km.

Wie drücken Worte das Unermessliche aus? Wie erfassen Worte überhaupt das Mass einer Sache? Jenseits des Gebrauchs reiner Zahlen wird die Sprache zur Metapher. Die Dimension, der hier Worte beizukommen versuchen, liesse sich als das Kosmische bezeichnen.

Diese beiden willkürlichen Beispiele zeichnen sich durch eine interessante Umkehrung bei der Wahl der Metaphorik aus. Das Universum wird durch das Bild einer die Namen aufsagenden Person nahegebracht. Der Körper wird durch die Vorstellung vom Erdumfang in den fernen Raum hinausverlagert.

Auf dem Rückweg von Bordeaux entschliesse ich mich, einen Freund in Paris aufzusuchen. Etwas paradox, wenn man bedenkt, dass er früher einmal ein Verfechter kinetischer und avantgardistischer Kunst war, erzählt er mir von seinem gegenwärtigen Interesse für das im 18. Jahrhundert in England beliebte Genre des Gesellschaftsstücks. Wieder zu Hause suche ich in meinem Bücherregal zwei alte Kataloge über englische Konversationsstücke von Zoffany und anderen heraus, um sie meinem Freund zu schicken. Dabei fällt mein Blick auf das in der Nähe stehende Buch über *Hogarth's Blacks* von David Dabydeen. Mir wird plötzlich klar, dass auch dieses Buch sich mit dem gleichen Genre befasst. Aus diesem Grund schaue ich es mir näher an. In seiner Einführung meint Dabydeen, William Hogarth habe von allen englischen Künstlern des 18. Jahrhunderts in seinen Bildern und Stichen am häufigsten Schwarze dargestellt, doch bislang habe «kein Kunsthistoriker den Versuch unternommen, die Schwarzen bei Hogarth in dem narrativen Zusammenhang zu betrachten, in dem sie in seinen Bildern figurieren». Als Beispiel nennt Dabydeen die «ansonsten vorzügliche» Dissertation von Robert Cowley über Hogarths Bilderzyklus MARRIAGE A LA MODE, in der der Autor jedes einzelne Bild bis ins kleinste Detail unter die Lupe nimmt, «bis hin zu den drei Nadeln, die im ersten Bild im Ärmel des Kupplers stecken, und den Spinnweben im Fenster im sechsten Bild, jedoch mit keinem Wort auf den Schwarzen eingeht, der im vierten Bild heisse Schokolade serviert, ja nicht einmal dessen Anwesenheit der Form halber zur Kenntnis nimmt».

Zurschaustellung und Zurückhaltung. War der schwarze Diener für Robert Cowley unsichtbar? Wahrscheinlicher ist, dass ihm die Worte fehlten oder dass er es sich nicht zutraute, die richtigen Worte zu finden, um diesen Aspekt des Hogarthschen Bildes zu beschreiben, obgleich Hogarth ein Künstler war, in dessen Bildern jedem Detail eine präzise Bedeutung im Rahmen einer genau ausgedachten Geschichte zukommt. Also überging er das Motiv. Konnte er irgend etwas sagen, das nicht die Tradition des Verschweigens verraten hätte? Es sei denn, er hätte sich zum Dilemma bekannt.

Wörter lassen sich, wie Michail Bachtin häufig betont hat, nicht einfach je nach Belieben aneignen. Viele widersetzen sich hartnäckig. Sie klingen fremd im Munde desjenigen, der sie benutzt. Jemand, der in einer Disziplin beredt und in seinem Element ist, wird in einer anderen «gezwungen, zu schweigen, oder mischt sich überaus ungeschickt ein».

Die Dimension, der hier Worte beizukommen versuchen, liesse sich als das Soziale bezeichnen.

Diese Beispiele sollen drei Dinge suggerieren, die mir im Zusammenhang mit dem Schreiben über Kunst wichtig sind. Erstens, sind die verwendeten Worte dem, was beschrieben wird, angemessen? Zweitens, kein Begriff ist absolut, kein Diskurs kann alles sagen, es gibt immer Normen und Konventionen. Die Redegewandtheit eines Autors in manchen Bereichen wird aufgewogen durch seine äusserste Zurückhaltung in anderen. Drittens, Erfahrung, Wahrnehmung, Erkenntnis stellt sich im Zuge der unermesslichen Komplexität der Ereignisse des täglichen Lebens ein. Dies betrifft jedoch alle. «Da das Bewusstsein», wie der japanische Zen-Autor D. T. Suzuki zu sagen pflegte, «unaufhörlich im Gange ist, kann niemand es anhalten, um es genau zu prüfen.»

Beim Schreiben über Kunst ist die Beziehung zwischen Worten und ihrem Objekt ein weit offenes Feld. Doch zu jedem bestimmten Zeitpunkt, in jedem gegebenen Umfeld gibt es eine akzeptable oder modische Form der Verbalisierung, eine Ausdrucksweise, die gerade in der Luft liegt. Diese muss dem beschriebenen Werk in keiner Weise angemessen sein. Neulich erhielt ich einen Katalog des Werkes eines jungen Malers aus Quito in Ecuador. Die Bilder erinnerten mich sehr stark an neoromantische englische, halbabstrakte Malerei im Stile John Pipers, die jederzeit innerhalb der letzten vierzig Jahre hätte entstanden sein können. Ich konnte mir zum Beispiel genau vorstellen, welche Art von Text diese Bilder in den 60er Jahren begleitet hätte. Deshalb war es befremdlich, aus diesem Katalog, einem Produkt der 90er Jahre, zu erfahren, dass sich die Bilder befassten mit «kulturellem Nomadentum», mit «künstlerischem Synkretismus», mit «dem Diskurs über Peripherie und Zentrum», mit «der Infragestellung der Malerei als tonangebender Ausdrucksform der modernen Kunst», mit «der Unterwanderung des vorherrschenden Diskurses der Moderne durch Erkundung der Subjektivität...» und so weiter. Die amerikanische Filmemacherin Maya Deren pflegte immer zu sagen, dass beim Erleben von Kunst «das Empfänglichsein vorrangig ist und jeder Analyse vorausgehen muss». Wie oft, frage ich mich, geht die Analyse der Empfänglichkeit voraus?

Dieser Ausdruck «Empfänglichsein» kommt mir vor wie ein Gegenstück zu der Aussage über das fortwährende Andauern des Bewusstseins. Beide begreifen Erfahrung als etwas, das sich im Fluss des Lebens einstellt, als die gelebte Erfahrung bestimmter Individuen, und beide begreifen das Objekt als etwas, das des Wandels, der Veränderung fähig und unabgeschlossen ist. Das Museum ist ein Ort, an dem sich eine bestimmte Analyse um ein Objekt herum etabliert hat, die dieses isoliert und seine kinetische Existenz lähmt.

Der brasilianische Künstler Hélio Oiticica bezeichnete seine Werke, wenn er überhaupt über sie sprach, selten als statische, für sich stehende Objekte, sondern als Teil eines veränderlichen oder körperlichen Erlebens, als Ereignisse. (Es ist in diesem Zusammenhang übrigens interessant, dass die frühe Kunstschriftstellerei grossenteils ein Zweig der Reiseliteratur war: Weil weniger Objekte in Museen gesammelt wurden, erlebte man sie im Rahmen einer übergreifenden Begegnung mit einer anderen Kultur.)

Oiticica beschrieb sein den Betrachter einbeziehendes Environment mit dem Titel EDEN, das er 1969 in der Londoner Whitechapel Gallery installierte mit Wendungen wie «Herumspazieren durch verschiedene Schauplätze», «Müssiggang im Innern von Zelten». «Geht man über den Sand weiter», schrieb er, «stösst man auf ein Areal, das Sand enthält, AREA BOLIDE 1, und auf ein anderes, das Heu enthält, AREA BOLIDE 2, und man legt sich nieder wie in Erwartung der inneren Sonne, der nichtrepressiven Musse...»

Ein zentrales Konzept seiner Kunst taufte Oiticica auf den Begriff «creleisure», den zahlreiche seiner Werke facettenartig beleuchten oder auch exemplarisch veranschaulichen. «Creleisure» ist ein zusammengesetztes Wort, das Kreativität, Musse (engl. *leisure*), Vergnügen (engl. *pleasure*) und vermutlich auch kreolisch miteinander vereint. Darin lag ein Versuch, jenseits des in der modernen westlichen Welt polarisierten Verständnisses von Arbeit und Musse sich eine Welt vorzustellen, «die im Zuge unserer Musse aus sich selbst heraus entsteht, die sich um unsere Musse herum kristallisiert, nicht in einem eskapistischen Sinne, sondern als Kulmination menschlicher Bedürfnisse».

Die AREA BOLIDES, von denen Oiticica in seiner Beschreibung sprach, waren schlicht rechteckige, von niedrigen bemalten Holzleisten eingefasste Bezirke. Seine Beschreibung ist, wenn man so will, reine imaginative Projektion oder eine Beschreibung von Möglichkeiten. Ist sie somit eine Phantasterei oder eine blosse Absichtserklärung?

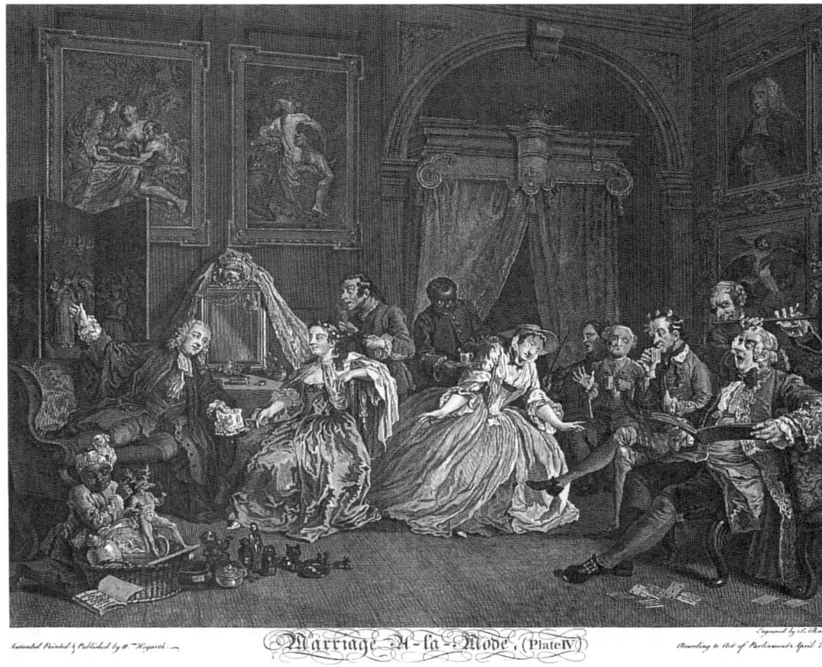

WILLIAM HOGARTH, MARRIAGE A LA MODE.

Diese Frage, so kann man sagen, trifft mitten ins Herz der Kunst des 20. Jahrhunderts. Es ist eine kuriose Tatsache, dass bei zwei berühmten Gerichtsfällen des späten 19. und des frühen 20. Jahrhunderts, die die Frage klären sollten, ob es statthaft sei, ein modernes Werk als Kunst zu bezeichnen (gemeint sind die Prozesse um die Malerei Whistlers und um die Skulptur Brancusis), von konservativer Seite jeweils die Auffassung vertreten wurde, dass diese Werke «zuviel der Phantasie überliessen». Diese Gerichtsfälle sind deshalb interessant, weil sie in stark reglementierter Form für einen die gesamte Gesellschaft durchziehenden Meinungsstreit stehen. Sie nehmen ihren Ausgang von Reglementierungen und führen vermutlich zu weiteren Reglementierungen.

Obgleich sowohl bei Whistler wie auch bei Brancusi das Werk, um das es beim Prozess ging, Leerräume andeutete, waren die gegen sie gerichteten Beanstandungen offenbar gegensätzlicher Natur. An Whistlers Bild NOCTURNE IN BLACK AND GOLD erzürnte seine Kritiker (neben der Anverwandlung eines musikalischen Titels) das Verschwommene, Formlose, Unfertige. Im Falle Brancusis dagegen drehte sich der Streit um die Frage, ob seine polierte Bronzeskulptur L'OISEAU DANS L'ESPACE als ein Stück bearbeitetes Material, ein Metallklumpen einzustufen sei, das als solches zollpflichtig war, oder als ein Kunstwerk, das zollfrei die Grenze passieren durfte. Das entsprechende Gesetz war ursprünglich entworfen worden, um die Verbreitung von Kunstwerken als Kulturgut zu erleichtern und sie deutlich von Gebrauchsartikeln abzugrenzen. Vor Gericht polarisierte sich der Diskurs im grossen und ganzen zwischen dem Poetischen, Einfühlsamen, Phantasievollen und Rhapsodischen auf der einen und dem Prosaischen, Pragmatischen, Materialorientierten auf der anderen Seite. Und das, obwohl sich die Gesetzgebung ursprünglich beim Versuch zur Trennung zwischen Kunst und Nichtkunst auf die Unterscheidung zwischen künstlerischer und zweckorientierter Materialverwendung gestützt hatte. Am Ende war jeder Massstab abhanden gekommen, und Metaphorik kam ins Spiel.

Der Fall Brancusi war eine Art Duell der Metaphern. Doch es gab schon von Anfang an eine starke Affinität zwischen Brancusis L'OISEAU DANS L'ESPACE und einem Klumpen Material. Die ursprüngliche Verwechslung oder Mehrdeutigkeit der Zeichen war schon für sich genommen bezeichnend.

Ich muss zugeben, dass mich diese Verwechslung reizt. In der einschlägigen englischen Literatur habe ich mich immer sehr stark zu zwei scheinbar entgegengesetzten Seiten hingezogen gefühlt, die seit langem ausgeprägt sind: eine, als deren Inbegriff sich die grossartige kosmische, visionäre, prophetische, glockenreine Diktion und dialektische Klarheit William Blakes anführen liesse, und die andere der skurrile, unprätentiöse, spöttische, selbstironische, nonchalante Tonfall einer Reihe von Kunstschriftstellern, an deren Ende heute ein Autor wie Stephen Fry steht. Ich bin mir nicht sicher, zu welcher Seite ich gehöre, mit anderen Worten: ich bin mir nicht sicher, ob die Sonne eine silberne Scheibe etwa von der Grösse eines Zehnpfennigstücks oder ein Chor von Engeln ist. Und weil ich mich ausserstande sah, diese Dichotomie aufzulösen, fühlte ich mich zu einer anderen Art des Schreibens hingezogen, von der ich glaubte (und nach wie vor glaube), dass sie als Modell dienen könnte für die heutige Gattung (oder Untergattung) der Kunstschriftstellerei. Dieses Modell war die Prosaliteratur der Antike und der Renaissance und das frühe Schrifttum wissenschaftlicher und technischer Traktate. Hier sind zwei Beispiele:

«Es dünkt mich von grösster Wichtigkeit, dass sich jeder, der über die Heilkunde spricht, auf Fragen beschränken sollte, die der breiten Öffentlichkeit vertraut sind, denn Gegenstand der Forschung und des Diskurses sind eben die Gebrechen, an denen sie selbst erkranken. Obgleich es für den einfachen Menschen kein leichtes Unterfangen wäre, für sich selbst die Art seiner Leiden herauszufinden und die Gründe, weshalb sich diese verschlimmern oder verbessern, so ist es doch leicht für sie zu verstehen, wenn ein anderer diese Befunde macht und ihnen erklärt, was vor sich geht. In diesem Fall braucht ein Mensch, wenn er von einer Krankheit erfährt, sich nur dessen zu entsinnen, wie er diese selbst erlebt hat. Wer jedoch abweicht von dem, was Allgemeinwissen ist, und sich seinen Zuhörern nicht verständlich macht, ist unpraktisch.»

aus dem *Penguin Book of Hippocratic Writings*

«Wenn dir einmal Musse zufällt, so wird es mich freuen, falls du diese meine kleine Schrift über die Malerei durchlesen würdest, die ich in toskanischer Sprache deinem Namen widme. [...] So mag es dir denn gefallen, mich mit Achtsamkeit zu lesen und falls dir etwas der Verbesserung bedürftig erscheint, verbessere es. Niemals war ein Schriftsteller so gelehrt, dass ihm gebildete Freunde nicht von grösstem Vorteil gewesen wären. Und ich besonders wünsche es, von dir in meinen Irrtümern berichtigt zu werden, um dem Angriff der Verleumder zu entgehen.»

aus Leon Battista Albertis Abhandlung *Della pittura* (15. Jahrhundert)

Aus ihnen spricht ein ausgeprägtes Selbstverständnis des Autors als jemand, der in der Mitte des Lebens steht, dessen Gedanken sich in der Mitte des Lebens herauskristallisiert haben. Und ein überaus ausgeprägtes Bewusstsein des angesprochenen Lesers. Das Geschriebene ist wie ein Segment aus einem anhaltenden Dialog. In die Art und Weise, wie Erkenntnis vorgebracht wird, spielt ein Wissen um das denkende, aber fehlbare Subjekt hinein. Ausserdem ist da die positive, spürbare Spannung innerhalb der Person des Autors selbst zwischen dem Spezialisten und dem einfachen Menschen, dem einen von vielen, weil die Spezialisierung noch nicht zu der privaten Profession, zu der, wie Tagore sagte, «Selbstsucht» geworden ist, die sie später wurde.

Der sokratische Dialog und die buddhistischen Dialoge liessen sich als weitere Beispiele anführen für das, worum es mir zu tun ist. Bachtin hat zu dieser Gattung (denn es handelte sich um eine literarische Gattung) zwei interessante Anmerkungen gemacht. Erstens sagte er, dass «beim sokratischen Dialog die Idee organisch mit dem Bild einer Person, ihrer Trägerin, verbunden ist». Und er meinte, dass der Bruch, der sich später zwischen dem «abstrakten wissenschaftlichen oder philosophischen Begriff und der künstlerischen Vorstellung» einstellen sollte, damals noch nicht eingetreten war.

Ich möchte nicht darauf hinaus, dass diese Gattung bewusst als Stil nachgeahmt oder kultiviert werden sollte, insbesondere nicht in einem nostalgischen Sinne. Und zwar aus eben dem Grund, weil sie sich nicht mechanisch kopieren lässt, sondern endloser Erneuerung fähig ist. Das Reizvolle an diesem Stil, an dieser Haltung ist meines Erachtens, dass wir durch sie uns unserer tatsächlichen Zeitgenossenschaft bewusst werden.

(Übersetzung: Magda Moses, Bram Opstelten)

Dieser Beitrag wurde ursprünglich als Vortrag auf dem von Rear Window organisierten Symposium *Writing Art* gehalten, das in diesem Jahr in London stattfand.

CUMULUS

From America

IN EVERY EDITION OF PARKETT, TWO CUMULUS CLOUDS, ONE FROM AMERICA, THE OTHER FROM EUROPE, FLOAT OUT TO AN INTERESTED PUBLIC. THEY CONVEY INDIVIDUAL OPINIONS, ASSESSMENTS, AND MEMORABLE ENCOUNTERS—AS ENTIRELY PERSONAL PRESENTATIONS OF PROFESSIONAL ISSUES.

Our contributors to this issue are GUY BRETT, art critic and writer based in London, and MARTHA FLEMING, artist living in Montreal. Both texts were first written as lectures for the symposium Writing Art, organized in April 1994 by Rear Window London and the Kent Institute of Art and Design.

THE SPIRIT & THE LETTER & THE EVIL EYE

MARTHA FLEMING

Manu sinistra. I am left handed. My heart always leaps when I see another person take a pen into his or her left hand. I am especially moved when the person is older, or brought up in a Catholic culture: The continued use of the left hand is a mark of resistance and survival in cases where a left hand may well have been strapped to the school bench. Repression of the use of this member can provoke serious neurological disturbances, including faintness, dizziness, and above all, speech difficulties. As the linguist Uldall makes evident, "The stream of air or the stream of ink" are both of the same language. The point of the finger. The point of the tongue. The point of the pen.

Manu sinistra. As a young girl, I sat beside my father at the circular dining room table on Sunday afternoons and practiced my handwriting. Dead now for over sixteen years, he was a skilled graphic designer and wrote with a perfect italic hand. This last was not and never would be the case of his left-handed daughter, and he did what he could to help me express myself articulately in a world which was not adapted to my particularities. I have ambivalent feelings and tender memories of his large, elegant right hand closing over my tiny left hand, his hand moving mine over the paper as if over a Ouija board, his hand setting mine right.

After a childhood of reading and writing—verbs I often even now confound—I began writing for publication, mostly in art magazines. But I ceased to publish shortly after I began to make art, apprenticed to Lyne Lapointe and others. I threw the act of writing out with the dirty bathwater of art magazines.

I continued to write, however, in several different ways that I did not originally see as linked. I wrote impossibly long letters to friends, which made it impossible for them to adequately reply. I regularly wrote complex grant applications and reports about the large-scale installation projects Lyne Lapointe and I produce; I wrote project proposals finely tuned to the different needs of our different collaborators on the projects, from City

Hall public works directors to historic preservation architects to museum curators: I wrote and designed all the posters, promotional and didactic material which was printed for these mainly self-produced projects. Above all, in all the projects Lyne and I have done—which at that time involved huge abandoned buildings such as a firehall, a central post office, and a vaudeville theatre—I wrote, designed, and painted the textual material which appeared in discrete works, in large interventions, and on the architecture itself.

My unconscious struggle to link apparently conflicting desires to write and to create images coalesced in the different lettering projects that I had done within the framework of these collaborative building projects, yet this activity of writing was so diverse and fragmented that I did not at first recognize it as a practice in and of itself. Gradually I began to see the complex connection between the narrative drive and an experience of "moving through" architecture.

It was only in 1991, when I sat down to begin a (still unfinished) book documenting the site projects already completed, that this practice began to take form in my consciousness as an experienced reality. The form it took at first was the form of tears. I was unable to put my hands to the keyboard without crying. Slowly I understood that these tears were coming to my eyes not only because of the stories I had to tell about the difficult conditions in which these projects had been produced, but that they were also tears of joy and release at returning to writing and to words, to the deep space of the printed page—so like, and so unlike, the celestial voids of the buildings themselves.

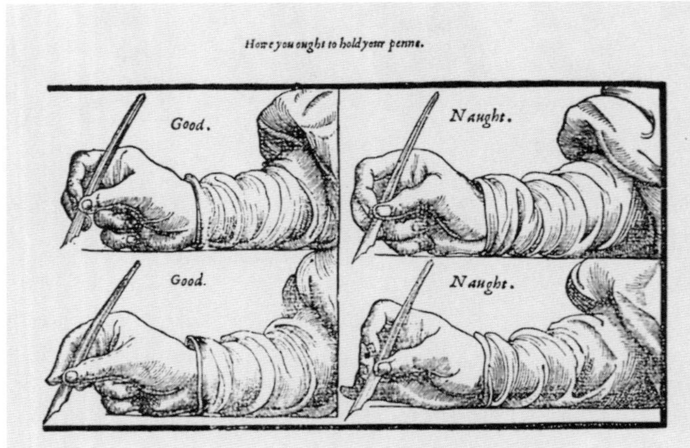

HOW YOU OUGHT TO HOLD YOUR PENNE,
in A New Booke of Copies, 1574.
Facsimile edited by Bernard Wolpe, Oxford, 1962.

What did I return to? What is writing? Is it the controlled act of taking a pen into hand with an opposable thumb and inscribing a piece of paper with ink? Is writing the construction of sentences? Is it the construction of meaning? Is it the act of legitimating and fixing that meaning and investing it with power? It is all these things, but it is also something more. Ultimately, it is something which issues forth from our luminous bodies.

In the following quote from Wittgenstein we see that his project was to open the idea of language to the cosmos it longs to embrace and which it also holds within it, as in a grain of sand.

> "If we take it for a given that human beings derive pleasure from our imaginations, we must be careful not to take this imagination to be a painted image or a plastic model; it is a complicated construction, composed of heterogeneous parts: words and images. Thus we will no longer oppose those operations which use signs spoken or written with those operations which use 'representative images' of events. We must plough the entire field of language."

Words and images: These are most exemplarily shown to be fused in the very letterforms of the Roman alphabet itself. In this Western tradition, which just as traditionally denies its own ideogrammatic origins, I see the fleeting, rainbow bridge between two worlds which have called to me, and see them as one. Here, so obvious as to be overlooked, so transparent as to be invisible, the floating world of letters on a page refuses reductive binarisms by embodying multiplicity. Individually fascinating, cabalistic, and in constant movement, each one of the 26 letters is both entire unto itself and is also an unassuming little nothing.

Among the grasses, wild and planted, in the entire field of language, there are blooming the images of the body which are the traces our own bodies leave as our writing hands move across the field of the page, quite apparent to our reading eyes as they sweep that same rich site. These images of the body are letterforms, invisible in their transparent ubiquity, and they are both signs written and representative images of events. Letterforms are the only thing I know, as an artist, how to draw. So intimately do I know their bodies, their legs and arms, their members, their joints, their articulations, their characters, that I draw them with the facility of a lover cartooning the face of the beloved. If this ideogrammatic status of the letterform is veiled as part of the Western discourse of denial which creates the binarisms essential to domination, what is the alphabet if not a form of screen memory? In its two-dimensionality, the page, the tablet, the stone, the etched glass, all that we write upon is a flat screen behind which surface we sense an immense and beckoning depth of field which is echoed in the muddy interior soundings of our own memories and forgettings. How is the authority of the written word used to repress the sensory memory which its very image embodies?

Writing both stands in for and blocks memories uniquely visual or oral. These last two, totally erotic, are both thwarted and referred to in the letterforms themselves (articulations) abstracted from the body and yet no longer entirely figurative, which hover about us like arms into which we would run and legs we long to feel wrapped around our waists and necks. We write to forget, and yet the very form of letters (characters) are haunted by our bodies, bodies whose senses are dulled by the very entry into language. How can writing bring us back to our bodies? How can it challenge the heavy grammar of perspective, the heavy perspective of grammar?

Another quote from Wittgenstein:

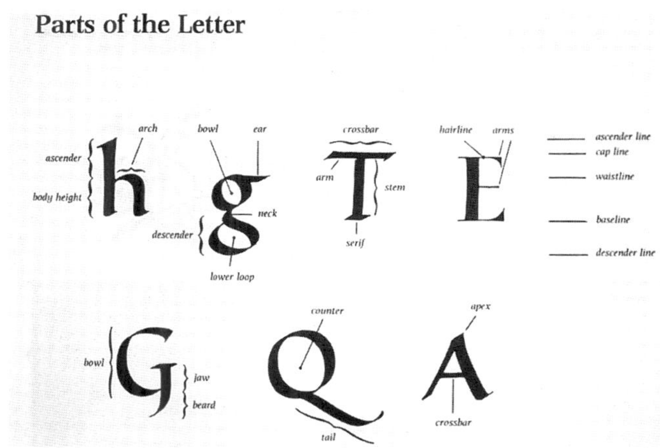

PARTS OF THE LETTER / DIE TEILE DES BUCHSTABENS, in The Calligraphers' Dictionary, edited by Rose Folsom, London, 1990.

> "An historical explanation, an explanation which takes the form of an evolutionary hypothesis, is only one way of putting together givens—that is, to give a synoptic schema. It is also equally possible to consider givens in their mutual relations and to group them in a general schema, without making a hypothesis concerning their evolution over time. (...) As one might illustrate the internal relation between the shape of the circle and that of the ellipse in gradually transforming an ellipse into a circle; *but not in order to assert that a given ellipse, in fact, historically, came from a circle* (evolutionary hypothesis), but only in order to tune our gaze to a formal correlation."

Let us go beyond the revolutionary proposal of the legitimacy of isometric or formal analyses as a diachronic, discursive antidote to chronological history. This formal correlation is the method of the most useful art, and its inherent teaching is to tune the gaze. Let us go beyond the proposal back to its origin and tune our gaze to the particular formal correlation that Wittgenstein has proffered as a paradigm.

What can his circle and ellipse be if it is not the round iris inside the almond shape of the eye of the beloved? What can it be if it is not the rows upon rows of o's and open l's made by school-children cramping their hands around the point of a pen as they learn to write?

There is no greater precision than that effected when the eye and the hand work together. Their precision effaces all the other organs between them and we send our hand out to that perfect point defined by the focusing eyes, to that one point of which Euclid spoke, atomic and yet ever-expanding, one of many on the waveline which defines Cos or Sine, or even the enigmatic trace of the writing hand.

What is the attainment of handwriting? We are being taught—as we are trained to hone our motor control to a maniacal precision in the acquisition of penmanship—to direct our many forms of desire into a point as precise.

Your touch.

The diffuse, polymorphous desire of the child must be channeled to enter the socially productive sphere. Eye/hand coordination is considered the apotheosis of motor control and ultimately, in this light, the precision act of writing—that act which appears most occulting of sensory memory—may itself be the first and prototypical engagement into the desiring machine's cogs. If we must learn that to have something within one's grasp is the only way to be fulfilled, what more accurate paradigm could there be for this than the hand with a pen? Total control and indelible proof. Yet the same parent will order a child to be silent by drawing an index finger to closed lips, and here the fusion of written and spoken language is shown to be fission. "Don't point," we are told, and yet this is how Moses gave so many other orders we are asked to follow. The point of the finger. The tip of the tongue.

The hand of Fahtma: a topographic rendering of eye/hand coordination. The hand of Fahtma, open as if to stop—or is it to greet?—an oncomer: In the dead-centre of its palm, where all the lines of the life, the heart, and the mind meet, there is an eye, alert and ever open. This, and the *manu in fica,* are apotropaic devices of protection against the evil eye in Indo-European cultures around the world, from Mesopotamia to the Amazon. *Manu in fica.* A fist with the thumb thrust between the index and the median. What are the many acts this gesture describes? What is its precision? Is the *manu in fica* a hand with a pen, or vice versa? Or is it at once both the inside and the outside of the same body, equally penetrating and penetrated? Is the hand of Fahtma a penetrating hand? Is the eye at its centre also infinitely penetrable and receptive to the loving glance? If the intent of amulets against the evil eye is to deflect the gaze, and the convention itself one of institutionalizing the fear of intimacy, how is it that these images of the mechanics of precision, that of the hand and the eye, are there conjoined in so polymorphous and intimate a fashion? Can it be that they, like the letterform created in the focal point their synchrony creates, conspire always to remind us of all the pleasure they always deny?

Wittgenstein again:

> "To kiss the image of the beloved. This is, naturally in no way founded on the belief that one produces a definite effect on the object represented in the image. It aims to provide satisfaction and effectively does. Or, rather, it aims at nothing; we act this way and thus we have a feeling of satisfaction.
> We could also kiss the name of the beloved, and then it would clearly be shown how her name replaces her."

Kiss the name of the beloved... The tip of the tongue. The point of the pen. Writing the name of the beloved absentmindedly—for she is absent—or addressing to her a "letter"—or letters, if only her initials—sealed with a kiss. Are kisses, formed with the lips, words themselves? And if letterforms are of the body, what act are we performing when we write her name?

It aims at nothing. Diffuse, abandoned, as receptive to sensory experience as it is desiring to act, finally the body admits to its equivalence with the letterform it has just written. As the hand brings the paper up to the lips, they at last seek the markings of the jetblack ink with which that same hand has just traced her name. The guiding eyes abandon their vigilant travail and close themselves, opening at once every other orifice they otherwise protect. We see that we can help Wittgenstein go further, be penetrable, and admit that not only does the name of the beloved replace her, but her name also is her.

A page from a vellum book painted by Nicolas Robert in 1641, entitled *The Garland of Julie:* In this little tome, the name of the beloved appears as a bower tressed of flowers by Amor. As they fall to earth, the blossoms bloom, and form the name Julie. On a more terrestrial plane, the *Harvest of Letters* of 1430 was also painted on skin in a bound book for Marguerite d'Orléans. Here are images of letters in their most integral materiality: living, organic, and rife with the imminent possibility of "sense." Odorant, ripe, and lush, both images show us rhizomes on the verge of forming from their magnificent fragments the brilliant name of the beloved.

Perhaps this is ultimately why we write: So that we may kiss this embodied name, these written words, with lips

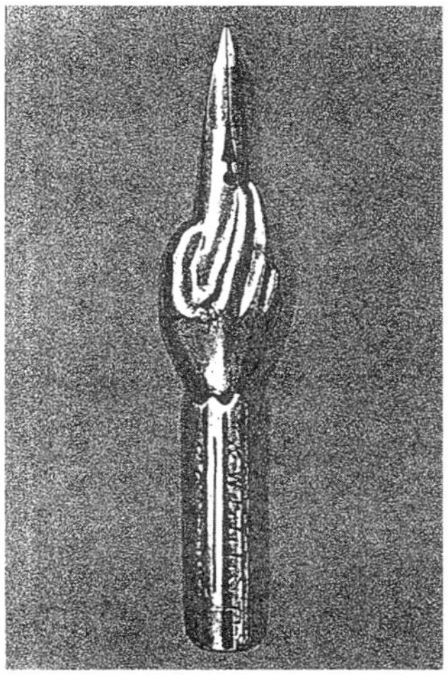 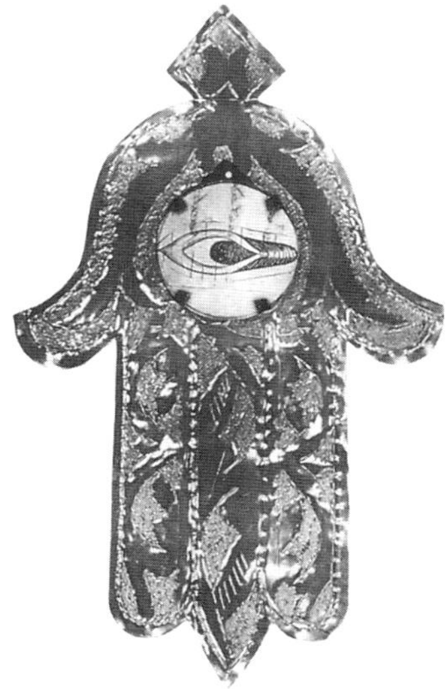 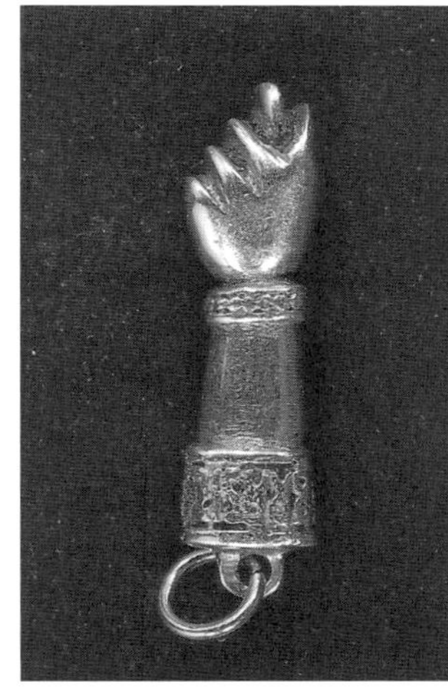

From left to right / von links nach rechts: PLUME D'ECOLIER, in Jean Brun, La Main, Paris, 1967. MARTHA FLEMING & LYNE LAPOINTE, FAHTMA HAND / FATIMA-HAND. MANU IN FICA, charm, collection of the artists / Talisman aus der Sammlung der Künstlerinnen.

too rarely silenced by the awesome magnitude of sensory experience, and embrace, with the abandoned closure of our eyes, the integrity of our bodies with every image we create—and go beyond the harnessing of motor control into an arm of attainment. Can it be that the letterform and the common experience of writing is the most complex and complete representation of sensory experience we know? For not only is writing as much of our bodies as the comet's tail is of itself, but each mark we leave stands in for and calls forth the unforgettable body of the absent beloved. Each stroke of the pen, then, designs the exact measure of our longing and, aiming at nothing, briefly brings two bodies together again, returning the writer at last to a body entirely composed of sense.

Yet even if this is all true, it is only one explanation. What would Wittgenstein say?

The lovelight of your eyes. Your touch. Your touch when you look at me. Talk to me.

If you can't hear me, I will drink to you only with my eyes from singing glasses: To make an elliptical wave of sound, I take the tip of my index and touch it to the tip of my tongue. Holding the base of the glass down against the table, I run my wetted finger lightly and smoothly in a perfect circle around the perfect mouth of the glass.

"I believe that the very project of explanation is already a failure... Compared to the impression made on us of that which is described, the explanation is too uncertain. All explanations are hypotheses. However, a hypothetical explanation will hardly be of help, for example, to someone tormented by love. An explanation will not appease."

The quotes are from Wittgenstein's *Comments on the Golden Bough,* manuscripts from 1930.

THE SPIRIT & THE LETTER & THE EVIL EYE is also the title of a site-specific project by Martha Fleming & Lyne Lapointe, commissioned by Antonia Payne and Angela Kingston for *Wellspring,* the 1994 Bath Festivals Trust exhibition. This project took place in The Book Museum, adjoining Bayntun's Bookbindery.

Der Geist & der Buchstabe & der böse Blick

MARTHA FLEMING

Manu sinistra. Ich bin Linkshänderin. Immer wenn ich jemanden sehe, der einen Federhalter in die linke Hand nimmt, schlägt mein Herz höher. Besonders berührt bin ich, wenn die betreffende Person schon älter ist oder in einem katholischen Umfeld erzogen wurde: Die Tatsache, dass sie nach wie vor ihre linke Hand benutzt, ist ein Zeichen des Widerstands und des Durchhaltens, obgleich es im jeweiligen Fall durchaus sein mag, dass die linke Hand an die Schulbank festgebunden wurde. Die Unterdrückung des Gebrauchs dieses Körpergliedes kann schwere neurologische Störungen hervorrufen, darunter Schwächeanfälle, Schwindelzustände und vor allem Sprachstörungen. «Der Luftstrom und der Tintenfluss» gehören, wie der Linguist Uldall deutlich macht, beide zur selben Sprache. Die Spitze des Fingers. Die Spitze der Zunge. Die Spitze der Feder.

Manu sinistra. Als junges Mädchen sass ich an Sonntagnachmittagen neben meinem Vater am runden Esszimmertisch und machte Schreibübungen. Er war ein versierter Graphiker und schrieb eine vollendete Kursivschrift. Letzteres konnte man von seiner linkshändigen Tochter nicht sagen und würde es auch niemals sagen können. Er tat aber alles in seiner Macht Stehende, um mir zu helfen, mich klar auszudrücken, in einer Welt, die nicht meinen spezifischen Bedürfnissen entsprach. Ich habe zärtliche und mit zwiespältigen Gefühlen durchsetzte Erinnerungen daran, wie seine grosse, gepflegte rechte Hand meine kleine linke umschliesst, wie seine Hand die meine über das Papier führt, als wäre es eine spiritistische Alphabettafel, und wie seine Hand die meine geraderückt.

Nach einer Kindheit, in der Lesen und Schreiben – Verben, die ich sogar heute noch oft verwechsle – im Mittelpunkt gestanden hatten, begann ich professionell zu schreiben, überwiegend für Kunstzeitschriften, hörte aber, kurz nachdem ich angefangen

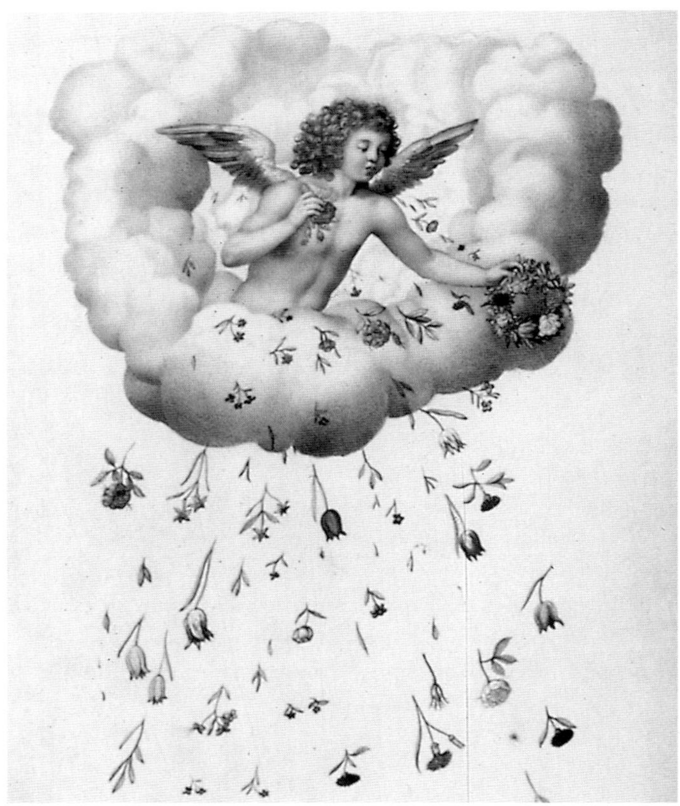

CUPID RAINING FLOWERS / CUPIDO LÄSST BLUMEN REGNEN, *in Nicolas Robert, La Guirlande de Julie, 1641.* (BIBLIOTHEQUE NATIONALE, PARIS)

hatte, Kunst zu machen, und bei Lyne Lapointe und anderen in die Lehre ging, bald wieder damit auf. Ich schüttete quasi das Schreiben mitsamt dem schmutzigen Badewasser der Kunstzeitschriften aus.

Dennoch schrieb ich weiterhin, und zwar in verschiedenen Formen, zwischen denen ich zunächst keine Verbindung sah. Ich schrieb Freunden unzumutbar lange Briefe, die es ihnen unmöglich machten, sie in angemessener Weise zu beantworten; ich schrieb regelmässig komplizierte Subventionsanträge und Gutachten im Zusammenhang mit den grossangelegten Installationsprojekten, die ich gemeinsam mit Lyne Lapointe mache; ich schrieb Projektvorschläge, die sich genau nach den unterschiedlichen Bedürfnissen derer richteten, die an unseren Projekten mitwirken sollten, von Leitern städtischer Ämter für Öffentlichkeitsarbeit über Architekten, die sich auf die Restaurierung historischer Bauten spezialisiert haben, bis hin zu Museumskuratoren; ich schrieb und entwarf sämtliche Plakate sowie das gesamte Werbe- und Informationsmaterial, das für diese grösstenteils in Eigenregie durchgeführten Projekte gedruckt wurde. Vor allen Dingen aber schrieb, entwarf und malte ich bei allen Gemeinschaftsprojekten von Lyne und mir, die damals riesige verlassene Gebäude wie eine Feuerwehrwache, ein Hauptpostamt und ein Varietétheater zum Gegenstand hatten, Texte und Beschriftungen, die in eigenständigen Werken, an der Architektur selbst und in Form von grösseren, aber zeitlich beschränkten Eingriffen zu sehen waren.

Die sich scheinbar widersprechenden Bedürfnisse des Schreibens und des Bilderschaffens, die ich unbewusst unter einen Hut zu bringen mich bemühte, fanden zur Synthese in den verschiedenen Beschriftungsprojekten, die ich im Rahmen dieser gemeinsamen Bauprojekte unternommen hatte. Dennoch war diese Schreibtätigkeit derart vielfältig und zersplittert, dass ich darin zunächst keine autonome Betätigung sah. Erst allmählich erkannte ich den komplexen Zusammenhang zwischen dem Drang zu erzählen und dem Sich-Hindurcharbeiten durch Architektur.

Erst 1991, als ich mich an ein (bis heute unfertiges) Buch machte, das die bereits abgeschlossenen architekturbezogenen Projekte dokumentieren soll, nahm diese Betätigung in meinem Bewusstsein allmählich als erlebte Realität Gestalt an. Das heisst, sie nahm zunächst die Form von Tränen an. Ich war ausserstande, meine Hände auf die Tasten zu legen, ohne zu weinen. Nach und nach begriff ich, dass mir diese Tränen nicht nur wegen der Geschichten in die Augen traten, die ich über die schwierigen Bedingungen zu erzählen hatte, unter denen diese Projekte zustande gekommen waren, sondern dass es zugleich Tränen der Freude und Befreiung waren ob der Rückkehr zum Schreiben und zu Worten, zum tiefen Raum der gedruckten Seite, der den himmlischen Leerräumen der Gebäude selbst so ähnlich und doch auch so unähnlich ist.

Wohin kehrte ich zurück? Was ist Schreiben? Ist es der kontrollierte Akt des Zwischen-Daumen-und-Zeigefinger-in-die-Hand-Nehmens eines Federhalters und des Beschreibens eines Blattes Papier mit Tinte? Ist Schreiben das Bilden von Sätzen? Ist es das Herstellen von Bedeutung? Ist es der Akt des Legitimierens und Fixierens dieser Bedeutung und des ihr Kraftverleihens? Es ist all dies, aber auch noch mehr. Letztlich ist es etwas, das unseren mit geistiger Energie begabten Körpern entströmt.

Das folgende Zitat von Wittgenstein zeigt uns, dass er die Sprache dem Kosmos erschliessen wollte, den zu umfassen sie sich einerseits sehnt und den sie andererseits einem Sandkorn gleich in sich trägt.

> «Wenn man es für selbstverständlich hält, dass sich der Mensch an seiner Phantasie vergnügt, so bedenke man, dass diese Phantasie nicht wie ein gemaltes Bild oder ein plastisches Modell ist, sondern ein kompliziertes Gebilde aus heterogenen Bestandteilen: Wörtern und Bildern. Man wird dann das Operieren mit Schrift- und Lautzeichen nicht mehr in Gegensatz stellen zu dem Operieren mit ‹Vorstellungsbildern› der Ereignisse. Wir müssen die ganze Sprache durchpflügen.»

Wörter und Bilder: Gerade in den Buchstabenformen des römischen Alphabets sind sie aufs anschaulichste miteinander vereint. In dieser abendländischen Tradition, die ebenso traditionsgemäss ihre eigenen ideogrammatischen Ursprünge verleugnet, sehe ich die ephemere Regenbogenbrücke zwischen zwei Welten, die mich gerufen haben, und erkenne sie als eine. In eben diesem Bereich – und das ist so offensichtlich, dass es schon wieder übersehen wird, so kristallkar, dass es unsichtbar ist – verweigert sich die fluktuierende Welt der auf einer Seite versammelten Buchstaben jeglicher reduktiven Dichotomie dadurch, dass sie Vielfalt geradezu verkörpert. Jeder einzelne der 26 Buchstaben, die jeder für sich faszinierend, mystisch und in ständiger Bewegung sind, bildet etwas völlig in sich Geschlossenes und ist zugleich ein anspruchsloses kleines Nichts.

Inmitten der wilden und angepflanzten Gräser des Feldes der ganzen Sprache erblühen die Bilder des Körpers, die die Spuren sind, die unser eigener Körper hinterlässt, während unsere schreibende Hand sich über das Feld der Seite bewegt, durchaus sichtbar für unser lesendes Auge, wenn es über eben dieses fruchtbare Gelände schweift. Diese Bilder des Körpers sind in ihrer transparenten Allgegenwärtigkeit unsichtbare Buchstabenformen, sie sind gleichzeitig Schriftzeichen und «Vorstellungsbilder» der Ereignisse. Buchstabenformen sind das einzige, was ich als Künstlerin zeichnen kann. Ich bin so vertraut mit ihren Körpern, ihren Beinen und Armen, ihren Gliedmassen, ihren Gelenken, ihren Nahtstellen, ihren Merkmalen, dass ich sie zeichne mit der Gewandtheit einer Liebenden, die das Gesicht des Geliebten porträtiert.

Wenn dieser ideogrammatische Status der Buchstabenform als Teil des abendländischen Diskurses der Verdrängung, der die Dichotomien schafft, auf denen jede Herrschaft fusst, verschleiert ist, ist dann nicht das Alphabet zwangsläufig eine Art Erinnerungsfilm? In ihrer Zweidimensionalität sind die Seite, die Tafel, der Stein, das geätzte Glas, ist alles, worauf wir schreiben, eine Projektionsfläche, hinter der wir eine unermessliche, lockende Tiefe erahnen, die in den verschwommenen inneren Klängen unserer eigenen Erinnerungen und Verdrängungen widerhallt. Wie wird die Autorität des geschriebenen Wortes instrumentalisiert, um die den Sinnen eingeschriebene Erinnerung zu unterdrücken, die es in seiner eigenen Gestalt ja gerade verkörpert?

Geschriebenes ersetzt und blockiert zugleich Erinnerungen, die ausschliesslich bildlich oder mündlich sind. Die beiden Arten der Erinnerung, beide ganz und gar erotisch, werden in den Buchstabenformen als solchen sowohl ausgeblendet wie auch angedeutet: Diese Buchstabenformen (Artikulationen), die vom Körper abstrahiert und dennoch nicht länger rein figürlich sind, umschweben uns wie Arme, in die wir uns stürzen würden, und wie Beine, die wir sehnlichst um unseren Leib und Hals geschlungen zu spüren wünschen. Wir schreiben, um zu vergessen, und dennoch klingt gerade in der Form der Buchstaben (Zeichen) unser Körper mit, ein Körper, dessen Sinne durch eben den Eintritt in die Sprache betäubt werden. Wie kann das Schreiben uns zu unserem Körper zurückführen? Wie kann es die lähmende Grammatik der Perspektive, die lähmende Perspektive der Grammatik in Frage stellen?

Ein weiteres Wittgenstein-Zitat:

> «Die historische Erklärung, die Erklärung als eine Hypothese der Entwicklung, ist nur eine Art der Zusammenfassung der Daten, ihrer Synopsis. Es ist ebensowohl möglich, die Daten in ihrer Beziehung zueinander zu sehen und in ein allgemeines Bild zusammenzufassen, ohne es in Form einer Hypothese über die zeitliche Entwicklung zu tun. [...] Wie man eine interne Beziehung der Kreisform zur Ellipse dadurch illustrierte, dass man eine Ellipse allmählich in einen Kreis überführt; *aber nicht um zu behaupten, dass eine gewisse Ellipse tatsächlich, historisch, aus einem Kreis entstanden wäre* (Entwicklungshypothese), sondern nur um unser Auge für einen formalen Zusammenhang zu schärfen.»

Gehen wir über die revolutionäre These der Gültigkeit isomorpher oder formaler Analysen als diachronisches, diskursives Gegenmittel zur chronologischen Geschichtsschreibung hinaus. In diesem formalen Zusammenhang besteht die Methode der sinnvollsten Kunst, und das, was sie naturgemäss lehrt, ist eben, das Auge zu schärfen. Gehen wir über die These hinaus zurück zu ihrem Ursprung und schärfen wir unser Auge für den spezifischen formalen Zusammenhang, den Wittgenstein als Beispiel anführt.

Was sind sein Kreis und seine Ellipse, wenn nicht die runde Iris im mandelförmigen Auge der/des Geliebten? Was könnten sie anderes sein als die unendlichen Reihen von «os» und offenen «ls», die von Schulkindern, die krampfhaft die Spitze ihres Federhalters umklammert halten, im Schreibunterricht hingeschrieben werden?

Es gibt keine grössere Präzision als die, die sich ergibt, wenn das Auge und die Hand zusammenarbeiten. Ihre Genauigkeit blendet alle anderen Organe aus, die zwischen ihnen liegen, und wir dirigieren unsere Hand exakt zu dem Punkt, den wir mit unseren Augen fokussieren, zu dem einen Punkt, von dem Euklid sprach, atomisch und doch unendlich, einer von vielen auf der Kurve, die für Kosinus oder Sinus oder gar für die geheimnisvolle Spur der schreibenden Hand steht.

Was ist die Errungenschaft der Handschrift? Während wir im Zuge der Aneignung des Schreibens lernen, unsere motorische Kontrolle bis zu einer irrwitzigen Präzision auszufeilen, bringt man uns bei, unsere vielfältigen Bedürfnisse auf einen ebenso exakten Punkt zu projizieren.

Deine Berührung.

Die diffuse, polymorphe Lust des Kindes bedarf der Kanalisierung, um in den gesellschaftlich produktiven Bereich einzutreten. Die Auge-Hand-Koordination gilt als das Ideal der motorischen Kontrolle, und angesichts dieser Tatsache kann man sich den Präzisionsakt des Schreibens – der Akt, der sich der den Sinnen eingeschriebenen Erinnerung am meisten zu entziehen scheint – durchaus als das erste und prototypische Ineinandergreifen des Räderwerks der Lust vorstellen. Wenn wir schon lernen müssen, dass es Erfüllung nur gibt, wenn man etwas im Griff hat, welches trefflichere Paradigma wäre hierfür dann denkbar als die einen Federhalter führende Hand? Totale Kontrolle und unauslöschlicher Abdruck. Doch die gleichen Eltern werden mit einem auf geschlossene Lippen gelegten Zeigefinger ihr Kind auffordern, still zu sein, und genau hier entpuppt sich das nahtlose Ineinanderübergehen von geschriebener und gesprochener Sprache als Bruch. «Nicht mit dem Finger zeigen», wird uns befohlen, und doch hat Moses auf ebendiese Weise so viele andere Gebote erteilt, die wir befolgen sollen. Die Spitze des Fingers. Die Spitze der Zunge.

Die Hand Fatimas: eine topographische Darstellung der Auge-Hand-Koordination. Die Hand Fatimas, geöffnet, als wollte sie einen Herannahenden anhalten – oder etwa begrüssen? Im toten Punkt der Handfläche, wo alle Linien des Lebens, des Herzens und des Geistes zusammentreffen, befindet sich ein Auge, wachsam und immer offen. Dieses und die *manu in fica* sind Sinnbilder zur Abwehr des bösen Blicks in indoeuropäischen Kulturen auf der ganzen Welt, von Mesopotamien bis zum Amazonas. *Manu in fica.* Eine Faust, bei der sich der Daumen zwischen Zeige- und Mittelfinger schiebt. Welche Vielzahl von Handlungen bezeichnet diese Geste? Worin

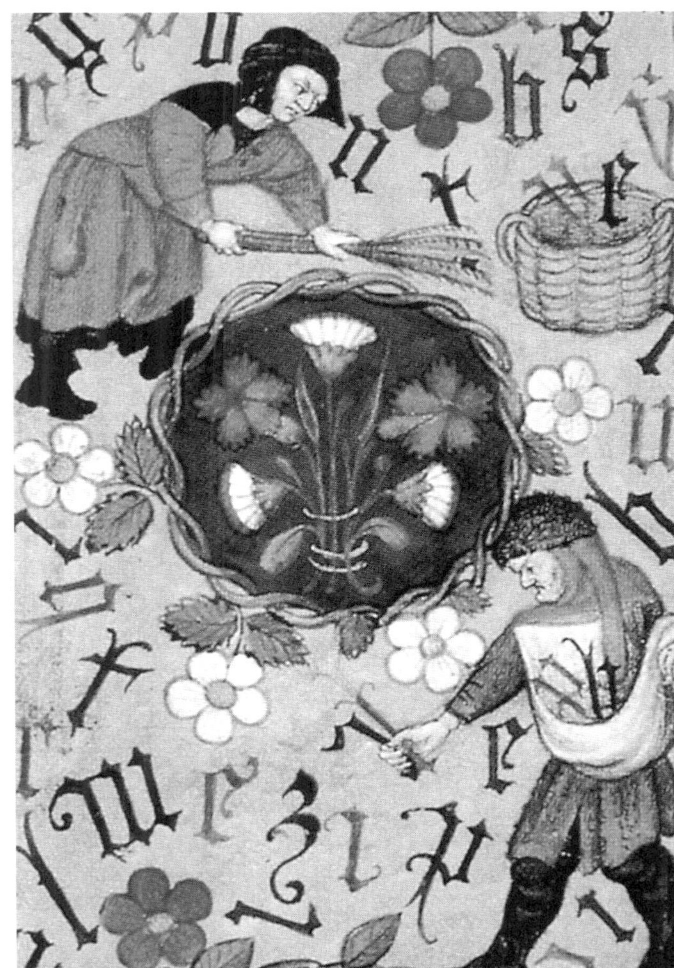

FLOWERS AND LETTERS / BLUMEN UND BUCHSTABEN,
in Les Heures de Marguerite d'Orléans, ca. 1430. (BIBLIOTHEQUE NATIONALE, PARIS)

besteht ihre präzise Bedeutung? Ist die *manu in fica* eine Hand mit einem Federhalter, oder umgekehrt? Oder ist sie zugleich das Innere und das Äussere des gleichermassen penetrierenden wie penetrierten Körpers? Ist die Hand Fatimas eine penetrierende Hand? Ist das Auge in ihrer Mitte ebenfalls unendlich durchdringbar und für den liebenden Blick empfänglich? Wenn der Zweck von Amuletten zur Abwehr des bösen Blicks darin besteht, den Blick abzuwenden, und der Brauch selbst der Institutionalisierung der Angst vor Intimität dient, wie erklärt es sich dann, dass diese Symbole des Präzisionsmechanismus, die Symbole der Hand und des Auges, in derart polymorpher und intimer Form miteinander verbunden sind? Könnte es sein, dass sie – wie die Buchstabenform, die in dem von ihrer Synchronie gebildeten Brennpunkt entsteht – zusammenwirken, um uns ständig an all die Lust und Freude zu erinnern, die sie uns stets versagen?

Noch einmal Wittgenstein:

> «Das Bild des Geliebten küssen. Das basiert *natürlich nicht* auf einem Glauben an eine bestimmte Wirkung auf den Gegenstand, den das Bild darstellt. Es bezweckt eine Befriedigung und erreicht sie auch. Oder vielmehr, es *bezweckt* gar nichts; wir handeln eben so und fühlen uns dann befriedigt. Man könnte auch den Namen der Geliebten küssen, und hier wäre die Stellvertretung durch den Namen klar.»

Den Namen der Geliebten küssen... Die Spitze der Zunge. Die Spitze der Feder. Geistesabwesend – denn sie ist abwesend – den Namen der Geliebten schreiben oder Geschriebenes an sie richten, und seien es nur ihre Initialen, versiegelt mit einem Kuss. Sind Küsse, mit den Lippen geformt, selbst Wörter? Und wenn Buchstabenformen aus dem Körper kommen, welchen Akt vollführen wir dann, wenn wir ihren Namen schreiben?

Es bezweckt nichts. Diffus, verlassen, ebenso empfänglich für Sinneserlebnisse wie nach Tätigkeit verlangend, bekennt sich der Körper endlich zu seiner Übereinstimmung mit der Form des Buchstabens, den er gerade geschrieben hat. Wenn die Hand das Papier an die Lippen führt, suchen diese endlich die Markierungen der pechschwarzen Tinte, mit der eben diese Hand gerade ihren Namen aufgezeichnet hat. Die steuernden Augen lassen ab von ihrer konzentrierten Arbeit und schliessen sich, im gleichen Moment jede andere Öffnung öffnend, die sie ansonsten schützen. Wir erkennen, dass wir Wittgenstein einen Schritt weiterhelfen können, durchdringbar zu sein und anzuerkennen, dass der Name der Geliebten nicht nur diese ersetzt, sondern zugleich sie selbst ist.

Eine Seite aus einer Pergamenthandschrift mit dem Titel *Guirlande de Julie,* die 1641 von Nicolas Robert illuminiert wurde: In diesem kleinen Band erscheint der Name der Geliebten in Form einer von Amor aus Blumen geflochtenen Laube. Die Blüten, die auf die Erde fallen, treiben neue Blüten und bilden den Namen Julie. In einem mehr weltlichen Kontext wurde die *Buchstabenlese* von 1430 in einem gebundenen Buch für Marguerite d'Orléans ebenfalls auf dünnem Pergament gemalt. Hier finden sich Darstellungen von Buchstaben in ihrer reinsten Körperlichkeit: lebendig, organisch und überbordend vom angedeuteten «Sinn»-Potential. Beide Bilder zeigen uns, duftend, reif und üppig, Rhizome, deren einzelne Triebe im Begriff sind, den strahlenden Namen der Geliebten zu bilden.

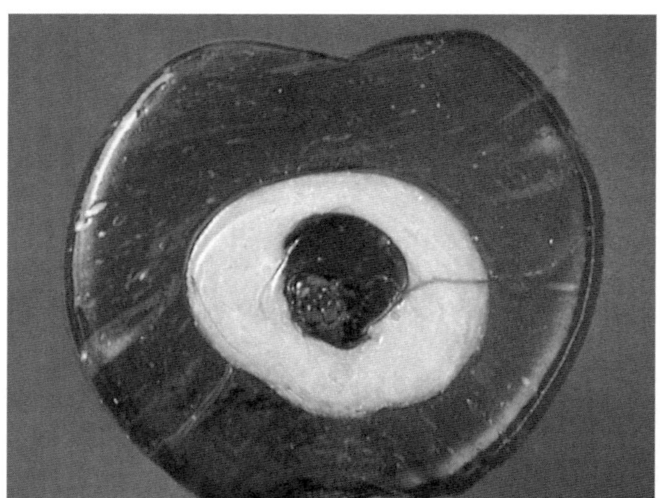

BLUE AND YELLOW EYE, amulet against the evil eye, Asia Minor / Blaugelbes Amulett gegen den bösen Blick, Kleinasien. (*SCHWEIZ. PHARMAZIEHISTORISCHES MUSEUM, BASEL*)

Vielleicht ist dies letztlich der Grund, weshalb wir schreiben: um uns die Möglichkeit zu verschaffen, diesen fleischgewordenen Namen, diese geschriebenen Wörter zu küssen mit Lippen, die allzu selten von der überwältigenden Bedeutung des Sinneserlebens zum Schweigen gebracht werden, und um die Ganzheit unseres Körpers mit jedem Bild, das wir schaffen, im Zuge des selbstvergessenen Schliessens unserer Augen zu umfassen und den Harnisch der motorischen Kontrolle zu einer Waffe der Vervollkommnung umzuschmieden. Könnte es sein, dass die Buchstabenform und die banale Betätigung des Schreibens die komplexeste und vollständigste Form der Sinneserfahrung darstellen, die wir kennen? Denn nicht nur entspringt das Schreiben dem Körper wie der Schweif dem Kometen, sondern jedes Zeichen, das wir hinterlassen, steht für und beschwört den immer gegenwärtigen Körper der/des abwesenden Geliebten. Jeder Federstrich vermisst also mit grösster Genauigkeit unser Verlangen und bringt, nichts bezweckend, für kurze Zeit zwei Körper aufs neue zusammen und führt den Schreibenden zu guter Letzt wieder zurück zu einem Körper, der ganz aus Sinn besteht.

Doch selbst wenn all dies zutrifft, ist es nur eine von mehreren möglichen Erklärungen. Was würde Wittgenstein dazu sagen?

«Ich glaube, (schon) das Unternehmen einer Erklärung (ist) verfehlt. (...) Die Erklärung ist im Vergleich mit dem Eindruck, den uns das Beschriebene macht, zu unsicher. Jede Erklärung ist ja eine Hypothese. Wer aber, etwa, von der Liebe beunruhigt ist, dem wird eine hypothetische Erklärung wenig helfen. – Sie wird ihn nicht beruhigen.»

Der Liebesglanz deiner Augen. Deine Berührung. Deine Berührung, während du mich ansiehst. Zu mir sprichst.

Wenn du mich nicht hören kannst, werde ich nur mit meinen Augen aus singenden Gläsern auf dich trinken. Um eine elliptische Schallwelle zu erzeugen, führe ich die Spitze meines Zeigefingers an die Spitze meiner Zunge. Während ich das Glas an seinem Fuss auf dem Tisch festhalte, lasse ich meinen angefeuchteten Finger leicht und gleichmässig in einem vollkommenen Kreis um die vollkommene Öffnung des Glases gleiten.

(Übersetzung: Magda Moses, Bram Opstelten)

Die Zitate entstammen Wittgensteins *Bemerkungen über Frazers Golden Bough (in Vortrag über Ethik und andere kleine Schriften,* Frankfurt 1989).

DER GEIST & DER BUCHSTABE & DER BÖSE BLICK ist auch der Titel eines standortbezogenen Projekts von Martha Fleming und Lyne Lapointe, das von Antonia Payne und Angela Kingston für die Ausstellung *Wellspring* im Rahmen des Bath Festivals 1994 in Auftrag gegeben wurde.

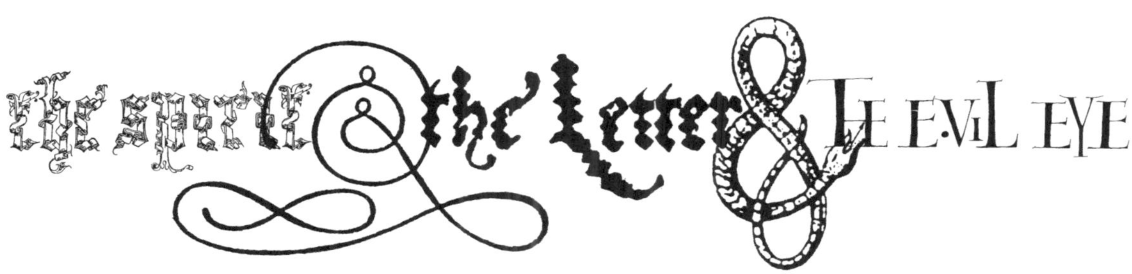

BALKON

Künstlerränke

ROBERTO OHRT

Das Buch[1] beginnt mit einer Photographie: das Innere eines Restaurants, ein Raum, der in irgendeiner klassischen Epoche unseres Jahrhunderts still, sauber und aufgeräumt, wie am frühen Sonntagnachmittag, ohne das geringste Zeichen von Ungeduld oder Nervosität auf seine Gäste wartet. Ofen und Ofenrohr, gedeckte Tische und Wein, «Richard» und Barhocker. Nur der Blick in die hinteren Räume erinnert an den Kater vom Morgen. Das «Exil» in Berlin.

Dann folgen einige orientierende Worte von Bruno Brunnet, ein ebenfalls orientierendes, aber schon auf den Zipfeln der Tischdecke geführtes Gespräch von **Michel Würthle** und Martin Kippenberger, und schliesslich öffnen sich die Nächte im Lokal. In 80 Zeichnungen geht es von 1972 bis 1979, also mitten durch die 70er Jahre. Erstaunlich. Weder die Photographie noch die Handschrift der Zeichnungen lassen an diese mittlerweile in die Erinnerung gerückte Epoche denken. Können sie auch nicht, denn erstens zeichnete man damals nicht, und schon gar nicht im guten illustrativen Ton der 20er Jahre, zweitens photographierte man nicht dokumentarisch-surreal – derartiges wurde gerade erst wieder in Büchern entdeckt –, und drittens sind die Zeichnungen nicht mehr als ein Jahr alt.

Thema, Strichführung, Papier und mitgelieferte Kommentare lassen Platz für jede Menge Legenden und Klischees. *Der Spiegel, Der Tagesspiegel* und sogar *Die Welt* waren angeregt: «Man fühlt sich automatisch an Liedzeilen von Reinhard Mey oder Hannes Wader[2] erinnert», stand da merkwürdigerweise... Ja, die Erinnerung stösst manchmal gegen die Beweise, die andere dafür aus dem Regal ziehen. Also erübrigt es sich, auch an dieser Stelle die geschichtlichen Tatsachen mitsamt ihren die Realität bereichernden Verwischungen nachzuweisen. Die *Aufzeichnungen eines bewaffneten Schankprinzen* sind hiermit ein aus Österreich eingeschmuggeltes Dokument der bundesrepublikanisch-berlinerischen 70er Jahre; nur wird man sich wahrscheinlich in einigen Jahren oder Jahrzehnten vor diesem, übrigens sehr präzisen Dokument wieder nicht vorstellen können, dass allein die Ausnahmen ihre Zeit überleben, immer noch. Berlin am Anfang der 20er Jahre bekommen wir mittlerweile ja auch als Dada- und Künstler-Hauptstadt präsentiert.

Der zeichnende Schankwirt hat seine Perspektive, meist leicht von oben, manchmal ganz extrem von oben oder eben umgekehrt, aus dem letzten Eck. Er zieht gerne Rahmen in Rahmen, höflich, wie es sich gehört, wenn die Herrschaften und das Bild ohnehin

---

ROBERTO OHRT lebt in Hamburg und ist Kunstkritiker und Ausstellungsmacher. 1991 veröffentlichte er sein Buch *Phantom Avantgarde* zur Geschichte der Situationistischen Internationale. 1993 war er Kurator der Ausstellung von Martin Kippenberger im Centre Georges Pompidou.

schon fertig sind. In seinem Blick ist immer etwas Vertrautes. Lampenschirm mit leuchtender Birne zum Beispiel und die Zeichnung der Lippen schaffen einfache und zuverlässige Anhaltspunkte im Geschehen. Das andere setzt sich drumherum, wie es in einem Lokal üblich ist, allmählich und sehr unterschiedlich oder zunächst mal «aneinander vorbeistarrend» und vielleicht am späteren Abend erst in «äusserst charmanter Körperhaltung.» Der Strich der Erzählung bringt es ohnehin wieder ins Ungelenke, sogar die Pose vor der Kamera, und glücklicherweise wird Verknicktes oder Gestolper nicht irgendeinem anderen ins Gesicht gezeichnet, sondern jedem, der sich in diesem Bohemetheater wohl fühlte oder nur kurz einfand, dem Zeichner Michel Würthle auch, dem «oiden Schlurf im Nodelstreif».

Michel Würthle hat auf seinem Weg in die Kunst inzwischen mit dreizehn Bildern zwei Schritte zugelegt: eine weitere Galerie und diesmal in Öl auf Leinwand. Birgit Küng zeigte in Zürich im Juni die «Hauptsorgen des alternden Schankprinzen: Verarmung, Verölung, Verkleidung».

Bei Brunnet, der die Wände seiner Galerie im Mai 1994 mit den 80 Exil-Zeichnungen regelrecht gepflastert hatte, wurde anschliessend eine Ausstellung von **Michael Krebber** vorbereitet. Ich war in Berlin, als gehängt und sonstiger Galerienhintergrund noch weggeräumt wurde, kannte also die Ektachrome seiner neuen Zeichnungen, bevor ich die Originale ansehen konnte, und hatte bei der Vernissage eine insofern etwas abgelenkte Wahrnehmung. Das war allerdings hilfreich, denn mitten drauf gucken bringt ja bei Krebber erstmal überhaupt nichts. Ausserdem hatte er die sechs Zeichnungen

Abbildungen aus: Michel Würthle. Aufzeichnungen eines bewaffneten Schankprinzen. Im Exil 1972–1979.

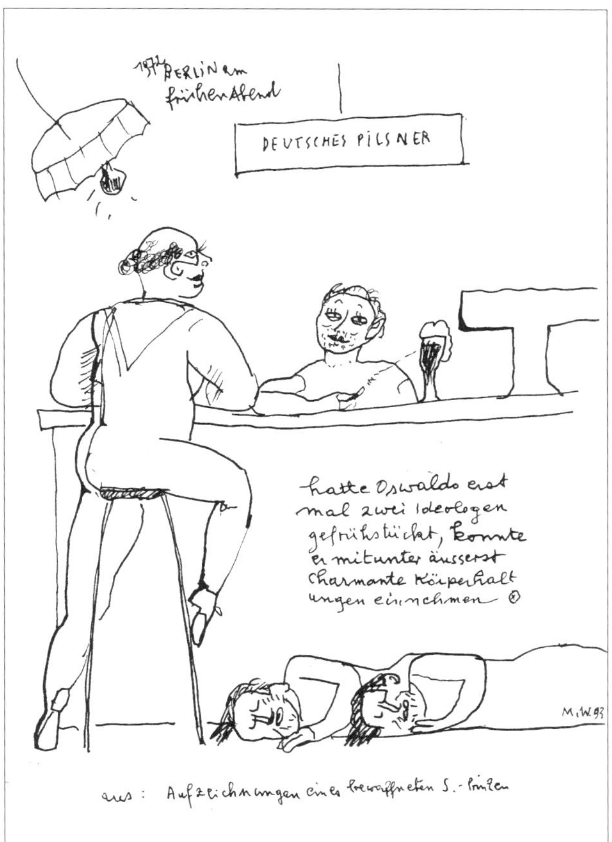

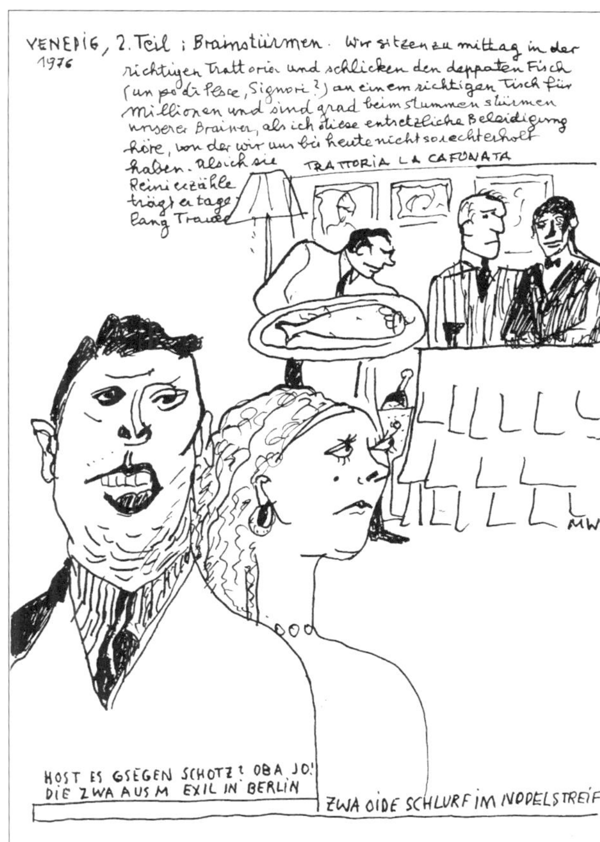

im Rahmen zum Teil auf ihre spitze Kante gestellt, um nachzuschauen, «ob die Post abgeht», und daher rutschte das Auge immer vom Blatt ab – oder hindurch... Vorn auf den Tuschen waren so wenige farbige Pinseltupfer angebracht, dass ich unwillkürlich dachte, ich sehe nur die Spuren eines Papiertests. Zu dieser Untersuchung würde dann auch die Beobachtung der Schatten gehören, die von irgendwelchen Malproben auf den Rückseiten durchschienen, und das Registrieren der leichten Feuchtigkeitsfalten dort, wo sich das Papier um die Farbe zusammengezogen hatte und wellig geworden war. Dieses ziemlich zittrige und dünne Arrangement setzte sich über die Rahmen hinweg auf der Wand fort, denn von etwa zwei Zuständen der Hängung waren die Spuren, kleine Löcher und einige überflüssige Nägel, nicht beseitigt worden. Und die endgültige Präsentation unterlief eine beruhigend genaue Ausrichtung der Bilder um feine oder auch deutlicher gesetzte Nuancen, hier ein halber, dort ein ganzer Zentimeter unter den Angaben der Wasserwaage.

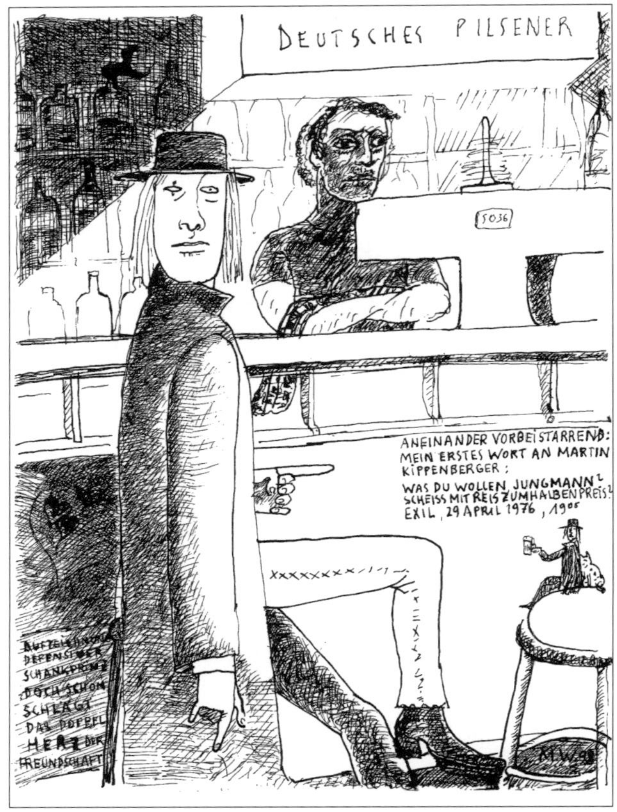

Abbildung aus: Michel Würthle. Aufzeichnungen eines bewaffneten Schankprinzen. Im Exil 1972–1979.

Über den Zeichnungen hingen vier Leinwände, hauptsächlich schieferschwarz. Auch hier war die matt schliessende Oberfläche aufgrund von Bearbeitungsspuren, Übermalungen und Materialkonsistenz der Farbe durchlässig geworden, und durch das poröse Monochrome der trockenen Ansichtsseite zogen sich noch einige leichte Farbspuren nach vorn. Das Ganze, besonders die Zeichnungen, liess an eine Wiedereinführung des Konstruktivismus der ersten Stunde, also mitsamt der Dynamik und Freizügigkeit seiner Entdeckungszeit, denken, demonstriert im Vokabular von Polke-Zeichnungen aus den 60er Jahren. Mit all den Flecken, Ecken und Ungenauigkeiten hatte Michael Krebber ein Mobile flach über die Wand gestreut. Die Elemente dieses Mobiles waren ebenso schwer zu bestimmen wie ihre unterschiedlichen Geschwindigkeiten, die leichten Ungleichgewichte und Schwankungen – und deshalb sagte ich «Mobile» oder «Konstruktivismus», obwohl sich damit natürlich einige schwere Missverständnisse im Raum befinden. Doch selbst die Missverständnisse, die Erinnerung an die Zeit der Mobiles, ihre Beiläufigkeit, die Durchsichtigkeit oder «der ganze Kitsch» des konstruktivistischen Gegenspiels sind hier gemeint, billig und einfach, locker zusammengefügt, aber mit kurzen und beherrschten Bewegungsmomenten versetzt. Michael Krebber erklärte auf Nachfragen ein weiteres Mal, dass es ihm darum ginge, die Tür – aus der Kunst raus – offenzuhalten. Er sagte es – auf die Bilder zeigend – gewissermassen von der anderen Seite der Wand, aber ganz so transparent, wie sein Gegenstand in diesem Moment erschien, kann seine Arbeit nicht sein, denn wenn man in seiner Umgebung fragt, was er da denn nun gemacht hat, beginnt das grosse Rätselraten.

1) Erinnerungen an das Dasein als Kellner in der Berliner Kneipe «Exil» verarbeitet der Österreicher Michel Würthle in seinen *Aufzeichnungen eines bewaffneten Schankprinzen. Im Exil 1972–1979* (Hrsg.: Martin Kippenberger, Berlin, 1994).
2) Populäre Sänger Deutschlands der späten 70er Jahre.

Intriguing Artists

ROBERTO OHRT

The book[1] opens with a photograph: the interior of a restaurant in some classical period of our century. A room quiet, clean, and tidy, waiting for guests as if on an early Sunday afternoon, without the slightest hint of impatience or nervousness. Stove and stovepipe, tables set and wine ready, "Richard" and bar stools. Only the view of the back rooms jogs memories of morning hangovers. The "Exil," a bar in Berlin.

There follow a few introductory words from Berlin gallerist Bruno Brunnet, an equally introductory conversation between **Michel Würthle** and Martin Kippenberger, conducted on the corners of the table cloth, and finally the night is open for business. In 80 drawings from the seventies, dated 1972 to 1979. Neither the photography nor the signature of the drawings suggest this decade, which has since been committed to memory. Nor could they because firstly, no one drew in those days and if they did, it was certainly not in the good old illustrative style of the twenties; secondly, no one shot surreal, documentary photographs—people were just rediscovering the likes in books; and thirdly, the drawings are less than a year old.

Subject matter (commentary included), delineation, and paper invite legends and clichés galore. The press, *Der Spiegel, Der Tagesspiegel,* and even *Die Welt,* were inspired: "one is automatically reminded of lines from songs by Reinhard Mey or Hannes Wader,"[2] a critic declared. Yes, memory sometimes trips up the evidence that others could theoretically pull off the shelves. So there's no point, here or anywhere, in checking out the historical facts replete with their reality-enriching obfuscation. *The Memoirs of an Armed Barroom Prince* are herewith a record of the German-Federal-Republic-Berlin seventies smuggled out of Austria; except that in a few years or decades, it is probable that, on seeing this incidentally extremely precise document, no one will be able to imagine that, as usual, only the exceptions outlive their age. Meanwhile early-twenties Berlin is also being served up as the headquarters of dada and artists.

The draftsman-bartender has his vantage point, usually slightly raised or from way above or—just the opposite—from way below, and he has a penchant for drawing frames within frames, politely, decorously, after the gentlemen and the picture are already finished anyway. There is something familiar about the view from the side.

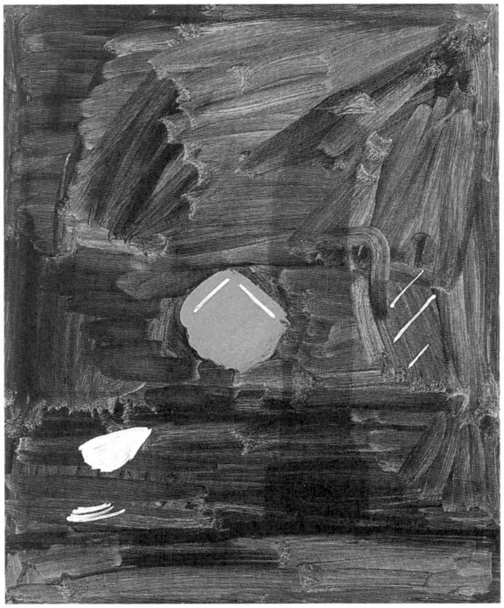

MICHAEL KREBBER, OHNE TITEL, 1994, 81 x 65 cm / UNTITLED, 32 x 25½".

ROBERTO OHRT lives in Hamburg; he is an art critic and freelance exhibition curator. He published the book *Phantom Avantgarde,* on the history of International Situationism, in 1991 and curated Martin Kippenberger's show at the Centre Georges Pompidou in 1993.

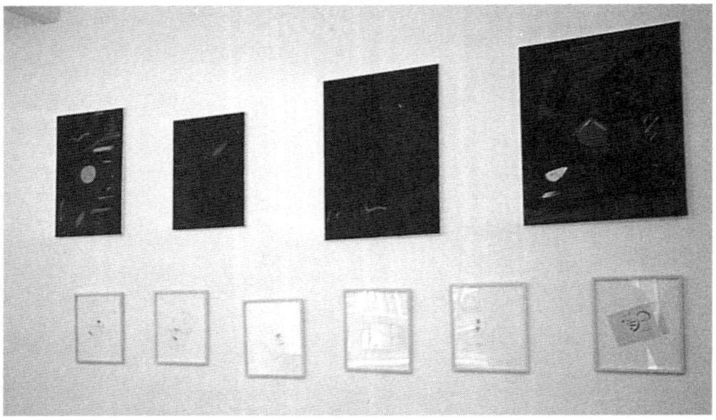

MICHAEL KREBBER, Installation bei Bruno Brunnet Fine Arts, Berlin.

Lampshade with burning bulb, for instance, and the drawing of the lips provide simple and reliable clues to what has transpired. The rest is draped around in a fashion typical of such establishments, gradually and very individualistically, or initially "staring at but past each other" and possibly, as the evening advances, in a "most charming pose." The line of the narrative will stiffen it up again anyway, even the pose in front of the camera, and fortunately wrinkles and faux pas do not show up on the faces of others but rather on all those who felt at home in this Bohemian theater or who just dropped in, including that "pin-striped gangster": draftsman Michel Würthle.

On his way, the bartender-turned-artist has taken two steps in thirteen pictures: another gallery, and oil on canvas, for a change. In Zurich, Birgit Küng shows an "Aging Barroom Prince's Chief Worries: Impoverishment, Impasto, Imposture."

After Bruno Brunnet had plastered the walls of his gallery with Michel Würthle's drawings, he proceeded with plans for a show by **Michael Krebber.** I was in Berlin when they were hanging the show and clearing away the miscellanea of behind-the-scenes gallery life. Having seen slides of the new drawings before seeing the originals, my perception of them at the opening was slightly deflected. Actually that proved helpful, because meeting up unprepared with a Krebber picture does not make for instant enlightenment. Besides, he had tipped some of the framed drawings—six in all—on to one corner to see if that would "do the trick" and so my eyes kept sliding off—or through—the picture. The dabs of color were so few and far between that it looked like a paper test, in which the paint shining through on the back was as important as the wrinkles formed around the dabs as the paper dried. This rather tremulous and thin arrangement spilled out of the frame on to the wall, where the traces—little holes and inoperative nails—of two other tries at hanging the drawings, had not been removed. Besides, extremely subtle or more conspicuous nuances in the final presentation undermined a comfortingly and conventionally squared arrangement. Four canvases, mainly slate-gray, loomed above the drawings. Here, too, traces of preparation, overpainted portions, and the consistency of the paint gave the impression that the edge-to-edge, matte surfaces had become permeable, so that it is small wonder how easily a few traces of color on the dry side of the pictures were still drawn towards us. The entire show, especially the drawings, evoked shades of reinstated constructivism of the first order, replete with the dynamic and abandon of its discovery—like the vocabulary of Polke's drawings from the sixties. With these patches, corners, and inaccuracies, Krebber had scattered a mobile flat against the wall, whose elements were as hard to define as their varying velocities—which is why I said "mobile" or "constructivism" although the terms naturally invite gross misunderstandings. But even the misunderstandings, the recollection of the age of the mobile, its casualness, the transparence or "all the kitsch" of constructivist counterplay are targeted here, cheap and simple, loosely combined, but mixed with brief and controlled bits of movement. On being asked, Michael Krebber explained once more that he wanted to keep the door—out of art—open. He said so, pointing at the pictures from the other side of the wall, so to speak. But actually, his work appears rather less transparent than his agenda did at that moment, because when someone around him asks just what it is that he has done, the great guessing game begins. *(Translation: Catherine Schelbert)*

1) Recollections of life as a waiter in the "Exil" bar in Berlin, recorded by Austrian Michel Würthle in his *Aufzeichnungen eines bewaffneten Schankprinzen. Im Exil 1972–1979* (ed. Martin Kippenberger, Berlin, 1994).

2) Chansonniers popular in Germany in the late seventies.

Each volume of PARKETT is created in collaboration with artists, who contribute an original work specially made for the readers of PARKETT. The works are available in a signed and numbered Special Edition. Prices are subject to change. Postage is not included.

EDITIONS FOR PARKETT

Jeder PARKETT-Band entsteht in Collaboration mit Künstlern, die eigens für die Leser von PARKETT Originalbeiträge gestalten. Diese Vorzugsausgaben sind als numerierte und signierte Editionen erhältlich. Preisänderungen vorbehalten. Versandkosten nicht inbegriffen.

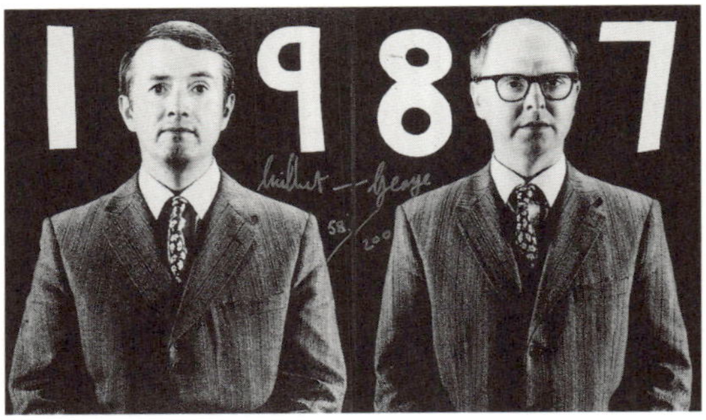

PARKETT 14

GILBERT & GEORGE, 1987

Photographie auf Karton aufgezogen,
in der Mitte faltbar, 25,5 x 42 cm,
Ed. 200, signiert und numeriert, **sFr. 1200.–**
Photograph, mounted on cardboard
folded in the middle, 10 x 16½" (25,5 x 42 cm),
Ed. 200, signed and numbered, **US$ 950**

Eindringlich und dramatisch spielt das Licht auf den Gesichtern von Gilbert & George im Photo-Diptychon zum Aufstellen auf Ihrem Schreibtisch oder Bücherschrank.

Memorabilia from an art world Hall of Fame. A provocative reshoot of the classic wedding photo, the alumni portrait, the religious diptych, Gilbert & George's stand-up self-portrait will be an asset to the mantelpiece of any self-respecting amateur.

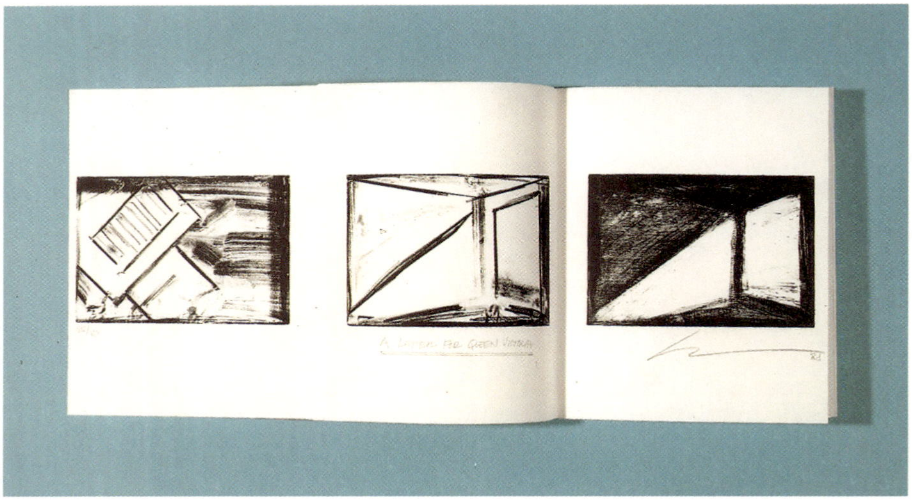

Mit minimalsten Licht- und Architekturakzenten öffnen sich traumhafte Bühnenräume, wie sie nur ein Robert Wilson erdenken kann.

The director's notebook. This animated three-part lithograph is a reminder that every one of Wilson's dramatic theater works has its genesis in a powerful, light-filled drawing.

PARKETT 16

ROBERT WILSON
A LETTER FOR QUEEN VICTORIA, 1988
Lithographie auf Rives, 25,5 x 61 cm, in Parkett eingebunden,
Ed. 80, signiert und numeriert, **sFr. 800.–**
Lithograph on Rives, 10 x 24", (25,5 x 61 cm), bound in the magazine,
Ed. 80, signed and numbered, **US$ 640**
Printed by Champfleury

Eine poetische Symmetrie oszilliert zwischen Flächigkeit, Stilisierung und Abbild der Natur.

Artificial nature. A deft exercise in Katz's ongoing exploration of pictorial flatness and poetic symmetry, this stylized woodcut on the most delicate of papers is a quiet moment of reflection from a preternatural world.

PARKETT 21

ALEX KATZ

SCHWARZER TEICH, 1989

Holzschnitt auf Goyu-Papier, 29,5 x 46 cm,
Ed. 100, signiert und numeriert, **sFr. 950.–**

BLACK POND, 1989

Woodcut on Goyu paper,
11⅝ x 18⅛" (29,5 x 46 cm),
Ed. 100, signed and numbered, **US$ 760**

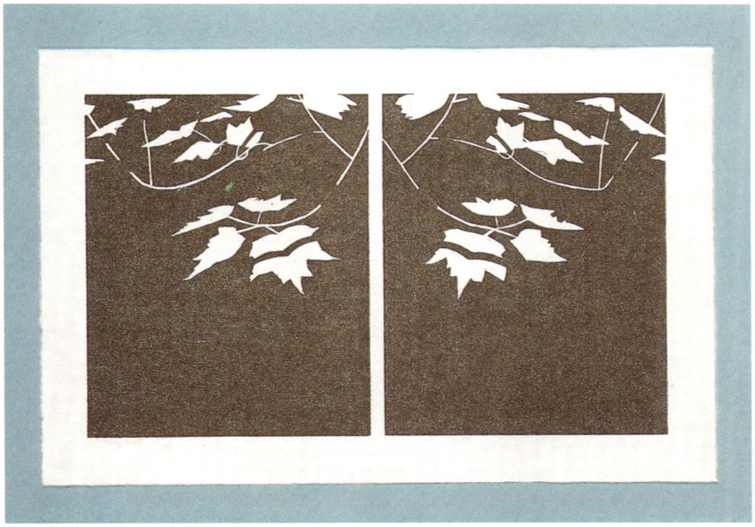

Der Künstler begibt sich auf die Spur von Verdoppelungen, lässt von zwei verschiedenen Händen die zweifache Ausgabe von Newsweek – die nationale und die internationale – abzeichnen.

Double trouble. A perennial obsession with dual identities and symmetry is manifested in the systematic rendering of twin subjects by two detectably different hands. A hand-applied flash of vicious scarlet completes this doubly complex Rorschach test.

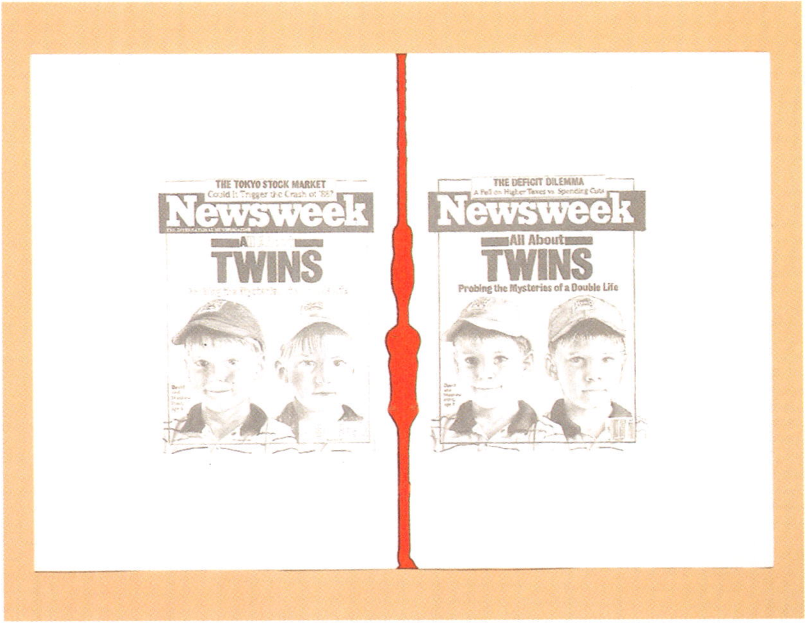

PARKETT 24

ALIGHIERO E BOETTI

AUF DEN SPUREN DER GEHEIMNISSE EINES DOPPELLEBENS, 1990

Lichtdruck (Granolitho), von Hand rot übermalt,
50 x 70 cm, Ed. 100, signiert und numeriert, **sFr. 1200.–**

PROBING THE MYSTERIES OF A DOUBLE LIFE, 1990

Collotype (Granolitho), overpainted by
hand in red, 19⅞ x 27½" (50 x 70 cm),
Ed. 100, signed and numbered, **US$ 960**

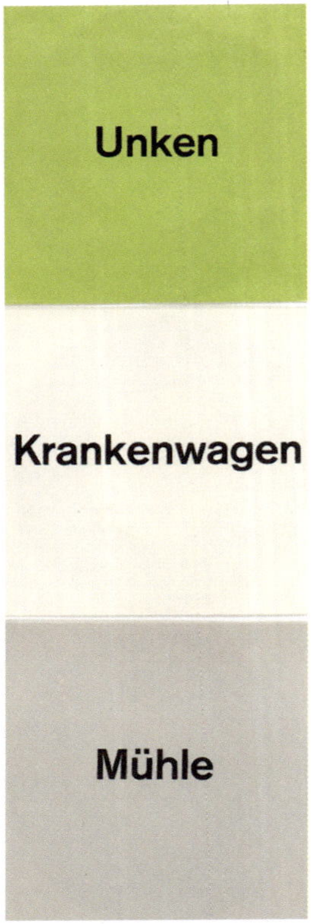

Klang- und Geräuschskulpturen, Erinnerungsbilder aus dem kollektiven Gedächtnis formen sich aus Ihren Lautsprechern heraus.

Music for the eyes. A set of three records, each pressed with a single ambient sound from the artist's aural memory—toads croaking, a watermill churning, a local ambulance siren wailing—and sealed with a corresponding emblematic color.

PARKETT 25

KATHARINA FRITSCH
MÜHLE/KRANKENWAGEN/UNKEN, 1990
Drei Single-Schallplatten, Ed. je 2000, unsigniert, zusammen: **sFr. 45.–**
MILL/AMBULANCE/TOADS, 1990
Set of three single records, Ed. of 2000 sets, unsigned, for set of three: **US$ 38**

Licht materialisiert sich zu geometrischen Körpern; für einmal nicht in einer von Turrells Rauminstallationen, sondern in einem traditionsgemäss für Hell-Dunkel-Effekte geschaffenen Medium.

Speed of light. These experimental forays into the medium of etching yield light as material, not illusion, in the contours of the printed image.

PARKETT 25

JAMES TURRELL
SQUAT, JUKE, CARN, ALTA, 1990
Vier Aquatinta-Editionen auf Zerkall 250 g, je 25,5 x 21 cm, in Parkett eingebunden, Ed. je 40 pro Aquatinta,
signiert und numeriert, **sFr. 1200.–** pro Aquatinta
SQUAT, JUKE, CARN, ALTA, 1990
Four aquatint editions on Zerkall 250 g, each 10 x 8¼"
(25,5 x 21 cm), bound in the magazine. Ed. of 40 each, signed and numbered, **US$ 960** per print

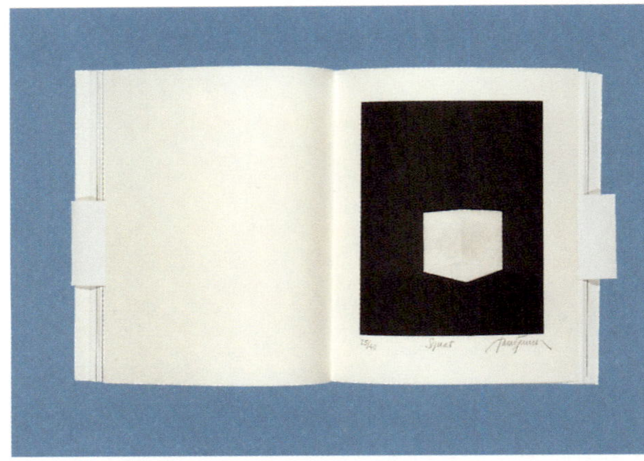

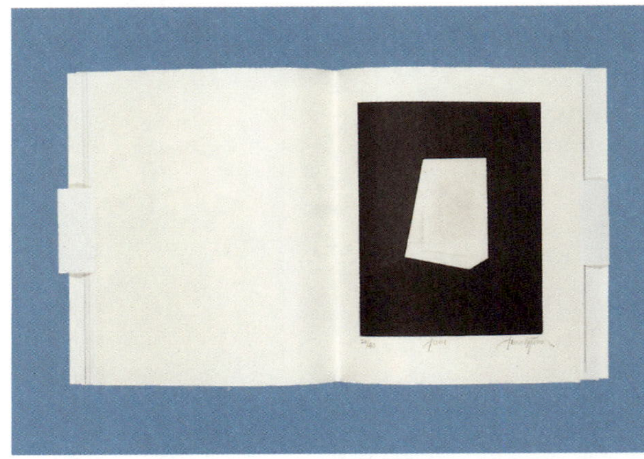

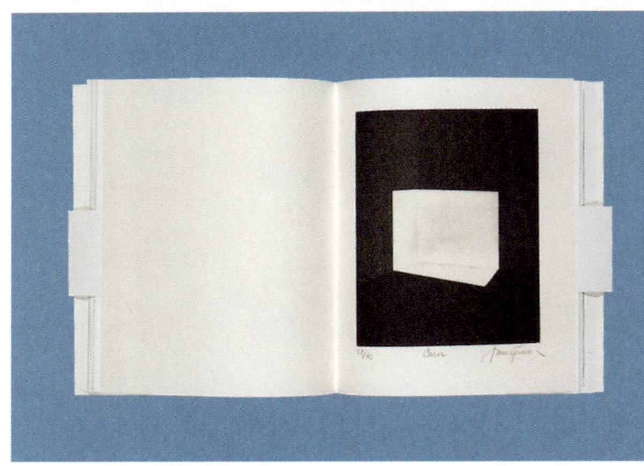

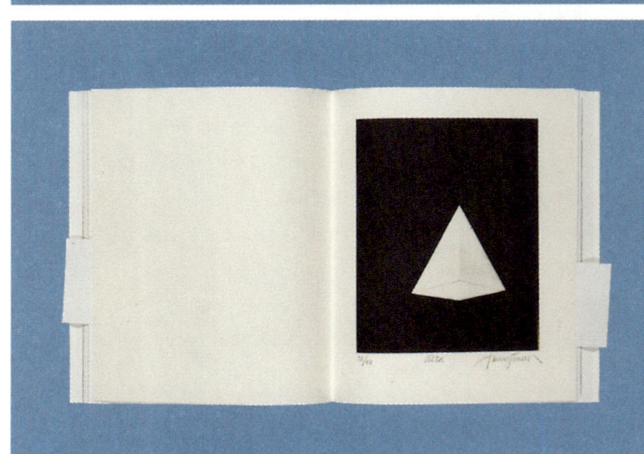

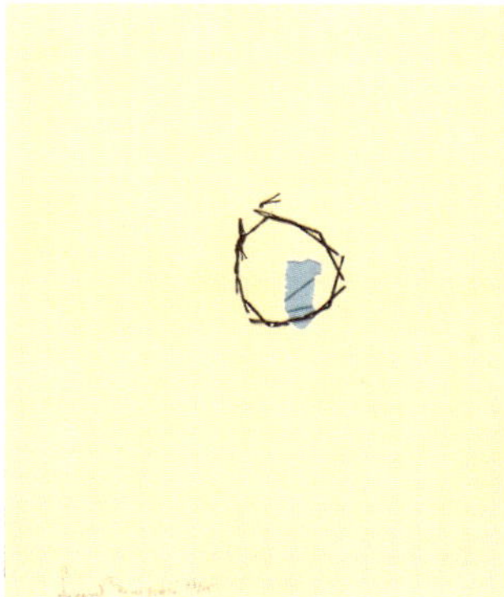

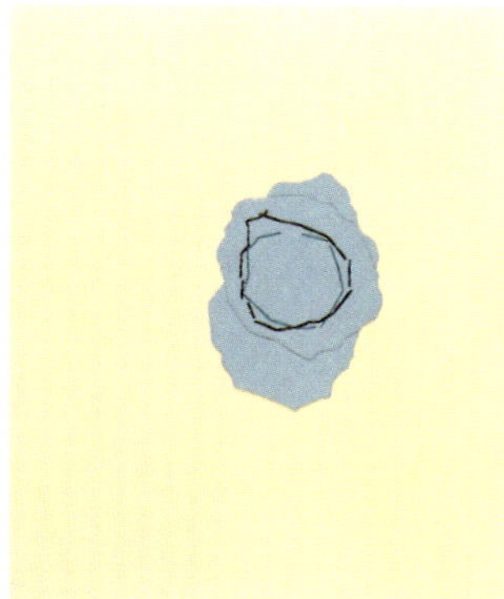

Die Künstlerin widmet Parkett mit seinem gestickten Schriftzug ein genähtes Flickwerk, das auf viele ihrer künstlerischen und ebenso biographischen Motive anspielt.

A stitch in time. A patched and mended page in a book fuses theory with biography—the sculptor's approach to assemblage as a reparative process and her origins as the child of tapestry-restorers.

PARKETT 27

LOUISE BOURGEOIS

FLICKWERK, 1991

Papier-Objekt aus bedrucktem und handgefärbtem Papier, von Hand gerissen, durchlöchert und mit Faden genäht, 25,5 x 21 cm, in Parkett eingebunden, Ed. 75, signiert und numeriert, **sFr. 1800.–**

REPARATION, 1991

Fabrication of printed and handcolored paper, hand-torn, pierced, and sewn with thread, 10 x 8¼" (25,5 x 21 cm), bound in the magazine, Ed. 75, signed and numbered, **US$ 1500**

PARKETT 28

THOMAS RUFF

C-PRINTS, 1991

2 C-Prints (Photos: ESO), je 50 x 50 cm, in Transparenthüllen, astronomische Daten in Siebdruck beidseitig auf Hüllen gedruckt, Ed. je 50, signiert und numeriert, **sFr. 1200.–**

C-PRINTS, 1991

Two c-prints (Photos: ESO), each 19½ x 19½" (50 x 50 cm), with astronomic data silk-screened on front and back of transparent wrappers, Ed. of 50 each, signed and numbered, **US$ 960**

Ruffs Sternenhimmel für einmal als Negativprint. Im Zentrum steht ein astronomisch bestimmter Stern.

Milky ways. Phantasmagoric photographs of the night sky and its galaxies are reversed into peppered white fields upon which a single lodestar is pinpointed by its astronomical data.

PARKETT 28

FRANZ GERTSCH

CIMA DEL MAR (AUSSCHNITT), 1990/91

Holzschnitt (Kobalttürkis und Ultramarin, halb und halb) auf Heizoburo-Japanpapier, 25,4 x 41,6 cm, gefaltet, nicht eingebunden, Ed. 80, signiert und numeriert, **sFr. 1350.–**

CIMA DEL MAR (DETAIL), 1990/91

Woodcut (cobalt turquoise and ultramarine, half and half) on Heizoburo Japan paper, 10 x 16⅜" (25,4 x 41,6 cm), folded, not bound in the magazine, Ed. 80, signed and numbered, **US$ 1080**

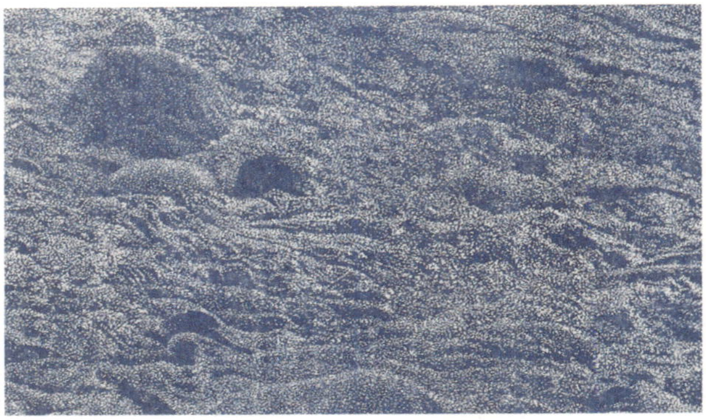

Detail aus einem über zwei Meter hohen Holzstock, an dem Franz Gertsch ein Jahr lang gearbeitet hat.

Against the grain. Every point of light on this minutely described surface corresponds to the removal of a sliver of wood. This fragment was taken from a gigantic woodcut measuring more than 5 x 6 feet (170 x 152 cm).

Ein Monster, gedruckt auf feinste Seide, quillt aus einem Goldrahmen.

The little house of horrors. A silken greasepaint grotesque rendered in startling 3-D threatens to burst from its keepsake frame.

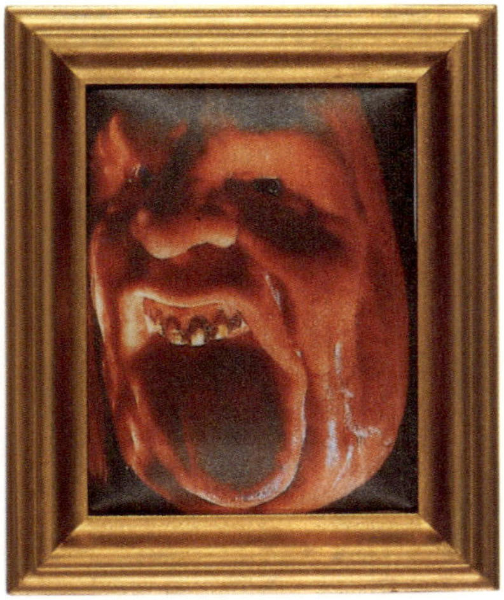

PARKETT 29

CINDY SHERMAN

OHNE TITEL, 1991

Bedruckte Seide, gepolstert, in goldfarbenem Holzrahmen, 15 x 11,5 cm (Bild), 21,3 x 17,4 cm (Rahmen), Ed. 100, signiert und numeriert, **sFr. 1380.–**

UNTITLED, 1991

Printed silk, padded, in gilded wooden frame, 8⅜ x 6⅞" (21,3 x 17,4 cm), with frame, Ed. 100, signed and numbered, **US$ 1100**

Basketball ist eine der Möglichkeiten für einen Afro-Amerikaner, reich zu werden. So trägt die Photographie des Objet trouvé den Titel «Geldbaum».

Readymade magic. A basketball hoop fashioned from the rim of a bicycle tire, embedded in a living tree in a Charleston backyard, testifies to the ingenuity of its anonymous maker.

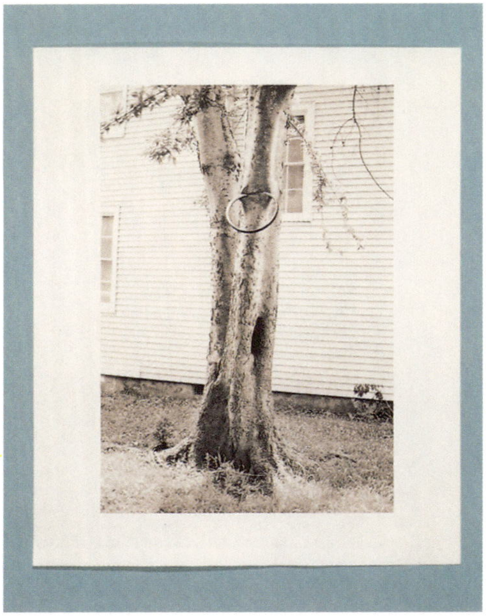

PARKETT 31

DAVID HAMMONS

GELDBAUM, 1992

Sepia-Print-Photographie, 42 x 28 cm, Ed. 70, signiert und numeriert, **sFr. 890.–**

MONEY TREE, 1992

Sepia-Print photograph, 16½ x 11" (42 x 28 cm), Ed. 70, signed and numbered, **US$ 720**

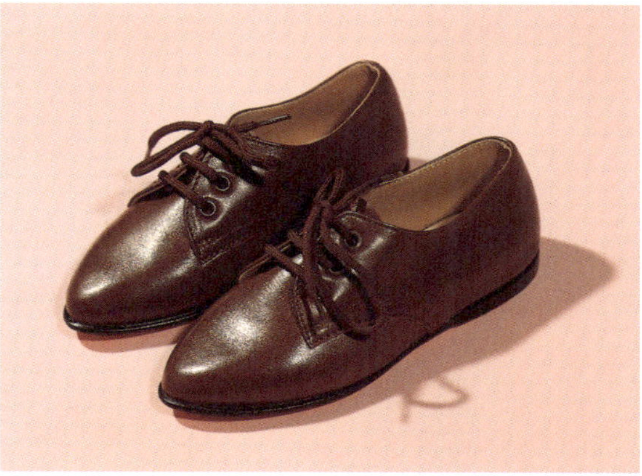

In den 16 cm kleinen Kinderschuhen vereinen sich Vorstellungen von Niedlichkeit und früher Uniformierung, von Androgynität und Standfestigkeit – als Bild der Einprobung in unsere Welt.

A new pair of shoes. Many years ago, Sherrie Levine found and sold pairs of small shoes in a gallery in New York. A refined version, handmade in Italy from softest leather and suede, retraces the artist's first steps.

PARKETT 32

SHERRIE LEVINE

2 SCHUHE, 1992

Ein Paar Kinderschuhe, braunes Leder, je ca. 16 x 6 x 6 cm, Ed. 99, signiert und numeriert, **sFr. 830.–**

2 SHOES, 1992

Pair of shoes, brown leather, each 6½ x 2½ x 2½" (16 x 6 x 6 cm), Ed. 99, signed and numbered, **US$ 670**

Greatest hits. Der Meister der Fiktion krönt sich selber mit der höchsten Auszeichnung der Unterhaltungsindustrie – die goldene Schallplatte – und fügt ihr ein Muster seiner Erzählkunst bei.

Greatest hits. A weaver of fictions awards himself the industry's highest accolade—a gold record—complete with winning cover design and haunting "lyrics."

PARKETT 34

RICHARD PRINCE

GOOD REVOLUTION, 1992

Goldene Schallplatte und graviertes Metallschild auf C-Print, montiert und gerahmt. Enthält zusätzlich eine beidseitig abspielbare Vinylplatte des Künstlers. «Good Revolution» (1,46 Min.) und «Don't Belong» (1,46 Min.) arrangiert und interpretiert von Richard Prince. Aufgenommen und gemischt auf der Harmonic Ranch von Mark Degliantoni, September 1992. 52 x 41,9 cm. Ed. 80, signiert und numeriert, **sFr. 1100.–**

GOOD REVOLUTION, 1992

Presentation gold record with engraved plaque mounted on C-Print, framed. Includes a playable vinyl record by the artist, recorded on both sides. "Good Revolution" (1:46) and "Don't Belong" (1:46), arranged and performed by Richard Prince. Recorded and mixed at Harmonic Ranch by Mark Degliantoni, September 1992. 20½ x 16½" (52 x 41,9 cm), Ed. 80, signed and numbered, **US$ 880**

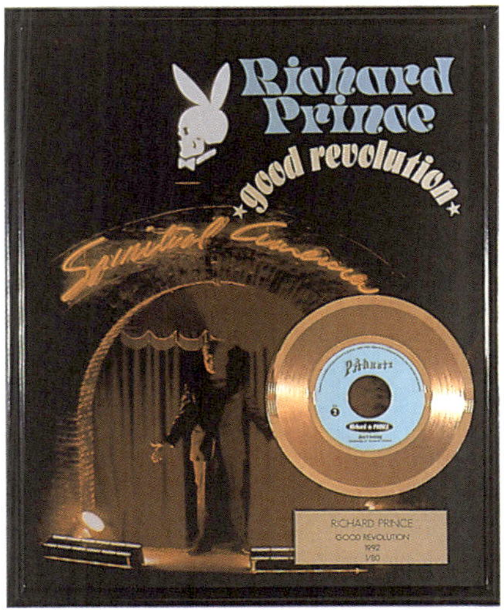

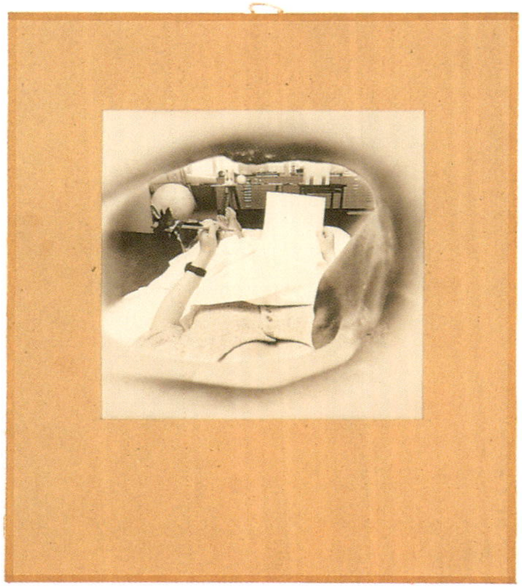

Teilen Sie mit Rosemarie Trockel die geheime Perspektive auf ihr Atelier als Hirnsicht durch die linke Augenhöhle.

Mind's eye view. An intimate perspective of the studio that places the viewer inside the secret cave of the artist's left eye.

PARKETT 33

ROSEMARIE TROCKEL

STUDIO VISIT, 1992

Photogravure in Strohpappe-Passepartout mit Prägedruck, säurefreies Folienfenster, auf Holz montiert mit Aufhänger, Bild: 21 x 21 cm, Rahmen: 38 x 33 x 0,9 cm, Ed. 80, numeriert und signiert, **sFr. 850.–**

STUDIO VISIT, 1992

Photoetching and acid-free transparent foil in embossed strawboard matte, mounted on wood with hanger, image: 8¼ x 8¼", frame: 15 x 13 x ⅜", Ed. 80, numbered and signed, **US$ 680**

Printed by Peter Kneubühler

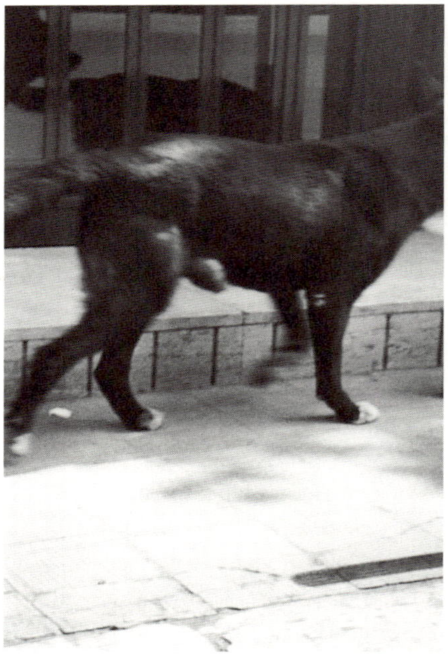

Die Verwandlung vom Wortbild RUN DOG RUN aus Christopher Wools Malerei zur bildmalerischen Momentaufnahme eines fliehenden schwarzen Hundes.

Word into image. RUN DOG RUN beat a tattoo in an earlier cycle of paintings; here it becomes a fleeting presence captured in a painterly snapshot.

PARKETT 33

CHRISTOPHER WOOL

OHNE TITEL, 1992

Schwarzweissphotographie, 25,4 x 20,3 cm, Ed. 70, numeriert und signiert, **sFr. 400.–**

UNTITLED, 1992

Black & white photograph, 10 x 8", Ed. 70, signed and numbered, **US$ 330**

Ein Bild mit Gewicht. In weiches, schweres Blei gegossen ist ein Mann flankiert von zwei mannshohen Echsen – Mensch und Tier vereint ohne Furcht und Hierarchie.

Graven image. A triumvirate of a man and two lizards cast in lead—a substance at once elemental and endearing—man coexists with beast, devoid of fear or hierarchy.

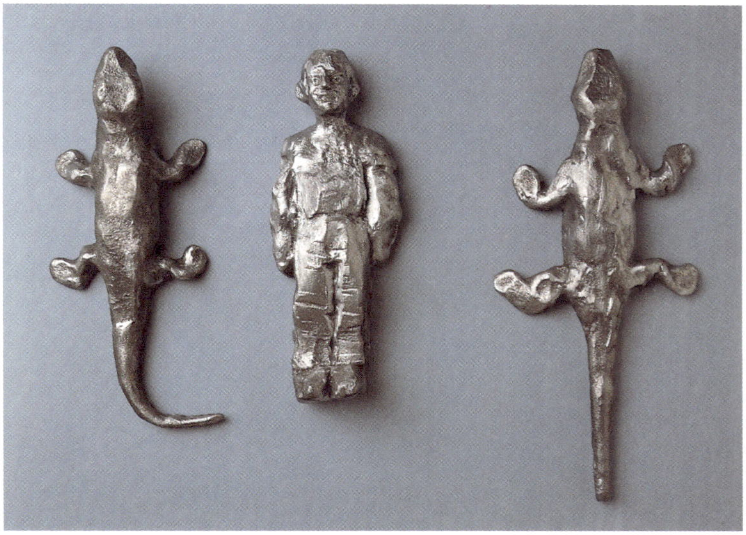

PARKETT 36

STEPHAN BALKENHOL

ZWEI ECHSEN MIT MANN, 1993

Dreiteilige Figurengruppe, gegossen in Bleilegierung durch Giesserei Bärtschi, Aefligen, Schweiz, je ca. 30 x 13 x 4 cm, Gewicht je ca. 2 kg, Ed. 85, signiert und numeriert, **sFr. 1900.–**

TWO LIZARDS AND A MAN, 1993

Group of three cast lead figurines, produced at the Bärtschi Foundry, Aefligen, Switzerland, each figure approx. 11⅞ x 5⅛ x 1½", weighing approx. 4.5 lbs, Ed. 85, signed and numbered, **US$ 1500**

Eine Seidenkrawatte war das erste von mehreren Kleidungsstücken, die Sophie Calle anonymerweise einem heimlich beobachteten Unbekannten zukommen liess. Die Geschichte dieser imaginären Beziehung ist auf der Krawatte niedergeschrieben.

Autobiographical story. A silken tie not only represents the first episode of a story in which a number of tasteful articles of clothing are sent to a badly dressed but attractive man; it also becomes the page on which the story itself is told.

PARKETT 36

SOPHIE CALLE

THE TIE, 1993

Krawatte mit aufgedruckter Kurzgeschichte «I saw him», Crêpe de Chine, braun mit blauem Text, hergestellt durch Fabric Frontline, Zürich, Ed. 150, signiert und numeriert, **sFr. 280.–**

THE TIE, 1993

Pure silk crepe-de-chine man's tie, printed with an autobiographical story, produced by Fabric Frontline, Zurich, Ed. 150, signed and numbered, **US$ 224**

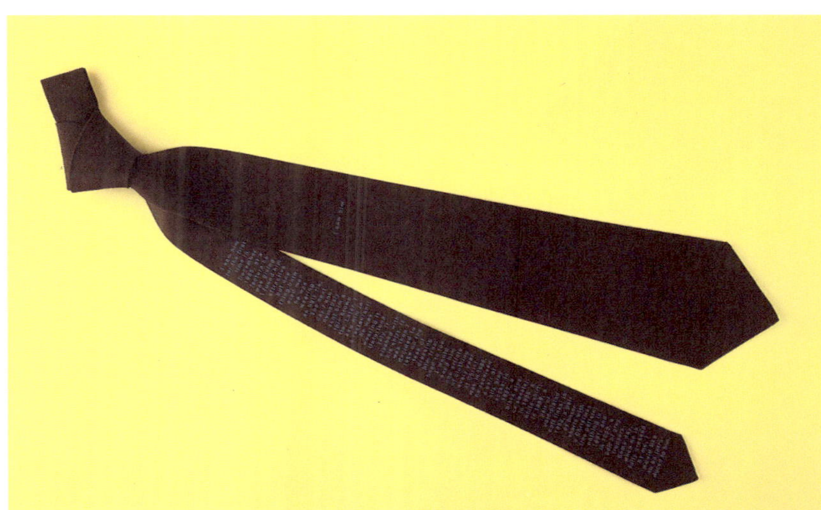

Über 500mal photographierte Charles Ray das Super-Model Tatjana Patitz für seine hobbyphotographische Subversion der Glamour-Technologie.

Between real and ideal. A relentless informal photo session with supermodel Tatjana Patitz yielded disarmingly familiar keepsake snapshots of an extraordinary girl next door.

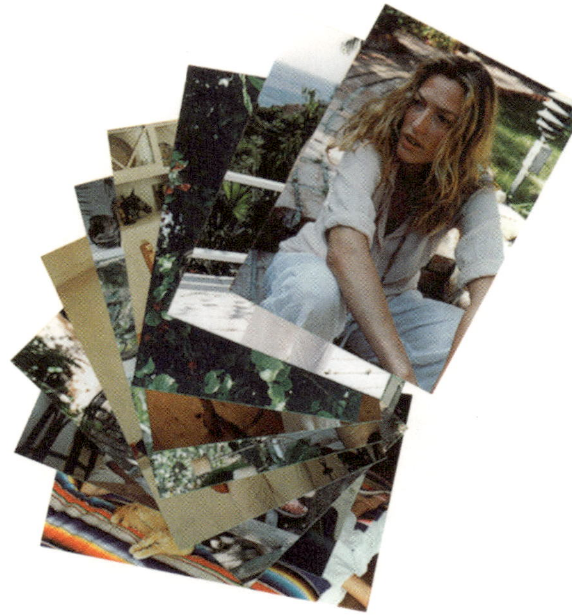

PARKETT 37

CHARLES RAY

DIE SCHÖNSTE FRAU DER WELT, 1993

Photoedition mit je neun Unikat-Farbphotos von Tatjana Patitz, 10 x 15 cm, Ed. 60, signiert und numeriert, **sFr. 1100.–**

THE MOST BEAUTIFUL WOMAN IN THE WORLD, 1993

Photo edition, each comprising a set of nine unique color snapshots of Tatjana Patitz, 4 x 6", Ed. 60, signed and numbered, **US$ 880**

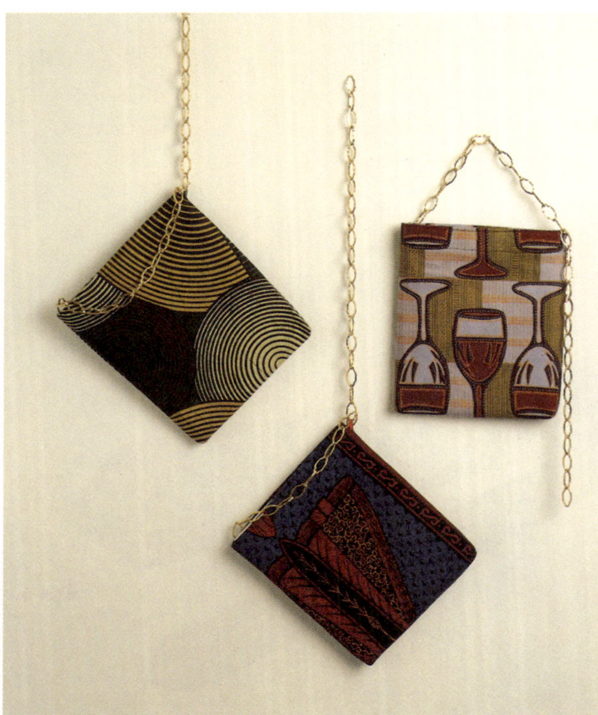

Franz Wests «Sackerl» bietet einen hintersinnigen Kommentar zum euroamerikanischen Zentrismus von Parkett.

Totem tote. A Parkett-sized pouch fashioned from hand-printed African fabric is a useful article for a specific purpose.

PARKETT 37

FRANZ WEST

ETUI FÜR PARKETT, 1993

Bedruckte afrikanische Baumwollstoffe, Kette, Ed. 180, numeriert und signiert, **sFr. 300.–**

POUCH FOR PARKETT, 1993

Printed African fabric, chain, Ed. 180, signed and numbered, **US$ 240**

Augenzwinkernde Vorurteilsbewältigung als drucktechnische Rhapsodie.

Archetypical exorcism. The crude silhouettes of street graffiti meet the painstaking processes of the handmade print, transforming familiar stereotypes into a luxurious triptych.

PARKETT 38

MARLENE DUMAS

THE BLACK MAN, THE JEW, AND THE GIRL, 1993

Gefaltetes Triptychon, hergestellt bei Marcel Kalksma, Amsterdam, in drei Durchgängen auf Arches (250 g): einfarbiger Holzschnitt (Silhouetten), zweifache Umdrucklithographie von einem Stein in zwei Farben, mit Tinte markiert, Augen und Geschlechtsteile ausgekratzt, handschriftlicher Text, 25,5 x 63 cm, Ed. 60, signiert und numeriert, **sFr. 1200.–**

THE BLACK MAN, THE JEW, AND THE GIRL, 1993

Triptych printed by Marcel Kalksma, Amsterdam, in three processes on 250 grs Arches: Blockprint in one color, two transfer lithographs from one stone rendered in two colors, inked and inscribed by hand, with eyes and organs scratched out, folded zigzag, 10 x 24¾", Ed. 60, signed and numbered, **US$ 960**

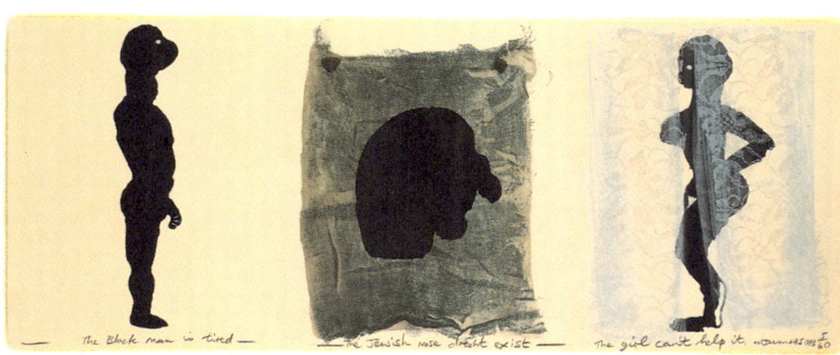

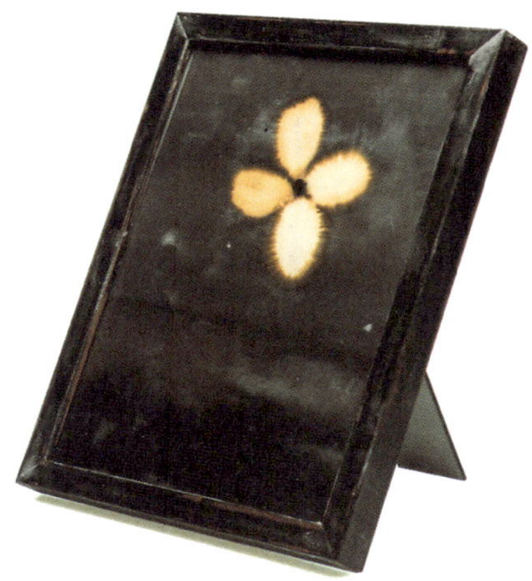

Ein Andachtsbild, eine lichte Blume im Dunkel, als gemalte Poesie einer indirekten Präsenz.

Forget me not. In handpainted portrait frames, a simple-petalled flower goes through a cycle of permutations, making each a unique and distinctive watercolor.

PARKETT 38

ROSS BLECKNER

OHNE TITEL, 1993

100 Originalblätter in Wasserfarbe, Tinte und Wachs auf Wasserfarbenpapier in handbemaltem, gewachstem Holzrahmen zum Aufstellen, 29 x 23 cm, Ed. 100, signiert und numeriert, **sFr. 1650.–**

UNTITLED, 1993

100 unique pieces, watercolor, inks, and wax on watercolor paper in handpainted and waxed wooden desktop picture frame, 11 x 9", Ed. 100, signed and numbered, **US$ 1320**

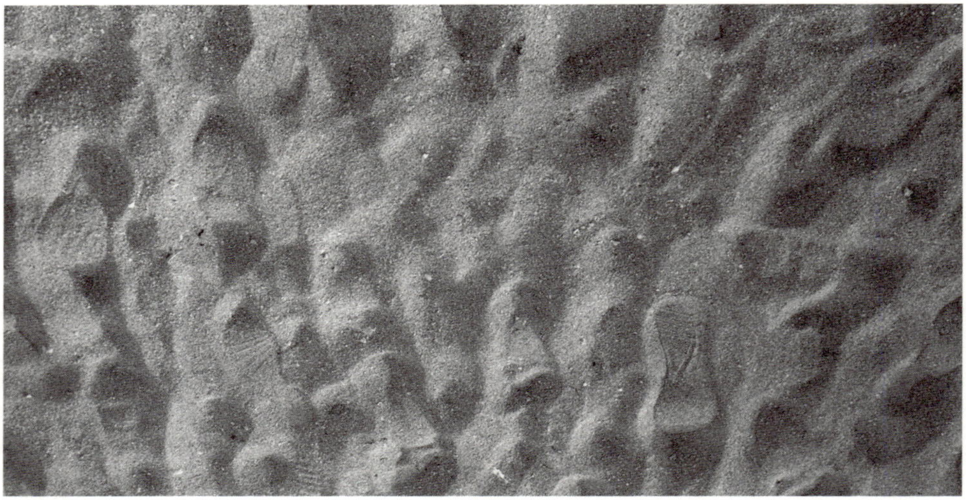

Wie durchlässig sind die Ränder unseres kollektiven Daseins? Felix Gonzalez-Torres hat ein gigantisches Bild geschaffen, das zugleich den Anspruch stellt, das stille «Bei-sich-Sein» wie das öffentliche «Nach-aussen-Dringen» zu symbolisieren.

Emotional propaganda. Ephemeral footprints in sand become an advertisement for the ineffable in a gigantic billboard.

PARKETT 39

FELIX GONZALEZ-TORRES

OHNE TITEL (FÜR PARKETT), 1994

Plakat in 30 Blätter unterteilt, Siebdruck auf imprägniertem (Appleton-)Papier, 317,5 x 690,9 cm, Ed. 84, signiert und numeriert, **sFr. 1200.–**

UNTITLED (FOR PARKETT), 1994

30-sheet billboard, silkscreen on Appleton coated stock, 125 x 272", Ed. 84, signed and numbered, **US$ 960**

Wolfgang Laib sucht sich einen Berg des europäischen Kontinents aus, um dort einen öffentlichen Ort der persönlichen Einkehr zu schaffen, und will ihn mit jenem «energetischen Gold überziehen, das Wachs heisst» (Jean-Marc Avrilla).

Trace elements. A delicate rendering in golden wax of a secluded place in the future, a mountain sanctuary to be built by the artist in the Pyrenees.

PARKETT 39

WOLFGANG LAIB

A WAX ROOM FOR A MOUNTAIN, 1994

Vom Künstler mit Ölstift überarbeiteter Siebdruck auf Rivoli SK2 (240 g), gedruckt bei Lorenz Boegli, Zürich, 49,3 x 41 cm, Ed. 75, signiert und numeriert, **sFr. 900.–**

A WAX ROOM FOR A MOUNTAIN, 1994

Silkscreen, oilstick on Rivoli SK2 (240 g), printed by Lorenz Boegli, Zürich, 19½ x 16⅛", Ed. 75, signed and numbered, **US$ 720**

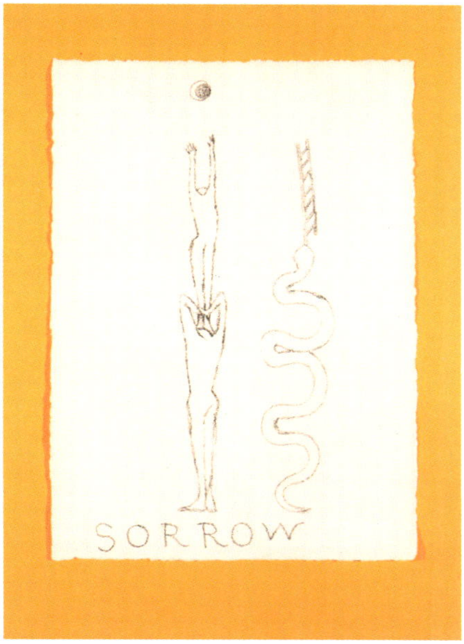

Im schwindelerregenden Balanceakt nach dem Mond greifen zu wollen und dabei zu scheitern ist die sich lohnende Wehmut aller.

Balancing act. A whimsical lyricism counter-weighted by an aura of impossibility haunts these simple figures.

PARKETT 40/41

FRANCESCO CLEMENTE

SORROW, 1994

Tiefdruck mit Photoätzung, 29 x 20,5 cm, gedruckt bei Peter Kneubühler, Zürich, auf handgeschöpftem Bütten-Papier, Ed. 60, signiert und numeriert, **sFr. 1500.–**

SORROW, 1994

Photo-etching, printed by Peter Kneubühler on handmade Vellum, 11⅜ x 8⅛", Ed. 60, signed and numbered, **US$ 1200**

Der Spiegel und die Kupferplatte, beide im Parkettformat, stehen in einem der spannendsten Kunst-Diskurse: gespiegelte Realität des Betrachters und seiner Architektur versus abstrakte Malerei, versinnbildlicht durch die Oxydationsflecken des Kupfers.

Reality abstracted. Lightning strikes between mirrored reality and the abstract pattern of oxidation on a copperplate, both in Parkett format.

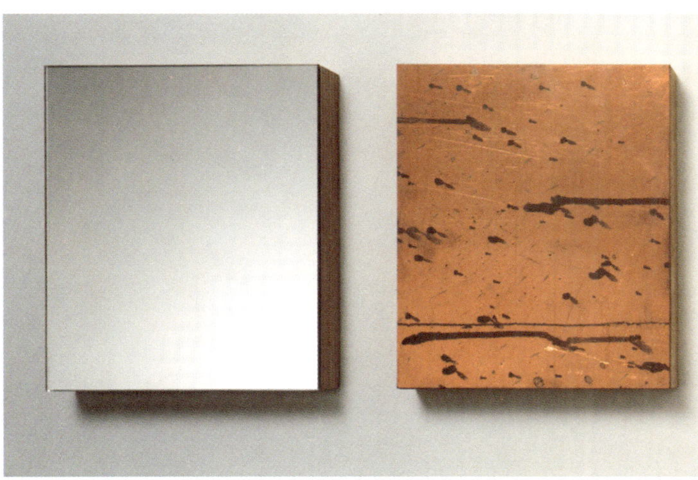

PARKETT 40/41

GÜNTHER FÖRG

OHNE TITEL (FÜR PARKETT), 1994

Zweiteiliges Objekt mit je einem Spiegel und einer Kupferplatte, auf Holz montiert, im Parkett-Format, je 25,5 x 21 x 3,2 cm, Ausführung Jürgen Zimmermann, Karlsruhe, Ed. 45, signiert und numeriert, **sFr. 2200.–**

UNTITLED (FOR PARKETT), 1994

Two-part object, consisting of one mirror and one copperplate each mounted on wood in Parkett format, each 10 x 8¼ x 1¼", produced by Jürgen Zimmermann, Karlsruhe, Ed. 45, signed and numbered, **US$ 1760**

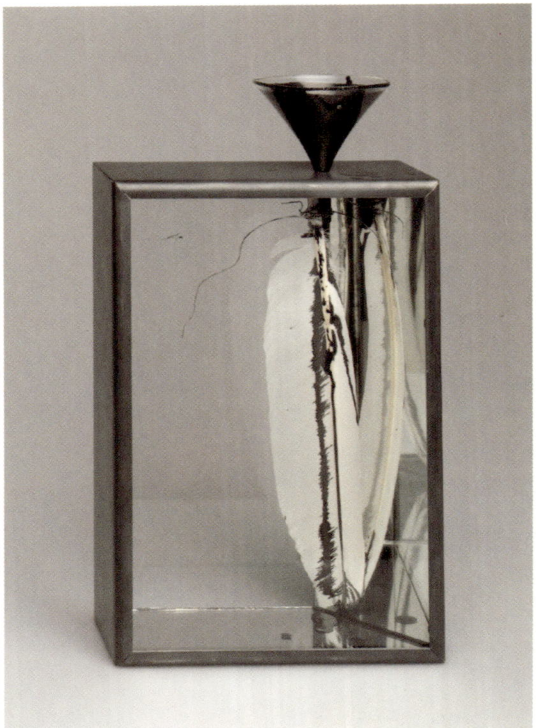

Die Welt, in der sich alles spiegelt, wo das Geschriebene jedoch nicht sichtbar und das Sichtbare nicht geschrieben ist.

Glass menagerie. Invisible written worlds, visible unwritten worlds reverberate in a cosmos of multiple reflections.

PARKETT 40/41

REBECCA HORN

SCHWANENLEITER, 1994

Schwanenfeder in Box mit Metallrahmen, Tinte, aufgesetzter Glastrichter, Glasfenster vorne und hinten, Spiegel. 31 x 21 x 8 cm, verpackt in Holzkasten mit Schaumstoff, 47,5 x 33 x 22,5 cm, Ed. 45, signiert und numeriert, **sFr. 5500.–**

SWAN LADDER, 1994

Swan's feather in metal-frame box with glass funnel, ink, glass windows front and back, mirror 12¼ x 8¼ x 3⅛", packed in wooden box with Styrofoam, 18¾ x 13 x 8⅞". Ed. 45, signed and numbered, **US$ 4400**

Persönlicher geht's nicht mehr, wenn auf den Überdrucken von Parkett der Zufall zuschlägt und uns gezeigt wird, wo der Meisterschütze den Apfel traf und wie die Währung gefährlich mitspielt.

Master marksman. Chance hits the mark on overprint paper in a fireworks of acrobatic multi-meaning.

PARKETT 40/41

SIGMAR POLKE

OHNE TITEL, 1994

Parkett-Band aus Überdruck-Makulatur, 25,5 x 21 cm, Ed. 25, signiert und numeriert, ca. **sFr. 2000.–,** und zusätzlich Ed. 25 mit Originalbeitrag, signiert und numeriert, **sFr. 4000.–**

UNTITLED, 1994

Volume of Parkett made of overprint paper, 10 x 8¼", Ed. 25 copies, signed and numbered, approx. **US$ 1600,** and Ed. 25 copies with an original contribution, signed and numbered, **US$ 3200**

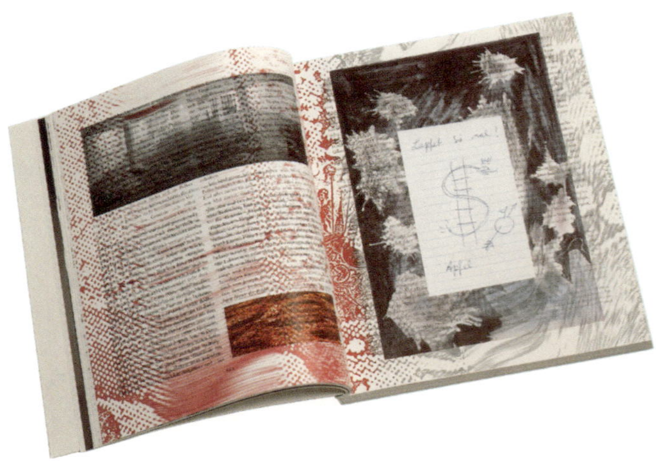

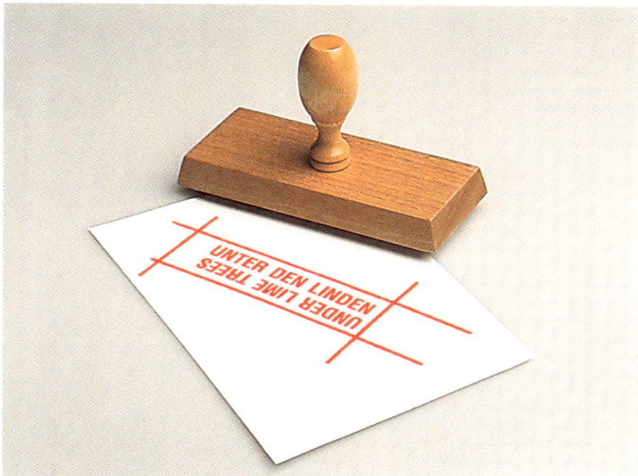

The meaning that comes away from the work of art. Berlin's historic street transforms—through the act of translation—into a metaphor of poetry and nature.

Bedeutungswandel. Der geschichtsträchtige Strassenname Berlins wird in der Übertragung zur romantisch poetischen Formel.

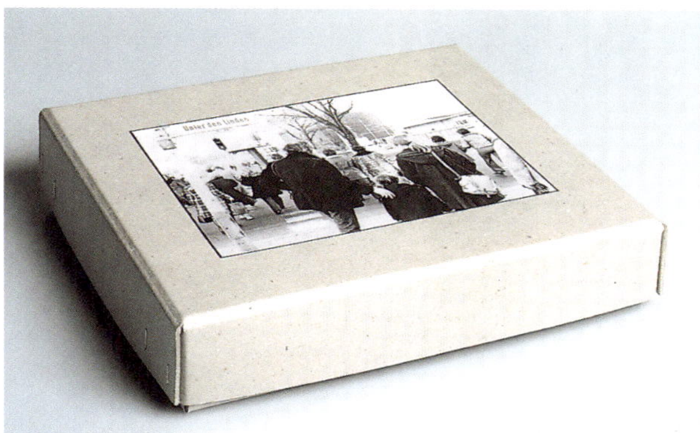

PARKETT 42

LAWRENCE WEINER

UNTER DEN LINDEN – UNDER LIME TREES, 1994

Stamp approx. 7½ x 3¾ x 3½" with red ink pad in silkscreened cardboard box.

Ed. 80, signed and numbered, US$ **680**

UNTER DEN LINDEN – UNDER LIME TREES, 1994

Stempel ca. 19 x 9,5 x 9 cm mit rotem Stempelkissen in Kartonschachtel, Feinrastersiebdruck.

Ed. 80, signiert und numeriert, **sFr. 850.–**

Negative charge. A domestic light switch box, cast inversely in delicate plaster, becomes an impenetrable source of embalmed energy.

Negativladung. Die Negativform eines Lichtschalters in fragilem Gips wird zur unzugänglichen Quelle einbalsamierter Energie.

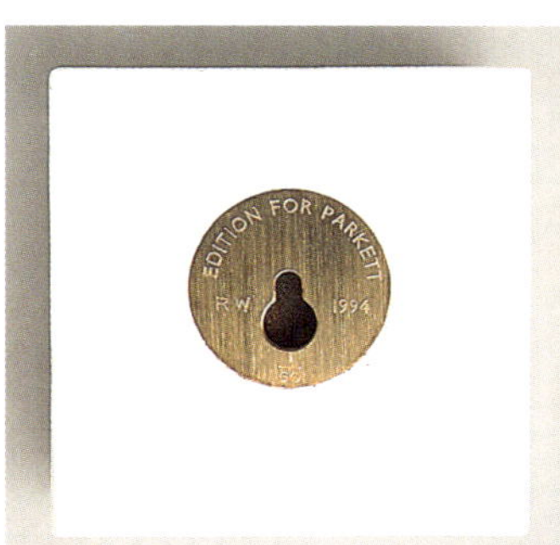

PARKETT 42

RACHEL WHITEREAD

SWITCH, 1994

Object, plaster (prestia-ortho) and brass, 3½ x 3½ x 1⅛"

Ed. 60, signed and numbered, **US$ 750**

SCHALTER, 1994

Objekt, Gips (prestia ortho) und Messing 9 x 9 x 3 cm.

Ed. 60, signiert und numeriert, **sFr. 950.–**

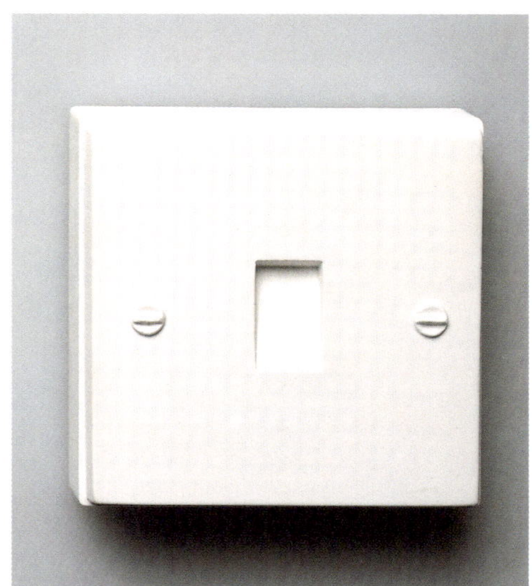

THE PARKETT SERIES WITH CONTEMPORARY ARTISTS
DIE PARKETT-REIHE MIT GEGENWARTSKÜNSTLERN

OUT OF PRINT / VERGRIFFEN: NO. 1 ENZO CUCCHI, NO. 2 SIGMAR POLKE, NO. 3 MARTIN DISLER, NO. 4 MERET OPPENHEIM, NO. 5 ERIC FISCHL, NO. 6 JANNIS KOUNELLIS, NO. 7 BRICE MARDEN, NO. 8 MARKUS RAETZ, NO. 9 FRANCESCO CLEMENTE, NO. 10 BRUCE NAUMAN, NO. 27 LOUISE BOURGEOIS, ROBERT GOBER, NO. 30 SIGMAR POLKE, NO. 31 DAVID HAMMONS, MIKE KELLEY

COLLABORATIONS

GEORG BASELITZ
REMO GUIDIERI, DIETER KOEPPLIN, ERIC DARRAGON, RAINER MICHAEL MASON, FRANZ MEYER, JOHN CALDWELL
INSERT: **BARBARA KRUGER**
GRAY WATSON: **DEREK JARMAN**
CAROL SQUIERS: **PHOTO OPPORTUNITY**
ROSETTA BROOKS: **TROY BRAUNTUCH**

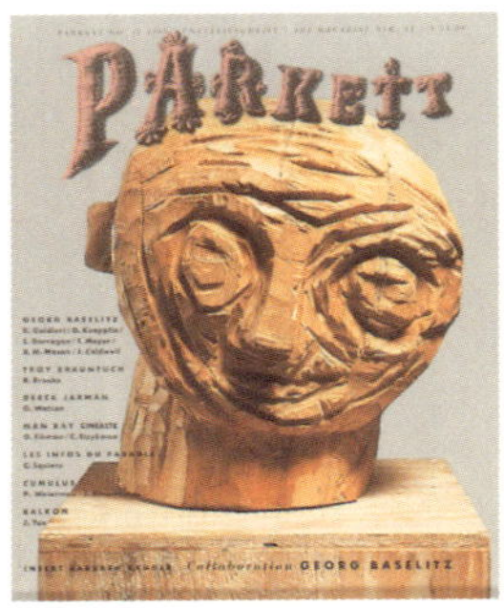

NO. 11

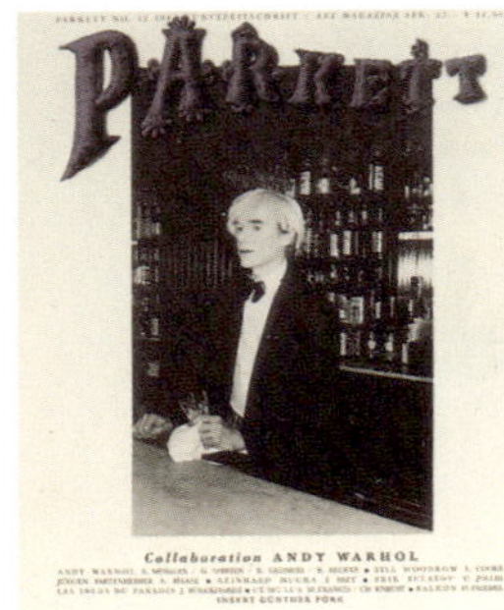

NO. 12

ANDY WARHOL
STUART MORGAN, GLENN O'BRIEN, REMO GUIDIERI, ROBERT BECKER
INSERT: **GÜNTER FÖRG**
LYNNE COOKE: **BILL WOODROW**
AMINE HAASE: **JÜRGEN PARTENHEIMER**
PATRICK FREY: **REINHARD MUCHA**

REBECCA HORN
BICE CURIGER, DEMOSTHENES DAVVETAS, MARTIN MOSEBACH, DANIEL SOUTIF
INSERT: **SIGMAR POLKE**
ALAIN CUEFF: **ALIGHIERO E BOETTI**
JEAN-PIERRE BORDAZ: **JENNY HOLZER**
JUTTA KOETHER: **KATHARINA FRITSCH**

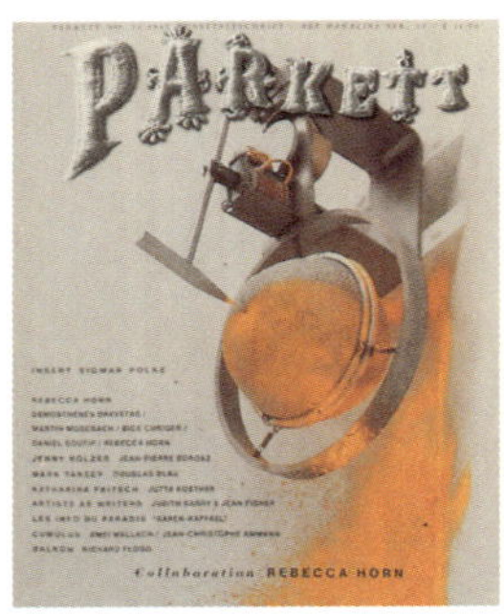

NO. 13

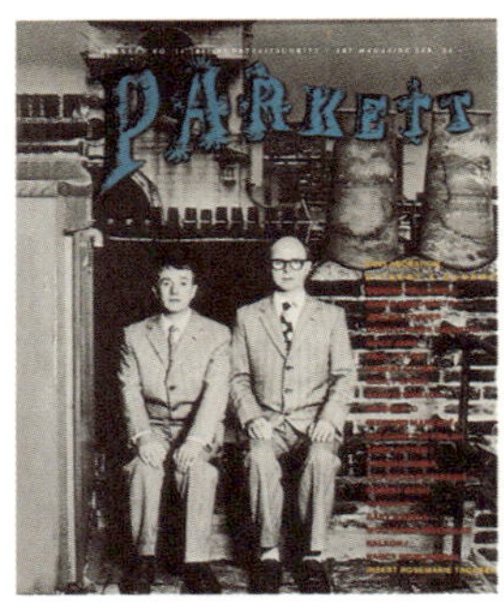

NO. 14

GILBERT & GEORGE
DUNCAN FALLOWELL, MARIO CODOGNATO, JEREMY COOPER, DEMOSTHENES DAVVETAS, WOLF JAHN
INSERT: **ROSEMARIE TROCKEL**
ROBERT STORR: **NANCY SPERO**
HAIM STEINBACH: **MANIFESTO**
JÖRG ZUTTER: **THOMAS HUBER**

MARIO MERZ
MARLIS GRÜTERICH, JEANNE SILVERTHORNE, DEMOSTHENES DAVVETAS, HARALD SZEEMANN, DENYS ZACHAROPOULOS
INSERT: **GENERAL IDEA**
MAX KOZLOFF: **GILLES PERESS**
FRIEDEMANN MALSCH: **GEORG HEROLD**
BRUNELLA ANTOMARINI: **FRANCESCA WOODMAN**

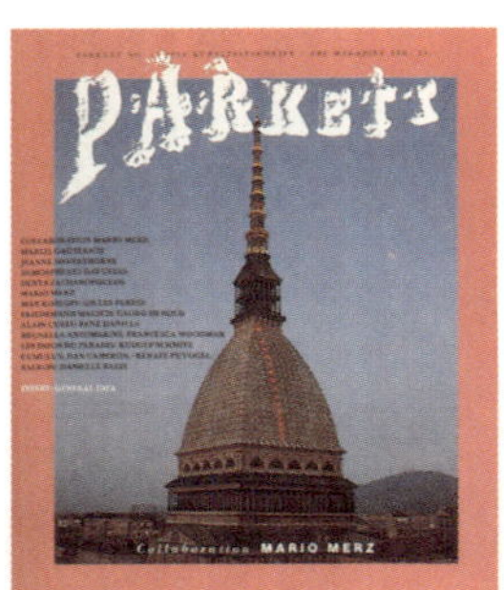

NO. 15

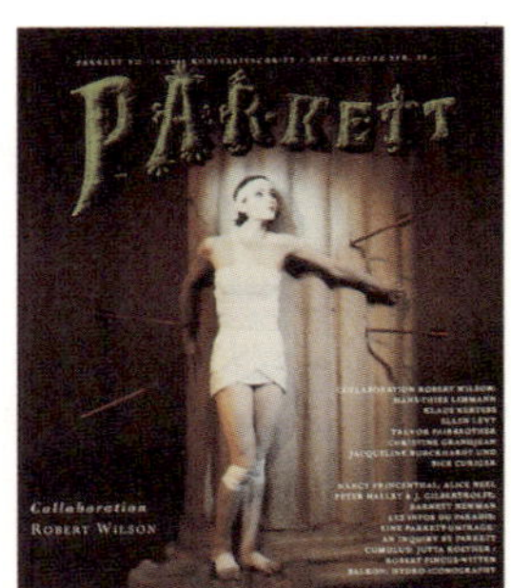

NO. 16

ROBERT WILSON
HANS-THIES LEHMANN, KLAUS KERTESS, ELLEN LEVY, TREVOR FAIRBROTHER, CHRISTINE GRANDJEAN, JACQUELINE BURCKHARDT, BICE CURIGER
INSERT: **SHERRIE LEVINE**
NANCY PRINCENTHAL: **ALICE NEEL**
PETER HALLEY & JEREMY GILBERT ROLFE: **BARNETT NEWMAN**
SYMMETRIEN – EINE UMFRAGE/ SYMMETRIES – AN INQUIRY

SPECIAL EDITIONS FOR PARKETT SUBSCRIBERS

42

The PARKETT-Series is created in collaboration with artists, who contribute an original work especially made for the subscribers in the form of a signed limited SPECIAL EDITION. The work is also reproduced in the regular edition of the magazine.

Each SPECIAL EDITION is available by order from any one of our offices in New York, Zurich or Berlin. Just fill in the details below and send this card to the office nearest you. Once your order has been processed, you will be issued with an invoice and your personal edition number. Upon receipt of payment, you will receive the SPECIAL EDITION. (Please note that supply is subject to availability. Parkett does not assume responsibility for any delays in production of SPECIAL EDITIONS. Postage is not included.)

- As a subscriber to PARKETT, I would like to order the following Special Edition(s), signed and numbered by the artist.

PARKETT No.	ARTIST	NAME:
PARKETT No.	ARTIST	ADDRESS:
PARKETT No.	ARTIST	CITY:
PARKETT No.	ARTIST	STATE/ZIP:
PARKETT No.	ARTIST	COUNTRY:
PARKETT No.	ARTIST	TEL:

- I have indicated my way of payment on the backside of this form.

Send this form to the PARKETT office nearest you:

PARKETT PUBLISHERS 636 BROADWAY NEW YORK, NY 10012 PHONE (212) 673-2660 FAX (212) 673-2887
PARKETT VERLAG QUELLENSTRASSE 27 CH-8005 ZÜRICH TELEFON 01/271 81 40 FAX 01/272 43 01
PARKETT VERLAG ROSSERTSTRASSE 16 D-60323 FRANKFURT A. M. TELEFON (069) 17 27 79 FAX (069) 17 27 70

VORZUGSAUSGABEN FÜR PARKETT-ABONNENTEN

42

Die PARKETT-Buchreihe entsteht in Zusammenarbeit mit Künstlern, die eigens für die Abonnenten einen Originalbeitrag in Form einer limitierten und signierten VORZUGSAUSGABE gestalten. Diese Editionen sind auch in der Zeitschrift abgebildet und können mit dieser Bestellkarte in jedem unserer Büros in Zürich, Berlin oder New York bestellt werden. Sie erhalten dann Ihre persönliche Editionsnummer und eine Rechnung. Sobald wir Ihre Zahlung erhalten haben, schicken wir Ihnen die Vorzugsausgabe. (Lieferung nur solange vorrätig. PARKETT übernimmt keine Verantwortung für allfällige Verzögerungen bei der Herstellung der Vorzugsausgaben. Versandkosten zuzüglich.)

- Ich bin PARKETT-Abonnent(in) und bestelle folgende VORZUGSAUSGABE(N), numeriert und vom Künstler signiert:

PARKETT Nr.	KÜNSTLER/IN	NAME:
PARKETT Nr.	KÜNSTLER/IN	STRASSE:
PARKETT Nr.	KÜNSTLER/IN	PLZ/STADT:
PARKETT Nr.	KÜNSTLER/IN	LAND:
PARKETT Nr.	KÜNSTLER/IN	TEL:

- Meine Zahlungsweise habe ich auf der Rückseite angegeben.

Schicken Sie diese Bestellkarte an das PARKETT-Büro in Ihrer Nähe:

PARKETT VERLAG QUELLENSTRASSE 27 CH-8005 ZÜRICH TELEFON 01/271 81 40 FAX 01/272 43 01
PARKETT VERLAG ROSSERTSTRASSE 16 D-60323 FRANKFURT A. M. TELEFON (069) 17 27 79 FAX (069) 17 27 70
PARKETT PUBLISHERS 636 BROADWAY NEW YORK, NY 10012 PHONE (212) 673-2660 FAX (212) 673-2887

PARKETT

SUBSCRIBE OR SEND A GIFT SUBSCRIPTION TO THE UNIQUE BOOKSERIES ON CONTEMPORARY ARTISTS

42

- I subscribe to the PARKETT series starting with issue No.: ______
  - for 1 year (4 issues) at US$ 75 (USA/Canada), sFr. 115.– (Europe), sFr. 130.– (Rest of the world; by air mail: sFr. 210.–)
  - for 2 years (8 issues) at US$ 135 (USA/Canada), sFr. 205.– (Europe), sFr. 240.– (Rest of the world; air mail: sFr. 395.–)
  - for 1 year (4 issues) at a 20% student discount (US$ 60 for USA/Canada, sFr. 92.– for Europe). A copy of my student ID is enclosed.
- Send a gift subscription in my name starting with issue No.: ______
  - for 1 year (4 issues) at US$ 75 (USA/Canada), sFr. 115.– (Europe), sFr. 130.– (rest of the world; by air mail: sFr. 210.–)
  - for 2 years (8 issues) at US$ 135 (USA/Canada), sFr. 205.– (Europe), sFr. 240.– (Rest of the world; air mail: sFr. 395.–)

  to the following person:
  (I have printed my name and address on the upper right side.
  A gift card in my name will be sent to the recipient.)

Postage included. All prices subject to change.

- I wish to complete my PARKETT collection and order the following issue No.(s) of the PARKETT series: No. ______
  at sFr. 30.– each, postage not included. Within the USA and Canada US$ 22.50 each, postage included. (Sold out: No. 1–10, 27, 30, 31)

NAME: ______

ADDRESS: ______

CITY: ______

STATE/ZIP: ______

COUNTRY: ______

GIFT RECIPIENT: ______

ADDRESS: ______

CITY: ______

STATE/ZIP : ______

COUNTRY: ______

- Charge my Visa Card
- Mastercard
- AMEXCO

Card No. ______ Expiration date ______

- Payment enclosed (US check or money order)
- Bill me

DATE SIGNATURE PRINT NAME

- As a PARKETT subscriber I would like to order the following Special Editions, signed and numbered by each artist. (See reverse side.)

Send this form to the PARKETT office nearest you:

PARKETT PUBLISHERS 636 BROADWAY NEW YORK, NY 10012 PHONE (212) 673-2660 FAX (212) 673-2887

PARKETT VERLAG QUELLENSTRASSE 27 CH-8005 ZÜRICH TELEFON 01/271 81 40 FAX 01/272 43 01

PARKETT VERLAG ROSSERTSTRASSE 16 D-60323 FRANKFURT A. M. TELEFON (069) 17 27 79 FAX (069) 17 27 70

PARKETT

ABONNIEREN ODER VERSCHENKEN SIE DIE UMFASSENDSTE BUCHREIHE MIT GEGENWARTSKÜNSTLERN

42

- Ich abonniere die PARKETT-Künstlerreihe ab Nr.: ______
  - für 1 Jahr (4 Ausgaben) zu: DM 122,– (BRD), sFr. 98. – (Schweiz), sFr. 115.– (übriges Europa).
  - für 2 Jahre (8 Ausgaben) zu: DM 222,– (BRD), sFr. 176.– (Schweiz), sFr. 205.– (übriges Europa).
  - für 1 Jahr (4 Ausgaben) mit 20% Studentenermässigung (BRD: DM 97,–/Schweiz: sFr. 78.–/Europa: sFr. 92.–). Eine Kopie meines Studentenausweises lege ich bei.
- Ich verschenke ein PARKETT-Abonnement ab Nr.: ______
  - für 1 Jahr (4 Ausgaben) zu: DM 122,– (BRD), sFr. 98.– (Schweiz), sFr. 115.– (übriges Europa).
  - für 2 Jahre (8 Ausgaben) zu: DM 222,– (BRD), sFr. 176.– (Schweiz), sFr. 205.– (übriges Europa).

  Meinen Namen habe ich rechts oben notiert. Das Geschenk-Abo geht mit einer Geschenkkarte in meinem Namen an:

Preise einschliesslich Versandkosten. Preisänderungen vorbehalten.

- Ich möchte meine PARKETT-Sammlung vervollständigen und bestelle die folgende(n) noch erhältlichen Ausgaben der Buchreihe zu je sFr. 30.–/DM 35,–, zzgl. Versandkosten:
  Nr. ______ (vergriffen: Nr. 1–10, 27, 30, 31)

NAME: ______

STRASSE: ______

PLZ/STADT: ______

LAND: ______

BESCHENKTE(R): ______

STRASSE: ______

PLZ/STADT: ______

LAND: ______

- Ich zahle mit Visa
- Eurocard/Mastercard
- Amexco

Karten Nr. ______ Gültig bis ______

- Mein Scheck über DM/sFr. ______ liegt bei.
- Bitte schicken Sie mir eine Rechnung.

DATUM UNTERSCHRIFT NAME (in Blockschrift)

- Als PARKETT-Abonnent(in) bestelle ich die folgenden signierten Künstler-Vorzugsausgaben (s. Rückseite dieser Karte).

Schicken Sie diese Bestellkarte an das PARKETT-Büro in Ihrer Nähe:

PARKETT VERLAG QUELLENSTRASSE 27 CH-8005 ZÜRICH TELEFON 01/271 81 40 FAX 01/272 43 01

PARKETT VERLAG ROSSERTSTRASSE 16 D-60323 FRANKFURT A. M. TELEFON (069) 17 27 79 FAX (069) 17 27 70

PARKETT PUBLISHERS 636 BROADWAY NEW YORK, NY 10012 PHONE (212) 673-2660 FAX (212) 673-2887

PETER FISCHLI/ DAVID WEISS
PATRICK FREY, GERMANO CELANT, KAREN MARTA, BERNHARD JOHANNES BLUME, JEANNE SILVERTHORNE, SIDRA STICH
INSERT: **LOUISE BOURGEOIS**
MAX WECHSLER: **IMI KNOEBEL**
PAUL GROOT: **MATT MULLICAN**
KATHY HALBREICH: **WOOSTER GROUP**

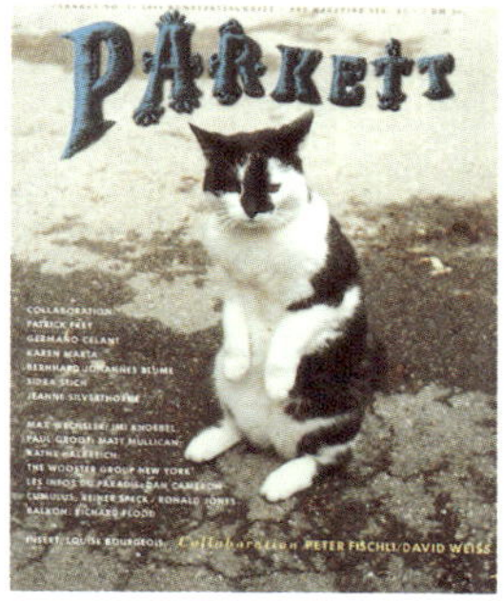

NO. 17

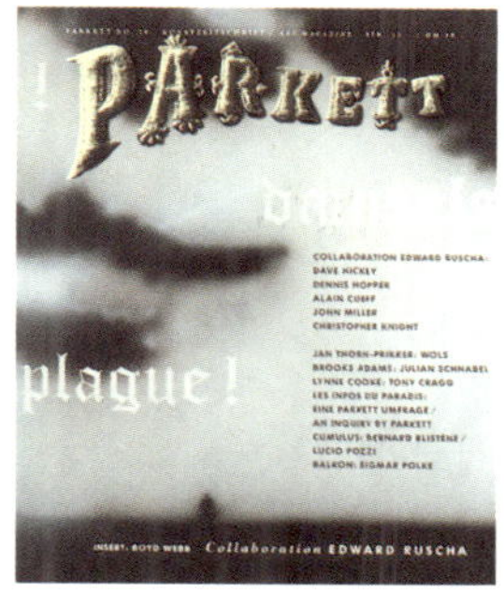

NO. 18

EDWARD RUSCHA
DAVE HICKEY, DENNIS HOPPER
ALAIN CUEFF, JOHN MILLER
CHRISTOPHER KNIGHT
INSERT: **BOYD WEBB**
JAN THORN-PRIKKER: **WOLS**
LYNNE COOKE: **TONY CRAGG**
BROOKE ADAMS: **JULIAN SCHNABEL**
DER KÜNSTLER ALS EXEMPLARISCH LEIDENDER? EINE UMFRAGE / THE ARTIST AS A MODEL SUFFERER? AN INQUIRY

JEFF KOONS MARTIN KIPPENBERGER
KLAUS KERTESS, BURKE & HARE, JEAN-CHRISTOPHE AMMANN, GLENN O'BRIEN, DIEDRICH DIEDERICHSEN, PATRICK FREY, MARTIN PRINZHORN/BICE CURIGER
INSERT: **ANSELM STALDER**
ANNEMARIE HÜRLIMANN: **BARBARA BLOOM,** HANNA HUMELTENBERG: **THOMAS RUFF,** FELIX-PHILIPP INGOLD: **RÉMY ZAUGG,** JAN-THORN PRIKKER: **GERHARD RICHTER**

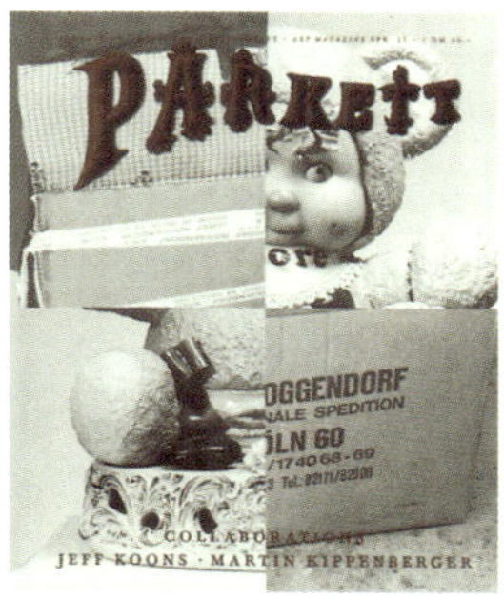

NO. 19

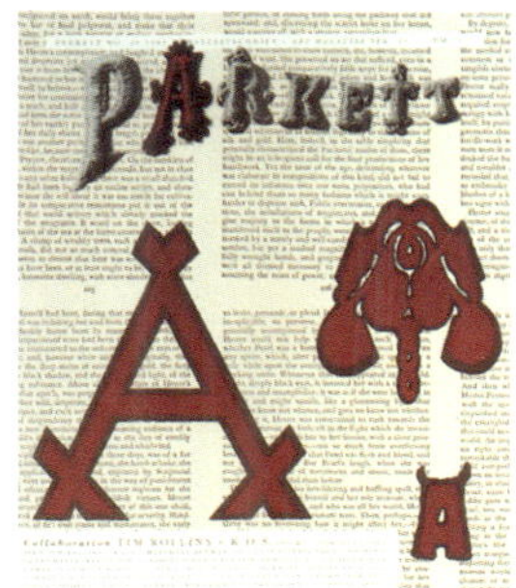

NO. 20

TIM ROLLINS + K.O.S.
MARSHALL BERMAN
TREVOR FAIRBROTHER
STATEMENTS, DIALOGUE 5
INSERT: **ANDREAS GURSKY**
MICHAEL NASH: **BILL VIOLA**
STEPHEN ELLIS: **ROSS BLECKNER**
KLAUS KERTESS: **TRISHA BROWN**

ALEX KATZ
JOHN RUSSELL, BROOKS ADAMS, DAVID RIMANELLI, FRANCESCO CLEMENTE, MICHAEL KRÜGER, RICHARD FLOOD, PATRICK FREY, CARL STIGLIANO, BICE CURIGER, GLENN O'BRIEN
INSERT: **WILLIAM WEGMAN**
LISA LIEBMAN: **ROBERT GOBER**
JACQUELINE BURCKHARDT: **GIULIO ROMANO**

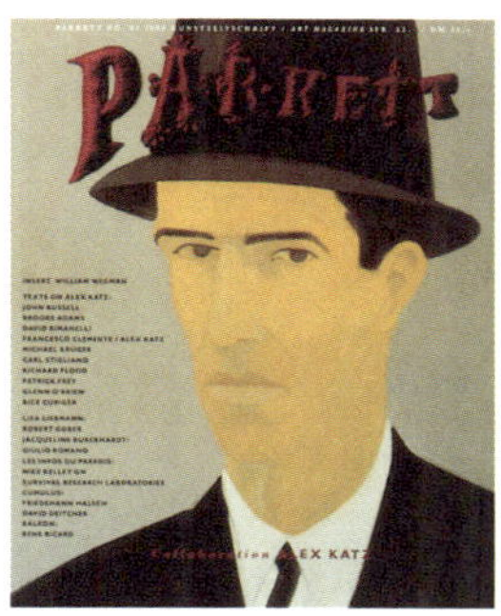

NO. 21

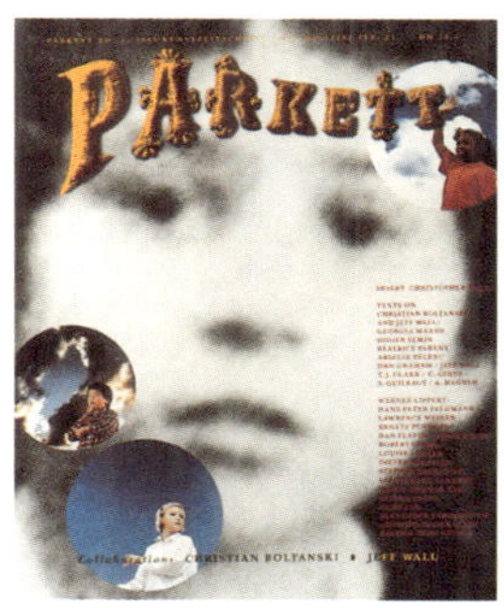

NO. 22

CHRISTIAN BOLTANSKI JEFF WALL
DIDIER SEMIN, GEORGIA MARSH
BÉATRICE PARENT, DAN GRAHAM
JEFF WALL, ARIELLE PÉLENC
INSERT: **CHRISTOPHER WOOL**
DIETER KOEPPLIN: **STEPHAN BALKENHOL**
RENATE PUVOGEL: **DAN FLAVIN, DONALD JUDD**
WERNER LIPPERT: **VARIOUS SMALL FIRES IN THE GUTENBERG GALAXY**

RICHARD ARTSCHWAGER
ARTHUR C. DANTO, GEORG KOHLER, MARIO A. ORLANDO, JOYCE CAROL OATES, WERNER OECHSLIN, ALAN LIGHTMAN, PATRICK McGRATH, DANIEL SOUTIF, LASZLO F. FÖLDENYI, JEAN STROUSE
INSERT: **DAVID BYRNE**
RENATE PUVOGEL: **ANDRÉ THOMKINS**
ULRICH LOOCK: **THOMAS STRUTH**
NANCY SPECTOR: **MEREDITH MONK**

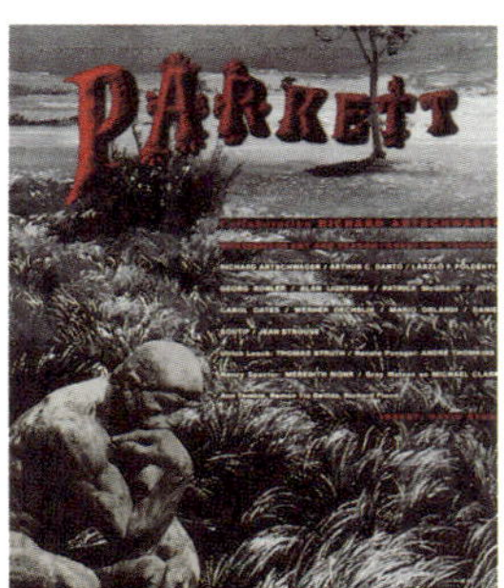

NO. 23

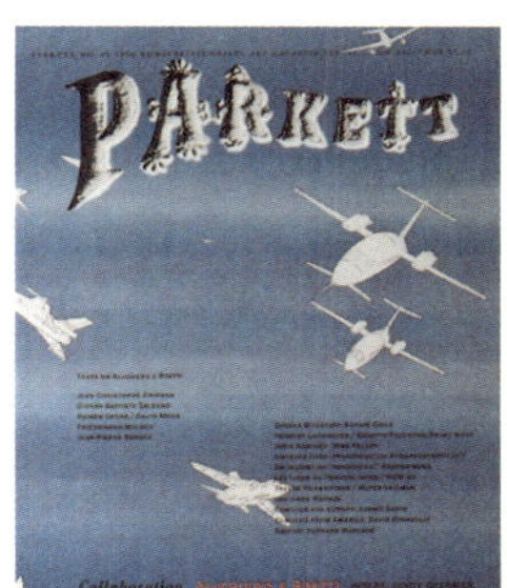

NO. 24

ALIGHIERO E BOETTI
JEAN-CHRISTOPHE AMMANN
GIOVAN BATTISTA SALERNO
RAINER CRONE & DAVID MOOS
FRIEDEMANN MALSCH
JEAN-PIERRE BORDAZ
ALAIN CUEFF
INSERT: **CINDY SHERMAN**
SHEENA WAGSTAFF: **SOPHIE CALLE**
HERBERT LACHMEYER/ BRIGITTE FELDERER: **FRANZ WEST**
JUTTA KOETHER: **MIKE KELLEY**

KATHARINA FRITSCH
JAMES TURRELL
GARY GARRELS
JULIAN HEYNEN, DAN CAMERON,
JEAN-CHRISTOPHE AMMANN,
DAVE HICKEY, RICHARD FLOOD &
CARL STIGLIANO, TED CASTLE
INSERT: **BEAT STREULI**
PATRICK FREY:
JEAN-FRÉDÉRIC SCHNYDER
DIETER SCHWARZ: **JAMES COLEMAN**
LYNNE COOKE:
RICHARD HAMILTON

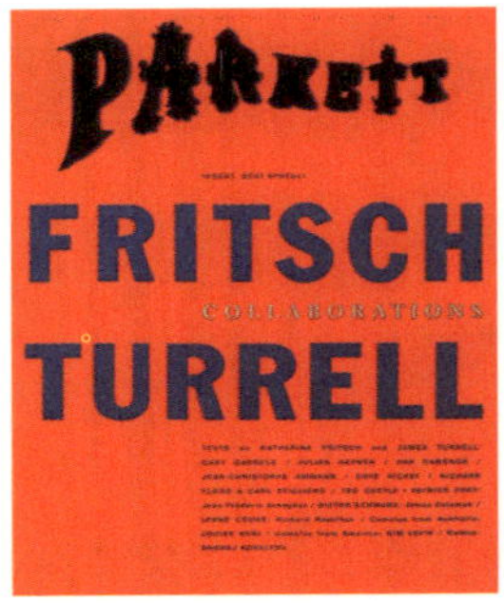

NO. 25

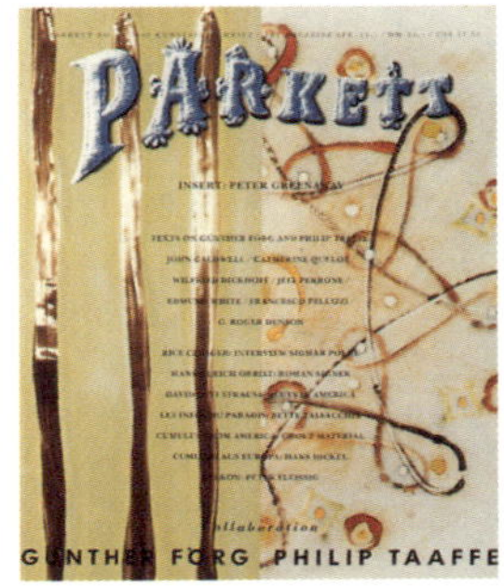

NO. 26

GÜNTHER FÖRG
PHILIP TAAFFE
JOHN CALDWELL, CATHERINE QUELOZ
WILFRIED DICKHOFF
JEFF PERRONE, EDMUND WHITE
FRANCESCO PELLIZZI
G. ROGER DENSON
INSERT: **PETER GREENAWAY**
BICE CURIGER: **SIGMAR POLKE**
HANS-ULRICH OBRIST:
ROMAN SIGNER
DAVID LEVI STRAUSS:
JOSEPH BEUYS

LOUISE BOURGEOIS
ROBERT GOBER
JOSEF HELFENSTEIN, CHRISTIANE
MEYER-THOSS, MIGNON NIXON,
MANUEL J. BORJA-VILLEL, HARALD
SZEEMANN, NANCY SPECTOR,
NED RIFKIN/THERESIA BUSH/
ROBERT GOBER, GREGG BORDOWITZ
INSERT: **ERNST CARAMELLE**
MARINA WARNER: **BUSH NATURAL**
CLAUDE RITSCHARD:
JOHN M ARMLEDER
HANS-ULRICH OBRIST:
DAVID RABINOWITCH

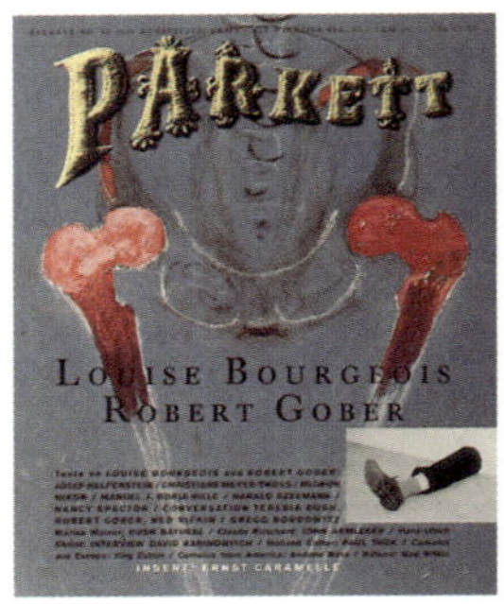

NO. 27

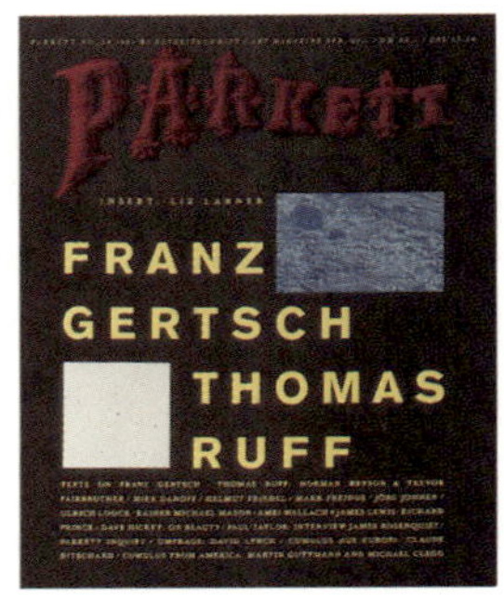

NO. 28

FRANZ GERTSCH
THOMAS RUFF
HELMUT FRIEDEL, ULRICH LOOCK
I. MICHAEL DANOFF, AMEI WALLACH
RAINER MICHAEL MASON
MARC FREIDUS, JÖRG JOHNEN
TREVOR FAIRBROTHER/NORMAN BRYSON
INSERT: **LIZ LARNER**
JAMES LEWIS: **RICHARD PRINCE**
DAVID HICKEY:
THE INVISIBLE DRAGON/
DER UNSICHTBARE DRACHEN
PAUL TAYLOR: **JAMES ROSENQUIST**

JOHN BALDESSARI
CINDY SHERMAN
HOWARD SINGERMAN, DAVE HICKEY;
THOMAS LAWSON, PATRICK FREY,
JAMES LEWIS, SUSAN DAVIS,
URSULA PIA JAUCH, NORMAN
BRYSON, ELFRIEDE JELINEK,
WILFRIED DICKHOFF, ABIGAIL
SOLOMON-GODEAU, RUDOLF
SCHMITZ, THEODORA VISCHER/
MARIA NORDMAN, CLAUDE
RITSCHARD, INSERT: **NIELE TORONI**

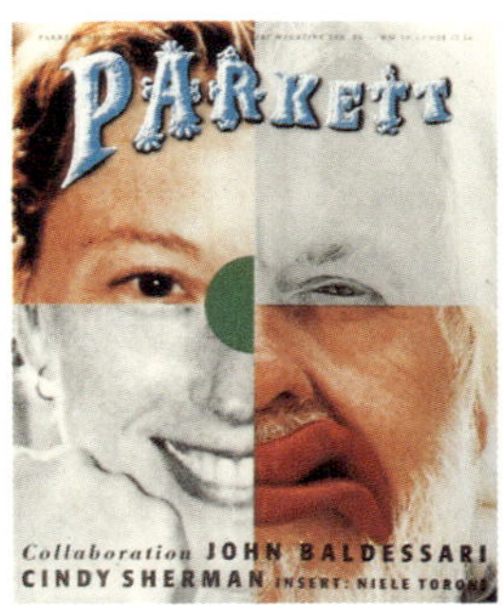

NO. 29

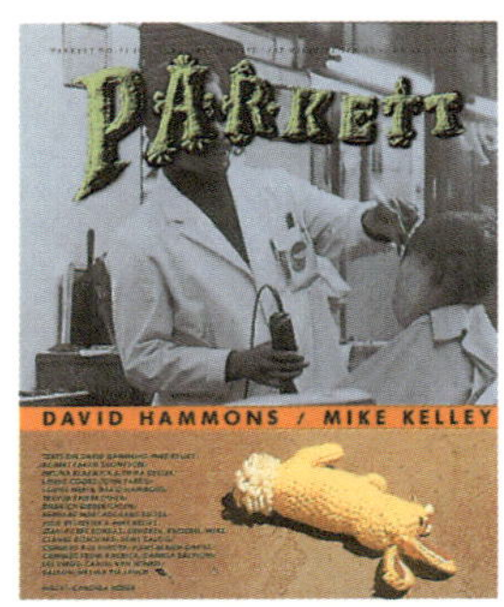

NO. 31

DAVID HAMMONS
MIKE KELLEY
ROBERT FARRIS THOMPSON
IWONA BLAZWICK & EMMA DEXTER
JOHN FARRIS, LYNNE COOKE, LOUISE
NERI, TREVOR FAIRBROTHER,
DIEDRICH DIEDRICHSEN, LANE RELYEA,
BERNARD MARCADÉ, JULIE SYLVESTER
INSERT: **CANDIDA HÖFER**
CLAUDE RITSCHARD: **RÉMY ZAUGG**
JEAN-PIERRE BORDAZ: **IMI KNOEBEL,**
ISA GENZKEN, GERHARD MERZ

IMI KNOEBEL
SHERRIE LEVINE
RUDOLF BUMILLER
RAINER CRONE/DAVID MOOS
LISA LIEBMANN, DANIELA SALVIONI
ERICH FRANZ, HOWARD SINGERMANN
INSERT: **DAMIEN HIRST**
SHEENA WAGSTAFF: **VIJA CELMINS**
JIM LEWIS: **LARRY CLARK**
LIAM GILLICK: **BETHAN HUWS**
THOMAS KELLEIN: **WALTER DE MARIA**

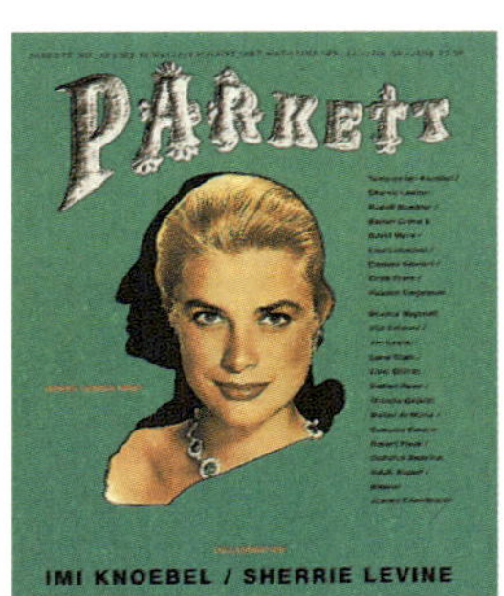

NO. 32

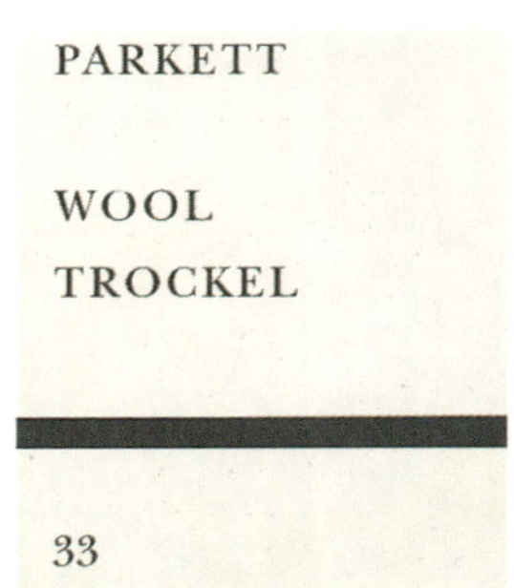

NO. 33

ROSEMARIE TROCKEL
CHRISTOPHER WOOL
VERONIQUE BACCHETTA,
BARRETT WATTEN,
ANNE WAGNER, JIM LEWIS,
GREIL MARCUS, JEFF PERRONE,
DIEDRICH DIEDERICHSEN
INSERT: **ADRIAN SCHIESS**
MARINA WARNER: **PENIS PLENTY**
G. ROGER DENSON:
DENNIS OPPENHEIM
CAMIEL VAN WINKEL

ILYA KABAKOV
RICHARD PRINCE
BORIS GROYS, ROBERT STORR
JAN THORN-PRIKKER
CLAUDIA JOLLES, EDMUND WHITE
SUSAN TALLMAN, DANIELA SALVIONI, KATHY ACKER
INSERT: **TATSUO MIYAJIMA**
GUDRUN INBODEN: **ASTA GRÖTING**
LYNNE COOKE: **GARY HILL**
PATRICK McGRATH: **STEPHEN ELLIS**

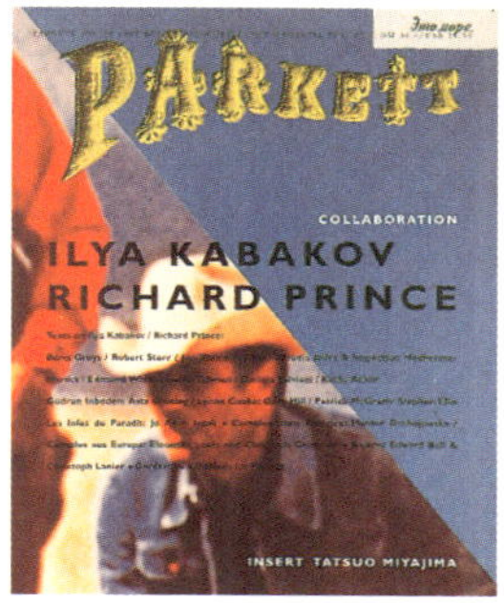

NO. 34

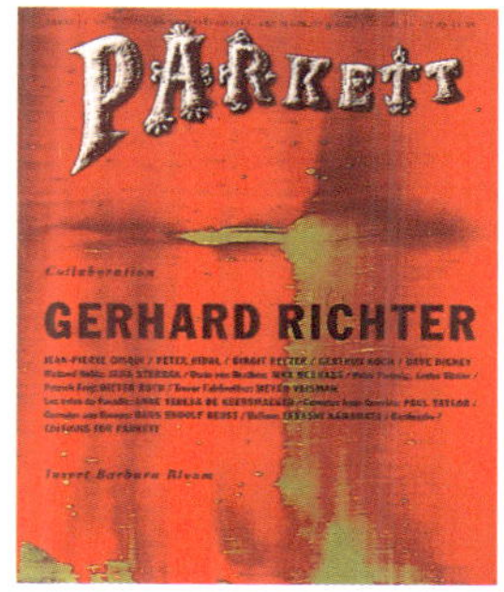

NO. 35

GERHARD RICHTER
JEAN-PIERRE CRIQUI
PETER GIDAL, BRIGIT PELZER
GERTRUD KOCH, DAVE HICKEY
INSERT: **BARBARA BLOOM**
RICHARD NOBLE: **JANA STERBAK**
DORIS VON DRATHEN: **MAX NEUHAUS**
TREVOR FAIRBROTHER: **MEYER VAISMAN**
PETER FLEISSIG: **LÈCHE VITRINE**
PATRICK FREY: **DIETER ROTH**

STEPHAN BALKENHOL
SOPHIE CALLE
NEAL BENEZRA, VIK MUNIZ, MAX KATZ
JEAN-CHRISTOPHE AMMANN
LUC SANTE, JOSEPH GRIGELY
PATRICK FREY, ROBERT BECK
INSERT: **RICHMOND BURTON**
URSULA PANHANS-BÜHLER: **EVA HESSE**
DOUGLAS BLAU: **JON KESSLER**
KIRBY GOOKIN: **LIZ LARNER**
LÁSZLÓ FÖLDÉNYI: **RUDOLF SCHWARZKOGLER**

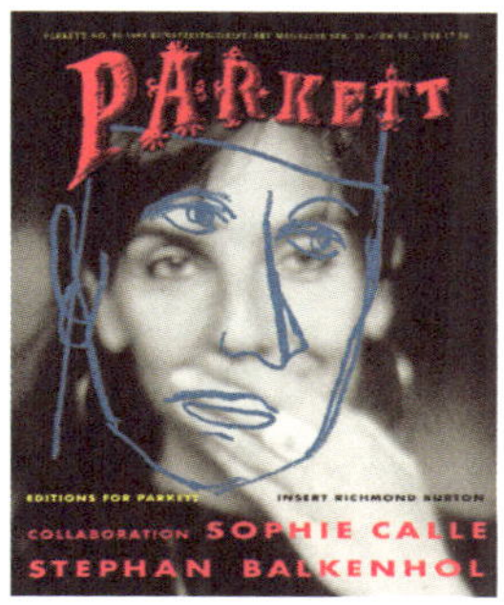

NO. 36

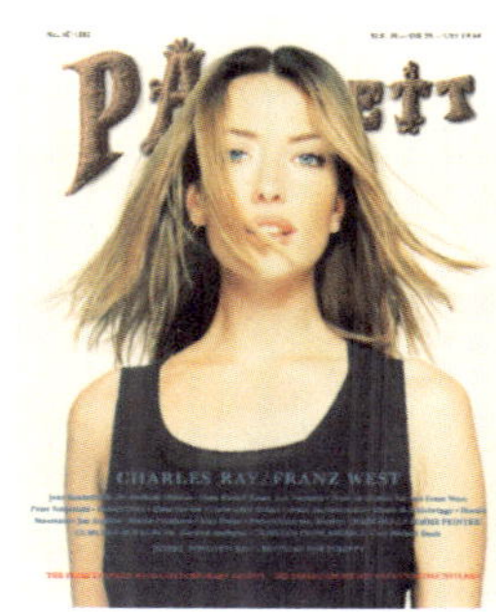

NO. 37

CHARLES RAY
FRANZ WEST
KLAUS KERTESS, CHRISTOPHER KNIGHT
PETER SCHJELDAHL, ROBERT STORR
JAN AVGIKOS, AXEL HUBER
MARTIN PRINZHORN, ELISABETH SCHLEBRÜGGE, HARALD SZEEMANN,
DENYS ZACHAROPOULOS
INSERT: **PIPILOTTI RIST**
JEAN BAUDRILLARD
HANS RUDOLF REUST: **LUC TUYMANS**
PARKETT INQUIRY:
CHERCHEZ LA FEMME PEINTRE!

ROSS BLECKNER
MARLENE DUMAS
EDMUND WHITE, SIMON WATNEY
JOSE LUIS BREA, MARINA WARNER
ANNA TILROE, INGRID SCHAFFNER
ULRICH LOOCK
INSERT: **RUDI MOLACEK**
HARTMUT BÖHME
MAX WECHSLER: **ADRIAN SCHIESS**
DORIS VON DRATHEN: **RACHEL WHITEREAD**

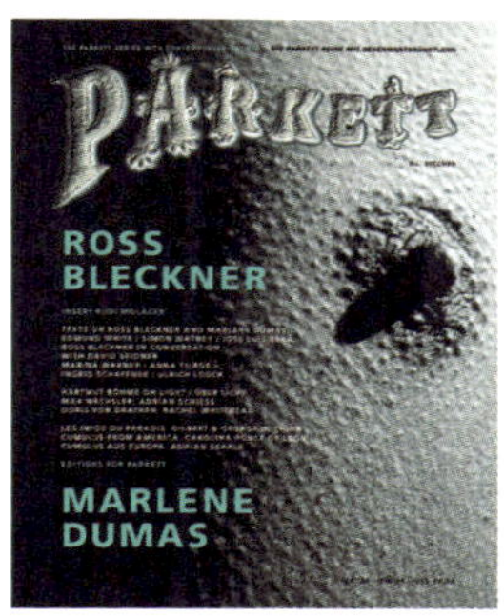

NO. 38

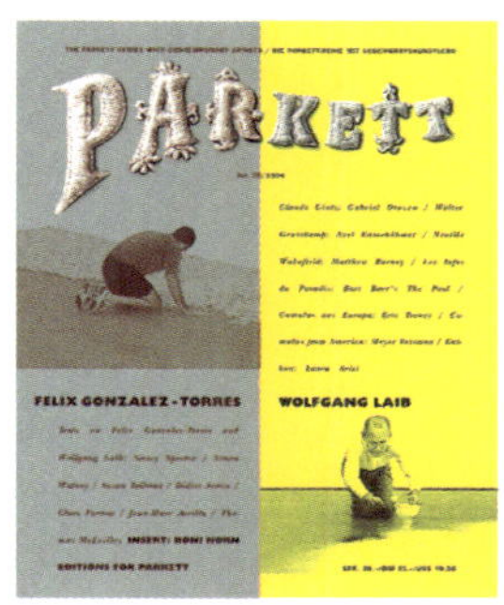

NO. 39

FELIX GONZALEZ-TORRES
WOLFGANG LAIB
NANCY SPECTOR, SIMON WATNEY,
SUSAN TALLMAN, DIDIER SEMIN,
CLARE FARROW, JEAN-MARC AVRILLA,
THOMAS McEVILLEY
CLAUDE GINTZ: **GABRIEL OROZCO**
WALTER GRASSKAMP: **AXEL KASSEBÖHMER**
NEVILLE WAKEFIELD: **MATTHEW BARNEY**
INSERT: **RONI HORN**
LES INFOS DU PARADIS: **BURT BARR**
CUMULUS: **MEYER VAISMAN**

FRANCESCO CLEMENTE
GÜNTHER FÖRG
PETER FISCHLI / DAVID WEISS
DAMIEN HIRST
JENNY HOLZER
REBECCA HORN
SIGMAR POLKE
HOLLAND COTTER, BORIS GROYS
MAX WECHSLER, DAVID RIMANELLI
JOAN SIMON, GORDON BURN
GILBERT LASCAULT, WERNER SPIES
BICE CURIGER, JEFF PERRONE
G. ROGER DENSON, VIK MUNIZ
DAVE HICKEY

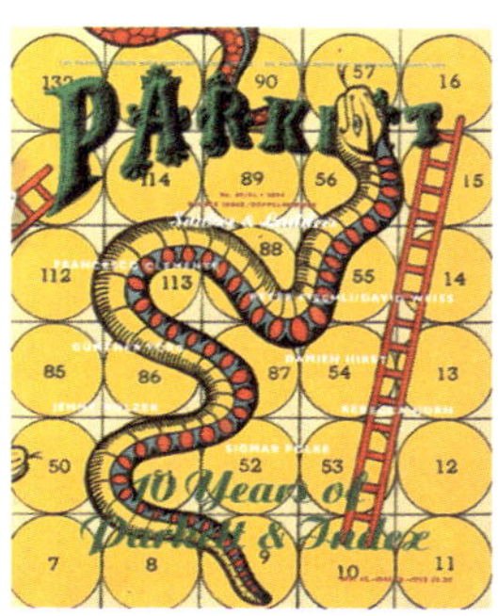

NO. 40/41

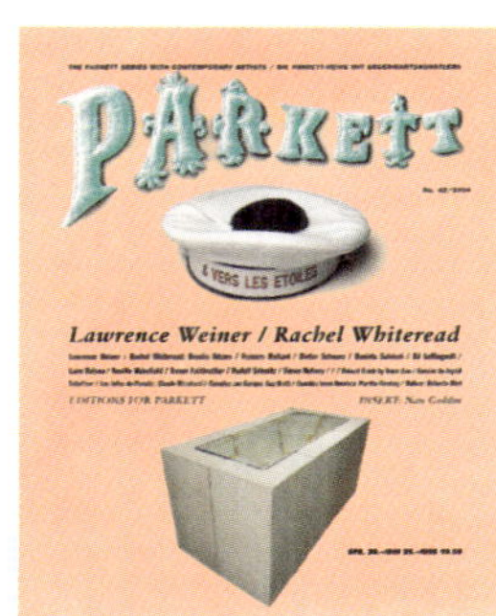

NO. 42

LAWRENCE WEINER
RACHEL WHITEREAD
BROOKS ADAMS, FRANCES RICHARD
DIETER SCHWARZ, DANIELA SALVIONI
ED LEFFINGWELL, LANE RELYEA
NEVILLE WAKEFIELD, RUDOLF SCHMITZ
TREVOR FAIRBROTHER, SIMON WATNEY
INSERT: **NAN GOLDIN**
VINCE LEO: **ROBERT FRANK**
CLAUDE RITSCHARD: **MARKUS RAETZ**

PARKETT IN BUCHHANDLUNGEN / *BOOKSHOPS*

AUSKUNFT UND ABONNEMENTS / *INFORMATION AND SUBSCRIPTIONS:*

«PARKETT»-VERLAG AG, QUELLENSTRASSE 27, CH-8005 ZÜRICH, TEL. 01/271 81 40, FAX 272 43 01; ROSSERTSTR. 16, D-60323 FRANKFURT A. M., TEL. 069/17 27 79, FAX 069/17 27 70

PARKETT, *636 BROADWAY, NEW YORK, N.Y. 10012, PHONE (212) 673-2660, FAX 673-2887*

SCHWEIZ

VERTRIEB
B + I BUCH UND INFORMATION AG
OBFELDERSTR. 35
8910 AFFOLTERN A. A.

BASEL
BUCHHANDLUNG STAMPA, SPALENBERG 2
BÜCHERSTAND STAMPA, KUNSTHALLE BASEL
W. JAEGGI AG, FREIESTR. 32

BERN
HANS HUBER AG, MARKTGASSE 59
BUCHHANDLUNG SCHERZ, MARKTGASSE 25
BUCHHANDLUNG STAUFFACHER, NEUENGASSE 25
BUCHHANDLUNG STAUFFACHER
IM KUNSTMUSEUM BERN, HODLERSTR.12

GENÈVE
LIBRAIRIE DESCOMBES, 6, RUE DU VIEUX-COLLÈGE
LIBRAIRIE PAYOT, 5, RUE DE CHANTEPOULET
LIBRAIRIE WEBER, 13, RUE DE MONTHOUX

LAUSANNE
LIBRAIRE BERNARD LETU,
MUSÉE D'ART CONTEMPORAIN
LIBRAIRIE PAYOT, 1, RUE DE BOURG

SCHAFFHAUSEN
BÜCHER-FASS, WEBERGASSE 13

ST. GALLEN
BUCHHANDLUNG COMEDIA, KATHARINENGASSE 20

ZÜRICH
BUCHHANDLUNG ZUM ELSÄSSER, LIMMATQUAI 18
BUCHHANDLUNG CALLIGRAMME, HÄRINGSTR. 4
SCALO BOOKS & LOOKS, WEINBERGSTRASSE 22 A
HEINIMANN & CO, KIRCHGASSE 17
BUCHHANDLUNG HOWEG, WAFFENPLATZSTR. 1
BUCHHANDLUNG AM KUNSTHAUS AG, RÄMISTR. 45
BUCHHANDLUNG KRAUTHAMMER, OBERE ZÄUNE 24
KUNSTKIOSK, LIMMATQUAI 31/HELMHAUS
ORELL FÜSSLI, FÜSSLISTR. 4
SEC 52, JOSEFSTR. 52

DEUTSCHLAND

VERTRIEB
GWP VERLAGSAUSLIEFERUNG
BEIENRODER HAUPTSTR. 3
38154 KÖNIGSLUTTER

BERLIN
BÜCHERBOGEN, AM SAVIGNYPLATZ
GALERIE 2000, KNESEBECKSTR. 56–58
WASMUTH GmbH & CO., HORDENBERGSTR. 9A
WERNER GmbH, EHRENBERGSTR. 29

BONN
CARL KAYSER, POSTSTR. 16
GALERIE PUDELKO, HEINRICH-VON-KLEIST-STR.

BREMEN
ANTIQUARIAT, BEIM STEINERNEN KREUZ 1
JOHS. STORM, LANGENSTR. 10
KUNSTBUCH, SPITZENKIEL 16/17
B. SIEBRECHT, PANORAMA, VOR DEM STEINTOR 136
KUNST UND BUCH,
AM NEUEN MUSEUM, WESERBURG, TEERHOF 20

BREMERHAVEN
KABINETT FÜR AKTUELLE KUNST, KARLSBURG 4

DÜSSELDORF
M. + R. FRICKE, POSTSTR. 3
WALTHER KÖNIG, HEINRICH-HEINE-ALLEE 15
MÜLLER & TILLMANNS, NEUSTR. 38

FRANKFURT
HUGENDUBEL, STEINWEG 12
KARL MARX BUCHHANDLUNG, JORDANSTR. 11
PETER NAACHER, SCHWEIZERSTR. 57
SCHUMANN & COBET, BÖRSENSTR. 2–4
WALTHER KÖNIG, DOMSTR. 6

HAMBURG
H. VON DER HÖH, GROSSE BLEICHEN 21
SAUTTER UND LACKMANN
ADMIRALITÄTSSTRASSE 71/72
PPS, FELDSTR./ HOCHHAUS

HANNOVER
BUCHHANDLUNG IM SPRENGELMUSEUM
KURT-SCHWITTERS-PLATZ

HEIDELBERG
KUNSTHANDLUNG W. WELKER, HAUPTSTR. 106

KARLSRUHE
KUNSTBUCHHANDLUNG JUST, WALDSTR. 85

KIEL
GALERIE + EDITION KOCH, HOLSTENTÖRNPASSAGE

KÖLN
WALTHER KÖNIG, EHRENSTR. 4

MÜNCHEN
ILKA KÖNIG, AM KOSTTOR 1
H. GOLZ, TÜRKENSTR. 54
L. WERNER, RESIDENZSTR. 18
INT. BAHNHOFSBUCHHANDLUNG, BAHNHOFSPLATZ 2
MAX SUSSMANN GmbH, ARNULFSTR. 1/II
BASIS ANTIQUARIAT, ADALBERTSTR. 43

MÜNSTER
HEINRICH POERTGEN
HERDERSCHE BUCHHANDLUNG, HÖLTENWEG 51

NÜRNBERG
HEINRICH HUGENDUBEL, LUDWIGSPLATZ 1

OSNABRÜCK
H. TH. WENNER GmbH, GROSSE-STR. 69

SAARBRÜCKEN
BOCK & SEIP, FUTTERSTR. 2

STUTTGART
WENDELIN NIEDLICH, SCHMALESTR. 9
GALERIE VALENTIEN, KÖNIGSBAU

TÜBINGEN
HUGO FRICK, NAUKLERSTR. 7

ULM
BUCHHANDLUNG UND GALERIE HOLM
HAFENBAD 11

WUPPERTAL
GRAEFF & HEINRICH, OBERGRÜNEWALDER STR. 13

ÖSTERREICH

VERTRIEB
LECHNER + SOHN, HEIZWERKSTRASSE 10, 1232 WIEN

GRAZ
BUCHHANDLUNG GALERIE
VERLAG DROSCHL, BISCHOFPLATZ 1

INNSBRUCK
PARNASS, SPECKBACHERSTR. 21
WAGNERSCHE UNIVERSITÄTSBUCHHANDLUNG
MUSEUMSTR. 4

LINZ
ALEX STELZER, HAUPTPLATZ 17

WIEN
JUDITH ORTNER, SONNENFELSGASSE 8
SHAKESPEARE & COMPANY
BOOKSELLERS, STEINGASSE 2

HOLLAND

DISTRIBUTION
IDEA BOOKS
NIEUWE HERENGRACHT 11
1011 RK AMSTERDAM

AMSTERDAM
ART BOOK, PRINSENGRACHT 645
ATHENAEUM NIEUWSCENTRUM, SPUI 14–16
MENEER KEES, PC HOOFSTRAAT 64-66
NIJHOF & LEE, STAALSTRAAT 13 A
PREMSELA, VAN BAERLESTRAAT 78
VERBEELDING, UTRECHTSESTRAAT 40

ARNHEM
HIJMAN, GROTE OORD 15
ARNHEMS GEMEENTEMUSEUM, UTRECHTSEWEG 87

BREDA
VAN KEMENADE & HOLLAERS, GINNEKENWEG 330

DORDRECHT
BENGEL, VOORSTRAAT 283

EINDHOVEN
MOTTA BERGSTRAAT 35
VAN ABBEMUSEUM, BILDERDIJKLAAN 10

ENSCHEDE
BROEKHUIS, MARKTSTRAAT 12

GRONINGEN
SCHOLTENS/WRISTERS, GULDENSTRAAT 20

HENGELO
BROEKHUIS, ENSCHEDESTRAAT 19

LEIDEN
GINSBERG, BREESTRAAT 127

MAASTRICHT
TRIBUNE, KAPOENSTRAAT 8
VELDEKE, KLEINE STAAT 14

ROTTERDAM
DONNER, LIJNBAAN 150
VAN GENNEP, OUDE BINNENWEG 131B

THE HAGUE
ULYSSES, DENNEWEG 108

TILBURG
DE PONT STICHTING, WILHELMINAPARK 1

UTRECHT
CENTRAAL MUSEUM, AGNIETENSTRAAT 1

BELGIQUE

ANTWERPEN
BRAMANTE, KOEPORTBRUG 4
F.N.A.C. GROENPLAATS
LANDSCHAP, WIJNGAARDSTRAAT 12
STANDAARD, HUIDEVETTERSTRAAT 57

BRUXELLES
PEINTURE FRAÎCHE, 10 RUE DU TABELLION
POST-SCRIPTUM, 37 RUE DES ÉPERONNIERS
TROPISMES, GALERIE DES PRINCES 11
GENT
COPYRIGHT JAKOBIJNENSTRAAT 8
INTELLECT, KALANDESTRAAT 1
KORTRIJK
THEORIA, ONZE LIEVE VROUWESTRAAT 22

ESPAÑA
BARCELONA
NOA NOA, CENTRE CULTURAL DE LA FUNDACIÒ
CAIXA, PASSEIG DE SANT JOAN, 108
NOA NOA LIBRES D'ART
CENTRE D'ART STA. MONICA
RAMBLA STA. MONICA 7
MADRID
LIBROS ARGENSOLA, DOCTOR MATA, 1
CENTRO REINA SOFIA, STA. ISABEL 52

FRANCE
AIX-EN-PROVENCE
LIBRAIRIE VENTS DU SUD, 7, RUE MARÉCHAL FOCH
BORDEAUX
LIBRAIRIE DU MUSÉE CAPC, ENTREPÔT LAINÉ
LIBRAIRIE MOLLAT, 9–15, VITAL CARLES
LYON
LIBRAIRIE LE RÉVERBÈRE, 4, RUE NEUVE
PARIS
LA HUNE, 170 BLVD ST-GERMAIN
«FLAMMARION 4», CENTRE GEORGES POMPIDOU
PLATEAU BEAUBOURG
LIBRAIRIE DU MUSEE D'ART MODERNE
9, RUE FERRIÈRE
GALERIE NATIONALE DU JEU DE PAUME
PLACE DE LA CONCORDE
TOULOUSE
LIBRAIRIE OMBRES BLANCHES, 50, RUE GAMBETTA

ISRAEL
TEL AVIV
BOOKWORM, 30 BASEL ST.

ITALIA
MILANO
A&M BOOKSTORE, VIA PLINIO 15
MILANO LIBRI, VIA G. VERDI 2
MODENA
LOGOS IMPEX
VIA CURTATONA, 5/F, 41010 SAN DAMASO/MODENA
ROMA
CENTRO DI GALLERIA NAZIONALE
D'ARTE MODERNA, VIA DELLE BELLE ARTI 131
FELTRINELLI, VIA DEL BABUINO 41
GALLERIA PRIMO PIANO, VIA PANISPERNA 203

PORTUGAL
LISBOA
COMICOS ESPAÇO INTER-MEDIA
RUA TENENTE RAUL CASCAIS 1B

SVERIGE
STOCKHOLM
BOK & BILD, KULTURHUSET, SERGELSTORG 3
NORDENFLYCHTSVÄGEN 70

GREAT BRITAIN
DISTRIBUTOR
CENTRAL BOOKS, 99, WALLIS RD. LONDON E9 5LN
LONDON
HAYWARD GALLERY BOOKSHOP, SOUTH BANK
ICA BOOKSHOP, NASH HOUSE
12, CARLTON HOUSE TERRACE
LIBERTY, BOOK DEPT., 210 REGENT STREET

USA
DISTRIBUTOR
D. A. P. (DISTRIBUTED ART PUBLISHERS)
636 BROADWAY, RM 1208 NEW YORK, NY 10012
BOSTON, MA
RIZZOLI INTERNATIONAL BOOKSTORES
100 HUNTINGTON AVE.
TRIDENT BOOKSELLERS & CAFE, 338 NEWBURY ST.
BERKELEY, CA
MOE'S BOOKS, 2476 TELEGRAPH
UNIVERSITY ART MUSEUM
2625 DURANT AVE.
BLOOMINGTON, IN
MORGENSTERN BOOKSELLERS, 2650 E. 3RD. ST.
CHICAGO, IL
MUSEUM OF CONTEMPORARY ART
237 EAST ONTARIO ST.
RIZZOLI INTERNATIONAL BOOKSTORES
835N. MICHIGAN AVE.
COLUMBUS, OH
WEXNER CENTER FOR THE ARTS
UNIVERSITY OF OHIO, 30 W. 15TH ST.
LOS ANGELES, CA
ART CATALOGUES, 625 N. ALMONT DR.
MUSEUM OF CONTEMPORARY ART
152 N. CENTRAL AND 250 S. GRAND
BOOK SOUP, 8818 SUNSET BLVD.
RIZZOLI INTERNATIONAL BOOKSTORES
3333 BRITSOL AVE., COSTA MESA
HOUSTON, TX
BRAZOS, 2421 BISSONNET ST.
MUSEUM OF FINE ARTS, 1001 BISSONET
KANSAS CITY, MO
WHISTLER'S BOOKS, WESTPORT SQUARE
427 WESTPORT ROAD
MINNEAPOLIS, MN
WALKER ART CENTER, VINELAND PLACE
NEW YORK, NY
149 PARKETT BOOKS, 149 WOOSTER STREET
BOOKS AND COMPANY, 939 MADISON AVE.
JAAP RIETMANN, 134 SPRING STREET
MUSEUM OF MODERN ART, 11 W. 53RD ST.
PRINTED MATTER BOOKSTORE AT DIA,
77 WOOSTER ST.
RIZZOLI INTERNATIONAL BOOKSTORES
31 W. 57TH AND 454 WEST BROADWAY
ST. MARK'S BOOKSHOP, 12 ST. MARK'S PLACE
WHITNEY MUSEUM OF AMERICAN ART
945 MADSION AVE.
OAK PARK, MI
BOOK BEAT, LTD., 26020 GREENFIELD
PHILADELPHIA, PA
PAUL CAVA GALLERY & FINE ART BOOKS,
22 N. 3RD ST.
SAN FRANCISCO, CA
SAN FRANCISCO MUSEUM OF MODERN ART
BOOKSHOP, VAN NESS AVE. AT MCALLISTER ST.
CITY LIGHTS BOOKSTORE, 2625 DURANT AVE.
JACK HANLEY GALLERY, 41 GRANT AVE.
ARIEL, 2901 LEAVENWORTH ST.
SANTA MONICA, CA
ARCANA, 1229 3RD ST. PROMENADE
HENNESSEY + INGALLS BOOKS
1254 SANTA MONICA MALL
SEATTLE, WA
ELLIOT BAY BOOKS, 1ST AND MAIN ST. S SOUTH
HENRY ART GALLERY BOOKSTORE
UNIVERSITY OF WASHINGTON
WASHINGTON, DC
BOOKWORKS – WPA, 400 7TH ST. NW
NATIONAL GALLERY, 6TH STREET
AND CONSTITUTION AVENUE NW

CANADA
CALGARY
TREPANIER BAER GALLERY, 999 8TH STREET
MONTREAL
ARTEXTE, 3575 ST. LAURENT
TORONTO
ART METROPOLE, 788 KING STREET WEST
ART GALLERY OF ONTARIO, BOOKSTORE
317 DUNDAS ST. WEST
EDWARDS BOOKS & ART, 356 QUEEN ST. WEST
DAVID MIRVISH BOOKS ON ART, 596 MARKHAM ST.
VANCOUVER
ART GALLERY STORE, 750 HORNBY ST.

AUSTRALIA
DISTRIBUTORS
MANIC EX-POSEUR, WORLD TRADE CENTER
MELBOURNE 3005
THE ARTS BOOKSHOP, 1067 HIGH STREET
ARMADALE, VICTORIA 3143
VICTORIA
HARTWIGS BOOKSHOP
245 BRUNSWICK STR., VICTORIA 3182

NEW ZEALAND
DISTRIBUTOR
PROPAGANDA, 44 COLLEGE HILL, AUCKLAND

HONG KONG
PUBLISHERS MARKETING LTD.
TUNG ON BUILDING, 171, PRINCE EDWARD ROAD
KOWLOON
TAI YIP ART BOOK CENTRE
HONG KONG MUSEUM OF ART
TSIM SHA TSUI, KOWLOON

JAPAN
TOKIO
EUROPA ART GmbH, KAMIOGI 4-16-4, SUGINAMI-KU
ON SUNDAYS, 3-7-6 JUNGUMAE, SHIBUYA-KU
AOYAMA BOOKCENTER, ROPPONGI STORE
MINATO-KU
HAKUO TRADING COMPANY
KOJIMACHI SHINE BLD., 8F, CHIYODA-KU
SANSEIDO BOOKSTORE, 7-11-8 KOHAKU, ADACHI-KU
MY BOOK SERVICE, AOI BLD. 5-8, SARUGAKU-CHO

E X H I B I T I O N S

BASEL

FILIALE BASEL	Kannenfeldstrasse 22 4005 Basel Tel./Fax 061 692 59 06	**FELIX STEPHAN HUBER**	**BIS 28.1.95**
		MARKUS SCHWANDER	**18.1.–4.3.95**
		ATTITUDES GENEVE PRESENTE...	**MÄRZ/APRIL 95**
		DOKUMENTATIONSSTELLE	**PERMANENT**

BERN

ERIKA + OTTO FRIEDRICH	Junkerngasse 39 3011 Bern Tel. 031 311 78 03 Fax 031 312 13 45	**ALEXANDER SCHLIEFFEN**	**25.11.94–13.1.95**
		MARK MANDERS	**20.1.–3.3.95**
		CHRISTIAN LINDOW, CHRISTOPH STORZ DRAWINGS	**10.3.–1.4.95**
SUSANNE KULLI	Nydeggstalden 30 3011 Bern Tel. 031 312 06 40	**BASIL LUGINBÜHL**	**27.11.94–4.1.95**
		ALFONSO HÜPPI	**14.1.–24.2.95**
		JÜRG LEISER	**11.3.–15.4.95**
		FRANZISKA MEGERT	**20.5.–2.7.95**

GENÈVE

DANIEL VARENNE	8, Rue Toepffer 1206 Genève Tel. 022 789 16 75 Fax 022 789 16 88	**PAINTINGS AND DRAWINGS 19TH AND 20TH CENTURY**	

ST. GALLEN

WILMA LOCK	Schmidgasse 15 9000 St. Gallen Tel. 071 22 62 52 Fax 071 22 62 24	**FRANZ ERHARD WALTHER, RECENT WORKS** **«Die Verlangsamung der Bilder» Ein neuer Werktypus (24.12.94–3.1.95 geschlossen)**	**5.11.94–7.1.95**

E X H I B I T I O N S

ZÜRICH

THOMAS AMMANN FINE ART	Restelbergstrasse 97 P.O. Box 922 8044 Zürich Tel. 01 252 90 52 Fax 01 252 82 45	**IMPRESSIONISTS & 20TH CENTURY MASTER**	**BY APPOINTMENT ONLY**
ARS FUTURA	Bleicherweg 45 8002 Zürich Tel. 01 201 88 10 Fax 01 201 88 11	**CARSTEN HÖLLER** **LOVERFINCHES**	**25.11.–24.12.94**
		ELISE TAK **Michael Okada: The Man Who Loves to Hate You!**	**20.1.–25.3.95**
MAI 36	Dufourstrasse 137 8034 Zürich Tel. 01 381 55 35 Fax 01 381 55 36	**ON KAWARA/RÉMY ZAUGG**	**19.11–7.12.94**
		ANKE DOBERAUER	**12.12–23.12.94**
		THOMAS RUFF / JÖRG SASSE	**7.1.–28.1.95**
ANNEMARIE VERNA	Neptunstrasse 42 8032 Zürich Tel. 01 262 38 20 Fax 01 262 38 26	**DONALD JUDD (1928–94)**	**26.11.94–11.2.95**
		RETROSPEKTIV I: **AGNES MARTIN & ROBERT MANGOLD**	**16.2.–11.3.95**
		JERRY ZENIUK	**14.3.–13.5.95**
JAMILEH WEBER GALLERY	Hardturmstrasse 110 8005 Zürich Tel. 01 272 74 70 Fax 01 272 23 83	**ANNOUNCING NEW LOCATION:** **WALDMANNSTRASSE 6, CH-8001 ZÜRICH** **TEL. 01 252 10 66, FAX 01 252 11 32** **INAUGURATION TO BE PUBLISHED**	

NOT VITAL

24 NOVEMBER 1994 – 20 JANUARY 1995

BERGGRUEN & ZEVI LIMITED

33 Davies Street London W1Y 1FN

Tel 0171 495 8867 Fax 0171 499 3906

Artists' Books

7 – 23 DECEMBER 1994

Christmas Exhibition

1 – 23 DECEMBER 1994

Dan Walsh

5 – 28 JANUARY 1995

Jennifer Bartlett

1 – 25 FEBRUARY 1995

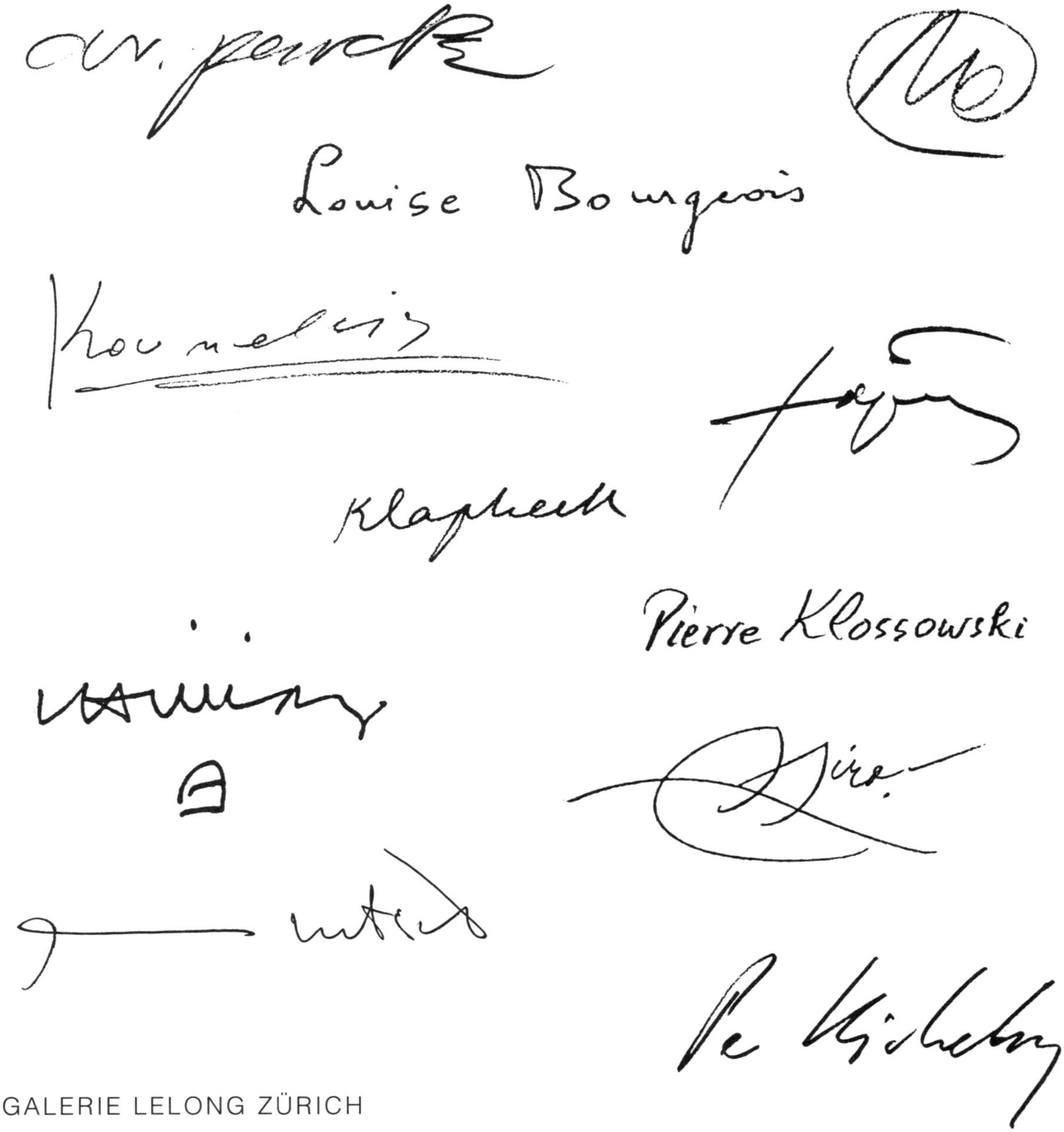

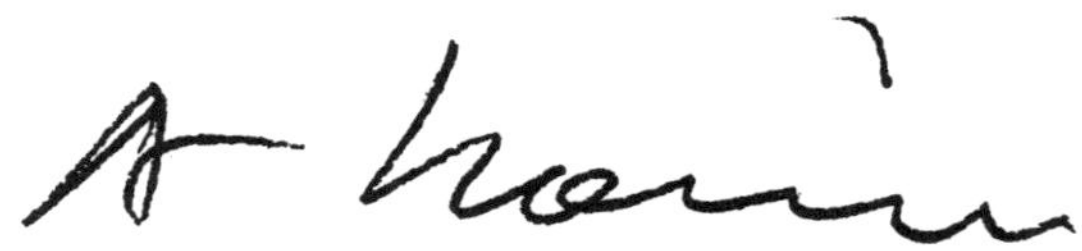

GALERIE LELONG ZÜRICH

PREDIGERPLATZ 2

8001 ZÜRICH

TELEFON 01 / 251 11 20

FAX 01 / 262 52 85

HARDTURM GALERIEN ZÜRICH

Hardturmstrasse 127
vis-à-vis kunsthalle

PETER FISCHLI/DAVID WEISS
Permanente Rauminstallation

hardturmstr. 127
tel. 01 273 50 70
fax 01 273 50 72
Sammlung Hauser & Wirth
mi - fr 14 - 18 uhr
sa 11 - 15 uhr

RICHARD ARTSCHWAGER – Archipelago
19.11.–Ende Januar

hardturmstr. 127
tel. u. fax 01 271 39 57
Peter Kilchmann
mi - fr 13.30 - 18 uhr
sa 11 - 16 uhr

FELIX STEPHAN HUBER – Ende Dezember
ZEICHNUNGEN – RITA ACKERMANN, JOHN LINDELL ROBERT MARSHALL, JACK PIERSON, BARRY RATOFF
14.1.–25.2.
WILLIE DOHERTY 3.3.–25.4.

hardturmstr. 124
tel. 01 273 01 12
fax 01 273 01 81
Mark Müller
mi - fr 12 - 18 uhr
sa 11 - 17 uhr

BEAT ZODERER 5.11.–7.1.
KARIN SANDER 14.1.–25.2.

hardturmstr. 124a
tel. u. fax 01 273 11 00
Bob van Orsouw
mi - fr 12 - 18.30 uhr
sa 11 - 16 uhr

MITJA TUSEK bis 7.1.
JOEP VAN LIESHOUT 14.1.–18.2.
BERNARD VOITA 25.2.–1.4.

KUNSTHALLE BERN

1995

28. JANUAR–12. MÄRZ 1995	RAYMOND PETTIBON
25. MÄRZ–30. APRIL 1995	VINCENT CHABLAIS RAOUL MAREK LAURENT SCHMID VERENA SCHWAB VÉRONIQUE ZUSSAU

HELVETIAPLATZ 1 CH-3005 BERN TELEFON 031/351 00 31 TELEFAX 031/352 53 85

BUREAU Castello di Rivara Center of Contemporary Art

via Pietro Micca 21, I-10121 Torino, tel., fax 011 562 60 67 / 0121 31122, tuesday–friday 13.00–19.00 p.m.

1994/1995

September 17
JOHN CURRIN MICHAEL BACH ANDREAS EXNER RAYMUND PETTIBON
ALESSANDRO RAHO WOLFGANG SCHLEGEL MAURIZIO VETRUGNO

October 20
ANDREAS EXNER

January 26
BERNHARD PRINZ

March 9
ANDREAS SCHÖN

April 13
HERMANN PITZ

Erwin Wurm 22°C

Museum moderner Kunst Stiftung Ludwig Wien
im 20er Haus
8. 12. 94 - 15. 1. 95

Kunstverein St. Gallen
im Kunstmuseum
4. 3. 95 - 7. 5. 95

FRANZ GRAF
HERWIG KEMPINGER

AUSTRIAN CONTRIBUTION TO THE
22ND INTERNATIONAL BIENNIAL OF SÃO PAULO, BRAZIL
OCTOBER 12TH - DECEMBER 10TH 1994
CURATOR: BRIGITTE HUCK

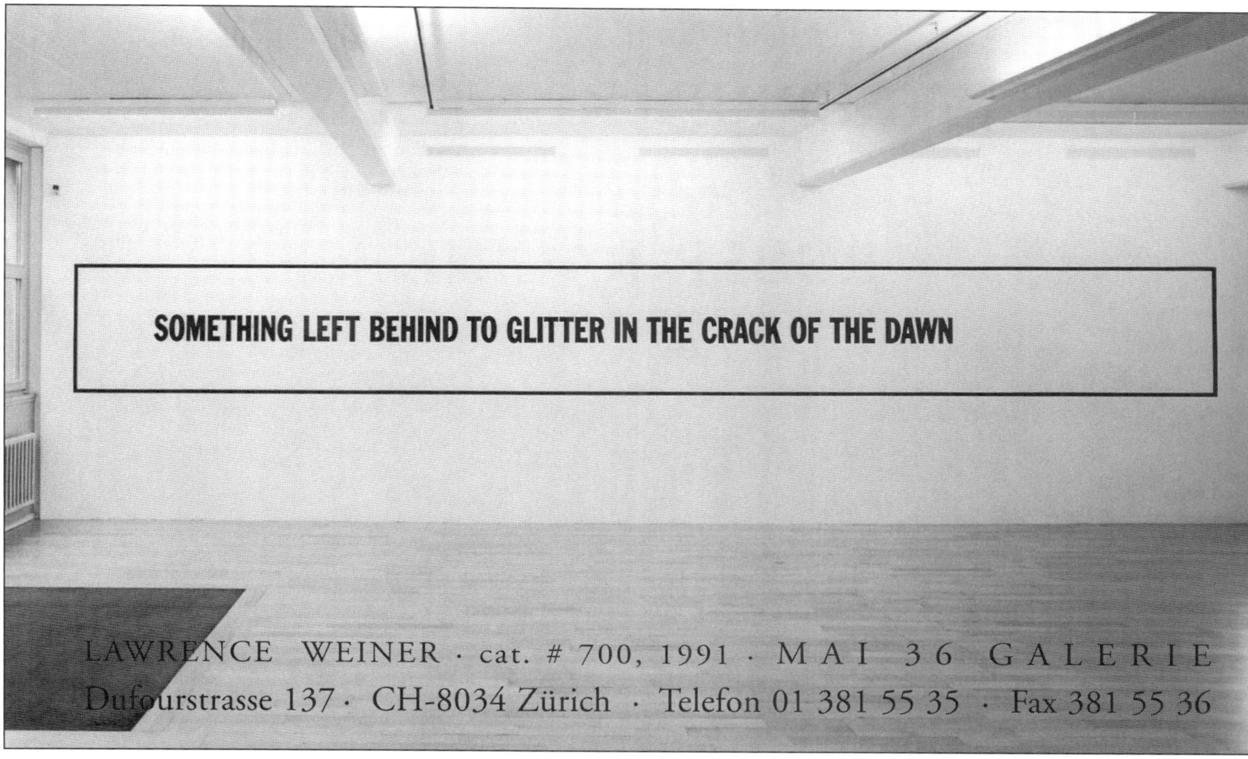

Nan Goldin is represented by Matthew Marks Gallery

Exhibition: February – April 1995

New photographs and
the slide installation
" The Ballad of Sexual Dependency "

at
522 West 22nd Street (between 10th and 11th Avenues) New York, NY 10011
Tel 212 861-9455 Fax 212 861-9382 Thursday – Sunday, 12 – 6

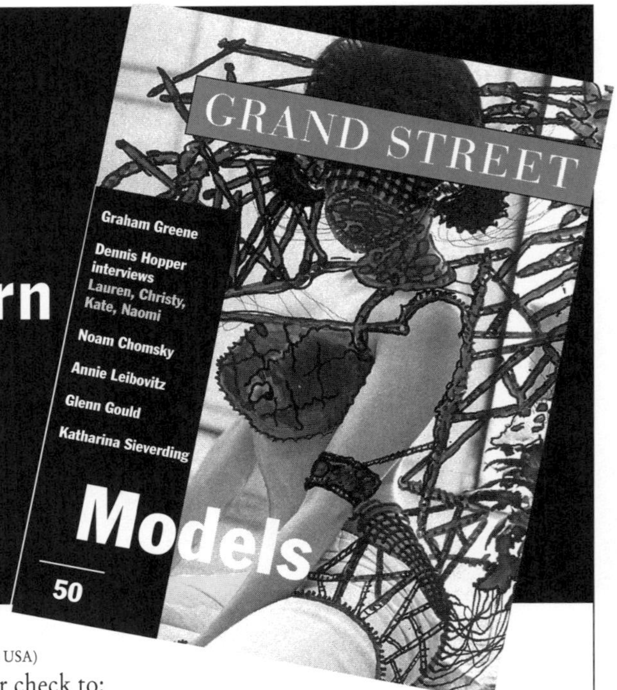

GRAND STREET
Graham Greene
Dennis Hopper interviews Lauren, Christy, Kate, Naomi
Noam Chomsky
Annie Leibovitz
Glenn Gould
Katharina Sieverding
Models
50

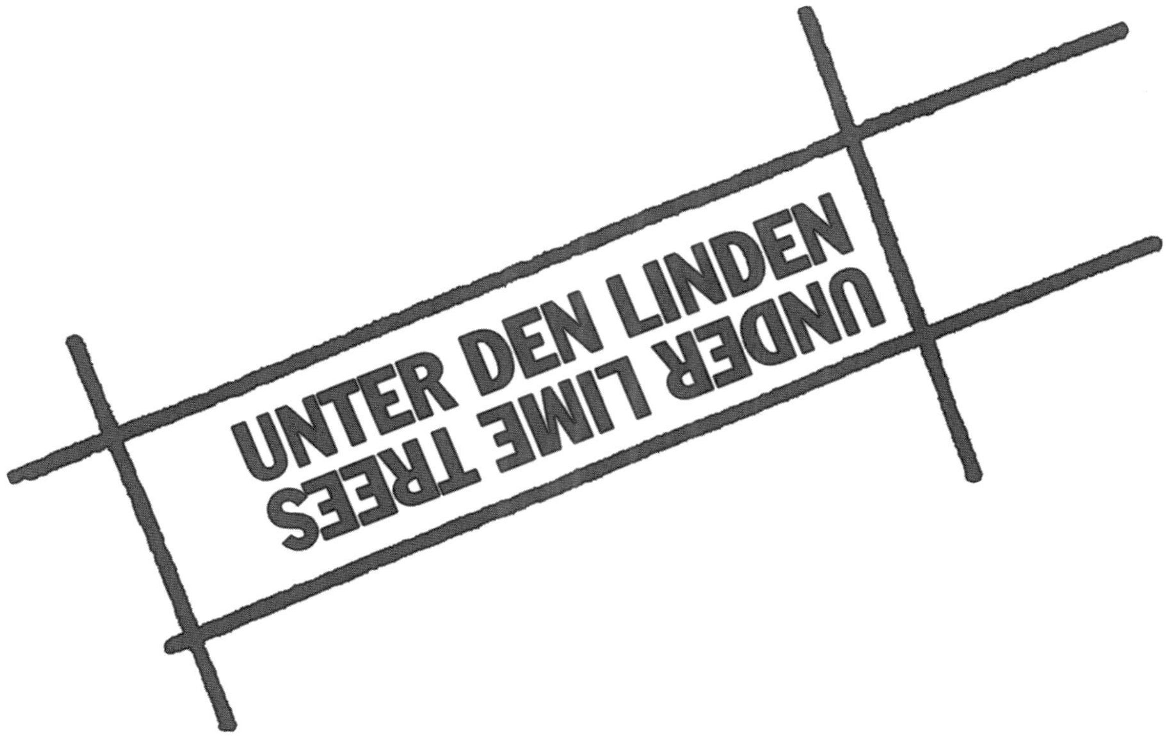

LAWRENCE WEINER

EDITION FOR PARKETT 42

MANUFACTURED BY

Speckert+Klein

SCHWEIZERGASSE 20   8023 ZÜRICH

GÜNTHER FÖRG

WANDMALEREI

NOVEMBER – DEZEMBER

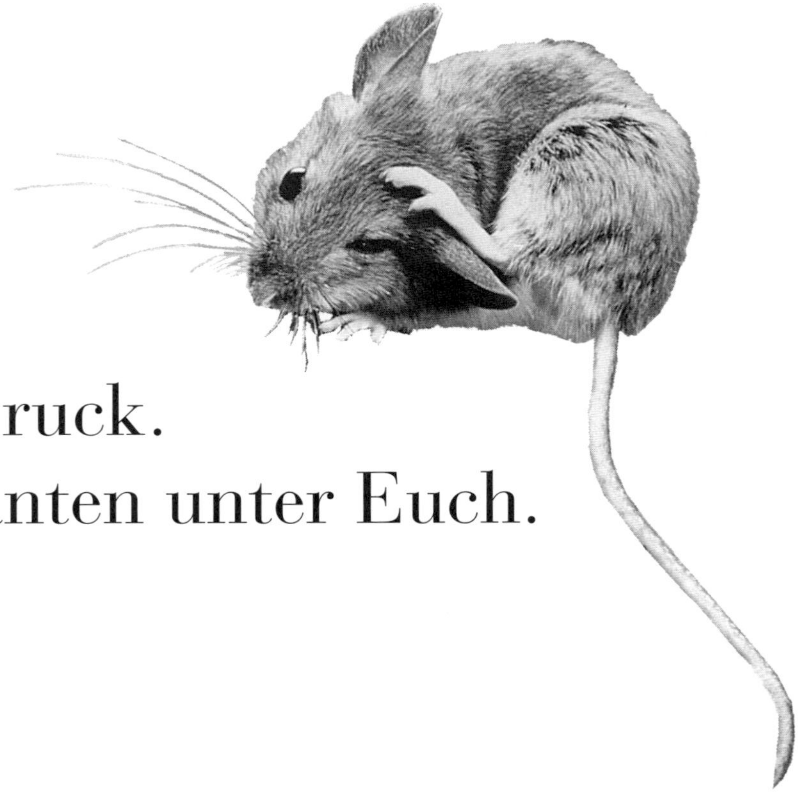

Wir machen Druck.
Auf die Ignoranten unter Euch.

We do presswork – pressurizing
the ignorants among you.

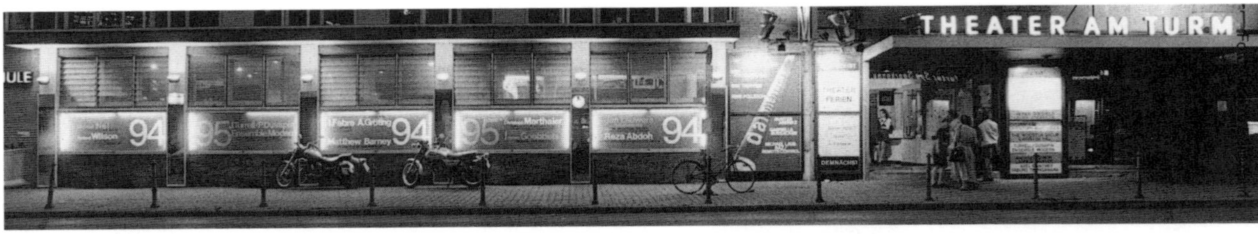

Das TAT

Bildende Künstler im Theater Am Turm Frankfurt

Kuratoren: Noemi Smolik und Hortensia Völckers

PHASE 1

ASTA GRÖTING
JAMES TURRELL
JAN FABRE
JANA STERBAK

22. bis 26. Feb. 1995

PHASE 2

MATTHEW BARNEY

Coproduktion mit dem Portikus, Frankfurt

u.a.

Nov. 1995

Info Tel. (069) 1545-104

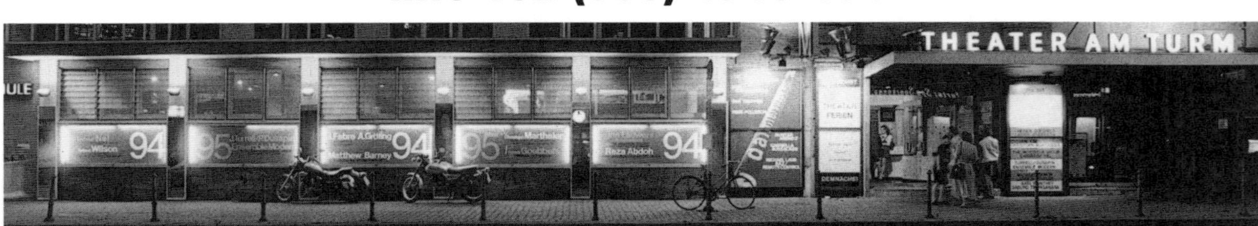

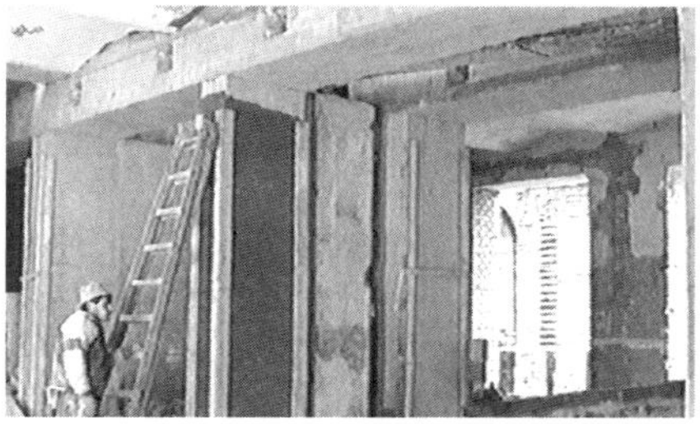

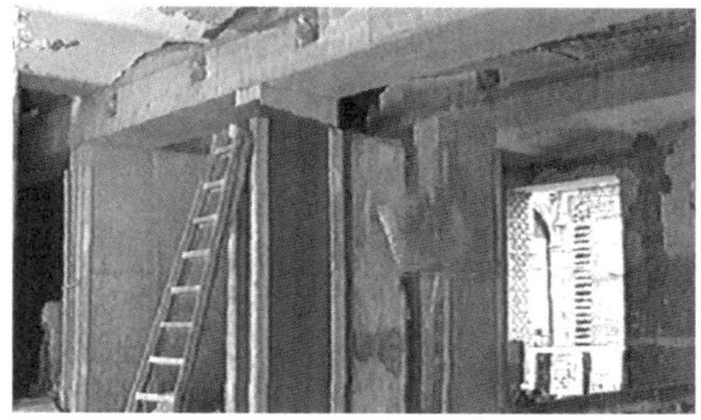

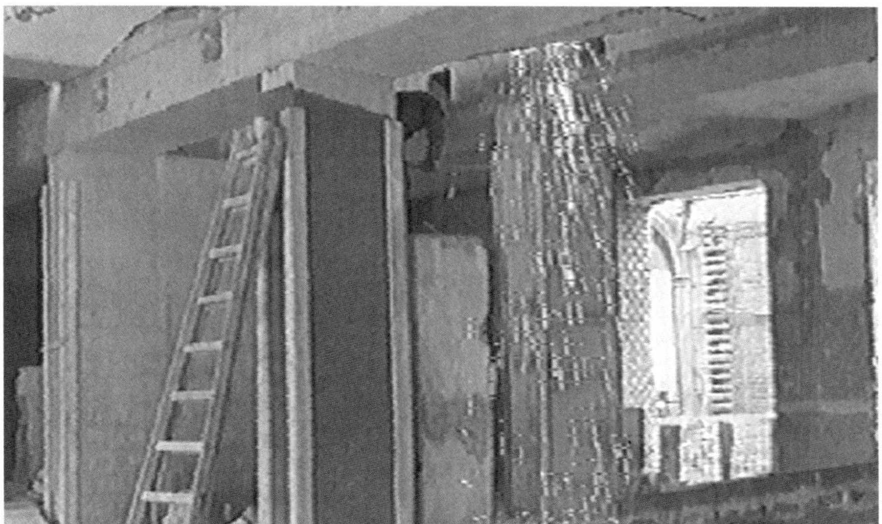

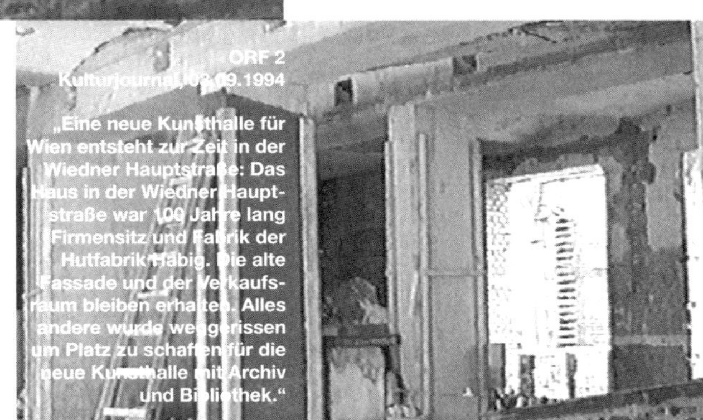

1995: Wiedner Hauptstraße 15, A–1040 Wien

Raumplan
Teil 1 als Video erhältlich

EA–Generali Foundation, Bauernmarkt 12, A–1010 Wien, Tel. +43 1 534 01-507, Fax +43 1 534 01-851

Armaly

ISSUE FOUR

BLIND SPOT

PHOTOGRAPHY

PHOTOGRAPH BY JAMES CASEBERE

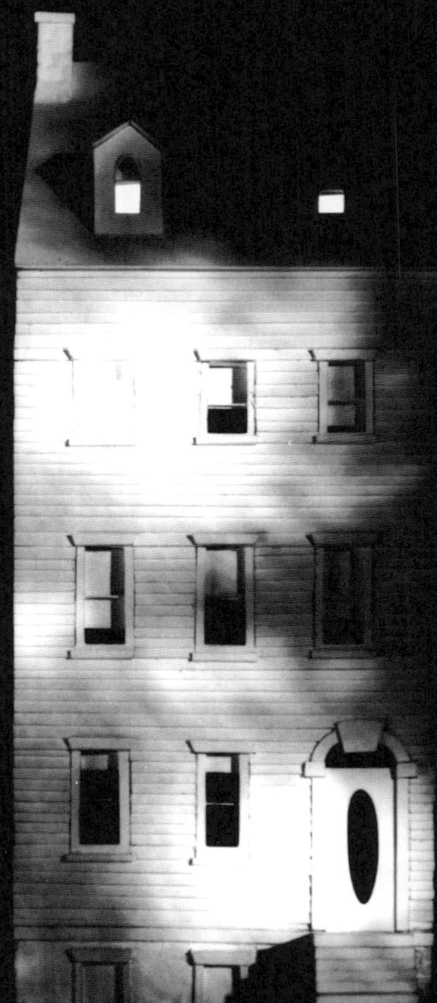

LYNN DAVIS
JOAN FONCUBERTA
ROBERT FRANK
ADAM FÜSS
DAVID HILLIARD
MARY ELLEN MARK
BEVERLY SEMMES
JEFF WALL
BOYD WEBB
BRUCE WEBER

PUBLISHED AT LEXINGTON LABS
49 WEST 23 STREET, NEW YORK CITY,
NEW YORK 10010
TEL: 212 633 1317 FAX: 212 691 5465

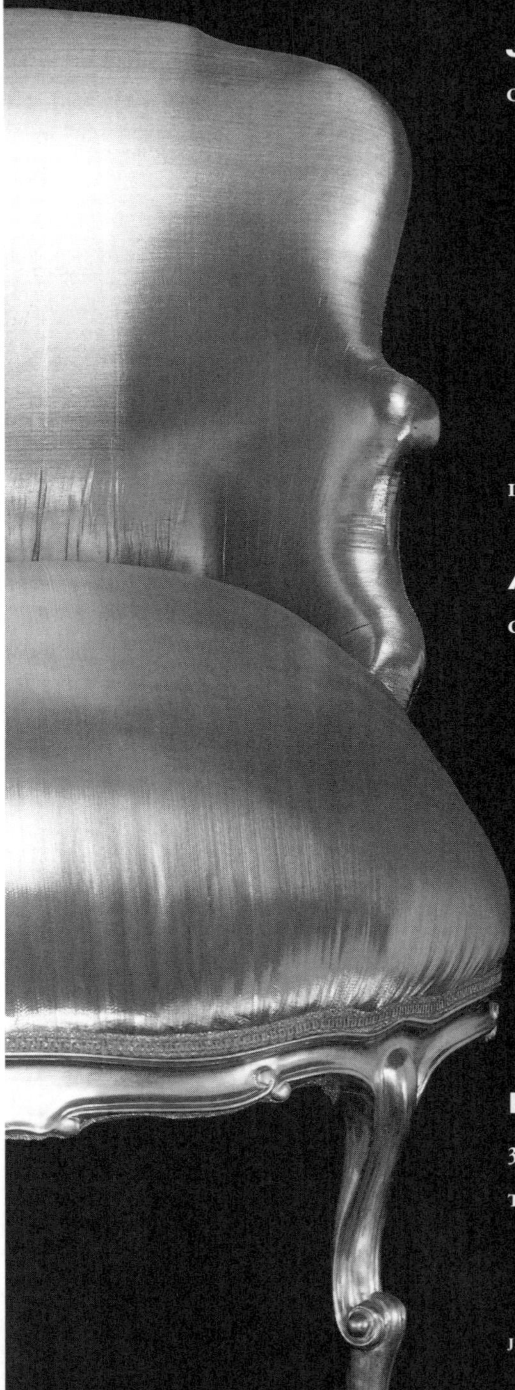

JAMES LEE BYARS. *The Golden Divan,* 1990.

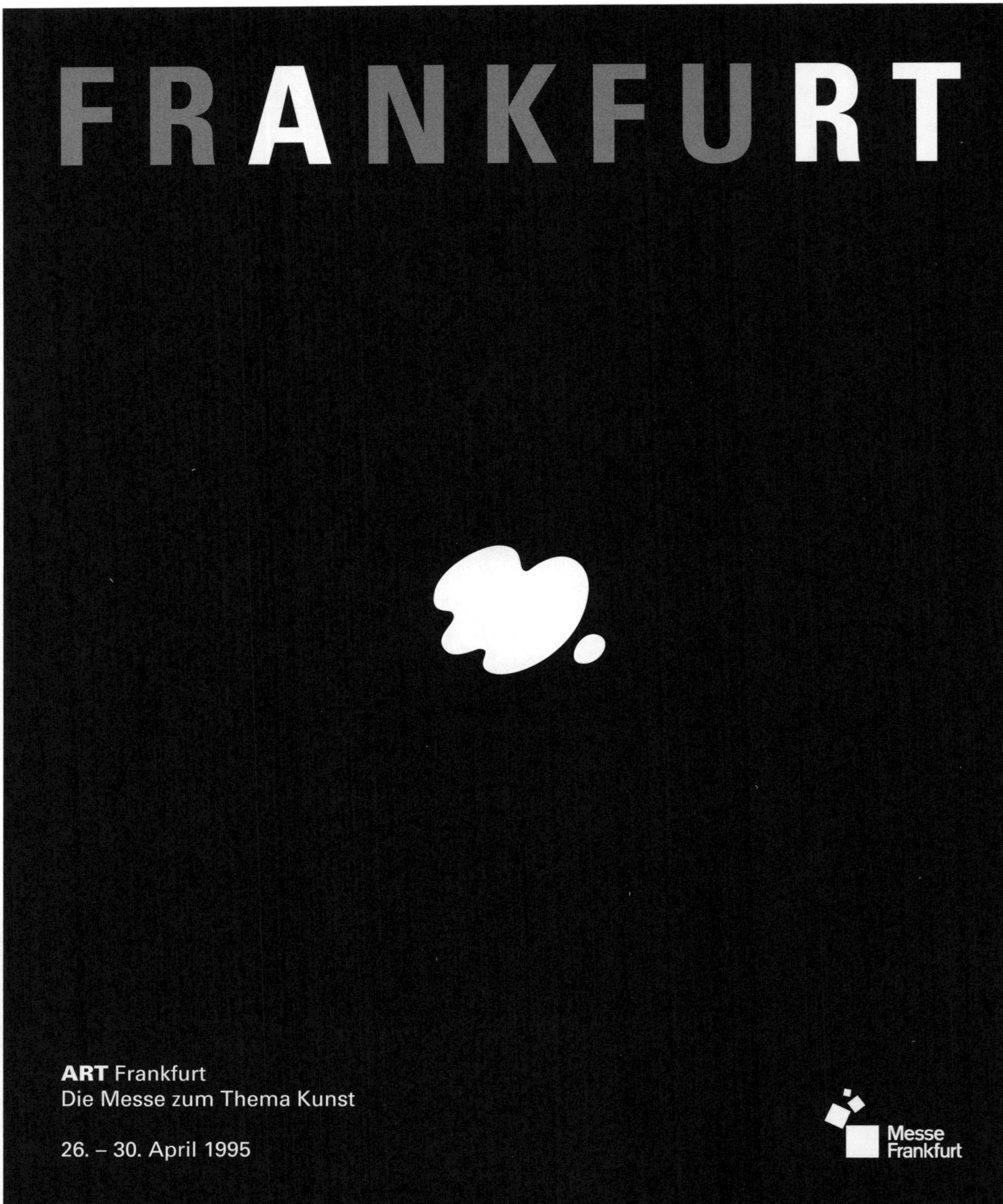
FRANKFURT
ART Frankfurt
Die Messe zum Thema Kunst
26. – 30. April 1995
Messe
Frankfurt

Öffentliche Kunstsammlung Basel

Jahresprogramm Kunstmuseum Basel

Kunstmuseum
St. Alban-Graben 16, CH-4010 Basel
Tel. ++41/61/271 08 28, Fax ++41/61/271 08 45
Dienstag bis Sonntag, 10–17 Uhr
Montag geschlossen

1994/95
17.12. – 19.3.95
Einblattholzschnitte des 15. und 16. Jahrhunderts aus dem Kupferstichkabinett Basel

1995
18.3. – 14.5.95
Lenz Klotz, Zum Siebzigsten Geburtstag
8.4. – 28.5.95
Neuerwerbungen des Kupferstichkabinetts Basel
10.6. – 27.8.95
zu Ende gezeichnet, Bildmässige Zeichnungen aus dem Kupferstichkabinett Basel
26.8. – 5.11.95
Bonifacius Amerbach (1495–1562)
Sonderpräsentation aus Anlass des 500. Geburtstags des Basler Humanisten und Rechtsgelehrten
9.9.95 – 15.1.96
Werke der Donauschule aus dem Kupferstichkabinett Basel
11.11.95 – 12.2.96
Studioausstellung ausgewählter Werke der Renaissance-Malerei nördlich der Alpen
17.12.95 – 9.3.96
Pablo Picasso, Die illustrierten Bücher

Öffentliche Kunstsammlung Basel

Jahresprogramm Museum für Gegenwartskunst Basel

Museum für Gegenwartskunst
St. Alban-Rheinweg 60, CH-4010 Basel
Tel. ++41/61/272 81 83, Fax ++41/61/271 05 36
Dienstag bis Sonntag, 11–17 Uhr
Montag geschlossen

1994/95
29.10 – 29.1.95
Gary Hill, Imagining the brain closer than the eyes
29.10 – 29.1.95
Claudia + Julia Müller
Es ist offengestanden sehr beruhigend
Manor-Kunstpreis Basel 1994

1995
1.4. – 16.7.95
Blinky Palermo, To The People of New York City
12.8. – 5.11.95
Ilya Kabakov
23.9. – 19.11.95
Roni Horn
28.10.95 – 5.2.96
Robert Gober

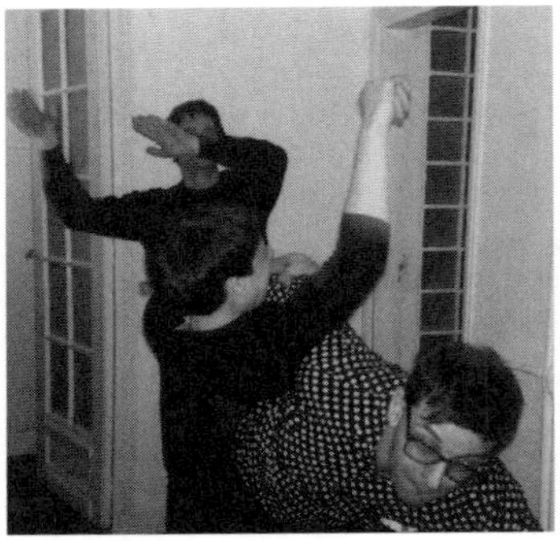

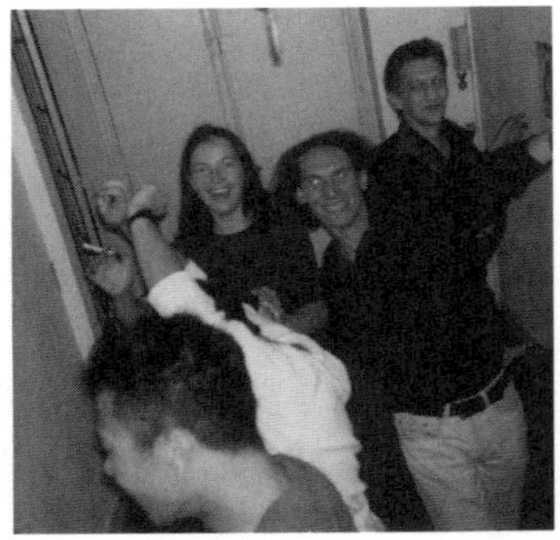

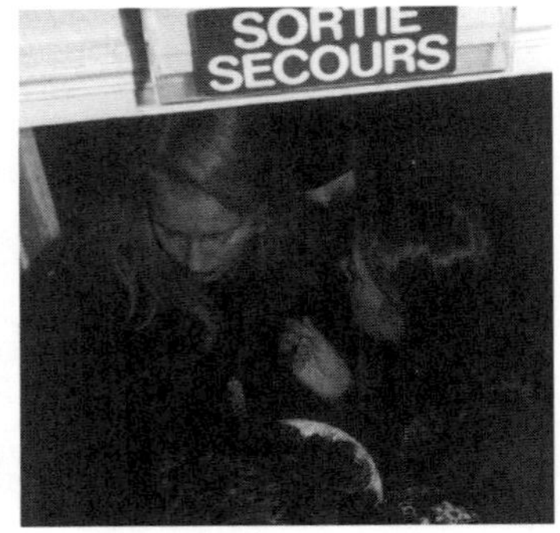
SORTIE
SECOURS

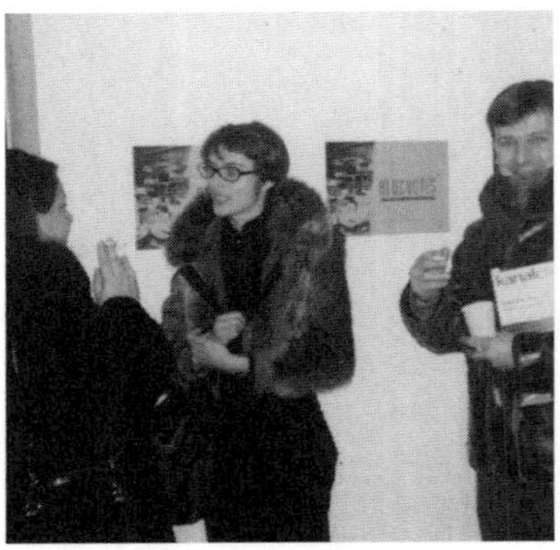

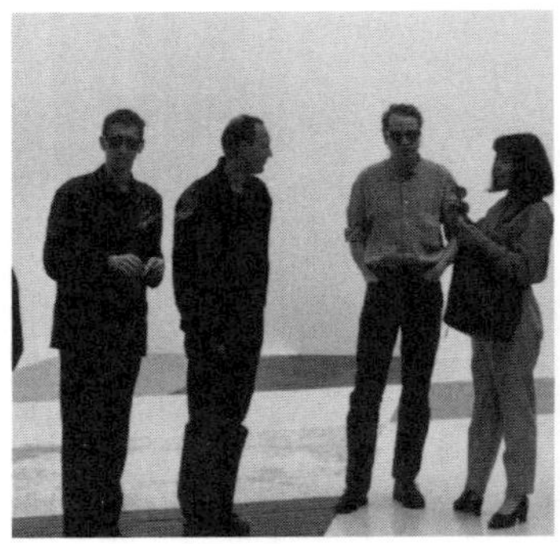

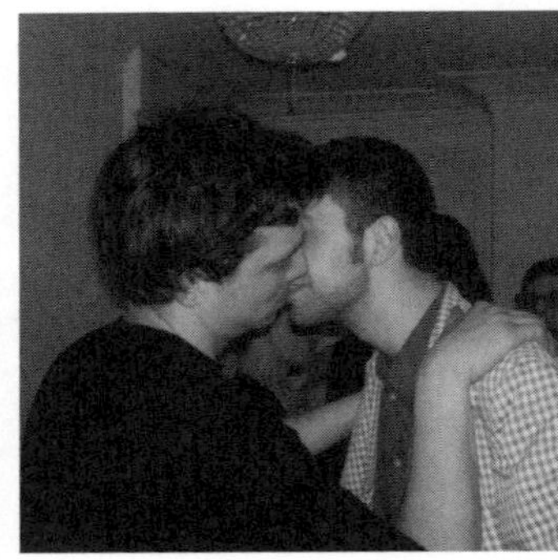

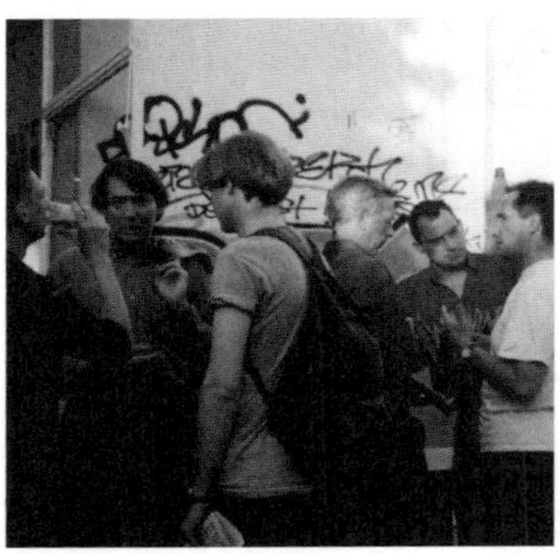

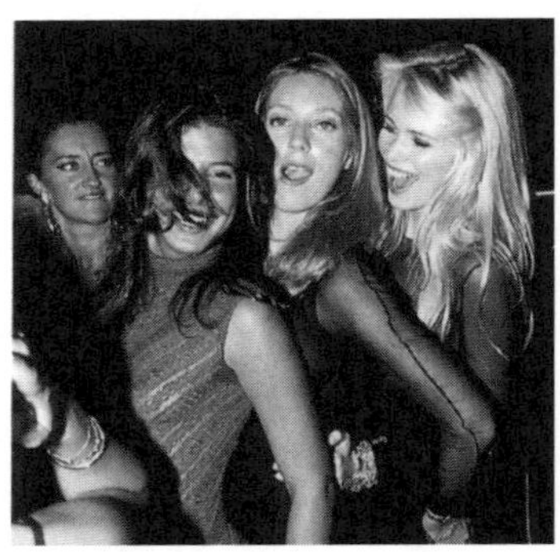

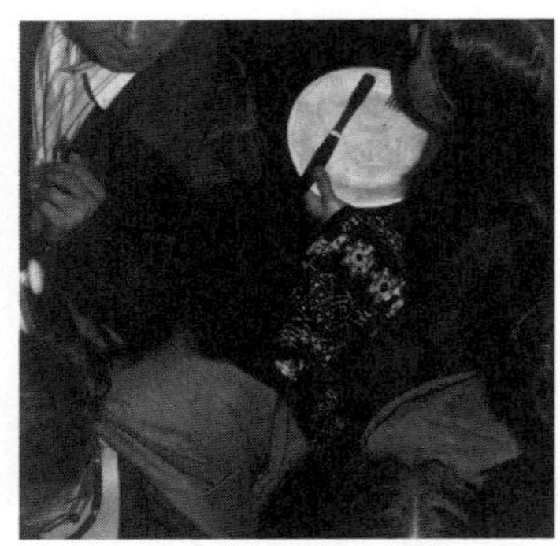

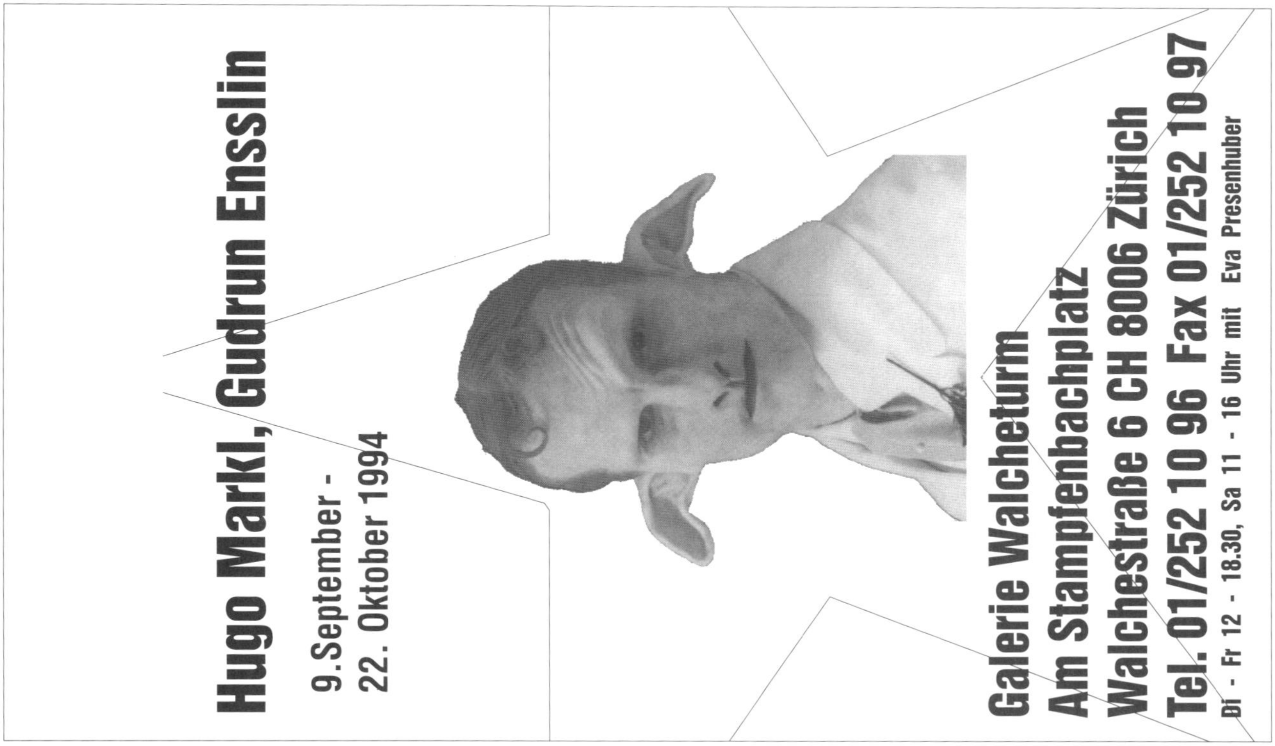
Hugo Markl, Gudrun Ensslin
9.September -
22. Oktober 1994
Galerie Walcheturm
Am Stampfenbachplatz
Walchestraße 6 CH 8006 Zürich
Tel. 01/252 10 96 Fax 01/252 10 97
Di - Fr 12 - 18.30, Sa 11 - 16 Uhr mit Eva Presenhuber

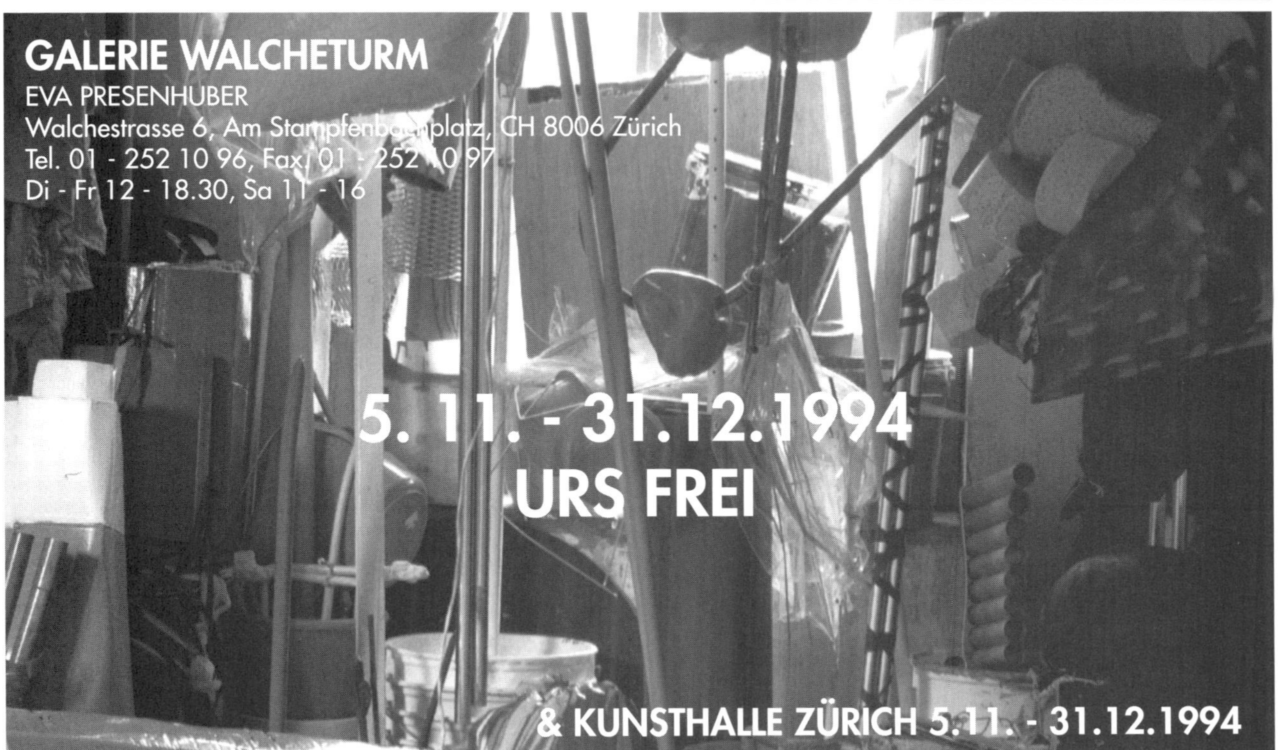
GALERIE WALCHETURM
EVA PRESENHUBER
Walchestrasse 6, Am Stampfenbachplatz, CH 8006 Zürich
Tel. 01 - 252 10 96, Fax: 01 - 252 10 97
Di - Fr 12 - 18.30, Sa 11 - 16
5. 11. - 31.12.1994
URS FREI
& KUNSTHALLE ZÜRICH 5.11. - 31.12.1994

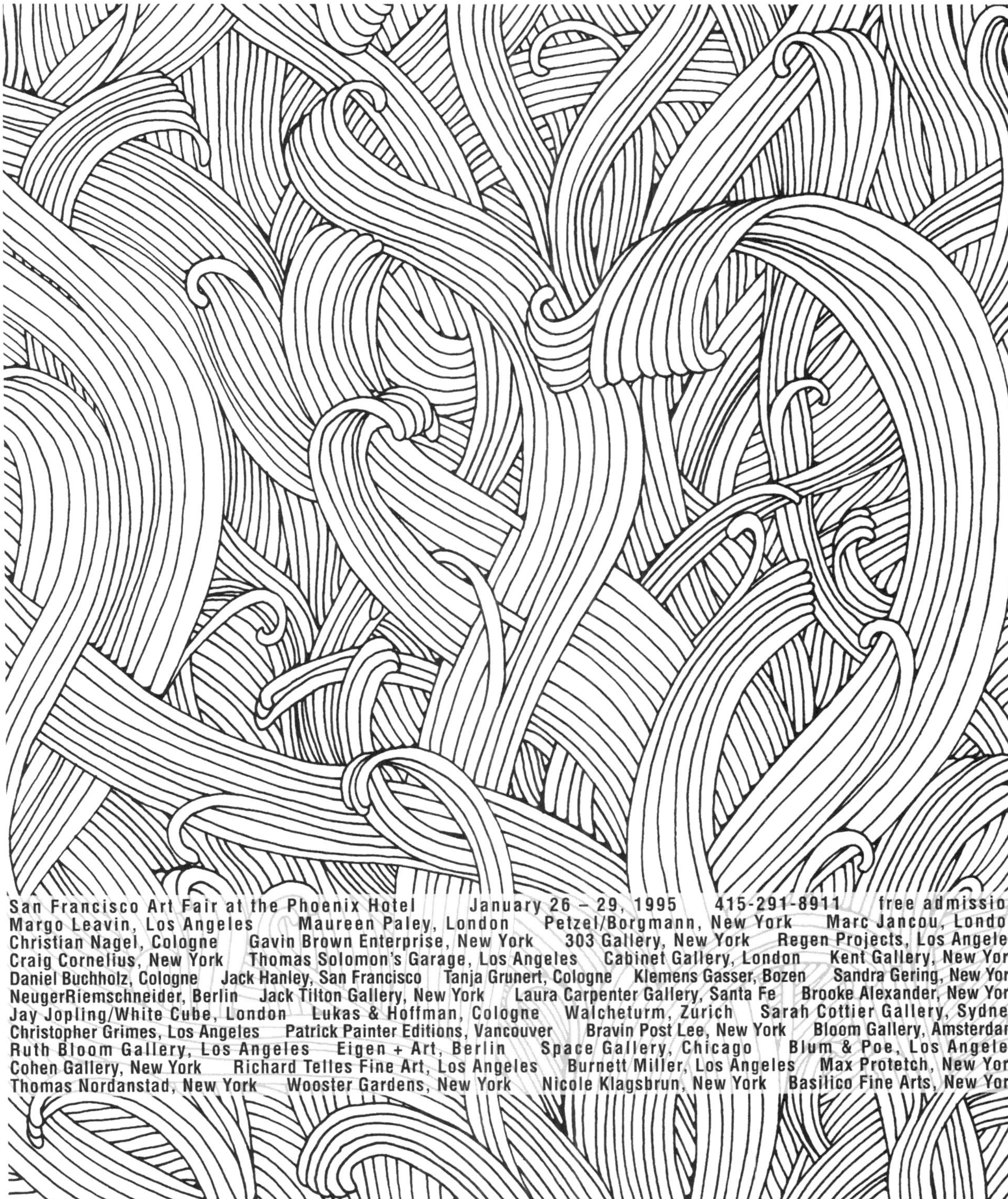
San Francisco Art Fair at the Phoenix Hotel January 26 – 29, 1995 415-291-8911 free admission
Margo Leavin, Los Angeles Maureen Paley, London Petzel/Borgmann, New York Marc Jancou, London
Christian Nagel, Cologne Gavin Brown Enterprise, New York 303 Gallery, New York Regen Projects, Los Angeles
Craig Cornelius, New York Thomas Solomon's Garage, Los Angeles Cabinet Gallery, London Kent Gallery, New York
Daniel Buchholz, Cologne Jack Hanley, San Francisco Tanja Grunert, Cologne Klemens Gasser, Bozen Sandra Gering, New York
NeugerRiemschneider, Berlin Jack Tilton Gallery, New York Laura Carpenter Gallery, Santa Fe Brooke Alexander, New York
Jay Jopling/White Cube, London Lukas & Hoffman, Cologne Walcheturm, Zurich Sarah Cottier Gallery, Sydney
Christopher Grimes, Los Angeles Patrick Painter Editions, Vancouver Bravin Post Lee, New York Bloom Gallery, Amsterdam
Ruth Bloom Gallery, Los Angeles Eigen + Art, Berlin Space Gallery, Chicago Blum & Poe, Los Angeles
Cohen Gallery, New York Richard Telles Fine Art, Los Angeles Burnett Miller, Los Angeles Max Protetch, New York
Thomas Nordanstad, New York Wooster Gardens, New York Nicole Klagsbrun, New York Basilico Fine Arts, New York

GIULIO PAOLINI

JANUARY

CHRISTIAN BOLTANSKI

FEBRUARY

GUISEPPE PENONE

MARCH